Driving Force
The Global Restructuring
of Technology, Labour, and Investment
in the Automobile and Components Industries

Published in cooperation
with the
United Nations Centre on Transnational Corporations

Driving Force

The Global Restructuring of Technology, Labour, and Investment in the Automobile and Components Industries

Kurt Hoffman
and Raphael Kaplinsky

Westview Press
BOULDER, SAN FRANCISCO, AND LONDON

Westview Special Studies in International Economics and Business

Cover design: Petra Böhr Rovendaal

This Westview softcover edition is printed on acid-free paper and bound in softcovers that carry the highest rating of the National Association of State Textbook Administrators, in consultation with the Association of American Publishers and the Book Manufacturers' Institute.

All rights reserved. No Part of this publication may be reproduced or transmitted in any form or by any means, electronic or mechanical, including photocopy, recording, or any information storage and retrieval system, without permission in writing from the publisher.

Copyright © 1988 by the United Nations

Published in 1988 in the United States of America by Westview Press, Inc., 5500 Central Avenue, Boulder, Colorado 80301, and in the United Kingdom by Westview Press, Inc., 13 Brunswick Centre, London WC1N 1AF, England

Library of Congress Cataloging-in-Publication Data
Hoffman, Kurt
    Driving force: the global restructuring of technology, labour, and investment in the automobile and components industries/by Kurt Hoffman and Raphael Kaplinsky.
      p. cm.--(Westview special studies in international economics and business)
    ISBN 0-8133-7502-9
    1. Automobile industry and trade--International cooperation.
2. Automobile supplies industry--International cooperation.
3. Automobile industry and trade--Automation. 4. Automobile supplies industry--Automation. 5. International division of labor.
6. International business enterprises. 7. Investments, Foreign.
I. Kaplinsky, Raphael. II. Title. III. Series.
HD9710.A2H64 1988
338.4'76292--dc19   87-28015
                                                                               CIP

Printed and bound in the United States of America

The paper used in this publication meets the requirements of the American National Standard for Permanence of Paper for Printed Library Materials Z39.48-1984

10   9   8   7   6   5   4   3

Contents

List of Tables and Figures	ix
Preface	xv
Acknowledgments	xvii

1 TRANSNATIONAL CORPORATIONS AND THE NEW
     INTERNATIONAL DIVISION OF LABOUR   1

    The Growth of Developing Country
       Industrial Production   2
    The Role Played by TNCs   3
    Situating the 1970s: A Change in Direction? .   19
    TNCs and the International Division of
       Labour in the Automobile Sector   26
    Notes   28

2 THE POINT OF TRANSITION -
     FROM MACHINOFACTURE TO SYSTEMOFACTURE   31

    Technology and Long-Waves   32
    From Mass Production to Flexible Specialization   36
    Transition Between Eras - Extending the
       Concept of Social Relations   40
    From the Era of Handicrafts to Manufacture . .   44
    From Manufacture to Machinofacture   46
    From Machinofacture to Systemofacture   49
    Patterns of International Integration
       in the Three Eras of Production   64
    Notes   70

3	THE AUTOMOBILE INDUSTRY	73
	Market Conditions in the Automobile Industry	73
	Corporate Response to the Rise in Competitive Temperature	96
	A Brief Overview of Automobile Production and a Categorization of Components	102
	Notes	110
4	TRANSITION IN THE JAPANESE AUTO INDUSTRY: THE EMERGENCE OF SYSTEMOFACTURE	113
	The Scale of the Japanese Competitive Advantage in the Auto Industry	115
	The Organization of Work: The JIT Labour Process	121
	The Transition to Computer-Integrated Manufacture	138
	Component Suppliers and Auto Assemblers	152
	Structure and Change in the Japanese Components Sector	158
	Notes	175
5	TECHNOLOGICAL TRANSFORMATION AMONG THE UNITED STATES AND WESTERN EUROPEAN MOTOR VEHICLE ASSEMBLERS	181
	The Search for a Technological Solution to Diminishing Competitiveness	184
	Selected Company Case Studies	201
	Will the Technological Solution Work?	216
	Notes	226
6	THE RESTRUCTURING OF ASSEMBLER-SUPPLIER RELATIONS AND THE GROWTH OF TECHNOLOGICAL INTENSITY IN THE UNITED STATES AND WESTERN EUROPEAN COMPONENTS INDUSTRY	229
	Complexity in Product Purchasing: the Growing Importance of Quality	232
	Restructuring Contractual Relations	237
	Restructuring the Design Relationship	244
	The Trend Towards Just-In-Time	253
	Technological Change in the Components Sector	265
	Technological and Organizational Learning Via Joint Ventures	277
	Notes	281

7	SYSTEMOFACTURE, INVESTMENT LOCATION AND OFF-SHORE SOURCING IN THE AUTOMOBILE COMPONENTS SECTOR	285
	The Locational Logic of Systemofacture in Automobile Components	287
	Short-term Competitive Dynamics in the Assembly Industry	294
	Component Suppliers, Offshore-Sourcing and FDI	309
	Is There a Future for Developing Country Component Exports?	318
	Notes	324
8	TNCs AND THE NEW INTERNATIONAL DIVISION OF LABOUR IN THE ERA OF SYSTEMOFACTURE	329
	The Transferability of the Japanese System of Production	332
	The Implications for Continued Industrialization in the Developing Countries	355
	TNCs in the Era of Systemofacture	361
	Notes	364
List of Abbreviations		369
Bibliography		371
Index		381

Tables and Figures

TABLES

1.1	The decline of United States industrial competitiveness (1960-79)	13
1.2	The percentage share of United States in the source and destination of FDI, 1970-71 to 1980-81 (two year moving averages)	14
1.3	Percentage annual growth rates of the three circuits of internationalization 1955-56 to 1981-82 (two year moving averages) . .	17
1.4	Historical rates of growth (1820-1979)	20
1.5	Productivity levels per person hour relative to United States (=100)	22
1.6	Unemployment rates in OECD economies	25
3.1	Extraregional automobile exports ('000s)	76
3.2	Per capita automobile penetration in selected economies, 1980	78
3.3	Automobile production - Western Europe, North America, Japan and selected countries ('000s) .	80
3.4	Worldwide car sales by major manufacturers, 1984	83
3.5	Automobile sales in the United States and Canada, 1978-1982 ('000s of units)	85

3.6	Employment in the motor vehicle and equipment industry in United States, Japan and Western Europe, 1970-1981	85
3.7	Import share of the United States, Western European and Japanese auto markets.	86
3.8	United States assembly capacities for United States and foreign firms, 1985-1990 ('000s)	92
3.9	New foreign auto producers exporting to the United States by 1990	93
3.10	Company and group integration, 1965-83 (%)	106
4.1	Vehicles per worker per annum, adjusted for vertical integration, capacity utilization and length of working year	117
4.2	Performance comparison for Japanese and United States engine plants, 1984	117
4.3	Performance comparison for Japanese and United States assembly plants	118
4.4	United States-Japanese comparison of output levels in two machining activities, 1980	119
4.5	Workers per shift to produce similar vehicle in Japan and two European countries, 1980	120
4.6	Domestic sales and imports in Japan 1951-1960	123
4.7	Shortening of set-up time and reduction of lot size in Toyota (1970-1980)	124
4.8	Percentage reduction in set-up time at Japanese subsidiary of United States auto component firms	126
4.9	Trends in inventory turns for United States auto assemblers and Toyota, 1973-1984	129
4.10	Inventories as a proportion of monthly production in a smaller Japanese auto firm	131

4.11 Suggestions submitted by employees for
     improvements in product and process at
     Toyota, 1979-1983 137

4.12 United States and Japanese auto industry use of
     numerical control tools by age of machine . . . 142

4.13 Nissan's inter-plant CIM system 148

4.14 JIT performance of Japanese component firms . . 156

4.15 Flexible manufacturing systems used by
     two Japanese component firms 163

4.16 R&D as a percentage of sales for
     two large Japanese component firms, 1978-1984 . . 167

4.17 Numerical control tools and robots installed
     by Japanese component firms, by firm size, 1983
     (units, number of employees) 172

4.18 Rate of growth of sales per employee in a
     technologically laggard small Japanese
     manufacturer of brakes, 1979-1984 173

4.19 Share of production value by capital
     classification of Japanese auto parts firms
     1979-1983 (% of total production sector) 174

5.1 Capital and R&D expenditures for United
     States auto firms, 1975-1985 ($ billion) 189

5.2 Selected investments in automation by United
     States and Western European component firms . . 192

5.3 GM and Ford affiliated leading-edge companies . . 194

5.4 Fiat's FIRE engine assembly plant,
     Termoli, Italy 208

5.5 Advanced computer projects at General
     Motors research facility 213

5.6 The main features of the saturn project 214

5.7	Comparison of product development efforts by United States, Western European and Japanese assemblers	218
5.8	Die change performance in selected United States and Western European assemblers	225
6.1	Selected examples of new Ford-supplier contracts in the US, 1985	240
6.2	Current and estimated reductions in numbers of auto parts suppliers 1980-1990 (units)	243
6.3	Targets for JIT at Buick city - mid 1986	256
6.4	Select examples of JIT practices adopted by United States and Western European component firms	258
6.5	Trends in R&D expenditure for selected component suppliers, 1979-1984	269
6.6	Support for component suppliers' R&D by Fiat, 1981-1984	270
6.7	Die change times for United States and Japanese component affiliates on comparable press 1981-1985	274
6.8	Flexible manufacturing lines installed by four United States component firms	276
7.1	Imports of auto components from non-OECD countries into Japan, 1981-1984 ($'000s)	291
7.2	Performance comparisons of Honda and Toyota United States assembly plants with GM and AMC, 1985	297
7.3	Current and planned imports of vehicles by United States assemblers from Japan, Republic of Korea, Brazil, Taiwan Province and Mexico	299
7.4	United States trade in motor vehicle parts and accessories, 1980-84 (in thousands of dollars; exports f.a.s. value, imports customs value basis)	302

7.5 Examples of outsourced products by Western European volume producer, 1985 304

7.6 Select joint ventures by United States firms in Republic of Korea, Mexico and Brazil, 1984-87 . . 314

7.7 Labour costs for engine machining and assembly . 321

FIGURES

1.1 Share of the developing countries in global manufacturing value added and manufactured exports 4

1.2 United States balance of payments (current dollars) 23

2.1 Pre-electronic organization of factory production 57

2.2 The three different types of automation 59

2.3 The three epochs of industrial development . . . 66

3.1 GM: Putting the world car together 99

3.2 Flow sheet of automobile production 103

4.1 Effects of automated die change technology . . . 125

4.2 If the river is deep there is no bottom in sight! 128

4.3 Division of labour in the Japanese auto industry 154

5.1 Recent technological changes in the Japanese automobile industry 185

6.1 Trends in perceived assembler criteria for selecting suppliers 234

8.1 Scale in production 347

8.2 Changes in the three dimensions of scale in the transition from machinofacture to systemofacture 351

Preface

One of the most striking features of the world economy in recent years is the rapid pace of technological change. New technologies have often been quite visible, as in the proliferation of personal computers, the growth of electronics components in automobiles, and the spread of a variety of consumer products whose performance is derived from computer chips. Less visible but potentially of greater importance are changes that are underway in how production is organized in key sectors of manufacturing, many of which are also linked to developments in electronics.

The United Nations Centre on Transnational Corporations (UNCTC) has conducted a number of studies on the role of transnational corporations (TNCs) in contributing to the economic development of developing countries. UNCTC has been especially interested in how TNCs transfer technology, and in how their activities can stimulate the growth of modern manufacturing industries in developing countries. The present study continues UNCTC work in this area. The study presents a detailed analysis of how production processes are being transformed in the manufacture and assembly of automobiles and automobile components, the role of TNCs in those transformations, and the possible implications for developing countries.

The automobile industry has long been thought to be accessible to many developing country producers, both to produce for domestic markets and to export components and finished vehicles to the large markets in the developed market economies. Although automobiles are a mature industry with product and production technologies that have been widely disseminated, this study shows that there is still substantial scope for TNCs to achieve competitive advantages through the application of microelectronics-based automation systems, and by virtue of the lower cost and flexibility gained from the re-organization of production. What is not clear is whether the advantages gained by firms will result in advantages to countries. This study raises the possibility that the new production methods, combined with increasing protectionist sentiment within the developed market economics, could lead to a reduction in the volume of automobile production within developing countries. While this remains a possibility, and is not yet a reality, the consequences of such a development are evident. For that reason, the present study deserves widespread attention.

The study was sponsored by UNCTC, and we are pleased to make it available to a wide audience. The methodology was devised and carried out by the authors and they are responsible for the research, writing and editing. The manuscript was not subject to United Nations editing procedures. UNCTC would like to thank Kurt Hoffmann of the Science Policy Research Unit and Raphael Kaplinsky of the Institute of Development Studies, both at the University of Sussex, United Kingdom, for their efforts in conducting the research and writing the study. Special thanks are due to Haleem Lone who assisted with the historical section in Chapter 2, Ludovico Alcorta who undertook the computations in Chapter 1 and Irene Williams who was responsible for the layout.

Peter Hansen
Executive Director
United Nations Centre on Transnational Corporations

1

Transnational Corporations and the New International Division of Labour

This book is, in the first instance, concerned with the past evolution and future direction of the international division of labour in manufacturing. More specifically we are trying to locate the role played by two major sets of actors in global manufacturing - the developing countries (DCs) and the transnational corporations (TNCs). Will the DCs increase their share of global manufacturing production? Which DCs will fare most successfully? Will the TNC be an important facilitator of the industrial progress of DCs, both in relation to producing for indigenous markets and as a conduit for production destined for industrially advanced country (IAC) markets? And will there be important differences between sectors?

These are complicated issues which find no easy answer. In part this is because the very complexity of the subject-matter clouds the crystal-ball, making accurate prediction difficult. But it also stems from the inherent indeterminacy of these events which will in the end be conditioned by a confluence of economic, social and political factors. These in their turn are subject to the decisions and actions of individual decision-takers - be they in the TNC or the state, in IACs or DCs.

In these first two chapters our primary concern is to set the background for the empirical study which follows in later chapters. The industrial advance of the DCs will be mapped out, pointing to the important role played in this by the TNCs. But these events must necessarily be recounted in historical context, especially in relation to the emergence of the economic downturn experienced by much of the global economy since the early 1970s. This downturn - often referred to as "crisis"[1] - began to manifest itself just as industrial production in many DCs assumed an outward orientation, culminating in the export-success of the Newly Industrializing Countries in the 1970s and early 1980s. As this downturn persists, important questions are inevitably raised about its effect not only on the maintenance of industrial growth in DCs, but also on the locational decisions of TNCs. Therefore the bulk of this first chapter is concerned with the historical context in which these events are occurring. Chapter 2 considers the dimensions which characterize the current economic crisis and the transition to a new social and economic order. In subsequent chapters we will focus on the way in which these events are being worked through on a global scale in a single sector - namely automobiles - and we will conclude with a consideration of the general impact of these events on other sectors and thus on the international division of labour in manufacturing.

THE GROWTH OF DEVELOPING COUNTRY INDUSTRIAL PRODUCTION

Broadly speaking, it is possible to distinguish two major periods in the post WW2 industrial performance of the developing world. Until the early 1960s most of this was inward-oriented, producing only for local consumers. In some cases this was predominantly a market-led phenomenon, but in others (most notably in the two giant Asian economies of China and India) the state played an important role in establishing the building-blocks for future industrial expansion. The early 1960s witnessed an important transition, beginning in the Republic of Korea in about 1963. In this the emphasis changed from an import-substituting to an export-oriented pattern of industrialization. This change in direction partly reflected the adoption of particular sets of policies in the Republic of Korea. But it also reflected an important change in the global economy in which production for world markets rather than national markets was becoming the norm in the IACs, and TNCs were adopting wider horizons in their production and sourcing strategies. The success of the Republic of Korea was rapidly emulated by Taiwan Province, Singapore and Hong Kong and these four economies soon saw a sustained expansion of both manufactured exports and overall industrial and economic growth.

Although these four economies were the primary success-stories, they were not alone. Other countries jumped upon the export bandwagon, whilst simultaneously serving a rapidly expanding local market. This included Brazil and Mexico in Latin America and Malaysia and Thailand in Asia. India and China continued their rapid industrial growth, but with a lesser emphasis being given to exports. Collectively this group of DCs (with a few additional countries such as Argentina, Venezuela and Indonesia) have come to be known as the Newly Industrializing Countries (the "NICs"). They accounted for an increasing share of manufactured exports which by the early 1980s had reached almost 80 percent of the DC total.

As a whole DCs saw an increase not only in its share of global manufacturing value added, but even more so in its share of global manufacturing exports (Figure 1.1). Whilst the absolute size of this industrial production and exports may not be so substantial (especially when it is considered that the developing world accounts for around 80 percent of the global population) it is the rising share of the global figures which is significant, especially in the case of manufactured exports.

This concentration in the share of the NICs in total DC production and exports of manufactures is mirrored by a concentration in the sectors within which these exports are to be found. In general upwards of 40 percent of DCs manufactured exports are in the traditional sectors of textiles, garments, shoes and leather products. There has however been a tendency for this share to decline in recent years as some of the NICs - notably the "gang of four" in Asia (that is Hong Kong, the Republic of Korea, Singapore and Taiwan Province) - have moved up the technological profile to produce products such as electronics, chemicals and automobiles. Their success has raised the problem of "graduation" in recent years, with many - most notably within the World Bank - arguing that these four Asian NICs no longer really qualify as "developing countries".

THE ROLE PLAYED BY TNCS

The genesis of the transnational corporation - loosely defined as a firm which has production sites in a number of countries - goes back to the nineteenth century. Its roots lay in the development of the mass market and the large firms in the United States in the nineteenth century,[2]/ a phenomenon which soon swept through many sectors of the United States economy. A large number of these firms quickly made the transition to producing in other countries, indeed, by the early twentieth century the share

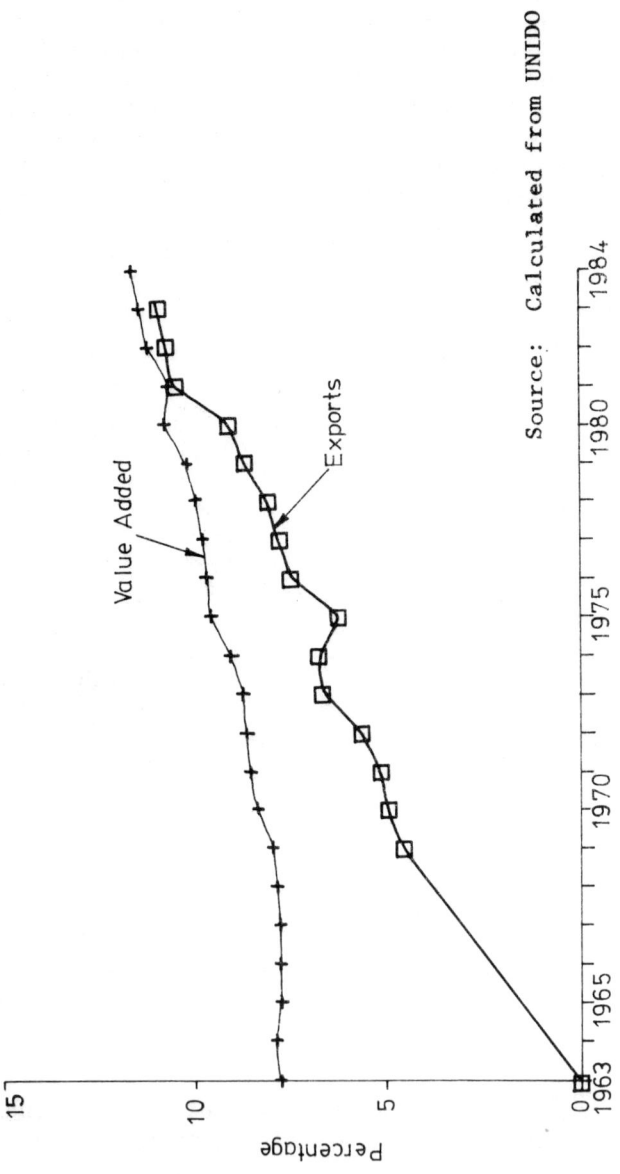

Figure 1.1 Share of the Developing Countries in Global Manufacturing Value Added and Manufactured Exports

Source: Calculated from UNIDO (1985)

[a]Taiwan Province is excluded from these calculations because it is not in the United Nations Family and adequate comparable statistics are not available. Its inclusion would increase not only the share of DCs in both categories, but also its rate of growth since Taiwan Province is the largest single exporter of manufactured goods among all DCs.

of outward direct foreign investment in the United States Gross Domestic Product (GDP) was not much different to that of the late 1970s.3/ This transnationalization of production spread not only through North America but also through Western Europe in the first half of the twentieth century and then, over the past two decades, through Far Eastern firms. Thus by 1976 there were something like 11,000 TNCs with some 82,600 foreign affiliates; of these the largest 371 accounted for around two-thirds of all TNC sales and by 1980 their liquid financial assets were equivalent to over three times total global gold and foreign exchange reserves.4/ In 1980 the total sales of the 350 largest TNCs were equivalent to 28 percent of the GDP of all non-communist economies, employing around 25 million people. This comprised approximately one-quarter of total manufacturing employment in these economies.5/ Perhaps most significantly, TNCs are estimated to contribute around one-third of total global industrial output and to account for a very significant proportion of world trade. In the United States, for example, TNCs are involved in around 97 percent of exports, and intra-firm transactions amount to about 36 percent of United States exports and over 48 percent of imports.6/ Overall, almost two-fifths of total world trade in manufactures occurs <u>within</u> international firms.

The TNCs are thus highly significant economic actors and their locational behaviour is necessarily of great importance to the developing world. If their behaviour is variant over time and sectors, this clearly holds important implications for DCs. Therefore, in addition to examining the role played by TNCs in a particular sector - which is the subject of discussion in later chapters - it is also necessary to examine the changing overall nature of this global pattern of foreign direct investment. We will consider here three important issues - the type of foreign direct investment (FDI) involved, the declining dominance of United States TNCs and the changing significance of the internationalization of productive capital in the post war period. All of these help to set in context the interrelationship between TNCs, the industrial progress of DCs and the international division of labour in manufacturing.

As we shall see, each of these three factors is important to our central concern of the future role to be played by the developing world in manufacturing for global markets. The type of FDI is at issue since it largely determines whether production will take place for the local or the foreign market. The declining dominance of United States TNCs is important since there is some evidence that they have been more likely to locate export-oriented production in DCs than foreign investors from other countries. And, finally, the changing patterns of internationalized production and exchange are relevant because some observers have argued that the phenomenon of TNCs producing in one set of countries for another set of markets is historically transient. It is important, however, to examine each of these sets of ideas in a little more detail.

Types of Foreign Direct Investment (FDI)

It is customary to distinguish between three major types of FDI.7/ The first is <u>horizontal</u>, involving the replication of production facilities in different countries in which essentially the same products are being produced. Often such enterprises are designed to serve the local markets. The second type of TNC is that in which different goods and services are produced in different countries - this is a <u>conglomerate</u> type of organization. <u>Vertical</u> foreign direct investment - which is the third type - occurs when the output of a plant in one country serves as an input into another plant in a second country.

The concept of the New International Division of Labour (NIDL) which achieved a great deal of prominence towards the end of the 1970s arises out of a particular type of vertical foreign direct investment. In this the production of a commodity is broken down and located in subsidiaries in different plants or countries. But the process of production which results is not sequential as it is in the case of producing bauxite in one country, smelting it into alumina in a second country, to aluminum in a third and into final products in a fourth country. Instead it occurs in a <u>disarticulated</u> form, which has two major constituents. In the first of these production occurs through the fragmentation across national boundaries of tasks, rather than sub-processes. For example, in this form of disarticulated FDI an integrated circuit may be manufactured in a number of countries with particular labour-intensive tasks such as inspection or bonding occurring in DCs. In the second type of disarticulated FDI, different components are produced in different countries for assembly in yet another country. Thus in the case of automobiles, a car may be assembled in one location with components which were produced or sub-assembled in other countries. The difference between these two types of disarticulated FDI are to be found in the types of activities which take place in national subsidiaries - in one it is only the labour-intensive parts of the production process; in the other it is the production of labour-intensive components and often also the incorporation of other locally-produced inputs and even, sometimes, technology.

Why is this distinction between sequential and disarticulated FDI germane to our discussion? The reason is that during the late 1960s and much of the 1970s disarticulated FDI became an important strand of internationalized production, especially insofar as it led to the incorporation of DCs in the international division of labour in manufacturing. It is also widely hypothesized (and believed) that this form of international integration presents a paradigm for the future, especially in the automobile industry where it is considered that DCs may become key suppliers of components for the cars which are being assembled in the IACs.

Since this hypothesis provides the analytical framework for the detailed case-study in later chapters it is useful to briefly survey the major aspects of this theory of the NIDL. The first major conceptualization was offered in 1977 (and subsequently translated into English in 1980) by Frobel, Heinrichs and Kreye.8/ They began with an historical framework, considering the evolution of contemporary capitalism over four centuries. From the sixteenth to eighteenth centuries the world economy was characterized by a putting-out system in Europe and the use of forced labour in the colonies and peripheral Europe to produce food. Then, in the latter eighteenth and throughout the nineteenth century, wage-labour began preeminent in Europe, the Americas were penetrated through the use of slave-labour, Indian industry was effectively destroyed and the Chinese and Japanese markets were opened up. This was followed in the first half of the nineteenth century by wage-labour spreading through the United States, Western Europe and Japan and a "peculiar" form of wage-labour being utilized in the colonies to produce raw materials and commodities; some import substituting industrialization also took place in these peripheral economies. Finally, in the most recent period capitalism penetrated throughout the global economy and the developing world provides the reserve army of labour for this pattern of global production.

In this schema Frobel et al argue that the most recent period finds its expression in the form of "world factories"

> The development and refinement of technology and job organization makes it possible to decompose complex production processes into elementary units such that even unskilled labour can be easily trained in quite a short period of time to carry out these rudimentary operations ...
> Usually vertically integrated into transnational enterprises world market factories produce, assemble or finish components, intermediate products or final products in processes which allow for the profitable utilization of the labour-force available at the respective sites . . . to produce for the world market.9/

Frobel et al substantiate their theory by reference to the locational strategies of garment producers from the Federal Republic of Germany. This is a powerful exemplar since in this sector there are many examples of truly disarticulated investments. In Sri Lanka, for instance, shirts are assembled with the cotton, material, collars and cuffs all originating in different countries. It is a similar process which takes place in the electronics industry where, for example, a personal computer may be assembled in the Republic of Korea with components and printed circuit boards being drawn from Japan, Western Europe, Singapore and the Republic of Korea itself.10/ Most pertinently for our case study it is also a stratagem which was widely believed to be occurring in the automobile industry with the "world car" being assembled from components manufactured in a series of "world factories" located in four continents - North America, Western Europe, Asia and Latin America.

Just how relevant this characterization of the production process is for the automobile industry will be considered in detail in later chapters. But it is important to recognize that this view of international location attracted increasing attention during the 1970s and early 1980s. Its credibility was reinforced by the recognition that in many cases it was not necessary for this international division of labour to be organized through the overseas productive operations of foreign subsidiaries since international subcontracting with locally-owned firms was becoming an increasingly important phenomenon, especially in Taiwan Province and the Republic of Korea. TNCs were thus critical to the development of this NIDL in two ways, as producers and as purchasers. Adams, for example, observed that

> International subcontracting - as opposed to the shift of industries or production plants - appears to be gaining ground. It may be implemented less spectacularly than the transfer of whole production units, for products which are inputs into final goods manufactured in DMECs [Developed Market Economy Countries], whether they be parts of footwear or electronic components, particularly if and when MNEs [Multinational Enterprises] are the producers of both components and final products... [It is thus] an irreversible process, an integral part of oligopolistic competition as well as ... the evolution of an international division of labour.11/

It is difficult to determine how large a share of total FDI was comprised of this disarticulated investment, or the extent to which it varied across sectors and countries. Whilst various studies have documented that the phenomenon was important in some countries (the Republic of Korea, Singapore, Taiwan Province, Brazil, Mexico, Malaysia and Thailand) and in some sectors (especially garments and electronics)12/ its precise contribution to the total is unclear. But it would appear that until the mid 1970s, at least, the significance of the NIDL in the total pattern of FDI in the developing world was not dominant. Franko, writing in 1975, estimated that around 97 percent of Western European firms in DCs produced primarily for local markets. Similarly, at about the same time Sabolo and Trajtenberg estimated that of total FDI in DCs and Southern Europe, 42 percent was in agriculture and extraction, 48 percent in manufacturing for the local market and only roughly 10 percent was invested to exploit low-labour costs to produce for world markets.13/ More recently MacEwan concludes a survey of United States FDI with the observation that "[t]hese data provide little support for the view that the search for cheap labour is a dominant feature of the activity of US based multinational corporations".14/

The proponents of this theory of the NIDL were not ignorant of these general figures on the stock of FDI, although they may possibly have overestimated the extent to which disarticulated FDI had taken root in the world economy. Their project was however a different one since it was one of the virtues of their historical approach that they were more concerned with future flows than with existing stocks. And it was their judgment that, at the margin, the trend would be more towards the disarticulated type of FDI with its output destined for foreign markets than either towards horizontal FDI or sequential FDI. It is relevant to note here that this viewpoint received increasingly widespread support and many countries adopted policies of industrial development designed to take account of this type of FDI, for example through the widespread introduction of Export Processing Zones.15/ Thus the OECD produced a report on trends in FDI in the early 1980s and concluded that

> A shift from investment to service local foreign markets to investment to service regional and worldwide markets, especially in South East Asia, was already discernible in the 1960s; and it had continued since then. Automobiles and electronics are the most obvious examples of large multinational firms with production units in different countries producing semi-products to be further processed by the same company or group in another location in the framework of regional or worldwide networks of integrated production units, rendered possible by modern information processing and transmission systems. (OECD, 1981, p 31)

The Declining Dominance of TNCs

If the eighteenth and nineteenth centuries were the era of United Kingdom economic hegemony, with the United Kingdom economy's needs dominating the organization of global production and exchange, the first three quarters of the twentieth century can appropriately be viewed as an era of United States hegemony. MacEwan, Brett and others 16/ have shown how the specific characteristics and needs of the United States productive system were mirrored in the organization of the international economy. This system of productive organization has a great many historically distinct features but the one which concerns us here is the arrangements for the mobility of international productive capital.

As we observed earlier, the modern TNC had its roots in the growth of the large national firm in the United

States in the nineteenth century. There the availability of mass markets and rapidly improving transportation networks provided the scale economies for the growth of large-scale production and this early development of efficiency and scale economies rapidly spilled over into FDI in Western Europe. Whilst we have already mentioned Wilkins' conclusion that by the early twentieth century the TNC's relative role in the United States was not much different to that in the 1960s, the growth of FDI as a <u>global phenomenon</u> is a particular historical characteristic of the post WW2 period. These four decades have been significant not only for the transnationalization of production but also for an important shift in the sectoral intensity of FDI. The earlier concentration of FDI in mining, oil extraction and commodity production had fallen and, by the 1960s, the share of these sectors in total FDI was around one quarter, equivalent to the share of the service sector. By then around half of all FDI was in manufacturing.

The bulk of this stock of FDI was of United States origin. By 1980, for example, 44.2 percent of all TNC affiliates in the DCs had United States parents, with the United Kingdom coming next with a share of 22.8 percent and Japan following far behind in third place with only 6.6 percent.<u>17/</u> This pattern of FDI reflects three major factors. The first and most obvious is the historical preponderance of, first, the United Kingdom and subsequently the United States economies. Being the largest and most dynamic economies in the world with the most technologically advanced firms, they were consequently the most likely to venture abroad. Second, especially in the case of the United Kingdom and France, their history of colonial rule gave them ready access to developing country markets. And, third, for reasons which will be explored in more detail in Chapter 2, it was the United States and United Kingdom firms which had the greatest propensity to invest in other countries, especially in DCs.

Underlying this outward movement of United States FDI - and especially its disarticulated component - was the development of institutional and legal arrangements to facilitate its expansion. Most pertinent was the introduction of specific tariff-legislation to make such arrangements feasible. This was first introduced in the United States in the 1960s and had the effect of only taxing the value added component of foreign production as opposed to the total nominal value of imports. This important piece of legislation contributed to the breaking up of the production process and in organizing particular sub-components of it to be produced in low-wage economies. It was of course not the only way in which FDI was facilitated and other important legal arrangements such as double-taxation agreements also played their part in the global expansion of FDI.

Most of this post WW2 environment - which saw the globalization of FDI - was an era of United States economic dominance. But as we shall see below, it was a period in which the relative economic strength of the American economy began to wane. One of the indicators of this waning industrial competitiveness in the United States (which was broadly mirrored in the United Kingdom) was the rapid growth of import penetration which substantially exceeded the overall growth in world trade and integration. Table 1.1 illustrates the extent and pervasiveness of this fall through the fifteen years which saw the peak and decline of United States economic dominance. It also illustrates the extent to which United States TNCs saw a decline in their global market shares in these sectors.

Consequently, insofar as the characteristics of this overall flow of FDI in the world economy reflected particular features of the United States system, so its patterns began to change. The clearest measurable change was to be found in the nature of overall flows, and as can be seen from Table 1.2, the decade of the 1970s saw very significant alterations in the pattern. Considered as a source of FDI, the share of the United States fell from 60.5 percent to 29.3 percent; as a point of destination, its share rose from 9.2 percent in 1970-71 to 42.9 percent in 1981. There are of course a variety of reasons why the United States share of these ratios changed, but it is at least suggestive of the conclusion that it reflects a decline in manufacturing competitiveness by United States TNCs, both in the home and foreign markets.

The overall national distribution of FDI thus changed as the relative position of the United States economy and its TNCs altered. What is less clear is whether this change in the type of FDI, specifically with respect to the extension of the disarticulated vertical FDI with which we are concerned, can be related to the decline in the dominance of United States TNCs. If so this not only enhances our general understanding of the behaviour of TNCs, but because many industrial strategies were consciously designed to take advantage of this perceived locational orientation of TNCs, it also has important policy implications. The case of the automobile sector is

Table 1.1
The Decline of United States Industrial Competitiveness (1960-79)

	United States Firms Share of Domestic Market		
	1960	1970	1974
Automobiles	96	83	79
Steel	96	86	86
Electrical Components	100	94	80
Farm Machinery	93	92	85
Consumer Electronics	94	68	49
Metal-cutting Machine Tools	97	89	74
Metal-forming Machine Tools	97	93	75
Textile Machinery	93	67	55
	United States Firms Share of Global Market		
	1962	1970	1979
Motor Vehicles	23	18	14
Aircraft	71	67	58
Telecommunications	29	15	15
Metal-working Machinery	33	17	22
Agricultural Machinery	40	30	23
Hand or Machine Tools	21	19	14
Textile or Leather Machinery	16	10	7
Railway Vehicles	35	18	12

Source: Reprinted from 30 June 1980 Issue of BusinessWeek by special permission, (c) 1980 by McGraw Hill.

particularly important here. As we shall see in Chapter 3, during the 1970s and early 1980s the United States industry moved towards a global-sourcing strategy in which the intent was to purchase wholly-made components from a large variety of DCs and to assemble them into final products in a different locale. Will these policies of United States TNCs endure in the latter half of the 1980s and during the 1990s, and will they be adopted by auto TNCs from other

Table 1.2
The Percentage Share of the United States in the Source and Destination of FDI, 1970-1 to 1980-1 (Two Year Moving Averages)

	1970-71	1971-72	1972-73	1973-74	1974-75	1975-76	1976-77	1977-78
As as Source	60.5	56.0	51.2	45.7	47.5	49.4	45.5	45.1
Point of Destination	9.2	5.4	12.5	21.7	14.6	22.2	23.9	21.7

	1978-79	1979-80	1980-81	1981-82	1982-83
As a Source	48.1	45.8	29.3	23.9	22.0
Point of Destination	29.2	32.6	37.8	41.5	41.6

Source: Calculated from International Monetary Fund Balance of Payments Yearbook

countries?
It is this which points to the relevance of our present study. Such speculations on the changing nature of FDI and the specific characteristics of United States TNCs are best undertaken on a sectoral basis. But so far, these have been limited in number. As we have seen, Frobel et al have done it for the Federal Republic of Germany garments industry and there have been a large number of studies for the electronics sector.[18] The importance of these sectoral investigations are particularly pointed at this period of historical transition. It is for these reasons - and also because the auto sector is the largest single industrial branch - that we have chosen to examine the evolution of these locational factors in the production of autos and auto-components for global consumption.

Changes in the Pattern of Internationalization in the Recent Global Economy

Economies of scale have been one of the major factors underlying the growth and expansion of TNCs. Despite the fact (as we shall see in the next chapter) that it appears as though there are many more diseconomies of scale than has often been thought, the search for larger markets has been an important component of post-war economic growth. Since the nature of scale economies is a complex phenomenon, it is important to disentangle three important dimensions - scale of plant, scale of product and scale of firm.[19]

There are three basic ways in which these scale economies can be realized. The first of these is to build large plants to serve transnational markets, and it is this which underlies much of the growth of global trade in manufactures, especially of the intra-industry variety.[20] In these cases the primary factor inducing specialization is scale economies at the plant-level and these largely explain the growth of the world-factories and world trade discussed above. A second way of realizing scale economies is to engage in horizontal FDI, this providing economies at both the product and firm-level.[21] This involves far less trade and international integration. And, finally, scale economies may arise with many plants in many countries - some of which may be independently owned - contributing to general firm-level indirect costs such as marketing, design and research. What is common about these three dimensions of scale is that each in its own way requires the internationalization of different elements of operation, be they of final products, technology or finance.

This internationalization cannot be realized in any single form and in fact it is possible to consider three terrains in which internationalization can occur.22/ These are the conduit of productive capital (of which FDI is the main constituent), that of commodity capital (by which is meant trade) and that of money capital (that is, financial flows). The TNC in fact often embodies all of these three elements, producing in various countries, trading the intermediate and final outputs and channelling funds around the globe. Yet it is not the only variant of internationalization and a variety of different forms have been developed, including international sub-contracting between related firms, joint-ventures, the licensing of technology, market-sharing arrangements and arms-length trade between wholly-independent buyers and sellers. Thus the realization of scale economies through internationalization need not necessarily involve the growth and expansion of the TNC.23/

Table 1.3 compares the rate of growth of these three elements of capital in the period between 1955 and the early 1980s. It contrasts the growth of commodity capital (trade) with productive capital and distinguishes between two elements of financial flows to developing countries, official government-to-government flows and via the commercial banks. A number of interesting and relevant points emerge. In the first place the growth of internationalization via trade was, over the whole period, the most rapidly-growing form. Second, during the 1970s private commercial flows were preponderant, reflecting the recycling of petro-dollars by the largest private banks and the growth of indigenously-owned manufacturing capability in the NICs. And, third, it was during the decade of the 1960s that the internationalization of productive capital grew most rapidly compared to the other elements of capital.

What this exercise does is to relativize and periodize the phenomenon of the TNC, especially in its relationships with DCs as a conduit for the disarticulated form of FDI. We hypothesized above that it was predominantly an expression of United States economic dominance and we see here that it saw its greatest growth in the decades of the 1960s and 1970s, a period in which the United States economy was at the height of its economic and political power. After that there is some evidence that the predominant form of internationalization was in the arena

Table 1.3
Percentage Annual Growth Rates of the Three Circuits of Internationalization, 1955-56 to 1981-82 (Two year Moving Averages).

| | Commodity Capital | Money Capital | | Productive Capital |
| | | (Official | (Commercial | |
	(Trade)	Flows)	Banks)	(FDI)^c
1955/6-1960/1	6.1	11.2^a	NA	NA
1960/1-1965/6	8.7	2.9	NA	11.6
1965/6-1970/1	11.3	3.9	NA	11.5
1970/1-1975/6	22.9	19.0	25.2^b	16.4
1975/6-1980/1	16.2	12.5	19.4	12.3
1981-1982	-5.9	NA	-21.5	NA

Note: These figures are in current dollars and are therefore more illuminating when comparing relative magnitudes between the three circuits than within each circuit over time.

Sources:
(i) World exports from GATT Annual Reports.
(ii) Official financial flows include OPEC and all non-CMEA developed countries and refers only to financial flows to DCs (OECD Annual Reviews). It excludes, therefore flows in the 1950s under the Marshall Plan.
   Private financial flows refers to net borrowings through the international capital markets (IMF International Capital Markets)
(iii) FDI outflows includes the 19 major investing countries plus (from 1972) outflows from DCs. DC outflows prior to 1972 were negligible (IMF Balance of Payments Yearbooks)

^{a} 1956/7-1960/1
^{b} 1970-1975/6
^{c} Gross flows

of trade, with independently-owned local firms - partly financed through international capital flows - becoming more imports.
   All these points are germane to the continued expansion of the NIDL. If this theory of international

specialization were to hold it would suggest that the internationalization of productive capital would continue to grow more rapidly than that of commodity capital or that of finance capital. But this does not emerge from the figures in Table 1.3 and through this periodization of the flow of these three elements of capital, it leads us to further question the likely overall advance of the NIDL. Moreover, these aggregate figures are in part recounting a distinct strategy adopted in a particular period by the dominant United States firms. As they began to run into increasing international competition in the 1960s and 1970s, and as the quest for some form of scale-economies became increasingly important, so internationalization was furthered in the form of FDI, a significant portion of which was of the disarticulated type in the developing world.

An interesting illustration of this strategy - as well as the different objectives of Japanese and United States TNCs - can be drawn from the case of the colour TV sector in the late 1960s and early 1970s.[24]/ The United States market was being rapidly penetrated by imports from Japan which were not only cheaper but of higher quality and reliability. The response of the major United States producers was to shift production (or parts of production) to low-wage south-east Asian economies with the intent of beating the Japanese back on the basis of price. The Japanese responded instead with a strategy of continuing to produce in Japan but with increasingly automated technology. This Japanese strategy soon triumphed over the American firms, most of whom were soon forced out of the market as independent producers. And when protectionism finally began to affect the location of FDI - making it difficult to continue serving the United States market from production platforms in Japan - the Japanese firms predominantly moved to the final markets rather than adopting the United States corporate stratagem of utilizing third country production sites.

In considering the overall role played by TNCs in the extension of the NIDL we thus hypothesize that it represents a particular confluence of factors in the 1960s and 1970s which need not necessarily endure, and more specifically, may not necessarily be evident as the world economy moves into an era when United States economic dominance dissolves. It was thus largely a temporal phenomenon, reflecting a period of extensive United States influence. MacEwan probably overstretches the point when he goes much further and argues that this was a much wider issue, affecting not just disarticulated NIDL-type foreign investment, but all FDI.

> ...whereas previous imperialist powers - Great Britain for example - exploited the international economy primarily through trade and finance capital, the establishment of operating subsidiaries abroad by multinational firms became the hallmark of US imperialism and its post-World War II heyday.25/

Before we proceed to examine in detail the evolving pattern of international specialization in the automobile sector, it is necessary to expand on the historical context within which these events are unfolding. In the last part of this chapter we will focus on the "crisis", the turning-point which is currently being experienced in the global economy. This enables us to situate the discussion in Chapter 2 which attempts to periodize this turning-point by comparing it to similar transitions in industrial history. Simultaneously we aim to draw-out the political and social dimensions of these events since they have an important bearing on the wider theme of the industrial trajectory of the world economy which we are exploring in this book. The continuing preoccupation in all of this discussion is with the international dimensions of the historically evolving pattern of industrialization - how were peripheral economies incorporated in the process of industrial accumulation and, more importantly, how will they continue to do so in the future?

SITUATING THE 1970S: A CHANGE IN DIRECTION?

As we have seen, the international dimensions of TNC locational decisions can only really be understood in historical context. Since it is our view that the most appropriate form of contextualization is one which takes a long view of historical developments (see Chapter 2), it is appropriate to go back some distance in time to gain a sense of perspective. Table 1.4, derived from an historical study of the major OECD economies by Maddison, provides a long time-series of relevant data (1820-1979). Maddison's periodization for the IACs leads him to distinguish between four major phases. Phase 1 between 1820 and 1913 he characterizes as the "Liberal Order", with little unemployment and a great deal of freedom for international trade and capital movements. Phase 2 (1913-

Table 1.4
Historical rates of growth (1820-1979)

	GDP	per capita GDP	capital stock	exports
1820-1870	2.2	1.0	(na)	4.0
1870-1913	2.5	1.4	2.9	3.9
1913-1950	1.9	1.2	1.7	1.0
1950-1970	4.9	3.8	5.5	8.6
1973-1979	2.5	2.0	4.4	4.8

Source: A. Maddison, Phases of Capitalist Development (Oxford University Press, 1985). Reprinted by permission.

50) is considered to be a "Beggar-Your-Neighbour" period in which unemployment is high, but trade barriers are erected and capital mobility is low. Phase 3, between 1950 and 1973, represents the "Golden Age"; priority is given to full employment, there is a strong move towards free trade and an increase in the international mobility of both capital and labour. Finally, and Maddison who writes in 1982 is unsure of whether this represents a momentary pause or a change in long run direction, there comes the post-1973 period of "Blurred Objectives" in which unemployment reappears, capital mobility and free trade are maintained and there are increasing restrictions on the mobility of labour. Arguably, were Maddison to be writing with the hindsight of the mid-eighties, he might have questioned the maintenance of mobility for commodities since protectionist pressures are becoming increasingly significant. He would almost also have reinforced his observation of a sustained slowdown in GDP growth.

What emerges from Maddison's estimates are two major observations. First, the rate of growth in the post World War II Golden Age was historically unprecedented. At 3.8 percent per capita it was almost three times that of any comparable period in history. But, secondly and perhaps more significantly, the rate of growth of world exports was not only over twice as high as any comparable period, but was also more than double the growth of per capita incomes. Thus the Golden Age not only represented boom conditions, but also a period of significant internationalization. It became increasingly difficult to speak of economies as separate entities and thus, for example, the ratio of trade to GDP rose almost everywhere in the industrially advanced world.26/

Reflecting on these events some observers have begun to speak of an "economic crisis" affecting not just the United States and United Kingdom economies, but global growth and order as well. Whilst the word "crisis" is often used in an apocalyptic and not very helpful sense to signify a process of collapse, a more accurate reading of its meaning provides a helpful insight into the nature of current events. Its dictionary definition (Concise Oxford Dictionary) is "Turning-point, especially of disease; moment of danger or suspense in politics, commerce; etc" and it was in this sense that the term was widely used in economics in the nineteenth century.

It is our contention - as we shall argue in Chapter 2 - that the world is indeed at just such a turning point in history, which we term the transition from machinofacture to systemofacture.27/ Before we proceed to map out the characteristics of this transition - and in particular to focus on the internationalization of productive capital in this transition - it is important to set the backdrop of some of the major dimensions of this contemporary crisis. The four which are most relevant to the discussion which follows - both at the general theoretical level and with respect to our case-study of the automobile sector - are the unevenness of productivity growth, the emergence of global trade imbalances, the uneven re-emergence of unemployment in the industrially advanced world and the growth of protectionism.

The Unevenness of Productivity Growth. Table 1.5 considers in detail the changing balance of productivity levels (measured in terms of output value per person-year of labour input) between the six major IACs and in general compares the United States levels with the fifteen major non-Communist IACs. It is illuminating at a number of levels. In the first place it illustrates the phenomenal relative productivity improvement of the United States economy between 1870 and 1950. It also shows how between 1950 and 1973, most of the IACs had begun to catch-up with the United States, a phenomenon which was particularly evident in the late 1960s when United States productivity growth began to slow.28/ Another important issue emerging from Table 1.5 is the rapid progress of Japan and the poor performance of the United Kingdom. The Japanese case is somewhat understated since its industrial progress - based on a policy of sectoral-targeting - has been uneven and in particular sectors (such as the automobile industry which

Table 1.5
Productivity Levels per Person Hour Relative to the United States (=100)

	1870	1913	1950	1973	1979	1981
United States	100	100	100	100	100	100
United Kingdom	114	81	56	64	66	78.2
France	60	54	44	76	86	95.5
Germany, Federal Republic of	61	57	33	71	84	95.5
Italy	63	43	32	66	70	NA
Japan	24	22	14	46	53	58.5
All 15 IACs	77	61	46	69	75	NA

Source: Drawn from Maddison (1982) and cited in Glyn et al (1986).

we will consider in later chapters) its progress has been phenomenal.29/

The Emergence of Global Trade Imbalances. One of the consequences of this unevenness of productivity growth - and specifically the relatively poor performance of the United Kingdom and the United States - has been the sharp growth of import penetration in some countries (see Table 1.1 for the United States). This has exceeded the general pattern of global trade growth in these countries and has been associated with a sharp deterioration in the balance of payments of these two countries. The trend in recent years in the external trade account of the United States is shown in Figure 1.2, and despite a growth in the net positive balance on service exports, the United States balance of payments current account deficit has also mushroomed over the past decade. In keeping with the large relative size of the United States economy this growing deficit has effectively dwarfed the balance of payments difficulties of all other IACs, and even of many of the large debtor DCs. Indeed from being the largest creditor (total external credits minus total external liabilities) in 1983, the United States had become the most debt-ridden by 1985 and at its current rate, the growth of its current annual liabilities exceeds the total stock of liabilities of Brazil, the next largest debtor country.

The Re-emergence of Unemployment. The third dimension

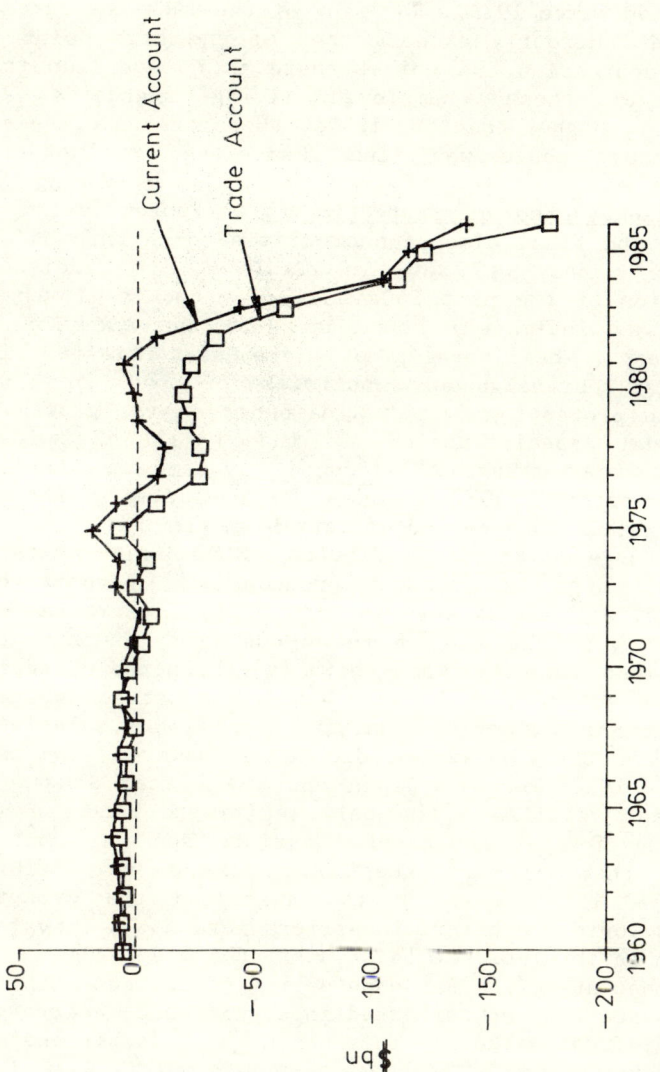

Source: International Monetary Fund Balance of Payments Statistics

Figure 1.2 United States Balance of Payments (current dollars)

of this contemporary "crisis" - or perhaps "turning point" might be a better phrase - is the changing structure of employment. It is here that important similarities and differences are to be found with the previous most recent crisis in the global economy. In the depression of the 1930s there was a collapse not just of employment but also of output. By contrast, in the most recent period output has held up whilst employment has fallen. Table 1.6 shows the extent to which employment has indeed fallen in the recent period since 1973. For many of the IACs the rate of unemployment currently exceeds that of the high point of the 1930s depression and whilst there is no question that for most of these unemployed living standards are significantly higher than the 1930s, there are nevertheless a great many people who find themselves involuntarily unemployed.30/

The Reemergence of Protectionism. Protectionism is the fourth and final dimension of crisis which informs our discussion. As we saw in Table 1.3, Maddison's periodization of the past 160 years of economic growth in the IACs was intimately bound up with the question of market access. The liberal pre-WW1 era was contrasted with the "beggar-your-neighbour" policies of the inter-war period when protectionism put a dampener on the growth of international specialization. Indeed it is widely recognized that the GATT-induced system of tariff-reductions after 1950 was one of the primary factors stimulating this long period of very high growth.

GATT targeted tariff protection as a primary obstacle to growth and in various rounds of negotiation, multilateral agreements were introduced to lower this form of barrier. By the end of the 1960s trade between the industrialized countries was generally unhampered by tariff restrictions and within Western Europe and between Western Europe and North America, market access was relatively uneven. When trade frictions did arise, however - as they did in the 1950s between Japan and the United States in garments and textiles - the only legitimate recourse was the introduction of non-tariff barriers such as quotas. But with the virtual exception of the multi-fibres agreement - first applying to Japan and then to the developing world - non-tariff barriers were not a prevalent phenomenon in the IACs, at least until the mid 1970s.

At that stage the Japanese policy of concentrating on particular sectors was reflected in significant penetration within individual markets. This was highly visible and had an easily-identifiable response - quota-barriers. Thus

Table 1.6
Unemployment Rates in OECD Economies

	1933	1959-67	1973	1977	1979	1981	1984
Belgium	10.6	2.4	2.9	7.8	8.7	12.9	13.3
Denmark	14.5	1.4	0.7	5.8	5.3	9.5	10.1
France	NA	0.7	1.8	4.8	6.0	8.9	9.3
Germany, Federal Republic of	14.8	1.2	1.0	4.0	3.4	6.7	8.3
Ireland	NA	4.6	5.6	9.2	7.5	11.5	16.0
Italy	5.9	6.2	4.9	6.4	7.5	9.6	10.4
Japan	NA	1.4	1.2	2.0	2.0	2.0	2.7
Netherlands	9.7	0.9	2.3	4.1	4.1	10.2	15.6
United Kingdom	13.9	1.8	2.5	5.7	5.8	11.3	11.7
United States	20.5	5.3	4.9	7.0	5.8	8.9	7.5

Source: Freeman, Clarke and Soete 1982; Freeman and Soete (1985)

began a series of Orderly Marketing Agreements (OMAs) and Voluntary Export Restraints (VERs) in which first the Japanese and then Western Europe, the Republic of Korea and Taiwan Province were given restricted access to the United States market. At the same time the EEC countries began to take action, sometimes as in the case of autos on an individual country-basis, but more often as a Community action. The Japanese had long had non-tariff barriers of this sort making it very difficult to export manufactured products to that market despite the low level of nominal tariffs.

The number of products covered in these agreements rapidly increased, particularly in the 1980s when it became obvious to many that the problem of unemployment would not be easily solved. Soon a wide number of sectors were covered by such non-tariff barriers including shoes, garments, textiles, steel, autos, colour TVs, agricultural products, video tape recorders, machine tools, photocopying machines, typewriters and semiconductors. Thus one of the primary factors underlying the growth of international specialization through the NIDL - that is, unrestricted market access - has come under threat.

In terms of a change in direction in the IACs, the new orientation in trade-regime is probably most visible in the United States. At the beginning of 1986 the United States

International Trade Commission had around 50 requests for protectionist barriers in particular sectors and by the beginning of 1987 the number of requests it was considering had doubled. Protectionism is on the political agenda and looks likely to be an issue of continuing importance in contemporary United States politics. All this of course has significant implications for the pattern of international location in manufacturing, a subject which we will explore in later chapters with respect to the automobile industry.

TNCS AND THE INTERNATIONAL DIVISION OF LABOUR IN THE AUTOMOBILE SECTOR

Our concern thus lies with the changing nature of the international division of labour in manufacturing and specifically with the role to be played by DCs. As we noted above it has been widely believed that the developing countries would increasingly be incorporated into production for global markets via a system in which they would assume responsibility for the labour-intensive components of products, and often even for the labour-intensive stages within component manufacture. This division of labour would be greased by the TNCs, either as the owners of production facilities in DCs, or as purchasers of sub-contracted manufactures. It would also have the effect of reinforcing the momentum of the export-oriented industrialization which had fueled economic growth in the NICs and would in time spread to other developing countries, beginning with the so-called second-tier NICs.

We have suggested some caveats in relation to this scenario. The whole phenomenon of FDI was seen to be related to a particular period of history, one of United States dominance. More specifically, it was suggested that the disarticulated component of FDI which is at the centre of the NIDL was of only limited overall significance and was most clearly related to the strategic behaviour of United States TNCs. Thus as United States technological, economic and political dominance ebbed, so this form of international location would be of reduced significance. Added to this strategic component of locational behaviour there is the additional question of the contextual environment in which these events are occurring. The world economy has moved off its historically unprecedented high-growth path and is now at a point of transition. This, as we shall see, is not so much a transition in the rate of growth (which may only be a temporary phenomenon) but one to a structurally different form of production and organization. Some of the characteristics of this transition - particularly the rising levels of unemployment and trade-imbalances - make it increasingly unlikely that such global locational horizons will be permitted, since protectionism is growing and market access is becoming increasingly problematic. Thus the "politics of location" will be altered. Moreover the nature of best-practice production in the new order also involves significant alterations in the economics of location.

* * *

These points are made at a general discursive level and are usually only considered as a macroeconomic phenomenon. Yet many of the actual decisions which shape the course of world events are made at the firm- and the sectoral-level. Thus in order to "test" which view of international location is valid requires some form of more detailed validation. We have chosen to do so through an analysis of the automobile sector, and will do so for two reasons. First, with its ancillary component-suppliers and the infrastructure required to support its use, the automobile industry is the largest single sector in manufacturing. And, second, the auto industry was considered to be a paradigm for the development and extension of the NIDL, both by outside academic observers and by insiders within governments and some of the firms themselves. It is useful to compare what is now emerging with these expectations. What shape it takes therefore has some significance for the general orientation of FDI and industrial growth in many countries.

Our primary intent is to explore the evolving division of labour in this sector by focussing on that part of its locational strategy which bears relevance to the NIDL. We are therefore not directly concerned with the phenomenon of horizontal FDI (that is, with auto TNCs producing the same products in different countries) as a central concern. Instead our primary interest lies with the extent to which auto assemblers utilize a system of international sub-contracting, either for components or for parts of components. The central topic for empirical investigation lies thus with the component sector and its locational strategy and with the purchasing policies of the assemblers. In the course of this research we visited most of the major automobile assemblers and a number of the major component-manufacturers in Japan, Western Europe and the United States. The results of this research are presented in Chapters 3-7, but before these results are pursued it is helpful to contextualize the discussion within a more detailed account of the current transition in the world economy. It is therefore to this subject that the analysis first turns.

NOTES

1. See Evans and Kaplinsky (eds) (1984) for a discussion of whether this is best characterized as "crisis" or "slowdown".
2. This process is described in great detail in Chandler (1977).
3. Wilkins (1974).
4. See Dunning (1981) and Brett (1985).
5. UNCTC (1983).
6. Brett (1985).
7. See Caves (1982) chapter 1 for an elaboration of these ideas.
8. Frobel, Heinrichs and Kreye (1980).
9. Frobel, Heinrichs and Kreye (1980) p 35 and pp 302-3.
10. These phenomena are described for the electronics sector by Ernst (1985b) and O'Connor (1985).
11. Adams (1975), pp 93-4.
12. See, for example, Finger (1975 and 1976), Frobel, Heinrichs and Kreye (1980), Helleiner (1973), Jarrett (1979), Nayyar (1978) and Sharpston (1975).
13. See Franko (1975) and Sabolo and Trajtenberg (1976).
14. MacEwan (1982), p. 51.
15. Between 1978 and 1980 the number of Export Processing Zones increased from 220 to 350. See Basile and Germidis (1984) for a wider discussion of these zones.
16. See MacEwan (1982), Brett (1985) and the references therein for a discussion of these issues.
17. See UNCTC (1983), Table II.17. This comprises analysis of a sample of 27,541 foreign subsidiaries.
18. See Ernst (1985b) and O'Connor (1985) and the bibliographies therein.

19. See Kaplinsky (1985) for a discussion of these strands of scale economies and how they now appear to be changing. These issues, as well as the discussion which follows, are considered further in the final chapter.

20. See Giersch (1979) for a discussion of the growing importance of intra-industry trade. This issue, as well as the discussion which follows, are considered in the final chapter.

21. Product scale economies reflect the length and extent of production of a single model. This can be met either through constructing more smaller plants or an enlargement of an existing plant. Firm scale economies reflect total vehicle production which may include any number of product combinations produced in a variety of plant sizes and countries. These three dimensions of scale - product, plant and firm - are treated extensively in Chapter 8.

22. See Palloix (1977) for an elaboration of such a perspective.

23. This issue is considered further in the final chapter.

24. See Sciberras (1979) and Baba (1985).

25. MacEwan (1982) p19.

26. In 1968-78 the trade/GDP ratio rose from 39 percent to 48.2 percent for the Federal Republic of Germany, from 10.6 percent to 18 percent for the US, from 43.7 percent to 57.3 percent for the United Kingdom, from 43.7 percent to 59.9 percent for Sweden and from 82.6 percent to 89.8 percent for the Netherlands.

27. And others, such as Piore and Sabel (1984) refer to as the transition from Fordism to Flexible Specialization. These views are also discussed in Chapter 2.

28. See Freeman, Clark and Soete (1982) and Bowles, Gordon and Weisskopf (1983) for a discussion of the periodization of the US slowdown.

29. See Lipietz (1987), Table 7, for details of sectoral productivity-variations between Japan and other countries.

30. A review of the literature examining the likelihood of these high levels of unemployment enduring can be found in Kaplinsky (1987).

2

The Point of Transition—
From Machinofacture
to Systemofacture

The post second WW2 boom - identified, as we have seen, by Maddison as the "Golden Age " - was followed by the downturn of the 1970s and 1980s. What at first looked like a short-run cyclical event, endured and increasingly became less amenable to correction via the fine-tuning of the Keynesian policies which had facilitated escape from the Great Depression of the 1930s. The concept of "crisis" - defined here as a turning point (see Chapter 1) - has come to be widely accepted as a useful way of situating the discussion of the prolonged economic downturn. But just what sort of a turning-point is it? What explains it? How can these economic difficulties be resolved? And, of primary concern to our discussion, how will the feasible changes affect the international division of labour in manufacturing?

Unless some theory can be provided to explain the origins and causes of this crisis it becomes very difficult to conceive of the necessary reorientations which are required to escape the prolongation of the unemployment, the unevenness of productivity-growth, the trade imbalances and the rise of protectionism which, as we saw in Chapter 1, are some of the major manifestations of current global economic problems. There is of course no shortage of explanations in the literature, each with its attendant policy implications, implicit or explicit. But the one which we will explore in this chapter is that which attempts to link the crisis with technological concerns. Here there has been a burgeoning debate in recent years, much of which is now at the forefront of public policy discussion, around the themes of long-waves and reindustrialization. Only once a view is reached on these complex phenomena will it be possible to develop a perspective on the likely implications for FDI, especially that incorporating the NIDL.

We begin, therefore, with a brief summary of the discussion of two sets of theories before proceeding to a presentation of our own interpretation of the relevant period of history. The first of these represents an attempt to link the observed long-waves in history to major technological developments. The second focuses more specifically on "social technology", that is on the organization of production in different periods of history and differentiates between the paradigms of mass production and flexible specialization. Each of these - as we shall argue below - offers a key important insight into the new wave and, from the two, it is possible to construct a more comprehensive view of the developments which are now occurring.

TECHNOLOGY AND LONG-WAVES

It was in the late 1970s and early 1980s that the theory of long-waves began to resurface. It had first been introduced in the early twentieth century by a Soviet economic historian (who later became a Minister in the Bolshevik government) named Kondratieff. In reviewing the history of industrialization, he had observed a series of "wave-like" motions of around fifty-year duration. Searching for an explanation Kondratieff looked to the longevity of infrastructural investments and the need for periodic renewal. These views were picked up by Schumpeter in the 1930s who provided a more convincing causal explanation for these observed long-term fluctuations. Schumpeter argued that the major cause of the cycles was the development and diffusion of a series of "heartland technologies", each of which spawned a cluster of related investments. In the case of these heartland technologies the clusters were sufficiently large as to unbalance the whole economic system, leading to phases of expansion when new clusters were diffusing and to stagnation when they had run out of steam.

By the end of the 1970s, when detailed sectoral studies were showing that demand-management alone was insufficient to rectify international imbalances and to bring supply into balance with demand, Chris Freeman and his colleagues at the University of Sussex picked up the issue of long-waves first raised by Kondratieff and then elaborated by Schumpeter.1/ In discussing the link between the cycles and technological change, they specified the respective heartland technologies as comprising of textiles and steam-engines in the late eighteenth century, railroads and steel in the mid-nineteenth century, the internal combustion engine, electricity and parts of the chemical industry in the first half of the twentieth century and microelectronics technology and parts of the chemical industry in the most recent cycle in the post WW2 Golden Age. The causal explanation offered for this cyclical movement was as follows. In the early phase of each cycle the new heartland technology was associated with new products; this led to an increase in demand and an expansion of (labour-intensive) production, which reinforced demand. So a virtuous circle of innovation and growth was established. But after a while the heartland technology ran out of growth-potential for new products, the scale economies inherent in production began to be realized and the technology came to be utilized for rationalizing the production of existing goods, as in the application of electronics to automation in the 1980s.2/ This soon led to the displacment of workers, a decline in demand and the intensification of competition and thus induced a downward spiral towards recession.

These views on the technological underpinnings of the long-waves provided valuable insights into an economic debate which was becoming bogged-down in a confrontation between monetarists and Keynesians, neither of whom were saying much of relevance to the issue of supply. What Freeman and his colleagues offered was a path to understanding the success of Japan and the Republic of Korea, both of whom had achieved success by focussing on technology and the supply-side of production. There can be no question that in this they were changing the framework of the policy-debate, providing for example a theoretical point of entry to the reindustrialization policies which became increasingly popular as the 1980s wore on.

Another particularly valuable outcome of this set of theorization was the identification of the major technological developments which Schumpeter first referred to as "heartland technologies". Freeman extended the initial insight of Schumpeter and offered a threefold classification of technological change.3/ The first of these are incremental changes, occurring continuously and representing minor changes in product and process. The second set are radical innovations which comprise a more significant set of technological breakthroughs as in the case of nylon and polyethylene.4/ The third and final set of technological changes are the <u>revolutionary</u> ones described earlier such as the steam engine, the railroads, the internal combustion engine and microelectronics.

But valuable as though this particular perspective of technologically-based long-waves is, it is not free from difficulties, of which three stand out in importance.<u>5</u>/ The first of the objections to this recent set of long-wave theorists arises out of the conception of technologies which they use, particularly in their earlier formulations. Their preoccupation lay with machinery, as can be seen from the list of the heartland technologies which they identified. Steam engines, textile machinery, steel, railroads, the internal combustion engine, chemicals and microelectronics - all of these are in the realm of embodied technology. (We will refer to this in later discussion as the "forces of production"). There seemed to be little space in their schema for "soft" or "disembodied" (as it is often called in the economics literature) technology, and which we will loosely term for the moment as "social relations". It is true that if pressed they could point to the social implications of the heartland technologies which they had identified. But this is a far cry from endogenizing the issue of organizational technology into their model of expansion, recession and depression. This is true for organizational technologies at the micro level - as on the shop-floor - and in the wider sphere of social interaction.

A second and related problem in these formulations of the long-wave is a pervasive sense of technological determinism. Given that social relations are in some way affected by the events which they are recording, their relationship to technological change "proper" (that is, in embodied technology) is generally considered by the long wave theorists to be unicausal. Changes in embodied technology are considered to <u>induce</u> changes in social relations, and in this perspective of technological determinism they were rather close to the earlier views of Marx - "The handmill gives you society with the feudal lord; the steam-mill, the society with the individual capitalist".<u>6</u>/

The third difficulty in these recent technology-oriented long wave theorists concerns the origins of the new heartland technologies. There was of course a long debate about whether they were induced by the extreme competitive pressures of the downswing or the rich surpluses of the upswing. There was also an interesting recounting of the change in Schumpeter's own views in which he began with a view of technical change which was exogenous to the system of accumulation - that is the firm - but as he recognized the increasing complexity of modern technology, this function was endogenized in his analytical model.7/ But despite these important observations there remains a sense of unease about the way in which these heartland technologies emerge. They tend to have a slightly mystical, *deus ex machina* quality about them. Why do they last fifty years? Do they necessarily run out of new products? Are "competitive pressures" a sufficient explanation for their emergence?

In a recent refinement of this discussion of technology and long-waves, Perez8/ goes some way to meet these problems with the initial formulation of her colleagues at Sussex. At the same time she builds a bridge towards the concept of flexible specialization which we will consider below. The major complement to their discussion which she offers is to recognize the importance of social relations - which she terms the "socio-institutional context" - in the transition between the waves. For Perez, each of the waves represent a "techno-economic paradigm" which becomes dominant when it fulfills the following conditions

- Clearly perceived low - and descending - relative cost
- Apparently unlimited supply (for all practical purposes)
- Obvious potential for all-pervasive influence in the productive sphere, and
- A generally recognized capacity, based on a set of interwoven technical and organizational innovations, to reduce the costs and change the quality of capital equipment, labour and products.9/

Long-wave recessions for Perez arise when there is a mismatch between the socio-institutional and techno-economic spheres, more specifically because

> ... the prevailing pattern of social behavior and the existing institutional structure were shaped around the requirements and possibilities created by the previous paradigm.10/

Thus we have the beginnings of an attempt to introduce social relations into the discussion and at the same time the suggestion that the forces of production need not necessarily determine the relations of production. In Perez's schema the new heartland technologies do not always produce the appropriate socio-institutional framework and in fact their diffusion may indeed be held back by the social structures of the past.

Whilst this recent development in the technology-based long-wave theory does make these important advances, it is still arguably deficient in the specification of this "socio-institutional" framework. Passing reference is made to "a new model for the management and organization of the firm"11/ and "the forms of organization of workers and major interest groups, together with the legal framework within which they operate"12/ but this is not spelled out in detail. Moreover, whilst they acknowledge that the forces of production do not necessarily cause changes in the relations of production, there is no hint that changes in the forces of production may themselves be induced by initial changes in the relations of production. It is for this reason that it is useful to focus on the emerging literature on "flexible specialization" since in contrast to the theorization of technology and long waves, it begins the discussion around the social organization of production.

FROM MASS PRODUCTION TO FLEXIBLE SPECIALIZATION

Once the concept of technology is opened out to include both social and physical technology, the possibility arises that the observed eras of historical progress may primarily be conditioned by the social equivalents of heartland technologies. In such a schema embodied technologies may be given a minor, subordinate role. This is the underlying theme of a recent explanation offered for the global economic crisis which sees it as reflecting the transition from an era of mass production to one of flexible specialization.

Piore and Sabel - who have been responsible for the development of this schema - focus in their analysis on the

> limits of the model of industrial development that is founded on mass production: the use of special-purpose (product specific) machines and of semiskilled workers to produce standardized products.13/

Although this schema takes some account of embodied technology - as does their specification of the renewed potential for flexible specialization which is linked to the new electronics-based automation technologies - their primary focus lies in the realm of social relations. They are concerned here to map out two major elements of this.

The first of these concerns the *weltanschaung* of production which focuses on the mass production of standardized commodities and is obsessed with cost reduction rather than product competition. This view permeates manufacturing horizons. For example, despite the fact that it is well-known that around two-thirds of production in the engineering and wood-based industries occurs in small-batches, the dominant perception of manufacturing is one of large-batch production. The consequence is that the "technological trajectory"14/ which has permeated modern manufacturing industry is one which incorporates an obsessive drive towards standardization of product and scale-economies in production. Yet, argue Piore and Sabel, there is often no necessary reason why this should be the case. Indeed once before, in the nineteenth century, the leading edge of manufacturing stood at the divide between the system of mass production and an alternative of craft-production based upon " a combination of craft skill and flexible equipment"15/. The balance at that time fell in favour of mass production and this occurred because it was in the United States - an economy experiencing a shortage of skilled labour - that the new systems were being forged. Thus

> [t]he recent historiography of technology clearly documents the vision of automatic machine production as a structuring principle of Anglo-American, particularly American, technological developments.16/

Now that the paradigm of mass production is running into difficulties, Piore and Sabel suggest a "Second Industrial Divide" with the possibility of flexible specialization being linked to the new breed of flexible electronics-based automation technologies. Here, as can readily be seen, the primary terrain of discussion is with social factors, involving a struggle between the political power of the craft-based industries and those premised on mass-production.

The second element of social relations considered by Piore and Sabel concerns a wider specification of what Perez loosely referred to as the socio-institutional structure. A distinction is drawn here between the development of the corporation (with its attempts to stabilize the market and to organize labour relations) and the emerging functions of the state (with its attempts to develop an appropriate regulatory mechanism which would facilitate the continued expansion of the mass production system).17/ The fundamental problem which both the state and the corporation have to contend with is that the growing scale economies of the mass production paradigm require a stable environment to ensure the conditions under which heavy expenditures on inflexible capital equipment can be written off.

In this schema the mass production paradigm runs into crisis because the external world is just too uncertain to allow for these scale economies to be realized. This situation arises for a combination of reasons which are both endogenous and exogenous to their model. The endogenous causes relate to the saturation of the available global markets for standardized products by the end of the 1960s; this was coincident with the rise of productive capacity in the NICs. There was also a growing strain on raw material supplies. Exogenously, there were a series of conjunctural factors which deepened the crisis - these included the growth of social unrest,18/ the uncertainties induced by flexible exchange rates, the two oil shocks of 1973 and 1979 and the growth of global debt which was exacerbated by high interest rates.

What all these factors did was to create an uncertain world. Yet the mass production paradigm required in the first instance a stable environment in which large-scale and inflexible investments could be written-off. The result has been a post 1973 slowdown which appears to have largely been immune to the conventional Keynesian demand-management policies which had been tried and tested in previous recessions. Piore and Sabel argue that there are two contrasting paths in the transition to a new stable era of high incomes and full employment. The first is the adoption of a strategy of international Keynesianism. Through coordinated international demand management, this will ensure that large, stable markets will continue to exist for mass produced homogeneous commodities, thereby allowing for the continued reaping of scale economies in mass production. The alternative is that of flexible specialization which "will be seen in retrospect as a turning point in the history of mechanization".19/

Whereas the long-wave theorists had put their primary emphasis on the forces of production, relegating the discussion of social relations to the role of fettering production, the flexible specialization schema throws the primary focus on social relations. It is argued that both in the first divide of the nineteenth century and in the second divide of the 1980s and 1990s, there are two possible paths of transition. Which triumphs is not a reflection of the inherent power of particular types of embodied technology to determine social relations, but will be resolved in the first instance within the realm of social relations. The forces of production which are subsequently developed will thus reflect the balance of power of these different sets of social actors. What is at issue in the differences between these two viewpoints is the underlying conception of technology - one set seems to focus almost entirely on the forces of production, the other on the social relations of production.

In comparing the long wave theorists with the emergent views on flexible specialization we can see that they have many similarities. They concur in beginning the discussion of contemporary crisis in an historical context. In contrast to the dominant neo-classical and Keynesian paradigms, both offer a supply-oriented perspective on crisis which centers around the issue of technology - its just that they possess different views on what constitutes "technology". They also both accept that from the mid-1970s the global economy has been at a major transitionary point - for the long-wave theorists this is the sixth turning-point in modern industrial history; for Piore and Sabel it is the second. They both also accept - sometimes only implicitly - that a full discussion of the issues means taking into account both the forces and the relations of production. But here their paths begin to diverge since, as we have seen, the long-wave theorists put their primary emphasis on the forces of production and often consign social relations to an adjunct discussion, whereas the flexible specialization schema places almost all its attention on the social relations of production and see embodied technology as being largely malleable to alternative sets of social organization.

What we aim to do is to characterize the current crisis as representing the movement between the eras of machinofacture and systemofacture. This latter concept is closely related to both the flexible specialization of Piore and Sabel and to Perez's concerns with techno-economic paradigms and "systemation". (It is also historically analogous to Marx's recounting of the previous transitions between the eras of handicraft and manufacture and between manufacture and machinofacture). But our account differs slightly from either of these two in that whilst we share Piore and Sabel's view that the fundamental motor of current change lies in the realm of social relations, we also put great emphasis on the historical significance of electronics-based automation technologies which is central to the analysis of Perez and Freeman. In addition, whereas Piore and Sabel are more particularly concerned with the dimensions of the previous era, we will take this as being largely given. Instead our concern will be to map out the evolving nature and dimensions of the new order, which we term systemofacture (the reasons for this nomenclature will become evident from later discussion). Thus, whilst this discussion is similar in many respects to those of Piore and Sabel and Perez, it should also be seen as complementary, adding flesh to many of the bones which they lay bare.

Our underlying concern in this book is also focused in a slightly different direction, that is with the locational decisions of the TNCs. We will therefore be primarily concerned to map-out the implications which each of these eras of technological development have for global integration via FDI. In later chapters we will explore the different patterns of FDI in the two eras of machinofacture and systemofacture with respect to a detailed study of the global production of automobile components. But before this is done we turn our attention to a more detailed specification of the new paradigm of systemofacture, and contrast this with the previous era of machinofacture. In addition, we will also describe two previous transitions in industrial history, that from handicraft to manufacture and from manufacture to machinofacture.

TRANSITION BETWEEN ERAS - EXTENDING THE CONCEPT OF SOCIAL RELATIONS

We have earlier asserted that in our view the explanation for the transition between the various eras of modern industry is to be found both in the realm of social relations and in the development of various families of embodied technology. We were sceptical of the view that the current transition is best seen as being induced by the autonomous maturation of electronics technologies, the exhaustion of new product possibilities and its use to rationalize the production of mature products. Instead we will try to show at great length in the coming chapters that the transition between the old era of machinofacture and the new era of systemofacture is more clearly captured in terms of the atrophy of a particular way of organizing production. Electronics-based flexible automation technologies do have a key historical role to play, but this is only within the context of a prior change in social relations.

It is helpful to place the current transition in historical context, considering previous transitions between the eras of handicraft and manufacture and between manufacture and machinofacture. This will be done rather briefly since our prime concern lies with the current transition between machinofacture and systemofacture. Once this schema is mapped out our attention will turn to the mechanisms of internationalization in each of these three periods of industrial history, focussing in particular on the role played not just by FDI in the international division of labour. All of this lays the basis for the detailed analysis of the auto sector which follows, as well as for the generalization of its conclusions to other sectors in Chapter 8.

Since most perspectives in this field are dominated by an undue emphasis on physical technology our analysis rests primarily within the realm of "social relations". But this is too general a term to be analytically useful and it is therefore desirable to first open-out this category to distinguish between two major components. In the final chapter we will lean on this analysis of social relations to try and obtain a better grasp of the likely spread of systemofacture to the older IACs and the developing world.

Piore and Sabel (as well as the French Regulationist school) concentrated on two levels of social relations, the organization of production and exchange by the corporation and the regulation of production by the state. These are important parts of the story and since they have covered the ground extensively there is little need to repeat their views. Instead, in our analysis of the transition between machinofacture and systemofacture it is necessary to focus on two other dimensions of social relations, both relating to the performing of tasks on the shop-floor. The first of these is the labour process and the second relates to the issue of "habituation".

The Labour Process

The concept of the labour process was first introduced by Marx, writing in the latter half of the nineteenth century. He had argued that the labour process is the social mechanism by which the interaction between human beings and the natural world is mediated by tools and machinery. It involves both the forces of production (that is, embodied technology) and relations of production. In much of Marx's writings - and certainly in the work of many of his modern interpreters such as Cohen[20]/ - this relationship is one of technological determinism. The interrelationship is such that the forces of production determine the relations of production, that is that machinery either requires or implies particular forms of social organization in work.

In this particular conceptualization of the labour process, there is little space for the explicit development of the concept of work-organization, thus making it impossible to understand how the same sets of machinery can be utilized in similar modes of production and yet nevertheless be associated with very different forms of work-organization. For this reason we prefer to use the concept of labour process more loosely, referring to the system in which human beings of different skill levels are brought together with different sets of machines. This allows for the fact that machines designed to serve the same physical function may be set up with alternative forms of control-devices, giving greater or lesser play to the control of workers over production. It is thus a _purposive_ concept, suggesting that each labour process arises from decisions by key individuals; there is nothing inevitable about the nature of work.

We will argue in great detail in later chapters that it is the realm of the labour process that the key events are taking place which allow us to understand the nature of the transition between machinofacture and systemofacture. These changes are particularly significant in the automobile industry since it was in this sector that the Fordist labour process which has come to dominate the era of machinofacture was forged. And it is in this sector that the alternatives to Fordism are being developed and transferred to other sectors.[21]/

Habituation

The labour process reflects one dimension of social relations at the point of production, where the nature of work is a consequence of purposive decisions by plant management. On its own it is doubtful whether any particular schema could ever operate effectively since both workers and management bring to their work-places a long history of aculturation. This affects their attitudes to work and to their superiors and subordinates. So if this wider level of aculturation is at odds with the attitudes being demanded in the work-place it is doubtful whether the labour-process being adopted by management can succeed. One concept which has been developed to make sense of the wider sphere of social relations which determines the process of aculturation is that of "habituation".

In this, a distinction is drawn between the labour process ("exterior conditioning) and a mixture of culture and ideology ("interior determination"),

> on the one hand, [there is] 'exterior conditioning' which consists of overt moves by capital directed against labour, normally at the point of production; and, on the other hand, [there is] 'interior determination' arising from those elements of culture and ideology which become accepted and transmitted, or even generated, by the institutions of proletarian culture itself.22/

The concern with this wider dimension of social relations is of obvious importance and it of especial significance when we come to focus on the reasons why these three eras of manufacture, machinofacture and systemofacture have different locational "centers of gravity", namely the United Kingdom, the United States and Japan respectively. The problem lies in distinguishing between its two primary components, culture and ideology. Thus, when is a particular attribute which facilitates the introduction of a new labour process and new machinery culturally determined? And if it is culturally determined, it suggests that the diffusion of these new labour processes and eras of industrialization may be inherently uneven. On the other hand if these sets of social relations are ideologically determined - that is, lending themselves to "correction" by the manipulation of elements of popular culture such as newspapers, TV and films - then the transition between these eras need not be problematic and will be less uneven. We will show in later discussion of the attempts by the Western European and the United States automobile industry to adopt the new labour process emerging from Japan that this is a key dimension in the analysis.

Before we proceed to map-out the characteristics of the era of systemofacture - and to try and understand the nature of the turning point between it and machinofacture -

it is first useful to focus on the nature of social relations in the two previous eras of industry. In both early points of transition the key differences were to be found in the nature of the labour processes involved and in the way in which these interacted with the wider sphere of social relations, including the question of habituation to work.

FROM THE ERA OF HANDICRAFTS TO MANUFACTURE

In the Western European feudal economy, industrial production for exchange was based in the towns and was undertaken in guilds and on a handicraft basis. The gradual growth of a merchant class after the twelfth century, which specialized in the exchange of these and other commodities, gradually ran this system of production up against its limits, for the restrictive practices of the craft-guilds increasingly forced the merchant organizers of production to develop an alternative form of production. From this developed the trend towards production in rural households (referred to variously as "domestic industry" or "proto-industry") which came to be the dominant type of industry from the fourteenth to the eighteenth centuries,23/ and took two major forms.24/ The first was the *Kauf* system involving the utilization by merchant capital of independent producers of industrial products. The second - and increasingly dominant - was the *Verlag* or putting-out system in which the merchant capitalist gradually imposed an increasingly intricate division of tasks on these rural domestic-workers, often advancing both raw materials and tools. In the process the producer's dependence on the putter-out was reinforced, since the fracturing of production meant that few rural households had complete products to sell. However the organization of the labour process itself was largely left in the hands of the domestic producer.

The inability of the putter-out to exert full control over the pace and quality of work in these proto-industries led to the development of the first factories, a period referred to by Berg as "centralized manufacture". For the first time the capitalist - who had initially concentrated on exchange and the organization of the putting-out system of production - was able to exert control over the activity of labour since hitherto it had not been confined within the bounds of the factory itself. It was this latter development which was key to the transition from handicraft production to manufacture. Marglin - in an article aptly-entitled "What do Bosses do?" - emphasizes that these first factories generally utilized the same technologies as domestic industry.25/ Since this largely depended upon the utilization of hand-tools by workers,26/ the pace and quality of work tended to be governed by the ability of the capitalist to control the activities of these newly-congregated workers.

Whilst the extent of control over the workforce naturally reflected the organizational and managerial skills of individual capitalists, the social conditions in which these first factories evolved was obviously the key to their long-term success. And it was for this reason that the first major and sustained transition from handicraft to manufacture occurred in England, for it was there that the social relations were most appropriately matched to this new organization of production. The growing imbalance between population and land - which had been evident once before, but had been reversed by the mass deaths of the Great Plague - was placing a limit on agricultural employment. And the enclosure movement - displacing "surplus" labour from the land - forced labour to seek alternative forms of employment in the new factories in the towns. Hence the primary conditions required to underwrite the development of these first manufacturing factories meant that it was in England, rather than elsewhere in Europe, that the key transition was made.

By providing an institutional mechanism by which workers could be controlled and profits could be realized, these first factories enabled the process of capital accumulation to occur on a sustained basis. But gradually they began to run into diminishing returns for a number of reasons. First, it proved difficult to maintain these profits once other capitalists began to replicate these primitive forms of organizational innovations. A second route to sustaining profits - the intensification of the working day - also had its limits. And, third, the lowering of real wages by the employment of women and children providing a respite to profit-erosion, but only a temporary one. Thus the search for an alternative form of production, and here the development of a new set of embodied technologies - the substitution of machines for implements - provided the key. In so doing, it also proved to be the transitionary stepping stone between manufacture and machinofacture.

FROM MANUFACTURE TO MACHINOFACTURE

The introduction of machinery was a phenomenon which became increasingly prevalent in the second half of the nineteenth century. The key innovation here was to remove the implement from the hands of the worker and to place it under the control of the machine. Once this was done the route was open to speeding-up the operation of these machines to rates of output which were previously thought unthinkable. Together with the substitution of mineral for vegetable and animal raw materials, 27/ a new era of industrial organization was opened-up, in this case largely because of changes in the forces of production, that is embodied technology.

A measure of the significance of these changes can be gained from a focus on the textiles industry. Traditionally, cloth had been made out of wool - in 1741, forty times as much wool was used in England as cotton. Yet partly because of the relative ease of mechanizing cotton-processing technology, and partly because of consumer preference for this light and smoother-textured raw material, a process of massive industrialization took place in the manufacture of cotton cloth. By substituting machine-power and machine-control for human-power and human-control, productivity was increased vastly, especially following a series of key innovations in the last quarter of the eighteenth century. Even the first spinning jennys and water-frames were between six and 24 times as productive as manual work, and by a factor of several hundred in the case of the spinning frame. 28/ These technological innovations stimulated complementary changes first in weaving, and subsequently in processing and harvesting in the colonies. The train of mechanization had been set in progress and was extended to other sectors, especially to metal-working.

But technological innovations on their own do not make for a new industrial order, and although the initial turning-point from manufacture to machinofacture had been stimulated by changes in the forces of production, it was the accretion of changes in the social relations of production which were critical for the subsequent global spread of this new era of industry. Over the next two centuries a series of changes in the organization of production and work were consolidated, in some cases building upon innovations which were introduced even before the first factories of the manufacturing era. This fabric of social relations at the workplace can be characterized as the Fordist labour process. The NIDL, which represents the Fordist labour process at the global level, began to be represented in new investments in the 1960s. And whilst it remained a relatively small segment of the total stock of FDI,29/ it was targetted by many firms and governments as being the area for extended activity in the latter half of the 1980s and beyond. Such a perspective was also to be found in the automobile sector, as we shall see in later chapters.

It is obvious therefore that this labour process of global Fordism is of considerable importance to subsequent analysis, and for this reason it is helpful to map out its six central features. At its root lies the division of labour, which began to be extended in the proto-industrial enterprises of the era of handicrafts and whose significance was remarked upon by Adam Smith in the eighteenth century. As a consequence of the ever more minutely-defined specialization of tasks, Smith argued that labour productivity would increase for three reasons - because the dexterity of each worker would improve through repetition; time would be saved by not having to lay down tools to change tasks; and the design and production of machinery would become more specialized.

The next logical step in the evolution of the Fordist labour process was the extension of the so-called Babbage-principle in the mid-nineteenth century. Babbage had shown that if the various manufacturing tasks could be redefined so as to separate out those which are unskilled (that is, that some of the work could be deskilled), then it would not only be possible to employ lower-waged labour, but also to exercise greater control over the labour process by sacking (or threatening to do so) recalcitrant workers. The third step was described by Marx and Ure who observed that skilled labour was inherently uneven in character so that the natural tendency was to try and mechanize these sub-processes. In Ure's words,

> whenever a process requires particular dexterity and steadiness of hand, it is withdrawn as quickly as possible from the "cunning" workman who is prone to many kinds of irregularities, and it is placed in charge of a particular mechanism, so self-regulating that a child could supervise.30/

The fourth stage is associated with F. W. Taylor in the late nineteenth century. Amongst other things, Taylor (who was an inventor and one of the founder members of the

American Institute of Mechanical Engineers) developed systematic procedures for the detailed control over work. There were four major principles in Taylor's schema. Management had to absorb and codify the traditional skills of workers and to reduce these to rules; "all possible brain work should be removed from the shop and centered in the planning and laying out department"31/; the increasing division of labour should lead to the separation of "direct" from "indirect" tasks such as machine set-up, preparation, maintenance and repair; and, finally, management should specify the tasks of workers in general. All this was to be done through the development of eight functional layers of management.

Then in the first part of the twentieth century, Henry Ford added to this evolving labour process a fifth stage, that of the mass production system in which these principles were fine-tuned within the realm of moving production lines, special-purpose machine tools and standardized products. The organizing principle was a supply-driven one and the emphasis was placed on the continued operation of production lines; to this end, inventories of work-in-progress were required just-in-case anything was to go wrong.

Finally, in the most recent period - after 1960 - this Fordist labour process (representing an accretion of four hundred years of factory organization) was extended at the margin on a global basis, giving rise to the New International Division of Labour which we discussed in the previous chapter. In this the principles of tasks-fragmentation and the employment of low-wage unskilled labour resulted in "world-factories" in developing countries, often employing women (who are, together with children, probably the cheapest source of labour in the world).

As in the transition between handicraft production and manufacture, it is important to bear in mind the social determinants of innovation. The first systematic introduction of machinery occurred in England in the late eighteenth century, initially in the textile sector and subsequently in metalworking. But as the nineteenth century progressed, the centre of accumulation began to shift, first to continental Europe and then decisively to the United States. It was in North America that three key features promoted the rapid growth of machinofacture - the development of a large, mass market, the shortage of skilled workers and the absence of a politicized tradition in the workforce.

As we saw in Chapter 1, the world was transformed during this era of machinofacturing production, not only in individual countries (and regions of countries) but also in the internationalization of production. It was an era which had begun with the most significant changes occurring in the realm of embodied technology, but as the centuries progressed it was the organization of the labour process and the whole cycle of production which provided the primary momentum for continued accumulation. Yet, as we saw in Chapter 1, this momentum not only faltered from the late 1960s, but became increasingly uneven in nature.

But why did this system run into crisis? The answer is both complex and difficult to resolve decisively. Nor is it our primary intent here to offer an explanation for the exhaustion of the Fordist mode of accumulation. If such an explanation were to be offered it would have to take into account the increasing difficulty of maintaining balance in both the national and global economies.32/ But it would also be necessary to point to the increasing difficulty being experienced in maintaining the conditions for accumulation on the shop floor. The growth of labour disputes, poor quality production and other elements of dissatisfaction and inefficiency are widely chronicled,33/ including in later chapters of this book. To put it starkly, the Fordist labour process had itself run out of steam. Moreover, the long-term concentration (especially following the innovations in Henry Ford's moving production line) on specialized single-purpose machinery made the machinofacturing system increasingly inflexible and unwieldy. The struggle for a resolution of these difficulties has now begun to provide the outline of a new industrial era, with the emphasis on systemic features.

FROM MACHINOFACTURE TO SYSTEMOFACTURE

In considering the transition from the era of machinofacture to that of systemofacture it is necessary to go into greater detail than in the discussion of the two previous points of transition. This is because this subject matter represents our primary concern and will be fleshed out in greater detail in subsequent chapters when we consider the process of international integration in the automobile industry. The ensuing discussion will therefore take the following form. First we will attempt to picture the new paradigm, despite the fact that it is still in embryonic form and that its specific characteristics will necessarily evolve in directions which cannot be predetermined. This requires consideration of the three basic pillars of systemofacture - the new labour process, the new electronics-based automation technologies and the new pattern of interfirm relationships. It is because each of these three elements have <u>systemic</u> components at their core that we refer to the new era as one of systemofacture. After this we will briefly consider the point of transition between this new era and the previous dominant one of machinofacture. Only when this is complete will it be possible to consider the forms of international integration which are implicit in each of these three eras of industrial production. In so doing, we will be able to develop a theoretical perspective on the NIDL and it is this which will be explored with respect to the internationalization of the automobile industry in later chapters.

The Labour Process in the Era of Systemofacture

Identifying <u>the</u> systemofacturing labour process is not an easy task. In the first place there is of course no single homogeneous labour process which can said to exist in any era of production. Differences occur over time, between countries, between sectors, between firms and even between different plants in the same firm's operations in a single country. Nevertheless the "inter-era variation" is considerably greater than the "intra-era variation" and it is therefore possible to describe an "ideal type" for each era, as we did in the case of the Fordist labour process in machinofacturing.

The labour process which we will be describing is that which has developed over the past two-to-three decades in the Japanese automobile and electronics industries.[34]/ Naturally it has particular characteristics associated with both the country and the sector involved, but it must be borne in mind that the same objections to generalization could have been made in discussing the system introduced by Henry Ford in the early twentieth century. What is significant is that the automobile industry remains the largest single industrial sector and has consistently pioneered organizational and embodied technologies which have subsequently spread to other sectors. In discussing this new labour process we will confine ourselves to a schematic presentation of its broad principles since its detailed description will be presented in Chapter 4.

It is difficult to know where to begin or what to call this new labour process since it presents itself as an organic system, each of whose pillars rest on the other elements of the same system. Some refer to it as Just-in-Time (or JIT) production35/ since one of its distinctive characteristics is its minimization of inventory levels as components are delivered on a just-in-time basis. Another organizing principle in this new labour process is its flexibility, and this is the element which is picked up in Piore and Sabels' concept of flexible specialization. Since this concept of flexibility points to a particularly important contrast with the Fordist labour process, it is probably best to begin a description of the schema at this point.36/

Arising from the small and fragmented nature of the Japanese market in the 1950s and 1960s - which contrasted sharply with the mass market available in the United States in the early twentieth century - the Japanese automobile firms were forced to adopt a more flexible attitude to automobile production. So instead of being able to take advantage of a supply-driven system in which the firm could concentrate on maximising the flow of homogeneous automobiles out of the factory which would be snapped up by an eagerly waiting public, the basis of production changed to a demand-driven one. Initially this was forced on the producers as a way of coping with a heterogeneous pattern of consumption, but as the system of production became fine-tuned to cope with variation in output, so this became a competitive-end in itself. Thus market-heterogeneity was actively encouraged by the automobile suppliers and the system has increasingly come to be characterized as one in which, by comparison with Fordism, the emphasis in competition has changed from price-competition to product-innovation.

The automobile sector is one of a major group of industries which can be characterized as the discrete-products industries. As we shall see in the final chapter, these branches are characterized by a flow of output of individual products, each distinct from the other. (This contrasts with the dimensional industries - such as textiles and chemicals - where output occurs in a stream which is measurable in volume or weight). In the discrete-product sectors, a change in the specification of output necessarily involves the resetting of machinery and this is one of the major factors accounting for scale economies in production. If the resetting of machinery takes time - "downtime" as it is usually called - then the introduction of flexible product schedules can be a costly innovation. Therefore one of the primary consequences of the introduction of a demand-driven system of production is the introduction of flexibility in work-patterns. This necessitates moving away from the historic trend towards the increasing division of labour since it is characteristic of the flexible labour process that the same laborers who are involved in operating the machines will also be responsible for changing the settings of machines and for routine functions of maintenance and repair. This not only represents a reversal of the historic trend towards the division of labour, but it also becomes imperative for workers to command a range of skills so that they can perform this multi-tasking work. Moreover, from this it necessarily follows that the new labour process is also a multi-skilling one, reversing the historic tendency towards the deskilling of work. Indeed it is a characteristic of this system that workers do not get paid according to what they do, but in relation to what they can do.

Because one of the functions of inventories in the Fordist labour-process was to ensure that the production line was kept moving at all costs, once the principle was accepted of interrupting production to ensure flexibility the possibility then arose of reducing inventory lines. This has been one of the major thrusts of the Japanese labour process and one which has possibly received the most attention in other countries. It has culminated in the JIT concept in which the final objective is to reduce inventories to close to zero. Yet the primary function of inventories in the Fordist system was to protect against any possibility of disrupting production - inventories were a buffer just-in-case anything went wrong. So that if the move was to be made to zero-inventories, than it should be imperative that some form of enhanced quality-control procedures be introduced. Nothing should be allowed to go wrong since there were no inventories to back-up the system - thus zero-defect policies were introduced as well as a complete reorganization of the way in which components were delivered. The previously haphazard procedure of piling an approximate number of components in a large container gave way to a much more careful packing system in specifically-designed pallatized containers[37]/ and together with the imperative of greater quality-assurance this led to a significant change in the relationship between assemblers and component suppliers (this will be discussed in greater detail below).

The emphasis on quality assurance meant that this function could no longer be left to a specialized group of workers at the end of the line, or in rectification bays, since the absence of buffer-inventories would mean that the whole line could be crippled before the quality control department could determine the source of the problem. (Complex products such as automobiles are also expensive items to rectify). Quality control thus necessarily had to become the concern of every worker. But this conflicted with the Taylorist schema in which all control over production was to be taken away from the line-worker and in some important respects control over production had to be given back to the detailed worker. Indeed in some assembly plants each worker was given a switch to close down the line of he or she noticed that anything was wrong - in fact they were not only given the possibility of stopping the line, but were actually expected to do so.

This principle of giving a measure of control back to the worker could only work in the context of a positive working environment. So partly for this reason and partly because quality itself was an important objective, quality-circles and other exhortatory activities - which in Japan often included the singing of company songs and exercising before work - were introduced. But these groups and activities served another important service. The switch from price-based competition to product-led innovation had changed the role of the R&D departments which now had to become more concerned with fundamental innovations - in the classically Fordist firms in the United States the R&D departments had concentrated on minor incremental changes in product and process. Thus, much of the responsibility for incremental technical change was given to the shop-floor worker and this was furthered through a scheme of suggestions for improvements, most of which were remunerated. Such an important schema could not be left to chance, however, and management characteristically set targets of suggestions which had to be submitted by the workforce.

Many parts of this new labour process are widely known outside of Japan. A great number of firms have come to be adopt JIT strategies, to adopt quality circles (QCs) or to introduce suggestion schemes. But what most firms have failed to do is to appreciate the systemic and interrelated nature of these various elements of the Japanese system. In one sense we could have begun to describe this new labour process through any one of its various components - beginning for example with QCs or with JIT or with the move to multi-tasking or multi-skilling. In each case it would have been necessary to describe almost all of the phenomena described above since all the elements relate functionally to one another and to the operation of this systemic labour process as a whole.38/

We have described so far the nature of the new labour process on the shop floor. There are also corollaries of these events in other spheres of relations between labour and management. This includes the phenomenom of lifetime employment (applying generally to those workers in the core assembly and component firms, making-up between one-quarter and one-third of the labour force) and the nature and function of trade unions. It is considerably more difficult here to draw any general conclusions since this topic is so substantively determined by historical and social conditions which are specific to individual countries and sectors. Nevertheless there are a few general principles which are important here. The first is that the old craft-unions which characterized many of the Fordist systems and which depended upon the trend towards the increasing division of labour are widely considered to be no longer appropriate. Enterprise-, firm- or sector-wide unions are probably essential if multi-tasking and multi-skilling work is to be introduced. Second, the old system of confrontation in work can no longer apply to a system in which cooperation and the two-way flow of information is essential. And, third, flexibility in work has wider dimensions than that of multi-tasking. It also requires greater flexibility of hours and management if a successful transition is to be made from a supply- to a demand-driven system. These are important issues and we will return to them later in this chapter (as well as in the final chapter) when we discuss the question of unevenness in the diffusion of this new labour process.39/

The Application of the New Heartland Technology to Products and Processes: The Diffusion of Microelectronics and the Importance of Systems in Production.40/

We have seen that some of those working in the domain of long-wave theories have argued that these long periods of boom and recession are associated with the emergence of revolutionary heartland technologies. In the early phase of its introduction, they argue, the new technology is primarily utilized for new products - demand expands, jobs are created and a virtuous circle of innovation and employment results. But after a while the technology comes to be used to rationalize production. Labour is displaced and the system declines first into recession, and subsequently into depression.

The most recent of these long-waves, it has been argued, has been in large part fueled by the development and diffusion of microelectronics technology. In the early years the technology found its major use in a series of new products, including consumer durables, telecommunications, information processing and military equipment. But as the decades wore on the technology has increasingly come to be applied in capital goods where it offers a number of important competitive advantages. It reduces the lead-time in product development, saves on material utilization, often saves in capital costs, makes possible what was previously impossible, saves on the use of material inputs and, perhaps most widely discussed of all, it also substitutes for labour. It is this latter phenomenon - that is the application of electronics to capital goods - argue the proponents of this theory, that explains the emergence of crisis in the world economy after the mid-1970s.41/

As we concluded in previous discussion, there is much merit to this schema. It points clearly to the central importance of electronics-based innovations in the recent period, even though we believe that it misspecifies the primarily causal explanation of the current crisis (which we have argued lies instead in the realm of social relations). Electronics really has been of substantial importance in a string of industries whose growth has resulted from its application in products - televisions, hi fi's, video tape recorders, computers, personal stereos, compact discs, electronic games, radar, medical equipment and aerospace are just a few of these new products. But in recent years the primary focus of attention has been the application of electronics to capital goods and it is this which is reflected in the strategic policies adopted in the early 1980s by the major Japanese conglomerates who saw themselves faced with declining growth in the market for consumer durables and one-by-one turned their attention to industrial electronics for their future prosperity.

There are a wide range of studies which show the significant competitive advantages arising from the incorporation of electronics in product and process and which show just why it is that this sector continues its rapid growth-rate when others are in decline. We concur, therefore, that electronics is the key embodied technology at this point of transition between machinofacture and systemofacture. There is no need, therefore, to repeat the results which emerge from the works on the economic benefits arising from the utilization of these new electronics-based automation technologies. But what is often missed in these analyses is the <u>systemic</u> characteristics of the new technologies and it is on this that we will focus our attention briefly.

Within the era of machinofacture, we can determine three vintages of automation. In the earliest the primary concern lay with the mechanization42/ of transformation - improved ways of cutting, bending, punching and other ways of transforming materials. Next, with the major innovations occurring around the turn of this century, was the automation of transfer, with the moving production line being the most significant innovation. The third phase of automation within machinofacture was that of control, beginning many years ago with mechanical cams, being boosted in the 1920s by the introduction of electrical relay switches and culminating in the utilization of electronically controlled equipment in the 1970s and 1980s.

Whilst this threefold classification of automation serves well as a taxonomy for understanding automation during machinofacture, it is too limited a concept for the new era. The problem is that its conception of production begins and ends with the process of transformation on the factory floor. But what of the indirect processes in production such as managerial organization and research and development? And what of the increasing importance of flows of information on the shop-floor? For, as we can see from Figure 2.1 there are three spheres of production in the modern firm. The first of these is design where the nature of the firm's output is defined and new production processes are explored. The actual transformation of these designs into a physical product occurs in a second sphere of production in which the raw materials and intermediate inputs are stored, processed into final products and ultimately delivered to the consumer. These two spheres of production - design and machinofacture - which are the kernel of an enterprise's activities could not operate effectively without some form of coordination and this comprises the third sphere of production.

Naturally the extent to which these spheres of production exist in any particular enterprise depends upon the nature of the activity involved. Firms producing simple products with relatively low technology will

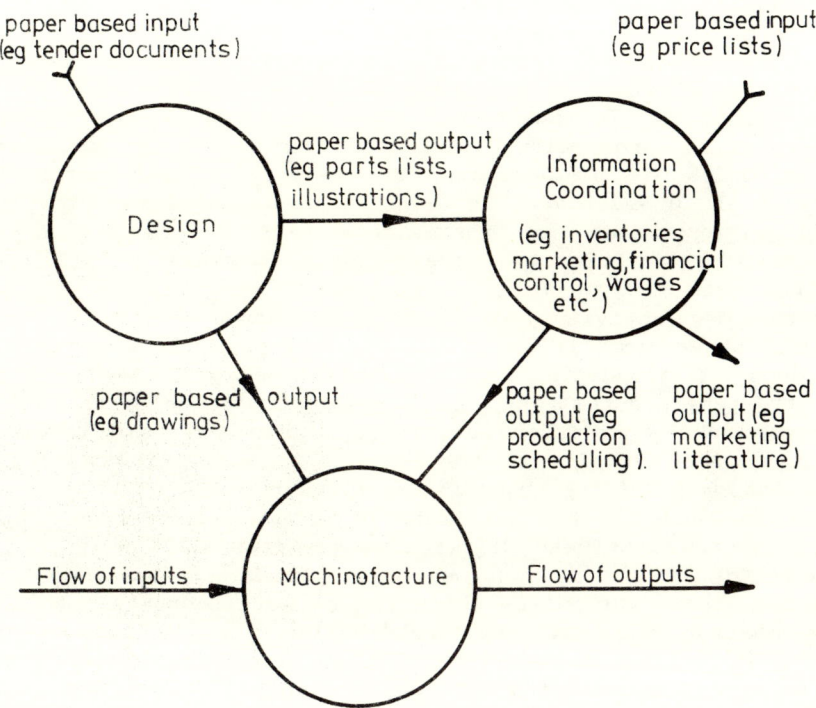

Figure 2.1 Pre-electronic Organization of Factory Production

obviously have a poorly developed design department whereas small, high-technology electronics firms may have a very well-developed design capability which requires little formal coordination. Nevertheless in almost all modern enterprises, whatever their sector or size, these three spheres of production will tend to be separated into different units (often in different towns, cities and even countries): the R&D block, the factory and the administration.

Within each of these three spheres of production there are a variety of separate activities. For example, within the design sphere, design itself is usually an activity distinct from drawing, copying and tracing; within the machinofacturing sphere there are important differences between handling, forming, assembling, control, storage and distribution; and within the coordination sphere, information has to be gathered, processed, stored, and transmitted. Whilst some activities are common to all enterprises - for example, handling in the machinofacturing sphere - there will inevitably be a variation in the number and type of other activities.

Once it is recognized that there are these three spheres of production, each with its particular sets of activities, it is possible to categorize three different types of automation. The first of these is <u>intra-activity automation</u>, that is, automation which occurs within a particular activity.<u>43/</u> The determining characteristic of this type of automation is that it is limited to a particular activity and that it is consequently isolated from other activities within or beyond, the particular sphere of production. The second type of automation is <u>intra-sphere automation, which refers to technologies which</u> have links with other activities within the same sphere. Indeed, the origins of the term 'automation' in the Ford assembly plant of the 1920s illustrated this type of automation well: the new transfer line mechanized the flow of materials between different activities such as lathes, drilling and boring machines. The third and final type is inter-sphere automation which is the most complete form of automation and involves coordination between activities within each of the different spheres. There are a wide variety of potential inter-sphere combinations. These may be of a relatively limited and simple nature, for example, using design parameters to automatically set machine settings; or they may be wide-ranging and complex such as in the linking of changes in the specification of production to parameters generated in redesign, and thus in continual adjustments made in machine settings.

The essential difference between these three different types of automation is shown in Figure 2.2. In (a) we illustrate the introduction of automation technologies into individual activities within each of the three sphere. In (b) we illustrate how an automation technology is introduced into a particular sphere with some form of interlinking (involving feedback in the case of the manufacturing sphere) between different activities. Finally in (c) we give an example of the merging of the three-sphere industrial enterprise back towards the single-sphere type of organization which characterised pre-industrial revolution enterprises. In this case automation technology links up different activities between different

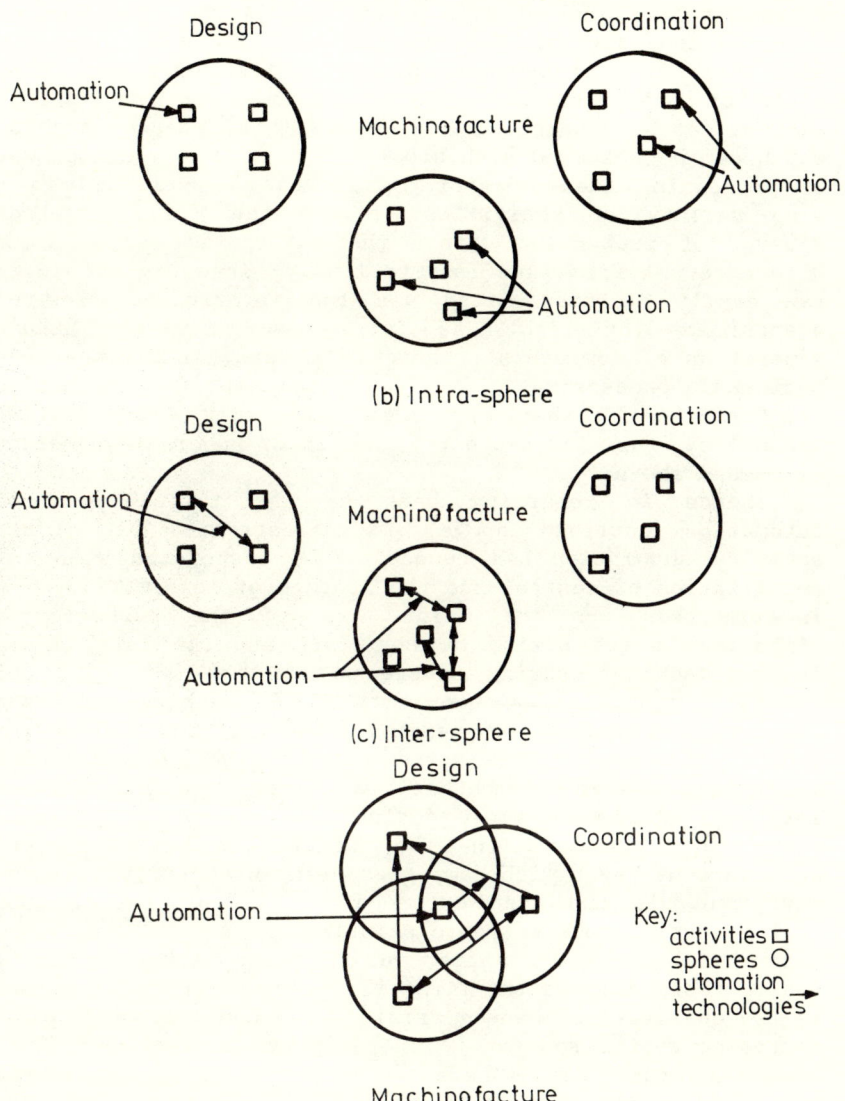

Figure 2.2 The Three Different Types of Automation

spheres of production.

The major factor accounting for the development of these systemic qualities in production is the emergence of a pervasive digital (often called 'binary') logic in electronic control devices. Binary systems operate on the basis of either/or logic in which counting and logical systems can be decomposed into a variety of states, each of which can be answered with binary logic. Thus a common way of processing ideas or information can be utilized in a wide variety of activities, across the full range of spheres of production within the enterprise, as well as with external firms and institutions. Since digital logic can easily be transmitted via the interrupted flow of electricity (or light, as is proposed for the future generation of computers), there is a ready interconnection between processing and transmitting information ('informatics') that provides the key facilitating technology for intra-sphere and inter-sphere automation discussed above.

Hence in referring back to the three types of automation outlined above, microelectronics in intra-activity automation has tended to be associated with the optimization of control and the storage of information. Indeed, this was the major area of the technology's diffusion in the period between 1960 and the late 1970s. In the machinofacturing sphere we saw the maturation of numerical control, beginning with simple machine tools and currently extending to assembly robots; in the design sphere, microelectronics systems began with batch-oriented mainframe design computers and have progressed to interactive computer-aided design (CAD) and computer-aided draughting systems; in the sphere of coordination, applications began with computers being used for stock-and-wage control, and then extended to word-processing and, most recently, to electronic printing.

Then towards the latter years of the machinofacturing era in the mid 1970s the first fledgling attempts were made at the qualitative changes arising from the introduction of microelectronics systems to intra-sphere automation. This trend towards intra-sphere automation is currently the major objective of most of the major machinery suppliers providing equipment for each of three spheres of production. In the design sphere, computer-aided-design and draughting systems are widely available. In the machinofacturing sphere, the target is the development of flexible manufacturing systems. And in the sphere of coordination, integrated multi-function workstations are being developed which cover the full range of activities. The early application of electronics in intra- and inter-sphere automation was however entirely compatible with the era of machinofacture - they merely substituted electronic control devices for electro-mechanical ones. But the introduction of full inter-sphere automation requires substantial changes in managerial approach, in organization and in the labour process and can no longer be contained within the realm of machinofacture. This is perhaps the major conclusions which emerges from out study of the auto sector in Chapters 2-7.

The New Pattern of Interfirm Relationships

The last of the three pillars of systemofacture relates to the changing relationship between firms. This, too, is becoming more systemic in nature, but in order to understand this phenomenon it is necessary to go back to the nature of interfirm relationships in the era of machinofacturing. Since the automobile industry set the pattern which was later adopted by most other mass production industries, and since it is the primary focus of this study, it is useful to focus on the pattern of interfirm relationships which developed in this sector, particularly between assemblers and component suppliers.

Henry Ford's Model T - the great success story which embedded the moving production line in the minds of corporate planners - was introduced in 1913 and its rapid growth in sales was initially founded upon the fundamental change in work-organization which was described earlier. But after the end of WW1 its continued growth largely arose from the establishment of the giant, integrated River Rouge complex covering the whole process of production from steel to the assembly of the final automobiles. This system of integrated production was soon copied by General Motors (GM) but after a gigantic write-down of inventory (involving $83m) in the recession of 1920-22, GM moved to a very different form of organization. This incorporated a multidivisional structure organized to produce different autos, each having its own functional departments. Economies of scale were realized through the specialization of component production, and each component affiliate was responsible for meeting the requirements of the different product divisions.

Over the years a number of specialized component firms developed in the United States to supplement the in-house production of components by affiliates of each of the major auto assemblers. GM - closely followed by Ford - had the greatest degree of vertical integration, whereas Chrysler and the Western European firms tended to buy-in a greater proportion of components from independent firms. What this system represented was a form of sourcing-schizophrenia. On the one hand a significant number of components were bought-in from captive affiliates which largely acted on an independent basis, producing component designs in isolation from their affiliates' development of final products. On the other hand the independent component producers were held at an arms-length basis. Contracts for individual items were renegotiated at regular intervals and under tough conditions. In general they were put out informally to tender by a number of component firms and, particularly in the 1960s and 1970s when industrial action came to be more of a problem, most automobile assemblers preferred dual-sourcing arrangements. Thus, to the extent that components were sourced from independent suppliers, the relationship between them and the assemblers was largely adverserial.

The Japanese by contrast developed a very different form of relationship between the component suppliers and the assemblers. In some senses there were similarities with the GM system, especially as most of the component suppliers were linked-in to particular assemblers. The banks played an important role in this, being involved in (and often initiating) a series of complex interrelationships with particular assemblers and their component suppliers in which cross-holdings of minor equity shares played an important role. However, the detailed relationships between the assemblers and component firms in Japan is of a rather different nature, as will be shown in later chapters. This form of organization provides a number of important benefits to the assemblers which were particularly important in the 1950s when the system was first being developed. Firstly, at a time when the assemblers were short of cash it allowed them to pass the financing costs for new investments on to others. Second, there was still some uncertainty in the mid-1950s as to whether the automobile industry would be able to continue its rapid growth of the early years of the decade; thus some of the risk of investment was passed on to others. And, finally, the subcontractors tended to pay significantly lower wages and this allowed a reduction in the costs of components.

We shall discuss the specific nature of this system in

Chapter 4. But at this general level of discussion, though, we can observe a number of important features which necessitate a different type of relationship between assemblers and suppliers firms to that which came to be the norm in the previous era of machinofacture.

In the first place the use of JIT inventory systems imposes a number of important requirements. Proximity between suppliers and assemblers is key, otherwise there is little prospect of maintaining tight delivery schedules and low inventories. JIT also requires detailed collaboration in the scheduling of production. Moreover, as we shall see in Chapter 4, the need for zero-defect components and precisely-packed containers not only necessitates a measure of harmony between the firms but also close cooperation when defects are found or when quality standards are not being met. These and other elements of the JIT principle rule out the traditional adversarial relationship between component suppliers and assemblers.

Secondly, a change in this relationship is also being dictated by the nature of technological progress. We referred earlier to the growth of systemic production technologies, but the same phenomenon is also occurring (as we shall see in Chapter 3) in relation to products. Largely - but not entirely - as a result of the use of digital-logic electronic control systems, it is becoming possible to take advantage of the systemic interdependence between different sub-systems in the final product. For example, engine control is now a complex system which draws together information from a variety of previously separate components such as the carburettor and the timing of the spark. The development of these systemic qualities in sub-assemblies of components requires a much closer level of coordination, not only between the assemblers and the component suppliers, but also between different component suppliers.

And thirdly, there has been a growing tendency for the technological content of the automobile - and indeed most other products - to increase. This requires specialized R&D, much of which involves a long lag between the conception and the supply of the final component or component sub-system. When a final product consists of many technology-intensive intermediates there is a much greater need for coordination than when the various inputs are relatively simple. So, once again, coordination and integration become important parts of the whole process of production.

Taken together these various attributes of the

relationship between firms take on a very different function to those which have evolved between the assemblers and the independent component suppliers in the latter days of the machinofacturing era. And whilst the vertically integrated production of components by affiliates of the same firm offered some of the potential for realizing these characteristics of the new order (especially the possibility of closer integration in design and scheduling), the reality was that few of the major firms took advantage of them. The net result is that the new system of interrelationships which will be described in Chapter 4, and which is very different to that of the old order, has many of this attributes of systemic and organic integration. It is as if automobile assembly comprises some form of organic holism, with a much closer measure of functional interdependence and coordination than has hitherto been known in this sector - or indeed in other sectors.

PATTERNS OF INTERNATIONAL INTEGRATION IN THE THREE ERAS OF PRODUCTION

The transition from handicrafts to manufacture was reflected in the development of the factory system. Machinofacture saw the substitution of human labour by machines, initially working on a stand-alone basis and subsequently in small groups of machines; it also saw the development and refinement of an historically distinct labour process and form of productive organization. In the most recent period the dominant characteristic of production is the prevalence of systems and integration - between machines (and groups of machines), between plants and firms, between workers and between tasks. Earlier in this chapter we also considered the factors which help to explain the transition between one era and the next. Here we contrasted the views of the "technological determinists" - that is, those who believed that the primary motive factor was the development, diffusion and maturation of a series of heartland technologies - with the views of others who had argued that it was in the realm of social relations that the key dynamic elements were to be found. Our own recounting of historical events was that the transition between handicrafts and manufacture had its origins primarily in changes in social relations. That between manufacture and machinofacture was initiated by changes in the forces of production and then consolidated by changes in social relations. In the most recent period the primary arena of change is to be found in the realm of social relations, although the development of a new set of embodied technologies is a key component of the development of the new order.

Consequently we have argued that the reason why the first decisive step in modern industry - that is, the transition from handicrafts to manufacture - occurred in England was because it was there that the social conditions were most conducive to change. Following an alteration in the relationship between land and population and the onset of the enclosure movement, labour had been displaced from agriculture and required proper employment. From the point of view of the capitalist, the putting-out system which had been utilized in the handicrafts era was no longer efficient because it was difficult to control labour. Thus arose the first factories in England, setting in motion the systematic application of organization and technology to production and hence the industrial revolution.

The transition from manufacture to machinofacture is also primarily explained by social factors of this sort. The new machine-based technology displaced both skilled and unskilled labour and whilst the first developments occurred in England, it was in the United States rather than Europe that the labour force was severely constrained and unschooled in shopfloor militancy. Moreover, it was also there that the large markets which were essential to exploit the underlying scale advantages of this inflexible form of mechanization were to be found. Hence the machinofacturing system first took root there. Now, in this new era of systemofacture, the social conditions which facilitate the new labour process and inter-plant and inter-firm relationships are to be found in the Far East and it is for this reason that the new paradigm is being forged there.

Figure 2.3 contrasts the major characteristics of these three eras of production. The era of manufacturing dates from the 16th century when the factories first became widespread until the latter quarter of the eighteenth century. The dominant labour process was one of "formal subordination" in which control over the worker involved detailed and constant supervision and whereby the quantum of work could only be increased through greater intensification of the working day - that is, harder work, or longer hours. Output was highly heterogeneous in nature, reflecting the craft-content of production and the diversification of the market. And since technology was

	Period	Labour process	Output	Locus of Production	Technology	Scale economies	Centre of accumulation	International integration
Manu-facture	16th century to 1770	Factory organization Flexible	Bespoke	Near market	Labour intensive	Small	Western Europe	Slight
Machino-facture	1770-1980	Rigid Division of Labour. Deskilling; Taylorism; Fordism	Standardised Mass production	Site of least cost	Capital intensive	High	North America	Liberal. New International Division of Labour
Systemo-facture	>1980	Flexible. Multi-tasking; Multi-skilling	Flexible	Near market	Capital intensive	Plant-scale falling; Firm-scale uncertain	Pacific Basin	Managed Trade

Figure 2.3 The Three Epochs of Industrial Development

relatively labour-intensive - being largely confined to the utilization of implements by the workforce - and scale economies were slight, the locale of production was close to the final market. International specialization was virtually absent, except in those commodities where climatic and ecological factors were decisive such as spices, salt and sugar.

The key early innovations at the onset of machinofacture during the latter quarter of the eighteenth century - such as the introduction of Hargreave's spinning jenny and Awkright's mule - grew out of the manufacturing era in England. But their rapid adoption and extension into other activities and sectors was held back by the accumulation of workpractices and the process of aculturation which had initially spawned and then grown out of the first factories. Thus the center of accumulation in the next era shifted to the United States where the social relations which underlay production were better attuned to the new labour process. This was one of "real subordination" - that is, instead of the implement being paced by the worker, the worker came to be paced by the machine. And now the quantum of production could not only be increased by an intensification of the working day, but it was also subject to mechanization. This mechanization was associated with a growth in scale economies along a number of dimensions - plants got bigger, product runs longer and small firms grew into TNCs. Inflexible mechanization was also facilitated by the development of mass markets for standardized goods in which the major competitive factor was price. As time wore on, and as the machinofacturing labour process (described earlier) evolved, so capital became more mobile. This mobility took a number of forms, as we saw in Chapter 1, comprising of the internationalization of commodity-, productive- and finance-capital.

Although there have been a number of phases in the machinofacturing era in which each of these forms of internationalization came to dominance, our central concern in this study arizes with the nature of the process of internationalization of productive capital. (These issues are discussed in greater detail in Chapter 1). One component of this internationalization was the NIDL. Although in terms of the overall stock of FDI this was a relatively minor item, it was becoming increasingly significant at the margin of international flows of productive capital. In the NIDL, capital went to the site of least cost production to produce for the world market.

In the extreme case this meant the employment of women in export processing zones in DCs, who represented the cheapest possible pool of labour. Specific tax provisions were enacted to make this possible and to maintain market access for production at the site of least cost. Hence we can observe the pattern of international integration in the latter era of machinofacture as being one in which both the TNCs and some developing countries played an increasingly prominent role in producing commodities for the world market.

The emergence of systemofacture, dating from the 1980s onwards, suggests some changes in this structure of production and trade may be imminent. Some aspects of this change are already clear. The labour process is changing to a more flexible, multi-tasking and multi-skilled one. Output is much more differentiated with the emphasis on product innovation to serve market niches. The technology is generally becoming more capital-intensive - although in some cases the new electronics-based automation technologies are also capital-saving - but unlike the era of machinofacture, this does not mean that scale economies are increasing along all dimensions. The flexibility of this technology is such that there are reasons to believe that in many sectors this may be associated with a reduction in plant and product scale economies; the question of firm scale economies is unclear. (We shall return to this subject in Chapter 8).

But it is in relation to the locale of production that our major concern lies. We know that the economics of location are changing significantly. Whereas in machinofacture it was economically rational to exploit scale economies in dedicated production lines and to ship the final products to world markets, in systemofacture the flexibility of organization and technology makes this imperative less intense. Moreover, it is in the logic of JIT that suppliers be clustered around the final assembler. Also, the introduction of labour-saving automation reduces the incentive to produce in localities of low-wage cost. On its own, though, these changes in the economics of location need not necessarily involve a change in the international division of labour in manufacturing since there is no reason why these clusters of production should not be established in the Republic of Korea, Brazil or China, taking advantage of low wage-costs (despite the relatively reduced importance of labour-costs in production). However, we noted in Chapter 1 that because of the unevenness of the transition between machinofacture and systemofacture we are witnessing the onset of barriers to market entry which create problems for the maintenance of the existing pattern of international specialization - the "politics of location" are also changing. Some have argued that this will lead to a breakdown in the world economy as we have come to know it and the development of regional trading blocs comprising perhaps of the EEC and Africa, the United States and Latin America, Japan and Asia and the USSR and Eastern Europe.44/

If protectionist barriers are to become more prominent, then it is likely that final production will be forced to occur near the market. Once this occurs, then the logic of JIT will result in the component suppliers following on. Moreover as markets become more differentiated it will also pay many producers to locate themselves near the final market, since this will be essential if they will be able to respond flexibly to changes in market conditions.45/ So, we hypothesize, this confluence of the changing economics and politics of location will lead to a significant change in the international division of labour in manufacturing. Renewed emphasis will be placed on production for the local market and diminished emphasis on production for distant markets.

* * *

Much of this remains at the level of conjecture and a number of important questions remain open. How significant are these changes in the economics of location? Will the protectionist pressures in the IACs endure? Will the TNCs continue to focus on the price-competitive mass production of standardized products at the point of least cost, or will they introduce flexible and highly-automated technologies near to the final markets and concentrate on product innovation in differentiated markets? Are we merely witnessing short-run changes reflecting the uneven pattern of transition between the eras of machinofacture and systemofacture?

Although these (and other important) questions can be worked through at a general level, it is only through the examination of particular sectors that we can determine whether these conjectures are accurate or fanciful. They have to be validated by reference to the real world, and it is for this reason that we have studied the automobile industry and the global-sourcing policies of the major TNCs. It is in an ideal sector for two major reasons.

First it is the largest single industrial branch and, second, many of the major TNCs adopted explicit policies of global-sourcing during the heyday of machinofacture. We therefore turn to the results of our research before concluding in the final chapter with some thoughts on the limits of generalizability of our findings, as well as on the implications for TNCs.

NOTES

1. See Freeman, Clark and Soete (1982) for a summary of their views, as well as those of Kondratieff and Schumpeter.
2. See Kaplinsky (1984) for a detailed discussion of the application of electronics to automation.
3. These more recent views are to be found in Freeman (1984).
4. In a recent paper, Perez (1987) argues that radical innovations are those which do not arise naturally out of a sequence of incremental innovations.
5. We consider here only those which are relevant to our wider and immediate concern with the nature of the current crisis and its international dimensions. Thus the debate about whether invention occurs in the downswing or the upswing is not considered (see Freeman, Clark and Soete 1982), and nor is the debate concerning the very existence of the long-wave cycles themselves (Rosenberg and Frischtak 1984).
6. Marx (1874) pp. 109-110.
7. See Freeman, Clark and Soete (1982), Chapter 2.
8. Perez (1985).
9. ibid. p. 444.
10. ibid. p. 445.
11. ibid. p. 444.
12. ibid. p. 446.
13. Piore and Sabel (1984), p. 4.
14. See Nelson and Winter (1977) and Dosi (1982).
15. Piore and Sabel (1984), p. 5.
16. ibid. p. 45.
17. For a discussion of the various characteristics of these regulatory devices - a perspective which has come to be known as the "regulationist school" - see Aglietta (1979) and Lipietz (1987).
18. In fact, one measure of social unrest was strife on the shop-floor arising out of the nature of the Fordist

labour process. This is best seen as an endogenous factor.
19. ibid. p 352.
20. For an orthodox Marxian recounting of the concept of forces of production, see Cohen (1983).
21. The concepts of Fordism and the Fordist labour process are discussed later in this chapter.
22. Henderson and Cohen (1979) p. 12.
23. Kriedte, Medick and Schlumbohm (1981).
24. Berg (1985).
25. Marglin (1976).
26. The word "manufacture" has as its root the Latin word for hand, "manus".
27. Landes (1969) regards these three features as being the critical components of the industrial revolution.
28. Landes (1969), p. 85.
29. See page 9.
30. Ure (1835), p. 19.
31. Taylor (1903), pp. 98-9.
32. Such discussions are pursued by Piore and Sabel (1984) and the so-called Regulationist School (see Aglietta, 1979, and Lipietz, 1987).
33. See, for example, Crouch and Pizzone (1978).
34. The inter-/intra-era differences are important here. Cusumano (1985) points out how much more rapidly and thoroughly Toyota has moved to the new labour process than Nissan. Yet the work-practices currently utilized at Nissan are considerably closer to those of Toyota than to that developed and utilized in the American and Western European auto firms. This will be discussed further in Chapter 4.
35. See, for example, Schonberger (1982).
36. It is interesting to note here that the major implementor of this system in Toyota - Ono Taiichi - ascribes its origins to the attempt to reduce inventories, rather than to cope with variable and low demand (see Cusumano 1985).
37. This aspect of the Japanese system is particularly clearly discussed in Schonberger (1982).
38. This systemic point was made in a recent survey of 100 firms introducing JIT production systems in the United Kingdom "The bad news is that even among the managers who are involved with JIT the overwhelming majority are at a very early stage in thinking about workflow, lack a proper understanding of the overall concept and are trying to introduce changes rather haphazardly and in small piecemeal packages". (Financial Times, 17 September, 1986).
39. In the final chapter we will also consider the

political dimensions of these changes in Japan, especially the destruction of the independent trade unions in the early 1950s.

40. These issues are treated in greater detail in Kaplinsky (1984).

41. It is however also a response to crisis since the declining rate of profit resulting from the increase in competitive pressures forces the search for greater efficiency in production - see Kaplinsky (1984) Chapter 1.

42. The literature on automation tends to concur with the definition of Einzig that "its loose use practically as a synonym for advanced mechanization may shock the economist, but serves the purpose of the economist" (Einzig, 1957, p. 2).

43. This is often referred to as "island automation".

44. Eatwell (1985) and Thurow (1985).

45. This phenomenon is becoming an important issue in the garments industry. Here the long and generally inflexible supply lines arising from production in DCs are inducing some IAC firms to relocate production near the final markets. Together with the sharpening of protectionism, it is also forcing some of the developing country firms to establish highly automated and flexible plants in the IACs. These issues will be discussed further in the final Chapter.

3

The Automobile Industry

This chapter sets the scene for the empirical analysis which follows. Except where it is germane to an understanding of later chapters or of our wider concerns with FDI and the NIDL, the discussion will be cursory and schematic. It is divided into three sections. The first relates to market conditions in the global automobile sector, beginning with a short history of automobile production and market structure; market-entry conditions - especially in recent years - are considered in somewhat greater detail. The second section considers the emergence of crisis-conditions in the United States and Western European industries and briefly describes three strategies adopted by the major producers, especially in relation to their component-sourcing policies. The importance of this is to be seen in relation to our concern with the locational decisions of TNCs and the NIDL, both of which were discussed in previous chapters. The chapter concludes with a description of automobile-assembly technology to help identify a way of classifying different types of components; this is of obvious importance in the discussion of sourcing-strategies which follows in later chapters.

MARKET CONDITIONS IN THE AUTOMOBILE INDUSTRY

A Short History

The internal combustion engine, the power unit which lies at the heart of the modern automobile and commercial vehicle, only became a commercial reality during the last quarter of the nineteenth century. Its incorporation into the automobile - which in some of its earlier versions was powered by a steam-engine - soon followed in Western Europe, but production levels remained limited. The concept of mass, national markets was not entrenched in this environment and "roads" were primitive. The automobile was seen as a luxury product and was manufactured in small batches for discerning users. By 1906, two decades after the first automobiles had appeared, a total of only 50,000 vehicles a year were produced throughout Western Europe.

These modest beginnings were important though, since the concept of a durable, autonomously moving vehicle was proven to be viable. It was in the United States, however, where the potential of mass, national markets was first realized in the nineteenth century$\underline{1}$/ and where as a result the commercial production of standardized automobiles developed. With the introduction of the Model T, Henry Ford ushered in the second phase in the history of the industry. The Model T was designed for mass manufacture as well as for ease of use and maintenance, and some six years after its 1908 introduction, it came to be produced on the moving production line, a major innovation in modern manufacturing history. Whereas only 6,000 Model Ts were produced in the first year - a significant number on its own when compared to total Western European output of around 50,000 - this jumped to 300,000 in 1914 and to 1.9m in its peak year in 1923. At that time total United States production had reached over 2m p.a., representing over 90 percent of global output. The automobile had thus been established as a mass consumption good, and the infrastructure required to make it a usable product (such as service stations and roads) was expanding rapidly.

The dominance of the United States industry in this period was high, but not absolute. The primitive nature of shipping technology - without the purpose-designed RORO (roll on, roll off) ships of today - offered a form of natural protection to Western European producers. This was complemented by a series of government policies which are not unfamiliar to contemporary ears. The desire to rebuild the war-shattered Western European economies, strengthened by the mass unemployment of the 1930s, saw its reflection in the adoption of high protective tariffs. These were often over 33 percent in nominal terms, and considerably higher as effective rates of protection. This not only provided space for indigenous Western European producers, but also forced the United States giants to locate abroad. By 1929, Ford had assembly plants in 21 countries and

General Motors in 16. Whilst inducing this transfer of United States manufacturing technology and protecting domestic industry, the small size of most Western European markets meant that few of their producers were able to reap the nascent economies of scale, and by the outbreak of the Second World War, the technological dominance of the United States producers remained.

Whilst the 1950s saw a familiar pattern of industrial regeneration in Western Europe, this was associated with a diversity of markets and numerous entry-restrictions. These disabilities were soon removed for most of the continental producers with the development of the Common Market. This not only continued to protect them from extracontinental competitors, but also allowed them to reap continent-wide scale economies. Over the 1950s and 1960s, therefore, a number of these Western European automobile firms expanded, each developing expertise in particular niches of the market.2/ By the 1970s they had matured into competitive producers, but unlike their United States counterparts whose product technology had degenerated into a standardized series of product differentiating facelifts, the Western European firms maintained a high rate of product innovation. Their emphasis on small-car technology made their automobiles particularly attractive in the United States and exports from Western Europe grew rapidly, penetrating 10.5 percent of the United States market by 1970. It also saw the first signs of cross-FDI, with Volkswagen and then Renault both moving to establish themselves as producers in the United States. At the same time, the United States multinationals which had established themselves in Western Europe in the 1920s and 1930s continued to act in virtual independence from their United States affiliates and maintained their relative market position.

The development of the Japanese automobile industry - which had been producing cars for almost as long as the United States with its first product available in 1902 3/ - slipped through almost unnoticed during these two decades. Early shipments of cars to the United States in the 1960s had proved disastrous - the cars were underpowered and consequently experienced a high rate of breakdown - and the Japanese industry retreated and regrouped. The second wave of exports proved to be phenomenally successful, and it was not long before Japan became the world's ascendent manufacturer and exporter of autos.

The trade implications of these changing patterns of

Table 3.1
Extraregional Automobile Exports ('000s)

	North America	Western Europe	Japan
1929	400	56	-
1938	149	96	-
1950	117	376	-
1960	107	1,213	7
1970	76	1,889	726
1980	171	1,276	3,947
1985	26	1,697[a]	4,427

Source: Compiled from Altshuler et al(1984) and Society of Motor Manufacturers and Traders (1985).

competitiveness is shown in Table 3.1. The prewar dominance of the United States was rapidly undermined by the protectionist barriers of the 1930s; Western European postwar competence was reflected in a surge of exports, tailoring off in numbers, but not in value in the 1970s; and finally the very rapid Japanese push into international markets has been a phenomenon of the past fifteen years.

The Size of the Automobile Sector

If sector size is considered in terms of final products, taking into account the production of intermediate inputs and capital goods as well as the costs of using and maintaining the final product, the automobile sector is clearly the largest single branch in global manufacturing. By 1985 there were over 360m in circulation globally, of which 40 percent were in Western Europe and 39 percent in North America;4/ more than 324 vehicles of all types were produced in the seven years between 1978 and 1985.5/ In 1979 - the peak year in the history of employment - 3.6m people were employed directly in automobile manufacture in the seven major producing countries (United States, Japan, the Federal Republic of Germany, France, Italy, the United Kingdom and Sweden), with an additional 2-3m in the production of capital and intermediate goods. In the United States in 1979, it was estimated that 9.1 percent of the labour force was employed in automobile-related occupations (1.2 percent in manufacturing; 2.8 percent in selling and servicing; 1 percent in road building and maintenance; and 4.1 percent in haulage).6/ In Argentina, Brazil, Mexico and Venezuela - all economies in which the automobile industry has a long history - it has been estimated that 7.5 percent of the industrial labour force was involved in the manufacture and servicing of autos and that the sector accounted for around 10 percent of industrial value added.7/ If employment in other countries, as well as people working in repair, maintenance, sales and the automobile service subsectors are considered, the numbers employed globally easily exceeded 10m. As a constituent of world trade in 1980, the sector accounted for 6.5 percent of total trade and for around 12 percent of global trade in manufactures.

One of the reasons why automobile-related employment is so much higher than the employment generated in the manufacture of automobiles alone arises from the large number of inputs contained in the final product. The linkage effects are therefore high. For example, in the late 1970s the United States auto industry consumed 20 percent of all steel and around 60 percent of all rubber. In Western Europe, in addition to similar quantities of steel and rubber, it is estimated that the industry consumes one-fifth of all machine tool output and five percent of all glass.8/ Moreover, the first major substantial user of industrial robots was the automobile industry, and it was also involved in pioneering the use and widening the market for Computer Aided Design.9/ Both of these latter technologies have been strategically important in the development of computer integrated manufacturing (CIM) technologies.

As can be seen from Table 3.2, the industrially advanced market economies display the highest level of per capita automobile penetration, with the United States - with more than one car for every two people - closely followed by other automobilized economies such as Canada, Australia and New Zealand, and then by other more densely populated industrially advanced economies with better developed public transport systems. It is significant that with such high levels of automobile penetration in these economies, combined with a steady improvement in durability and hence the life of automobiles, market growth has slowed. In the 1960s, the growth rate was around 8 percent p.a., falling to 4.5 percent in the 1970s, and around 2 percent in the 1980s. In these economies, therefore, it is predominantly a replacement market. By contrast, in the socialist bloc and the developing world where penetration

Table 3.2
Per Capita Automobile Penetration in Selected Economies, 1980

Automobiles per 000 Population

Developed Market Economies	1980	1985
United States	537	555
New Zealand	406	455
Canada	428	435a
Australia	407	435
Germany, Federal Republic of	377	417
France	357	385
Italy	310	385
United Kingdom	276	345
Japan	203	233
Centrally Planned Economies		
German Democratic Republic of	151	189
Czechoslovakia	148	170
Hungary	85	133
USSR	31	40
China	0.05	0.1
Developing Economies		
Venezuela	95	121
Argentina	115	116a
Brazil	67	64a
Mexico	47	74
Korea, Republic of	6	14
India	1	2

Source: Compiled from Altshuler et al(1984) and Society of Motor Manufacturers and Traders (1985).

a1984

is much lower, it has been argued that the prospects for market growth are much higher.

Market Structure

The automobile industry has been through a number of phases since its inception at the turn of the century. In the initial period before the Ford-inspired standardization of production, there was a plethora of small scale producers. The trend towards oligopolization first developed in the United States and was consolidated by Ford's mass production line.10/ Concentration was further reinforced by the development of firm-economies of scale, based upon organizational changes. This became an important phenomenon in the early 1920s when (as we saw in Chapter 2) Alfred Sloan at GM rationalized production between divisions, and between GM and independent component suppliers. The first wave of foreign direct investment to Western Europe in the 1930s reinforced the global dominance of the major United States producers. This was essentially maintained through the early 1960s, since although Western European production had advanced considerably, a significant proportion was accounted for by subsidiaries of GM and Ford, as well as by the somewhat moribund activities of Chrysler.

It was in the late 1960s that global corporate market shares began to alter. Not only were some Western European firms rapidly expanding their domestic output, but they were also building up both exports and foreign production. Of considerable importance here were the international activities of Volkswagen (in the United States and Brazil), Fiat (Brazil, Spain and Eastern Europe) and Renault (Spain and the United States). But even more significant was the phenomenal expansion of output by the Japanese firms, producing almost exclusively in their home country. Coupled with the retreat from some foreign operations by Fiat, the sharp decline in output by the indigenous United Kingdom industry and the building up of predominantly foreign-owned capacity in Spain by the United States multinationals,11/ there has been a major change in corporate shares in the past decade.

In 1985 the ten largest auto producers were General Motors (7.1m), Ford (3.8m), Toyota (2.6m), Volkswagen (2.1m), Nissan (2m), Renault (1.6m), Peugeot-Citroen (1.6m), Chrysler (1.3m), Fiat (1.2m) and Honda (1.1m).12/. However, there is unfortunately no long time-series on corporate market shares. But a glance at geographical production figures (Table 3.3) provides an insight into the changing pattern of oligopoly. At the onset of the Second World War, the United States accounted for something like

Table 3.3
Automobile Production – Western Europe, North America, Japan and Selected Countries (000s)

	1929	1938	1950	1960	1970	1980	1984	1985
North America	4,791	2,143	6,950	7,001	7,491	7,223	8,673	9,257
Western Europe	554	879	1,110	5,120	10,379	10,372	10,726	10,849
Japan	na	na	2	165	3,178	7,038	7,073	7,647
Czechoslavakia	na	na	25	56	143	184	174	185
German Democratic Republic	na	na	10	64	127	177	200	175
Poland	na	na	0	12	24	79	279	300
USSR	na	na	65	139	344	1,327	1,300	1,260
Argintina	na	na	0	30	163	216	142	114
Brazil	na	na	0	62	344	978	695	770
India	na	na	7	19	37	31	64	102
Mexico	na	na	25	137	303	245	251	
Korea, Republic of	na	na	0	0	15	57	255[a]	650
Taiwan Province	na	na	0	0	132	134	158	na

Source: Compiled from Altshuler et al (1984), Financial Times, 11 September 1985 and 20 February 1987, Society of Motor Manufacturers and Traders (1985), L'Argus (1985 and 1986).

70 percent of global production. This was even higher - about 85 percent - in the immediate aftermath of the Second World War, but declined rapidly through the next two decades. By 1970, Western Europe produced more automobiles than the United States (although it must be borne in mind that a sizable proportion of Western European output was accounted for by United States TNCs). Although the Japanese producers had almost reached the aggregate production levels of the United States by 1980, the most striking feature of their performance is their disproportionate share of world trade. Whereas their 1980 output was only three-quarters that of Western Europe (Table 3.3), their exports were three times as much (Table 3.1).

A further significant trend in recent years has been the very rapid rise of production in four newly industrializing countries - Spain, Brazil, Mexico and the Republic of Korea. Spain, whose production in 1985 of 1.2m exceeded that of the United Kingdom and approached that of Italy, had fared particularly well as a production base for small cars by Ford and GM, and soon by Volkswagen. Brazil became an important centre of production by subsidiaries of TNCs, not just for the indigenous market, but also for exports of engines to the United States and Italy and complete cars to marginal markets, often backed by government subsidies and the countertrade arrangements which are characteristic of the new protectionist environment. Mexico has increasingly become incorporated within the United States industry, and may play a very different role to that of Brazil in the future.

Finally, the Republic of Korea stands out as a major potential producer in the late 1980s. Its auto production capacity grew from less than 100,000 in the early 1980s to 650,000 in 1986 and jumped further to over 1m in 1987. Most of the output gains were made by an indigenous firm, Hyundai. Its capacity rose from 150,000 in 1984 to 500,000 in 1986 and 750,000 in 1987. As can be seen from Table 3.3, this puts both Hyundai and the Republic of Korea in the big league of producers. The significance of the Republic of Korea's effort arises because although it has received technology from United States and Japanese firms, it is a predominantly locally-owned and controlled industry, the first such case since the rise to prominence of the Japanese producers in the late 1960s and early 1970s. But perhaps even more significantly, unlike Japan where auto production goes back over eight decades, the recent Republic of Korean entrants have had little prior experience in the industry.

Corporate market shares are more difficult to track over time. Table 3.4 records recent data for the share of final markets in the major consuming countries. It is clear that the two largest United States TNCs continue to exercise dominance over global markets, followed by the biggest Japanese producer (Toyota) and then by a clutch of medium/large firms such as Nissan and the larger Western European corporations. The most significant feature of the current oligopolistic market structure in many of the major consuming countries (especially the United States, the United Kingdom and the Federal Republic of Germany) is the growing presence of Japanese producers, especially over the past decade. The issues that this aspect of market structure raises for the industry and for our main arguments are pursued further in the next section.

Market Entry

The Rise of Protectionism. Despite the historically distinct reduction in trade barriers in the two and a half decades after 1950 - associated with a rapid rise in trade in the automobile and other sectors - it is important to bear in mind the pre-war experience of the global automobile industry. As we have seen, the technological dominance of United States-based producers counted for little when it came to serving the Western European market in the inter-war period. Entry into this market required local production and this drove the larger American firms to establish subsidiaries there, as well as in other markets such as South Africa, Australia and Latin America where tariffs had the effect of restricting entry. In the mid-1930s - the high point of unemployment in the Great Depression - nominal tariffs on automobile imports were 70 percent in Japan (1937), 45-70 percent in France (1932), 40 percent in the Federal Republic of Germany (1937), 101-111 percent in Italy (1937) and 33.3 in the United Kingdom (1924-1950).13/ Effective rates of protection were of course much higher.

Immediately after World War II and up until 1960, tariffs on automobile imports in the main producing nations remained at about 30 percent. Thereafter successive rounds of GATT-orchestrated improvements in trading conditions took the form of tariff reductions, in the automobile industry as in other sectors. By 1983 nominal external duties in all of these countries had fallen, to 2.8 percent

Table 3.4
Worldwide Car Sales by Major Manufacturers, 1984

	United States	Canada	Japan	Western Europe	Other Countries	Latin America	Total
General Motors	4,588	346	2	1,123	129	263	6,450
Ford	1,979	143	1	1,301	191	275	3,890
Toyota	558	68	1,275	228	149	39	3,317
Volkswagen-Audi	249	26	16	1,223	29	341	1,881
Nissan	485	43	805	287	85	65	1,771
Fiat	0	1	2	1,288	1	124	1,415
Renault	12	14	0	1,108	15	137	1,287
Peugeot-Citroen-Talbot	20	0	1	1,169	5	37	1,232
Chrysler	987	147	0	0	0	70	1,204
Honda	508	71	246	115	30	0	970
Mazda	170	22	215	201	61	0	668
Mitsubishi	131	12	198	112	68	0	521
Daimler-Benz (Mercedes)	79	4	.7	332	19	0	442

Source: Compiled from Financial Times, 11 September 1985

in Japan, 7 percent in the United States and 10.5 percent throughout the EEC. The same pattern extended to United States-Canada auto trade as the Auto Pact of 1965 significantly liberalized trade between those two countries.

A number of factors contributed to this process of liberalization. Rapid growth in the world economy accompanied the rapid expansion of world auto trade. So a decline in market-share in any one country was compensated for by a combination of growing absolute sales (as the total market for cars was expanding) or growing market-shares in other countries. The strength of the United States economy was also important since the growth in auto-imports there was masked by a positive overall trade balance.

All of these developments contributed to an atmosphere of freer trade. That is, up until the late 1970s. At that point, the emergence of the dimensions of economic-crisis in the industrial sector noted in Chapter 1 (uneven productivity-growth, trade imbalances and a slowdown in growth-rates) began to affect the automobile industry. The general slowdown in the Western European and United States economies was reflected in the automobile sector which began to experience a decline in production and a significant drop in employment. Table 3.5 shows, for example, the sharp decline in motor vehicle sales in the United States and Canada between 1978 and 1982. Table 3.6 illustrates that was paralleled by an even larger fall in employment in most IACs (with the notable exception of Japan where production continued to climb). This latter table highlights the substantial job losses in the United Kingdom and the United States of 23 percent and 26 percent respectively between 1979 and 1981. The decline continued in the United Kingdom through 1984 while Fiat in Italy and Peugeot and Renault in France also registered substantial reductions in the 1980-1984 period. In Fiat, for instance, 36,000 workers lost their jobs between 1980-1983.14/ Although automobile production began to rise again in some of these affected countries after the 1979-82 recession, there was not a corresponding increase in employment. The protectionist fuse had been lit.

It was only in Japan where production continued to climb and employment failed to fall. This, as we have seen, was associated with a continued increase in production and a growing share of global markets. The extent of this growth of import-penetration in the United States and Western Europe by the Japanese (and of import-

Table 3.5
Automobile Sales in the United States and Canada, 1978-1982
('000s of units)

	1978	1979	1980	1981	1982	Percentage Decline 1978-1982
United States	11,310	10,670	8,980	8,540	7,980	29%
Canada	990	1,000	930	900	710	28%

Source: Federal Task Force, 1983.

Table 3.6.
Employment in the Motor Vehicle and Equipment Industry in United States, Japan and Western Europe, 1970-1981

	1970	1973	1975	1978	1979	1980	1981
United States	799.0	976.0	792.0	977.1	982.2	773.8	723.2
Japan	580.0	634.4	601.2	637.8	651.3	682.8	704.3
Germany, Federal Republic of	605.7	625.4	566.3	650.2	673.3	684.1	670.0
France	476.4	528.5	507.4	534.1	523.5	503.0	505.2
United Kingdom	512.4	510.0	457.1	471.3	456.7	424.0	347.7
Italy	258.8	290.1	252.6	282.2	289.3	285.1	269.5
Sweden	46.2	53.5	60.8	62.3	66.1	67.1	60.7

Source: Altshuler et al (1984).

penetration in general) is shown in Table 3.7. The growth in Japanese market-share was particularly marked between 1973 and 1981. The first date represents the onset of higher oil-prices and the extra attractions to the consumer of the fuel-efficient Japanese automobiles; the latter date reflects the slowdown in Japanese exports as a series of protectionist quotas began to be imposed in most of the major markets. It is striking that although Japan had the lowest nominal external tariffs of any of the three major trading-regions, its levels of imports - 2.17 percent in 1986 - was insignificant.

The combined effect of these developments in Western

Table 3.7
Import Share of the United States, Western European and Japanese Auto Markets

Imports to	United States			Western Europe	Japan
Exported from	Western Europe	Japan	World	Japan	Rest of World
1962	4.8	0.1	4.9	n.d.	1.4
1968	8.9	1.6	10.5	0.6	0.5
1969	8.7	2.5	11.2	n.d.	0.4
1970	10.5	4.2	14.7	1.1	0.5
1971	9.0	5.9	14.9	1.6	0.5
1972	7.6	5.7	13.3	2.7	0.6
1973	9.0	6.2	15.2	3.6	0.8
1974	9.0	6.7	15.7	4.0	1.1
1975	8.9	9.3	18.2	5.2	1.1
1976	5.6	9.2	14.8	5.6	1.0
1977	6.3	12.0	18.2	6.2	1.0
1978	5.9	11.9	17.8	6.3	1.2
1979	5.6	17.0	22.6	7.2	1.3
1980	5.4	22.8	28.2	9.8	1.0
1981	5.8	23.0	28.8	9.1	0.7
1982	5.4	23.2	28.6	8.6	0.7
1983	6.3	19.7	26.0	9.9	n.a.
1984	5.2	18.3	23.5	10.1	1.62
1985	5.6	20.1	25.7	10.7	2.17
1986			28.3		

Source: Compiled from Altshuler et al (1984), Cusumano (1985), Financial Times, 20 February 1987

Notes: n.d. = no relevant data available

Europe and the United States was a rapid change in attitude concerning the virtue of free trade in autos - particularly with regard to the "Japanese Challenge". In Western Europe import restrictions against the Japanese began at a national level, sometimes via Voluntary Export Restraints (VERs)15/ negotiated with the Japanese industry, and at other times via formal restrictions on the number of imports allowed. Italy maintained its pre-GATT limit on Japanese exports of 2,200 vehicles a year. In 1975 the United Kingdom government negotiated a VER with the

Japanese limiting their share of the United Kingdom market to 11 percent. Other Western European nations soon followed the same path with France imposing a 3 percent share limit in 1977, the Federal Republic of Germany (previously a major supporter of free trade) imposing informal restrictions in 1979, Belgium a 7 percent limit in 1981, the Netherlands acting similarly also in 1981, and Spain and Sweden following suit in 1983.

The culmination of this process of national market closure came with a warning from the EEC in 1983 concerning regional market closure. It stated that unless the Japanese exercised restraint and kept their Western European-wide share to the 9 percent achieved in 1982, further limits might be imposed. Then in 1984 - when the Japanese began to respond to the growth in protectionism by announcing plans to assemble autos in Western Europe - the tack changed to a warning about the dangers of "screwdriver operations". Sixty percent local content - the figure specified by the existing EEC Rules of Origin - were inadequate, it was argued, and could easily be covered by the import of kits, local assembly costs and profit. A more "realistic" figure of 80 percent would be required to ensure that genuine manufacture was occurring in Western Europe. The call for protectionism by the Western European industry was led by the Chairman of Ford Europe. He called upon the European Commission to monitor the nature of growing Japanese assembly in Western Europe very closely to ensure a minimum of 80 percent local content measured by weight since

> Japan had built up its motor industry behind a protectionist wall for 25 years because it was an infant national industry . . . we should not be reluctant to do the same thing to promote the rebirth of industries in the West.16/

It is, however, in the United States - by far the largest national market - where the most crucial protectionist battles are being fought. This battle began in 1979 when pressure for a curb on Japanese imports began to emerge and culminated in a VER agreement being negotiated between the United States and Japan in April 1981. This limited imports to 1.76 million units and represented a drop of 7.7 percent on the 1980 totals. This level was maintained until 1983 when it was raised to 1.876 million units, and further relaxed to 1.94 million units for the year beginning April 1984.

In April 1985, after a vociferous battle in which the big three producers and the unions were aligned in support of maintenance of the VER against a Reagan government with a strong free trade bias, the decision was finally taken to relax the VER further. Contributing to this decision to relax import quotas were the high profits earned in this protective environment by the major United States producers - $9.8bn in 1984 and around $8bn in 1985. But it was accompanied by highly-publicized warnings from the United Auto Workers Union (UAW) that a minimum of 200,000 jobs would be eliminated by this relaxation of import quotas and threats from Chrysler to significantly cut back on its level of vehicle production in the United States. In 1986, following the attempt by President Reagan to trade-off access to the United States auto market in return for United States access to the Japanese timber, pharmaceuticals and agricultural markets, the Japanese quota rose to 2.3m autos, a level which was maintained in 1987.

What is especially interesting about this experience of rapid Japanese penetration into a market free of entry restrictions, is that it is not dissimilar to recent experience in Canada, this time involving a new Republic of Korea automobile producer, Hyundai (in which a Japanese firm, Mitsubishi Motor Company, has a 15 percent equity share). Hyundai is making a concerted attempt to enter the world automobile industry. It is particularly targeting the United States market where it is currently unaffected by import quotas facing its Japanese small-car manufacturing rivals. Lacking a large domestic market of its own -and fearing a repeat of the early failure of Toyota and Nissan in the United States who had failed to test their products operating in United States conditions - Hyundai has tested its product on the Canadian market. It targeted sales of 6,000 autos in 1984, but due partly to its tariff-free status and thus low prices, its actual level of sales was more than 25,000. Its 1985 target was 60,000, but in the first eight months alone its actual sales were 48,556, compared with 12,388 in the same period in 1984. This made Hyundai the largest importer by a substantial margin, selling 10,000 cars more than its nearest Japanese rival, Honda. (This strategy of test-marketing in Canada seems to have paid dividends. Hyundai aimed at United States sales of 100-120,000 in 1986 and actually achieved sales of 168,882).

The Response to Protectionism. The recent United States experience of protection and investment-response in the automobile industry presents a particularly rich case study of the political-economic intricacies of protectionism and the effect of this phenomena on the investment location issues with which we are centrally concerned. By far the most important development arising out of the introduction of the VERs and the threats of local-content legislation in the United States (and also present in a more limited fashion in Western Europe) was the response of the major Japanese auto firms. All of these firms have now decided to establish auto production in the United States and they have done so largely because of their belief that rising trade barriers are inevitable. This behaviour contrasts very significantly from the two earlier foreign investments in the United States in the 1970s, in which Volkswagen had established production facilities in order to keep costs down, and Renault had bought up a major share of American Motors equity to obtain a customer base.

Even before United States protectionist sentiment led to the establishment of the VERs, Honda had tested the United States waters by establishing a motorcycle plant in 1979. The success of this venture and the imposition of VERs led them to invest $250m in a new plant to build 150,000 Accords in Ohio in 1981. There were two major reasons why it was Honda that first took this step. The first was that it had been less successful in implementing new work-practices and JIT philosophy (described in Chapter 2) than Toyota and the other Japanese producers17/ and it was consequently less difficult for Honda to transfer production abroad. And secondly, Honda's foreign sales account for the largest percentage of revenue (64 percent on total sales of 1.2m in 1984) of the Japanese producers. This made it particularly sensitive to import restrictions and protectionist sentiments and, combined with its small quota allowance (which was based on its historic rather than recent performance),18/ Honda was particularly anxious not to upset the United States industry and unions in their moment of deep crisis in 1980. This latter desire also accounts for the relatively low-key way in which it went about setting itself up in the United States with as little publicity as possible - a style that contrasted sharply with the fanfare that accompanied VW's announcement of its United States assembly plans in 1977 or that of Nissan in 1984. By 1987 Honda was assembling 320,000 autos a year in the United States and planned for this to rise to 500,000 by 1990.19/ Most intriguingly, it is planning to serve the Western European market - where its sales are limited by quota restrictions against imports from Japan - from this United States plant in the knowledge that the Western European countries will be much more reluctant to bar imports from the United States. Moreover with the sharp decline in the value of the dollar during 1987, it is likely that United States produced autos will be cost-competitive in Western Europe.

The other Japanese majors were not so far-sighted as Honda and were at first much more reluctant to bow to the pressures towards local production. This was particularly true of Toyota whose production system of JIT and new work-practices was judged to be most difficult to transfer to the United States. All of the Japanese firms would have preferred to source the United States markets from Japan because of their demonstrated ability to produce vehicles there at a much lower cost than they can do anywhere else in the world. Nevertheless the seeming permanence of the VERs in the early 1980s soon forced their hand and they began to follow Honda in rapid fashion.

Nissan was first, feeling its way with a less risky light-truck plant and then announcing in May 1984 a plan to build 100,000 Sentras starting in May 1985. The next wave of investments was seemingly induced by United States firms. GM, unable to produce its own small car competitively, struck up a joint venture called NUMMI (New United Motor Manufacturing Inc) using a disused plant in Freemont, California. For GM it was an opportunity to acquaint itself with Japanese organizational techniques; for Toyota an opportunity to test United States waters at low cost. Then, two other Japanese firms which had close equity links with United States producers, Mitsubishi (with Chrysler) and Mazda (with Ford), made similar decisions. Meanwhile Toyota, having convinced itself that in the long run it had no alternative to local production, not only decided to add a further model to its NUMMI joint venture, but also announced plans to build its own $800m assembly plant in the United States and another one in Canada. Anticipating further protectionist pressures, in late 1987 Toyota announced plans to build a $300m engine and transmission factory to feed this assembly plant.[20]/ Subaru and Isuzu have also taken the plunge and plan to share the costs of a 200,000 unit plant. In addition to this, Honda has announced plans to increase its output to 360,000 units by 1988, as well as building another 150,000 in Canada - and Honda's president has been quoted as saying they would like to be producing one million units in North America in 15 years time.[21]/ The million figure has also been cited as a Nissan aim - and Toyota and Mazda must be assumed to be entertaining similar ambitions.

Leaving aside their long-term aspirations, if all goes according to announced plans, by 1990 these Japanese-owned plants will have the capacity to build at least 1.3m - and possibly even 2m - cars in the United States, equivalent to around 13 percent of the domestic market (Table 3.8). Moreover, this figure assumes that they will also be exporting a further 3m autos to the United States. If protectionism makes this level of imports impossible (which must be a distinct possibility) and some of the long-term plans are brought into action more quickly, it is possible that within a short space of one decade the Japanese automobile industry will move from 100 percent home production to a 50:50 split - and in the process could quite possibly satisfy 40 percent of the United States market's need from local United States production. In this case we might eventually be faced with the irony of Japanese firms operating as major producers in the United States (and therefore employing substantial numbers of United States workers) and clamouring for protection against the efforts of United States producers to import cars into the United States from their offshore export platforms! Given the level of trade supplanted by these foreign investments (over $30bn) and the cost of building assembly plants abroad (approaching $1bn under present plans) these are among the most significant developments to have taken place in the world auto industry in the last thirty years.

As if the Japanese invasion was not enough, United States assemblers have also to confront the prospect of a rapid growth in the number of other foreign firms building cars destined for sale in the United States. In 1985, this number stood at 28. In addition there exist announced plans for a further seven domestic projects or joint ventures with foreign companies producing in the United States, bringing the total number of new projects whose output is destined for the United States market to 35, offering some 172 carlines. By 1990 at least 12 new foreign companies hope to export more than 750,000 cars to the United States. Those with formally announced plans are listed in Table 3.9, but the table does not include the unannounced plans of specialist producers such as AC (United Kingdom), Panther Co (United Kingdom), Reliant (United Kingdom), VW's entry level model from Brazil, and Suzuki (Japan). In 1985, car imports (at 2,680,000) accounted for 24.2 percent of the 11,063,000 cars sold in

Table 3.8
United States Assembly Capacities for United States and Foreign Firms, 1985-1990 ('000s)

	1985	1986	1988	1990
CAPACITIES:				
General Motors	5,000	5,000	5,150	5,400
Ford	1,800	1,800	1,800	1,800
Chrysler	1,350	1,350	1,350	1,350
AMC	135	135	135	135
Volkswagen	115	115	115	115
Honda	150	150	300	300
Nissan	70	70	125	125
NUMMI	80	250	250	250
Mazda			240	240
Diamond Star*			180	180
Toyota			200	200
Total Capacity	8,700	8,870	9,845	10,095
US Manufacturers	95.2%	93.4%	85.7%	86.1%
Foreign Manufacturers	4.8	6.6	14.3	13.9
US Auto Sales	10.70	10.75	9.75	10.80
Imports	2.71	3.11	3.00	3.40
MARKET SHARE:				
Imports	25.3%	38.9%	30.8%	31.5%
Local by Foreign Firms	29.7	34.6	40.7	41.6
Local by Domestic Firms	70.3	65.4	59.3	58.4

Source: Salomon Brothers, quoted in The Financial Times, 5 September 1985. Reprinted by permission.

*Chrysler-Mitsubishi

the United States - an additional 750,000 units would raise the import share to more than 31 percent. Adding North American production by Japanese firms would leave the share available to United States producers to less than 50 percent.

A similar process of protection being met with a response of FDI has occurred in Canada. As we saw earlier, Hyundai launched its North American strategy by testing the waters of the Canadian market, and with considerable success. The response from the Canadian unions and component manufacturers was to demand protection. The

Table 3.9
New Foreign Auto Producers Exporting to United States by 1990

Company	Country	Carline(s)	Date of Entry	Anticipated Volume	Building Cars for
Austin Rover	United Kingdom	XX, 2nd Model	1987	20,000	Self
Daewoo	Republic of Korea	Opel Kadett-derived	1987	80,000	Pontiac
Daihatsu	Republic of Korea	Charade, other	1987	50,000est	Self
Lio-Ho	Taiwan Province	Small Car	1988	40,000	Ford
Usines Chausson	France	Sports Car	by 1990	5,000est	Ford
Hyundai	Republic of Korea	Poly Excel, Stellar	1986	100,000	Self
		Excel	1987	30,000	Mitsubishi
Kia	Republic of Korea	Minicar	1987	70,000	Ford
		Minicar	1988	40,000	Mazda
AIM	Greece	Desta APV	1986	20,000	Self
SEAT	Spain	Malaga	1988	50,000	Self
Skoda	Czech	Small Car	by 1990	40,000est	Self
Yue Loong	Taiwan Province	March	1988	50,000	Nissan
Zastava	Yugoslavia	Yugo	1986	150,000	Self
Total				745,000	

Source: Ealey, "Twelve Foreign Car Makers to Enter US by 1980" (Automotive Industries, 1985). Reprinted by permission.

Ontario state government - concerned at the fate of its own auto industry - claimed that the C$2,000 tariff concession on Hyundai's cars should be removed and asserted, in addition, that the Republic of Korea no longer portrayed the characteristics of a developing country and should no longer receive these types of concessions.22/ Hyundai's first response to these stirrings of protectionism was to announce plans for a C$25m components plant in Canada. Then as pressure built up, it widened these plans to include an R&D facility to design engine components. And then, finally, Hyundai buckled to the protectionist pressures and announced a plan for a C$200m plant to assemble 100,000 autos per year, beginning in 1988. Then, towards the end of 1987, these protectionist pressures were strengthened in Canada. GM's and Ford's Canadian subsidiaries claimed that Hyundai was dumping autos in Canada and a 36 percent countervailining duty was imposed.23/ Hyundai's decision to produce in Canada has been matched by a number of Japanese firms. In addition to Honda (which will be assembling 80,000 autos per year by 1987), Toyota has committed itself to a 50,000 (on a single-shift basis) assembly plant to be in operation by 1988. Nissan announced plans to invest C$3-500m in a plant to come on stream by 1990-1, GM plans a joint-venture with Suzuki to produce 200,000 small cars for the North American market. The issue of local content in these autos has not yet risen in public debate, partly because the two parties agreed that the assembly plants would be a *quid pro quo* for voluntary export restraint by the Japanese. Under the existing terms of the Canada-United States auto pact, duty-free access to the United States market is conditional upon a local content of only 50 percent which, as we have seen, is relatively easy to achieve with only limited incorporation of local components. But these investments in Canada are all additional to current Canadian production and in the context of the extensive over-capacity in the United States it is inconceivable that local-content pressures will not force the renegotiation of the relevant clauses in the Canada-United States auto pact.

This sort of interaction between protection and investment location is not confined to North America. Similar conditions have arisen in Western Europe with Japanese auto firms seeking ways round the European-wide quotas. In this case, the United Kingdom is attracting the most interest as a means of providing the Japanese with unrestricted access to Western Europe's 10 million units a year car market. Nissan rather than Honda was the first, with a $420m, 100,000 unit per annum plant. But Honda has also taken steps to increase local production, starting initially with its joint design and assembly venture with the Rover Group, and then in 1987 deciding to build an engine-plant production (and, perhaps, full assembly later) partly to feed its United Kingdom customer (RG) and partly in an attempt to get round the quotas which threaten sales of its autos which are assembled by RG in the United Kingdom.24/ Even Toyota (the Japanese firm most reluctant to invest abroad) has undertaken at least two feasibility studies regarding the prospects for setting up a 120,000 unit assembly plant in the United Kingdom. The Japanese are active elsewhere in Western Europe as well. Nissan had a joint venture with Alfa Romeo in Italy, and holds a majority share of Motor Iberica in Spain. Mazda, through its close links with Ford, is expected to participate in plans to export vehicles from Portugal into the EEC as well. And Mitsubishi and Mercedes Benz cooperate in the production of trucks in Spain.

Although similar forces are at work in both Western Europe and North America, there are some European twists in the above described situation. Whereas the state in the United States has offered no incentives to encourage Japanese FDI, the United Kingdom government has anxiously courted the Japanese auto manufacturers. It strongly endorsed the RG/Honda link and, to the dismay of all the existing United Kingdom producers, also provided Nissan with $157m worth of incentives; it will probably be similarly receptive to overtures from Honda. This action in turn set off a chain reaction of protest from elsewhere in Western Europe. First the Italians protested that the 60 percent local content rule being applied to the RG/Honda joint venture was too low for the final car to qualify as an EEC product. Although this objection was initially overruled by the EEC Commission, Ford Europe, as we have already noted, again took up this theme and pressed for an 80 percent local content - needless to say, Ford's position on this matter must be seen as somewhat equivocal given that it had previously berated Western European governments for their protectionist tendencies and also because the local content of the autos it assembled in the United States and the United Kingdom had recently come under attack.25/ Despite Ford's delicate position on this matter, it is clear that local content legislation will be an increasingly important issue in the protectionist environment in Western Europe, as well, no doubt, as in the United States.

So, the response by the Japanese to the reemergence of protectionism in the industrially advanced countries has been to invest in automobile assembly in those countries. The question is how "deep" these activities will be. Will they be mere screwdriver operations with the Japanese assemblers bringing their components from Japan or from low-wage developing economies? Will the host-country firms be forced to maintain their assembly operations in the home-countries, but feed these plants with components produced abroad? These important issues are not yet clear, but are of course of considerable significance, not least for the expectations of export-led industrialization in the developing world. They will be addressed in detail in later chapters.

CORPORATE RESPONSE TO THE RISE IN COMPETITIVE TEMPERATURE

In the 1950s and 1960s when markets were expanding at a rapid rate and the world auto industry was on an upward trend everywhere, there was room for a great many producers. As the years progressed there was a steady trend towards oligopolization, especially in the United States and the United Kingdom where the minor actors were taken over by the industry majors. Nevertheless, right through to the mid-1970s, automobile production remained a profitable industry. Then, as the Western European industry began its process of interpenetration and as first the Europeans, and then the Japanese, began to move into the North American market, many of the major actors began to experience a considerable squeeze on their operations. A sharp fall in profitability in the late 1970s in the United States was arrested by the introduction of VERs, and the United States TNCs once again moved into profitable operation. In Western Europe, the United Kingdom industry experienced a continual crisis of profitability and as the competitive temperature began to increase, the French firms, too, passed through a series of very unprofitable years. The Western European subsidiaries of Ford and GM also experienced a fluctuating pattern of profit and loss, with the losses becoming more sustained in the early 1980s. Fiat, in Italy, after a major restructuring in the late 1970s experienced a significant turnaround into profit. Only the Federal Republic of Germany and Swedish industries - largely buoyed by profitable exports of "up-market" autos to North America - seemed to be able to escape the continual drift into unprofitability.

As the industry enters the second half of the 1980s, the continued profitability of some of the major producers must be open to question. We have already observed that the picture looks bleak for the United States industry. For, in addition to a large rise in production in foreign countries of autos directly destined for the United States market and to the existing share of the market held by imports, significant domestic production by foreign manufacturers is scheduled to come on stream before the end of the decade. If all these short-term plans are realized (leaving aside the grander, medium-term plans of some of the non-United States firms), the United States manufacturers will be left with only slightly more than one-half of their domestic markets. Matching planned investments in the United States with the anticipated domestic market - and excluding the 750,000 cars being built abroad specifically for the United States market - suggests levels of excess capacity which are likely to grow from 8 percent in 1985 to 14 percent in 1986, 31 percent in 1988 and 27 percent in 1990.26/ The result is that the United States industry is likely to see very significantly higher rates of competition than it has hitherto experienced.

A very similar situation already prevails in Western Europe in that there exist high levels of excess capacity and growing pressures on profitability. To some extent, however, the Western European industry has not yet seen the worst of these competitive pressures. Its exports to the United States have not yet been affected by protectionist pressures, diverting a considerable share of higher-value (and traditionally, until the appreciation of the dollar in 1986-7, more profitable)27/ production abroad. The Japanese have also not yet brought on stream plants in Western Europe, but no doubt as soon as they have come to terms with the plants they are establishing in the United States, this will be their next objective. And, thirdly, the NICs such as the Republic of Korea, Brazil and Taiwan Province have not yet begun to export large numbers of autos to Western Europe or to third country markets which are currently served from Western Europe. Nevertheless, despite these bleak future portents, the existing picture is problematic enough for the Western European industry. In 1986 Western Europe accounted for around 2.5m on the estimated 5m units of global excess capacity, and its volume sector alone lost $1.8bn in 1984, the fifth successive year of unprofitable production. Many of its domestic firms were "propped up" by governments with

Renault alone losing $3.35bn between 1984 and 1986.

"Restructuring" has thus become imperative for the global industry, but it clearly means different things for different firms. For the Japanese firms it involves a new step, that of FDI in order to obtain market access. For the American firms it requires steps to cope with increasing competition in their home market, a problem that they have to meet both with lower costs and new products. And for the Western European industry - with a strong portfolio of product technology - the primary problem at present is meeting the pressures of price-competition. But longer term restructuring is required to cope with the possibility of restricted access to the North American market, to the growing strength of Japanese product innovation, to the likelihood of Japanese production on Western European soil and to the emergence of the NICs and Eastern Europe as low-cost producers.

Aside from market-exit, there are three potential responses to these growing competitive pressures, each of which has different locational implications for TNCs and for the developing countries who are the primary focus of our attention. One option for the TNCs is to develop a "world car" strategy, aiming to maximize economies of scale by producing a single design of auto for all markets, reaping maximum economies of scale at all stages of production. In this strategy the design and development of the autos would be globalized, with production occurring largely on a national (or continental, in the case of the EEC) basis. This was indeed the approach adopted by the major United States TNCs when the crisis in the industry first began to display itself in the mid 1970s. The idea was to produce mechanically "identical" cars in different markets, but to fine-tune the design of each to meet the particular characteristics of each of the markets. The same principle of scale economies was extended to incorporate a "world-firm" strategy in which a number of different types of "floor-pan" - each representing a different size of "world-car" - would be produced to help the firm maximize corporate economies of scale. The logic behind these "world" strategies was to take maximum advantage of scale economies in production and design. Were it to have been a reality, it would have meant the disappearance of the smaller automobile manufacturers. Indeed, in the late 1970s this was a widely-held belief and it was commonly thought that firms manufacturing less than 1.5-2m cars per annum would be unable to survive.

Thus, Ford - in the design of their Escort/Erika range

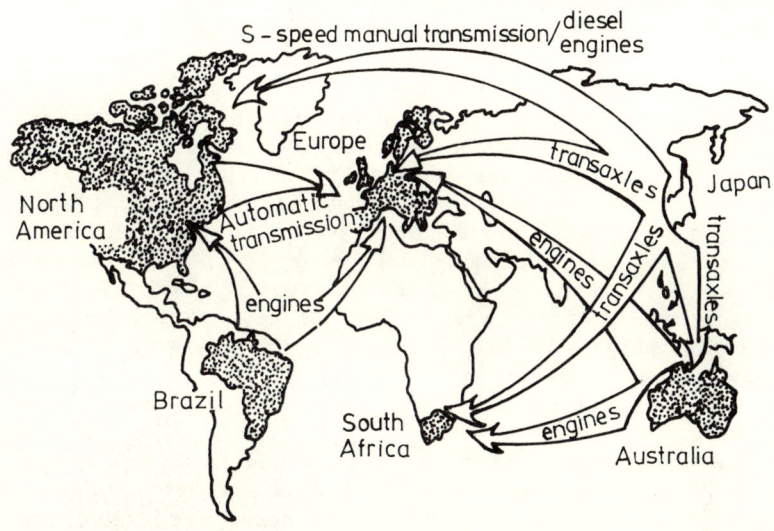

Source: Stuart Sinclair, <u>The World Car: The Future of the Automobile</u> (Euromonitor Publications, 1983). Reprinted by permission.

Figure 3.1 GM: Putting the World Car Together

of cars - and GM - in their design of the Cavalier/Ascona range - initially set these design concepts in train. GM went so far as to specialize the production of engines in three geographically spread-out locales - Brazil, Australia and Austria. (Figure 3.1 illustrates GM's plans for one of the "world cars" it developed during the 1970s). Yet, against all expectations, the "world car" failed to materialize, at least in the form which was initially proposed. Ford has virtually completely abandoned the concept - its United States Variant range, though touted as a "world car" continued to source 95 percent of its components domestically and in the end the project was more notable for its commonality of design effort than in manufacturing. The United Kingdom and United States versions of the Escort - another Ford "world car" - have only six common component parts.

The demise of the "world-car" was fairly rapid. Corporate planners soon discovered that markets are much more heterogeneous in the real world than they might appear on paper. As the MIT study documents graphically,[28]/ this has meant that each of the major Western European markets has an accentuated demand for particular types of automobile. While the Western European consumers placed great stress on product innovativeness and, partly for geographical reasons, preferred small- and medium-sized cars, their United States counterparts have traditionally demanded much larger and more powerful vehicles. Moreover, the growing technological intensity of the automobile has meant that another and better way of spreading the high fixed costs of design and development is to push part of the process of technological change on to component suppliers. This has the added advantage of developing technologies which are appropriate for individual environments.29/ Through this strategy the smaller producers are able to withstand the concentrating tendencies inherent in the process of technological deepening.

The consequence of these trends has been the survival - and indeed in some cases the flourishing - of those smaller firms such as BMW, Mercedes, Honda and Jaguar whose extinction had been so confidently predicted by the proponents of the "world car" a mere decade ago. Moreover, at the same time their success provided a strategic perspective which allowed many of the larger automobile producers to weather the crisis which subsequently hit the industry. This involved choosing the shelter of a particular market niche, allied to continual product innovation and a strong and technologically competent components industry. Thus it is fairly common to find manufacturers retreating from the world-firm concept in which every type of floorpan was feasible, to a more selective approach in which only a partial range of options is being pursued.

The second major strategy open to the automobile firms is to try and reduce costs by locating production in low-wage economies. This strategy fits the picture of the NIDL which we sketched out in Chapter 1 and which was in part responsible for a significant portion of the export-led industrialization strategies adopted successfully by the developing countries in the heyday of the machinofacturing era. As a general industrial strategy this approach is more closely allied to the classically Fordist strategy of standardization and price-competition than to the higher value-added approach embodied in the flexible specialization characteristic of the era of systemofacture.

Production in these low-wage locales may take a number of forms. This may either involve the production of autos by a subsidiary or an affiliate, or the purchasing of completed vehicles from a largely independent firm. As we shall see in Chapter 6, after the failure of their world-car strategies, the United States TNCs have chosen both of these routes (whilst simultaneously exploring a range of other options). Another possibility is to develop a strategy involving the selective off-shore sourcing of components which are combined with locally-made components during final assembly. This particular strategy most closely fits into the disarticulated FDI characteristic of the NIDL which was outlined in Chapter 1. Of course, for any element of this overall strategy to operate successfully, continued access to markets is key - protectionism spells the death of such an approach to global production.

The third major strategy available to cope with these competitive pressures involves a comprehensive programme of innovation, with production taking place close to the final market. Continual innovation is necessary both in relation to product and process technology, involving the adoption of new electronics-based automation technologies and new work-practices. As we saw in Chapter 2, it necessarily also involves a different set of relationships with component suppliers, who are required to be both proximate to assembly and more closely linked into production and design. We have termed this cluster of strategic innovations as one of systemofacture.

The widespread adoption of such a strategy obviously has important implications for developing countries since their prospect of incorporation into the international division of labour is remote under this scenario. The implications for TNCs, though, are less clear. A continual process of R&D-intensive innovation is costly and obviously suggests that scale-economies will be important. If these scale economies are captured all by a vertically integrated firm - a strategy pioneered by GM in the 1920s - then the transnational auto firms will continue to flourish and the global industry will come to be dominated by a few giant companies, much as now occurs in the oil, pharmaceutical and computer industries. On the other hand, if these scale economies are covered through a series of technology-sharing joint ventures or via a process of technology-deepening in the components sector, then the possibility of a larger number of smaller and less integrated auto firms enduring is high.

The analysis which follows in the next three chapters is designed to explore which of these three scenarios seems likely to dominate the auto industry. We hypothesized in Chapter 1 that the first two options - the world-car and the global-sourcing strategies - which are characteristic of the late era of machinofacture would be supplanted by the third strategy which is associated with the forthcoming era of systemofacture. But this was largely based upon *a priori* conjecture and requires detailed substantiation. Chapter 4 explores the pattern of innovation and location of the Japanese industry. Chapter 5 considers the first response of the Western European and United States firms to the Japanese challenge which was to automate their way to competitiveness. Their subsequent attempts to restructure their relationships with suppliers is discussed in Chapter 6. Then in Chapter 7 we consider the specific implications which these developments in the Japanese, Western European and United States industries have for the incorporation of the developing countries into the international division of labour in this sector. However, before we can proceed to this analysis, it is necessary to briefly describe the process of automobile production and to determine various categories of components which might lend themselves to global sourcing.

A BRIEF OVERVIEW OF AUTOMOBILE PRODUCTION AND A CATEGORIZATION OF COMPONENTS

Automobile production is a multi-stage activity with each step comprising of a variety of manufacturing processes, some of which are common to different stages. Roughly speaking, the process is initiated at the design and engineering stage. The design phase begins with the specification of basic vehicle-concept - what market-niche is being targeted, what size floor-pan is intended, and so on? At this stage thought is given to the engineering relationship between these conceptual ideas, the detailed functional characteristics of the car and its major components. "Design for manufacture" is becoming an increasingly important philosophy here.30/ In the detailed design and engineering phase, the production process itself and the schedule (of output mix and volume, and in-house versus external component delivery) are determined.

The physical transformation of the design into final vehicles is illustrated in Figure 3.2. It begins with the purchasing of raw materials and some ready-made components; the extent of component-purchases varies between firms (see below). After inspection the raw material inputs are

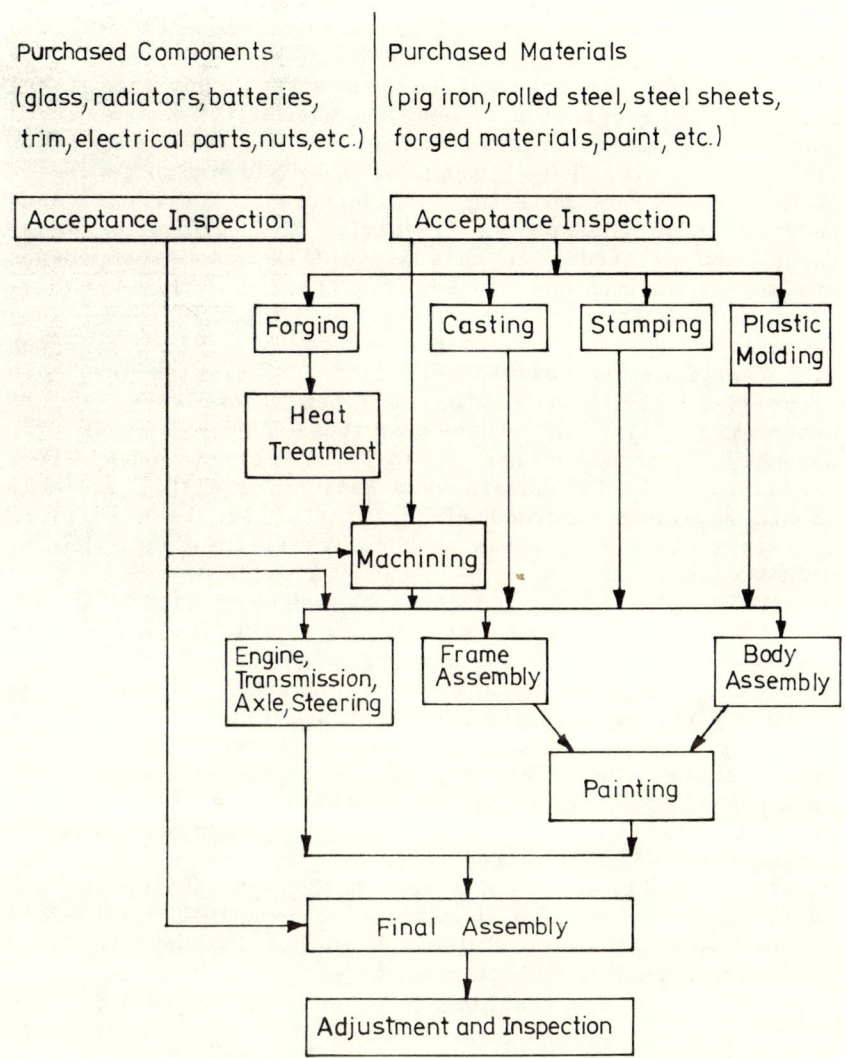

Figure 3.2 Flow Sheet of Automobile Production

subject to four major forms of treatment - they may be cast, forged, stamped or molded into a variety of shapes. After this the forged and cast work-in-progress may be subject to heat-treatment to temper and strengthen the materials which are then machined into components. The various components - some of which may have been produced in-house, others of which may have been obtained from affiliates and yet others from independent suppliers - are assembled into a series of sub-assemblies. These included gearboxes, axles, engines, doors, dashboards and other items of trim. These groups of sub-assemblies generally occur in different buildings or factories. The chassis and body are then constructed (involving the welding of metal parts) and painted. At this stage the various components and sub-assemblies are brought-together onto the assembly-line, where the car is actually put together. In some factories a special quality-control bay may exist, together with rectification bays to set-right errors which have been identified. The final autos are then stocked and sent to customers. In all these various stages except for assembly, automation has steadily displaced labour from production. It is only in very recent years that assembly robots have been introduced, but these have been confined to relatively simple tasks such as installing spare-wheels, windows and seats.

This pattern of production has changed little in any basic sense since it evolved in the first two decades of the century. There are however signs that after eight decades of refinement, a series of changes are occurring which may render this picture of production obsolete within the next two-to-three decades. Three elements of technological change are especially important. The first relates to the general trend towards flexibility which we have observed in earlier chapters. Arising partly as a consequence of the introduction of the new systemic and flexible electronics-based automation technologies and partly as a result of a fundamental change in manufacturing philosophy (both of which were described in Chapter 2),31/ there are signs that the whole concept of product and plant scale economies are changing. For example, whereas it used to be thought that an engine plant would have to produce around 500,000 engines per year over a substantial period in order to pay-off the high costs of dedicated machinery, many new engine plants (such as the Rover Group's 800 series engine-line) will produce only around 150-200,000 engines per year and will pay for itself by also being able to produce very different designs.32/. Similarly the rule of thumb for minimum assembly plant sizes used to be 250,000 plus cars per year, but as can be seen from Table 3.8, most of the new state-of-the-art assembly plants being built by the Japanese in the United States are smaller than this. It is unclear just what the implications of this trend towards flexibility holds for the whole concept of auto production.

A second factor suggesting that the nature of auto production will change relates to the introduction of new materials. The system outlined in Figure 3.2 has evolved to fit the needs of machining and joining metal. This necessitates distinct processes such as casting, forging and welding. But if the basic material used to produce autos changes - for example to plastics - then the processes inherent in production will also change. Plastics are in fact finding increasingly widespread uses in autos. But the same point may apply even if metal continues to be utilized, such as if adhesives can be substituted for the welding or joining through fasteners of body-parts.

The third area of technological change which may affect the organization of production as mapped out in Figure 3.2 relates to a change in production philosophy. As the figure shows, the idea is for the assembler to build the chassis and body and then to install a series of separate components bought-in from outside suppliers or produced in other parts of the factory. In the new philosophy the idea is to turn the process on its head - instead of buying-in individual components, complete sub-assemblies will be purchased (for example, complete dashboards rather than individual instruments). Then the auto-body will be built around these sub-assemblies rather than having the component installed after construction. This important change in philosophy, it is believed, will facilitate the automation of assembly, the one area which has remained stubbornly labour-intensive. If this change does occur, then once again we are likely to see a very different form of factory organization to that which has evolved historically.

Important inter-firm differences in construction philosophy continue to exist now, as they did in the past. One of the major areas of difference arises from the extent to which components and sub-assemblies are bought in from outside firms, some of which are subsidiaries or affiliates. Broadly-speaking it is possible to contrast the highly vertically-integrated policies of GM and Ford with those of the Japanese firms and Chrysler. The Western

Table 3.10
Company and Group Integration, U.S.-Japan, 1965-83 (%)

	Nissan In-House	Nissan Group	Toyota In-House	Toyota Group	GM In-House	Ford In-House	Chrysler In-House
1965	32	54	41	74	50	36	36
1970	29	52	35	66	49	39	36
1975	22	50	30	73	45	36	36
1979	26	70	29	74	43	36	32
1980	26	73	29	76	-	-	34
1981	26	71	28	75	-	-	31
1982	26	75	26	70	-	-	34
1983	26	78	26	70	-	-	28

Source: Reprinted from <u>The Japanese Automobile Industry: Technology and Management at Nissan and Toyota</u>, by Michael A. Cusumano (Council on East Asian Studies, Harvard University, 1985) by permission of the publisher.

European firms are in an intermediary position, probably closer to the United States than the Japanese position. The Japanese firms and Chrysler tend to buy-in substantially more components than do GM and Ford (Table 3.10). In-house production in the first group accounted for between one-quarter and one-third of total vehicle costs versus around two-fifths for the two American TNCs. However, when account is taken of purchases of components from affiliates - which in many senses represents a form of more decentralized production - the percentage of value contributed by group activities is in fact higher in the Japanese case.

In the context of these different policies towards the purchase and manufacture of components it is possible to distinguish between the following five categories of components, each of which are subject to ongoing processes of technological change. The point of distinguishing between these categories of components is to help determine which are most likely to be purchased and which are likely to be manufactured in-house, given the general policies of each assembler as to the appropriate make/buy mix which they adopt. The distinction is also important since it provides some clues as to the possible role which developing country producers may play in any international division of labour which may evolve in this sector.

<u>Generic components</u>. These are components that are

common to many industries - nuts, bolts, screws, fasteners, and so on - and which are used in multiple numbers in vehicles but comprise less than five percent of total component cost. In general this type of component tends to be physically small so that the transport-to-value ratio in production and distribution is low. Moreover, because their mass production allows the use of dedicated machinery, plant scale economies are high, production is specialized and often concentrated geographically, with output distributed on a wide, often global basis.

There is only limited evidence that this category of components is as yet undergoing significant change in product or process technology, (such as flexible automation in screw production) but in the medium term they are likely to be substantially altered by changes in materials technology in automobile production itself. Most important here is the trend towards the use of plastics (which is self evident) where the ability to mould complex shapes means that single products can be substituted for groups of components which are currently often joined with generic industrial fasteners.

Bulky, non-mechanical parts. These include mufflers, glass, stampings, seats, fueltanks and radiators. Such parts are low in both product and process technological content. By their nature they are tailored to the specific characteristics of the product and, because they also tend to have a relatively high transport-to-value ratio, it is common to find these parts produced near the final market. Individual components amongst this group are seeing significant technological change. In some cases these are occurring through changes in production processes. This is the case with products such as fueltanks and mufflers in which the introduction of electronic controls allows for rapid readjustment of machine-settings, and therefore facilitates the flexible automation of production. In other cases there are important changes in design and in materials technology, such as in the introduction of plastic fueltanks and aluminum/copper radiators, or the development of molded seats.

Various items of trim and wiring. These components are traditionally characterized by low technology and low transport costs - they include wiring harnesses, window handles, switches, exterior trim, interior upholstery material as well as spark plugs, points and windscreen wipers. As both their technological content and their unit transport costs tend to be low, production of these components has historically been considered as an appropriate form of international specialization for low-wage economies.

Technological change is likely to have some impact in this category of components. In the case of wiring harnesses, the move towards centralized computer control and multiplex wiring in automobiles is likely to eradicate the need for this labour-intensive product. Similarly, the trend towards systems in window control - with centralized consoles and electrically operated windows - is likely to obviate the need for forged handles. Points have been rendered obsolete by electronic engine controls, and switches are becoming much more complex. Moreover, the introduction of electronically controlled flexible production systems is injecting scale economies into small batch production and making it considerably more complex and capital intensive in nature. It is possible that many of these types of components will be particularly significantly affected by the introduction of electronically-controlled systems in product technology.

<u>Electro-mechanical and systems components</u>. This comprises of items such as carburettors, clutches, starter motors, ignition systems, brakes, shock absorbers and steering mechanisms. Traditionally their relative technological complexity and low transport-to-value ratio has seen these components being produced in the industrially advanced countries. However, as technological capability in some NICs has increased, so has production begun to be transferred to these locales. It is here that we can conjecture - and hope to provide evidence in later chapters to substantiate this view - a particularly acute impact of technological change on DC sourcing, since three related factors are rapidly impinging on the organization of production. First the introduction of flexible manufacturing systems, together with improvements in assembly automation are transforming a labour-intensive industry into a capital-intensive one. The second type of technological change having an impact on this type of component is the modularization of production through the development of subsystems, generally electronically controlled. Thus by facilitating mechanization, by requiring systemic assembly and by being more technologically complex, the scope for sourcing in DCs is likely to be substantially reduced by technological developments. And, thirdly, we have suggested that the relationship between component-suppliers and assemblers will be changing and become much closer, especially at the design stage. To the extent that this occurs, the

importance of this phenomenon is likely to become greater in the more technology-complex items such as these.

<u>Core technologies</u>. By general acknowledgement, the core technologies comprise of engines, transmissions and gearboxes. These have been characterized in the past by labour-intensive assembly, scale economies in production and heavy indirect costs in design. There have been three locational tendencies arising out of these characteristics. In the first case, labour-intensive production has provided the opportunity for taking advantage of low wage costs and government subsidies and therefore engines are produced and exported from developing countries such as Brazil and Mexico. Second, the high minimum economies of scale in production has tended to enforce international specialization and trade, often as we shall see in later chapters, of an intra-firm nature. And, third, heavy design costs (which represent a factor inducing firm-, rather than plant-economies of scale) have led to a plethora of technological collaborations and the buying-in of engines. This, too, will be illustrated in later chapters.

* * *

In the first two chapters we considered the general context in which the locational behavior of the TNC could be located. This involved an elaboration of various theories which have attempted to explain the current crisis - or turning point - in industrial history. Our view was that we are witnessing the transition between two industrial eras - that of machinofacture and systemofacture. From this it was possible to develop a number of hypotheses concerning the incorporation of the developing countries in the international division of labour in industry. This has important implications for the general orientation of industrial strategies, especially those based upon export-oriented industrialization. But these were inherently speculative, based upon *a priori* analyses of the macro-economic environment. To have any credibility these views needed to be tested in the real world.

We have chosen to do this via a case study of the automobile industry. This sector was chosen partly because it is the largest single branch of modern industry, but more importantly because it was ideally-suited to the disarticulated FDI which had powered much of the industrial success of developing countries in the latter years of the machinofacturing era. In this chapter we have set the automobile sector in context, considering its size, its changing market conditions and its changing technology. Two particularly important conclusions which we reached concerned the growth of protectionist pressures in the major importing markets and the increasing competitive pressures. Both have a direct impact on the extent and nature of the component-sourcing activities of TNCs. Given the demise of the "world car" concept two major alternative strategies are available to the auto assemblers - either to cut costs by off-shore sourcing of components and/or autos from developing countries (that is, an extension of the NIDL which had fostered export-oriented industrialization in the developing world) or to move to automated production near the final markets in the industrially advanced countries. It is to these issues that we now turn.

NOTES

1. See Chandler (1962 and 1977).
2. See Altshuler et al (1984).
3. Odaka (1983) and Cusumano (1985)
4. L. Argus (1986).
5. Automotive News, April, 1986.
6. Altshuler et al (1984).
7. O'Brien and Aleu (1983).
8. ibid.
9. Kaplinsky (1984).
10. The concept of mass production in automobiles was not in fact that of Ford. It had been pioneered by Ransom Olds, with the introduction of first mass produced cars - the Oldsmobile - for the consumer market in 1902.
11. Although the indigenous auto producer SEAT - initially linked with Fiat and then subsequently taken-over by Volkswagen - also added to Spanish auto production.
12. These figures - drawn from Financial Times, 22 October 1987 - refer only to passenger cars.
13. Altshuler et al. (1984).
14. Silva, Ferri and Enrietti (1984).
15. These VERs are sometimes known as Orderly Marketing Arrangements (OMAs).
16. Financial Times, 11 September 1985.
17. Cusumano (1985).
18. In the long-saga of protectionist pressures and

responses, conflict amongst the Japanese auto producers has been an important element. The major issue has been that in the markets where protectionism has been in play for some time, the share of imports allocated to individual producers was based upon their historic market shares. The newer and more rapidly-growing producers - such as Honda, Mitsubishi and Mazda - found themselves stuck with small quotas and naturally objected.

19. Financial Times, 10 November 1987.
20. Financial Times, 10 November 1987.
21. Ealey (1984).
22. This was especially alarming to the Republic of Korea's government since at the same time there were rumblings in the World Bank and elsewhere that it had "graduated" into an industrialized economy.
23. Financial Times, 27 November 1987.
24. Honda's Western European sales - affected by its late arrival to a closing market - are limited to around 100,000 autos p.a.
25. Jones (1985).
26. Industry estimates reported in Financial Times, 5th September, 1985.
27. A measure of the profitability entailed for the Western European industry can be obtained from the comparison of prices in the United States market for luxury cars in early 1985, before the dollar's international strength fell. The cheapest Mercedes Benz was on sale in the United States for more than two times the price of a high specification Cadillac.
28. Altshuler et al (1984).
29. The head of R&D at the Volkswagen/Audi Group emphasizes that Japanese consumers are much more attracted by gadgetry electronic components than are the Western]#European consumers. He also believes that Japanese consumers are also much more tolerant of untested technological innovations. (Financial Times, 27 March 1987).
30. In a recent attempt to utilize computers in this design for manufacture philosophy, Ford claims a 30 percent reduction in the number of parts in assembly. "Fewer parts mean easier assembly, which cuts labour costs and boosts quality., It also reduces the material costs needed to produce a part" (Automotive News, 2 February 1987).
31. Electronics are of course simultaneously finding their way into the final product.
32. The development of this engine line illustrates the interaction between electronics technologies and

flexibility. In the past the design and construction of such a line would take four-to-five years since the engine design would have to be built into a prototype which had then to be tested and developed before the design was finalized. Only then could the construction of the production line begin. With the new flexible lines which are under construction, the same production line can produce a variety of different engine types. It thus became possible for the RG's machinery-supplier to begin construction of the line before the design of the engine itself was finalized, since any developments and modifications could easily be handled by the new, flexible system. This cut the process down from about five to just under two years.

4

Transition in the Japanese Auto Industry: The Emergence of Systemofacture

There are two reasons why the historical and current experience of the Japanese auto industry are of particular interest. First, the roots of Japanese success in the auto industry lie in the evolutionary development and perfection of a unique system of production organization in which flexibility and change substituted for standardization and status. The scale of the competitive advantages that Japanese firms derived from these organizational innovations have been a key factor in triggering the present phase of restructuring in the United States and Western European auto industry. Moreover, a prime objective of this restructuring involves a creative absorption of the Japanese model of production by auto producers in these countries. This move by United States and Western European auto producers has important implications for the strategy of offshore sourcing, since as we shall see, the rigorous implementation of the Japanese organization of production militates against the import of components from DCs.

Second, the Japanese system of production has not remained static but has continued to evolve in recent years, taking advantage of the opportunities afforded by electronics-based automation technologies and new materials for product and process improvement. Thus, new embodied technologies are now being combined with the unique organizational features of the Japanese system which developed between 1950 and 1975 to define a new mode of best practice in the 1980s which we have termed systemofacture. These new developments pose problems and opportunities for all motor vehicle manufacturers. More importantly from our perspective, this also injects a significant number of new elements into the equation determining the future pattern of offshore sourcing and investment in the components sector.

In this chapter we shall draw both on our empirical research in Japan and on the wider literature to explore the key characteristics of the Japanese model and the developments which are pushing it in the direction of systemofacture. This focus means we will be concentrating our analysis largely on Japanese developments in production organization and process technology rather than the perhaps equally significant changes occurring in product technology.1/

Before proceeding to this analysis it is essential to bear in mind a point made in Chapter 2 in which we considered the contrasting characteristics of the eras of machinofacture and systemofacture. We observed there, that in each case the paradigm of production continued to change and that there were necessarily important differences between the specific features of individual plants and firms. However, as a general rule, the inter-era differences were more significant than the intra-era differences. This is an important point to keep in mind when considering the experience of the Japanese auto industry. For while its general operations are quite distinct from those of classical Fordism in other parts of the world, at the same time there are important differences in the approaches adopted by individual Japanese auto producers. Most significantly Toyota and Nissan - the two largest firms - have placed a distinctly different emphasis on changes in the forces and relations of production. Toyota - the most efficient of the Japanese producers - has concentrated on organizational changes and a restructuring of work-organization and has only given subsidiary importance to the adoption of radically new embodied technologies. By contrast Nissan, whilst also making major changes in the nature of work and in organization, has tended to place more faith in the adoption of new embodied technologies as a source of competitive advantage.2/

This chapter is divided into five sections. We begin by briefly presenting some evidence on the scale of competitive advantage enjoyed by Japanese producers. The next section reviews those features of the production organization and labour process which make the Japanese system distinct, putting some flesh here to the bones of the analysis presented in Chapter 2. This is followed by a discussion which shows how Japanese auto firms are integrating computer-based control systems and automation technologies into their production systems. In the next section we consider the distinctive features of the relationship between component-suppliers and assemblers in Japan since together with changes in the labour process and the new relationships between assemblers and component-suppliers, this completes a discussion of the three central features of systemofacture. The chapter concludes with an analysis of the way in which these factors are influencing the components industry in Japan since our wider interests with developing world industrialization are partly affected by the locational decisions of these firms, and their locational decisions will of course reflect the momentum of their current and projected operations.

THE SCALE OF THE JAPANESE COMPETITIVE ADVANTAGE IN THE AUTO INDUSTRY

In Chapter 2 we briefly described the basic principles of the Japanese approach to car production and need not repeat these here. However, it is worthwhile to review some of the available evidence on the manifold competitive advantages enjoyed by Japanese auto producers as a result of their unique approach. The most striking feature is that Japanese auto producers enjoy a substantially higher degree of labour productivity for every category of employee compared to the United States and Western European firms. Equally important are their much lower unit capital costs that derive from the greater utilization of fixed capital, the lowering of inventory related costs and lower fixed investment costs. The considerable emphasis placed on final product quality in Japan is a further key element, as is the ability to respond to changing market conditions derived from its flexible production systems.

Whether these factor-productivity differentials and other factors lead to a price-competitive advantage compared with other producers very much depends upon relative exchange rates. Thus, at least until the latter part of 1986 - and certainly when much of our research was undertaken between 1984 and 1986 - the dollar-yen rate was such (approximately ¥225=$) that there was a substantial cost differential between cars produced in Japan and those produced in the United States and Western Europe. In the early 1980s the Japanese cost advantage was estimated to be roughly $2,000 per car in relation to the United States and $500-700 in relation to Western Europe.3/ By 1984 Toyota's cost advantage on a Tercel-sized car had risen to $2,200-2,300 4/ with a confidential report commissioned by the United Auto Workers in the United States, suggesting that the cost-gap was even higher, more in the order of $2600. It is uncertain how much of this cost advantage was eroded by the dollar's devaluation in late 1986-early 1987.

There is of course a considerable debate within the industry and among analysts as to the size of these gaps and the precise share of the differential accounted for by different factors. We do not propose to enter into this debate here since it is difficult to draw definitive conclusions from the information that is available.5/ It is, however, much less difficult to misinterpret or refute the differences in the physical output indicators that are detailed in Tables 4.1 to 4.3.

Comparing the total number of vehicles produced per worker is not easy since there are a variety of distorting factors such as the extent of outsourcing (GM and Ford, as we have seen, tend to buy in fewer components than do Chrysler and the Japanese firms), the degree of capacity utilization and the length of the working years.6/ Table 4.1 shows the trend at industry level in the total hours taken to assemble a vehicle in the United States and Japan between 1970 and 1981, adjusted to remove the affect of differences in capacity utilization, the length of the working year and the degree of outsourcing.7/ The period between 1970 and 1979 is of particular note since this was the period in which the Japanese auto manufacturers entered the United States market with such success. In fact the *improvement* over this period in Toyota's labour-productivity (4.1 vehicles per year per worker) almost equalled the absolute level of labour productivity of all three United States assemblers in 1979 (that is, 5.5 cars per worker per year). It is worth noting how important these adjustments for capacity utilization, outsourcing and working hours are. Without them the apparent superiority of the Japanese firms is much greater. Calculated on the basis of gross figures, Toyota's superiority over GM was a factor of 5, and of 4.1 over Ford in 1983. This compares with the adjusted ratio of "only" 2.2 by Toyota over the whole United States industry.

The impression of a significant productivity differential in the early 1980s is reinforced if we look at Tables 4.2 and 4.3 which compare characteristics of Japanese and United States assembly and engine plants. The differences in labour-productivity per engine between the Toyota plant and the Chrysler plant are especially illuminating given the fact that the Toyota plant uses no robots to achieve five times the equivalent level of

Table 4.1
Vehicles per Worker per annum, Adjusted for Vertical Integration, Capacity Utilization and Length of Working Year.

	GM, Ford, Chrysler[a]	Nissan	Toyota
1965	4.7	4.3	6.9
1970	4.6	8.8	10.9
1975	5.3	9.0	13.7
1979	5.5	11.1	15.0
1983	5.7[b]	11.0	12.7

Source: Reprinted from The Japanese Automobile Industry: Technology and Management at Nissan and Toyota, by Michael A. Cusumano (Council on East Asian Studies, Harvard University, 1985) by permission of the publisher.

[a] Average figures on worldwide operations
[b] gm and Ford figures assume 1979 levels of vertical integration

Table 4.2
Performance Comparison for Japanese and United States Engine Plants, 1984

	Toyota Kamingo Engine Plant	Chrysler Trenton	Ford Dearborn
Products:	2.4-L 4-cyl 2.0-L 4-cyl	2.2-L 4-cyl incl. turbo	1.6-: 4-cyl HO; turbo; EFI
Plant size:	310,000 ft	2.2 million ft	2.2 million ft
Hourly employment:	180	2,250	1,360
Line rate:	1,500/day	3,200/day	1,960/day
Manhours per engine:	.96 hrs/engine	5.6 hrs/engine	5.55 hrs/engine
Shifts:	2	2	1 assembly 2 machining
Robots:	None	5	NA

Source: Automotive Industries, September, 1984. Reprinted by permission.

Table 4.3:
Performance Comparision for Japanese and United States Assembly Plants

	SUZUKI Kosai completed 10/83	MAZDA Hofu completed 10/82	GMAD Lake Orion completed 12/83
Plant size:	553,270 ft^2	1.5 million ft^2	3.7 million ft^2
Products:	Cultus (Chevy Sprint)	626	Cadillac, Olds C-car
Line rate:	30/hour 60,000/year	62.5/hour 240,000/year	75/hour 260,000/year
Employment:	600[a]	1800	6700
Man-hours per car:	20[b]	14[c]	48.7
Robots:	137	155	157

Source: <u>Automotive Industries</u>, April, 1985. Reprinted by permission.

[a] one shift
[b] includes stamping and engine & transmission assembly
[c] includes stamping

output. As we have seen, in part this reflects the historic (but rapidly changing) attitude of Toyota towards embodied automation technologies. These tables reveal not only the above-mentioned variation in output per employee and person-hours per car or engine assembled, but also differences in the scale of the physical facilities involved. Implicit in this difference in plant size are the lower fixed investment costs characteristic of Japanese plants. This particular point was underlined by an example given during an interview. The Ford Motor Company was considering making a $300 million expansion investment to produce a new trans-axle. Mazda - with whom Ford has an equity-link - was asked for an estimate to build a plant for an equivalent level of output. Their bid was $100 million. Lower fixed investment costs in these Japanese

Table 4.4
United States-Japanese Comparison of Output Levels in Two Machining Activities, 1980

	Japanese	United States
Facing and centering of transaxle shaft		
machine efficiency	80%	54%
output pcs/hr	96	59
Green grinding transmission shaft		
cycle time (minutes)	0.50	0.55
percentage loss of machine time[a]	20%	49%
output pcs/hr	96	56

Source: Interviews.

[a] Composed of time for loading/unloading, tooling change, maintenance, breakdown, scrap, etc.

plants was also associated with a more productive utilization of the capital which had been invested (Table 4.4), arising from the greater flexibility of the Japanese labour force (see below). In this comparison of fixed capital utilization in 1980, the Japanese plant was producing around 70 percent more output from essentially the same machines.

Finally, the comparison is particularly significant because the car assembly plants shown in Tables 4.2 and 4.3 are among the newest in full operation. It is notable that whilst there has been some improvement on the part of the United States, the differentials are still considerable in every category.

These labour-productivity differentials were not confined to a comparison between the American and Japanese industry; they apply also to the Western European industry. Table 4.5. offers a comparison made by a major TNC between the labour-productivity by function in two of its Western European plants and that in a Japanese plant which it visited in 1980. (The figures are not directly comparable with those in Table 4.1 so they provide no basis for the overall comparison between the auto firms in these three countries, nor for those between the United States and Western Europe). Producing similar numbers of vehicles,

Table 4.5
Workers per shift to produce similar vehicle in Japan and in two European countries, 1980

	Japan	Europe 1	Europe 2
Daily Volumes	360	379	308
Direct Labour per Shift:			
Stamping	135	58	39
Metal Assembly and Body Shop		362	221
Paint Shop	40	151	82
Trim and Final	175	453	301
Total Direct Labour per Shift	350	1024	643
Indirect Labour per Shift:			
Inspectors:			
Body	1	28	31
Paint	2	6	7
Trim	2	12	7
Final and Repair	10	37	23
Total Inspectors per Shift	15	83	68
Material Handling and Line Feed	10	328	113
Other	35	601	174
Total Indirect Labour per Shift	60	1012	355
Total Direct and Indirect Labour per shift	410	2036	998
Workers/vehicle			
Direct	1.0	2.7	2.1
Indirect	.2	2.7	1.2
Direct and Indirect	1.1	5.4	3.2
Absenteeism	1%	6.1%	5.1%

Source: Interviews.

the Japanese plant employed between one-half and one-third of the direct labour, and between two-fifths and two-tenths of the indirect labour. Their overall labour productivity was between three and five times higher than those of the two European plants. What is also of considerable interest is the much lower level of absenteeism in Japan, reflecting the interaction noted in Chapter 2 between social relations at the point of production and in the wider social sphere.

THE ORGANIZATION OF WORK: THE JIT LABOUR PROCESS

The above discussion establishes the large disparities in performance between the Japanese and United States and Western European auto assemblers. Our interviews in Japan gave us the opportunity to examine the factors at work within the Japanese auto industry and within the auto plants themselves which explain these differences. As many others have noted, the essential character of the Japanese model is that it is a tightly integrated and finely tuned system of production that has evolved over the last 25 years. And, as is widely noted, it is at the level of the organization of the individual components of the system where the key to the Japanese success during the last decade are to be found. We will briefly explore these features below with the aim of highlighting those aspects of particular relevance to our specific concerns with component sourcing and FDI.

The Japanese system of motor vehicle manufacture is now commonly referred to as Just-In-Time production (JIT). Underlying this is a philosophy of production developed in Toyota in the 1950s that rests on three pillars - the reduction of cost by eliminating waste; the use of minimum amounts of equipment, materials, parts and working time, and the full use of workers' capabilities. As noted in Chapter 2, the key feature of this labour process is the tightness of its organization and the interdependence of its constituent parts. Not only is it difficult to isolate a single feature as being of central importance, but it is also possible to characterize the organizing principle as being one of flexibility rather than inventory reduction. It is possible to identify seven key features to this labour process.

Flexibility of output: production is demand driven

The Fordist system of production organization was supply driven, with the emphasis being placed upon continuity of output in order to obtain the full benefits of scale-economies in production. Taken to its logical extreme it required the unchanging production of a single specification of product - the Model T Ford was the archetype. This was not possible in post-war Japan since as can be seen from Table 4.6 the domestic market for all vehicles only exceeded 200,000 for the first time in 1959. The principles of mass production were therefore inappropriate and a more flexible pattern of production was therefore essential.

In the face of this small (and variable) pattern of demand, the Japanese auto firms substituted a demand-driven system at an early stage of the industry's development. Moreover, as the transition was made to this demand-oriented system and as production expanded, the resultant flexibility in production allowed the auto firms to offer an increasingly bewildering range of alternatives to customers. Japanese auto producers, keen to increase market share at home and abroad, opted for a strategy that sought to exploit emerging product-niche opportunities by producing a wider range of cars and accessory permutations, coupled with frequent model changes. For instance, Toyota increased its number of basic models from 24 to 50 between 1974 and 1979 and introduced a completely new model range every four, as opposed to every seven years. Greater variation was allowed within individual models as well. When the Toyota Corolla was first introduced, it was available only as a sedan with an 1100cc engine. Today it is available in five body types (sedan, lift-back, hard-top, van or coupe) with a choice of five engine types - 1300, 1500, 1600, 1800 or 2200cc - and when the various specification and accessory options are put together there are 10,000 potential varieties. Other companies now offer the same range of choice - Mazda's Capella was produced in 2300 varieties in 1983. One of the Nissan assembly lines we visited is capable of handling 100,000 variations of automobiles based on three different floor pans.

Flexibility of output takes a number of forms. In some cases the modifications are trivial, but they also involve more substantial changes reflected in an increasing rate of product innovation. Some examples illustrate this ability to vary the nature of output at short notice; in the case of Nissan, although there is a three month rolling

Table 4.6
Domestic Sales and Imports in Japan 1951-1960.

	Sales	Imports	Import Penetration (%)
1951	63,654	28,419	44.6
1952	57,491	15,988	27.8
1953	76,185	27,406	36.0
1954	75,659	16,317	23.1
1955	75,659	6,748	8.9
1956	133,050	9,103	6.8
1957	176,690	6,719	3.8
1958	198,285	6,702	3.4
1959	279,860	7,111	2.5
1960	407,963	4,329	1.1

Source: Derived from Cusumano (1985).

production plan, final production-line scheduling allows for changes within 10 days of production, to direct customer order; Toyota has a similar system but allows domestic customers to change their minds within four days of manufacture; one of Toyota's main models (the Crown) is available in over 10,000 different specifications. The consequence of producing for (an increasingly differentiated pattern of) demand - rather than to fill pre-determined supply inventories - is that flexibility in production is essential.

Flexibility in product and process

These changes in product mix - both with respect to product innovation and product differentiation - have major implications for flexibility in production and thus for the labour process. If the Fordist labour process was built around unchanging production structures the Japanese alternative in the auto industry is focused on flexibility in manufacturing process and in work. So the first point is to observe how flexible the system has become. One of the more organizationally complicated aspects of production concerns the use of dies to shape the flat sheet-metal used for body panels. This frequently involves a series of 300-500 ton hydraulic presses, through which the pressed sheet

Table 4.7
Shortening of Set-Up Time and Reduction of Lot Size in Toyota (1970-1980).

Division		1970	1975	1980
Stamping	Set-up time (mins)	40-150	20-30	5-15
	Lot size (no of items)	5,000	1,500	500
Forging	Set-up time (mins)	100-200	20-50	10
Casting	Set-up time (mins)	60	20	4

Source: Information supplied by Toyota Motor Corporation.

passes. Each new model of car requires a change of these heavy dies, and in the traditional Fordist system which was designed to produce a single shape for a long period of time, die-changing was a specialized task and took around 8 hours. Similarly the forging and casting of engine parts also involved organizationally-complex changes in dies. Table 4.7 illustrates the rapidity and extent of progress within the Toyota company in Japan and shows how the initial decision to reduce batch-size (that is, to increase diversity) is linked to the reduction in change-over time.

In Nissan the pattern was similar. With the use of movable bolsters, it took three people 20 minutes to change five dies in 1984 - this compared with 50 minutes in 1979. In Mitsubishi - where changeovers in the stamping plant occurred every 1-1.25 hours in 1984 - the changeover time had been reduced to 5-7 minutes compared with 15 minutes in 1979. These shortening changeover times enabled Mitsubishi to change the stamping line when enough parts had been produced for less than four shifts production. In recent years, these changeover times have been reduced even further with the introduction of new mechanical devices to facilitate changeover and in one plant we visited (see below, Figure 4.1) it had been brought down to just over two minutes.

Another case, showing the rapidity of progress in the 1970s when many Japanese firms moved to adopt more flexible

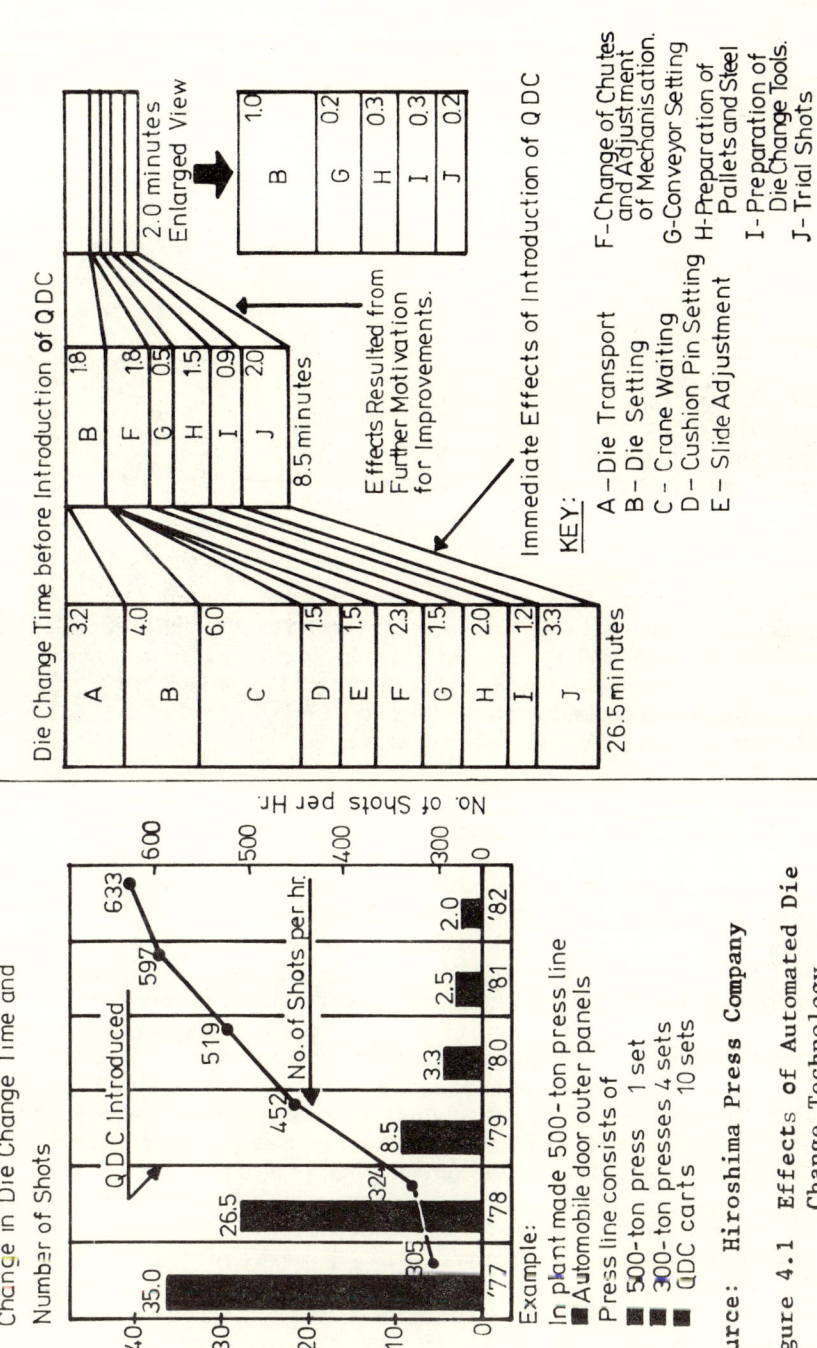

Source: Hiroshima Press Company

Figure 4.1 Effects of Automated Die Change Technology

Table 4.8
Percentage Reduction in Set-Up Time at Japanese Subsidiary of United States Auto Component Firm

Set-Up Time	1976	1977	1980
>60 min	30	0	0
30-60 min	19	0	0
20-30 min	26	10	3
10-20 min	20	12	7
5-10 min	0	17	16
100 sec - 5 min	0	17	16
<100 sec	0	41	62

Source: Wantuck (undated).

work-practices is shown in Table 4.8 in relation to a Japanese subsidiary of a United States auto-component manufacturer. What is especially striking about this is that this example was utilized in the mid 1980s in an attempt by the American parent to change work-practices in its own United States subsidiaries.

Multi-skill and multi-task work

The speed of these production changes is critically dependent upon the division of labour. It can only be achieved if workers undertake a number of tasks and possess a number of skills. For example, whereas die-changing had become a specialized skill in the Fordist labour-process - in which the production line came to a standstill and the specialized die-changers began their work - in the Japanese body-stamping lines noted above the production workers are also responsible for the changing of dies. Similarly, they are also responsible for routine maintenance of their machines and will have undergone specific training for these and a range of allied tasks. As part of this system of work-organization, therefore, workers are characteristically employed in a general category and not for specific tasks.

It is readily apparent that this represents a major break from two of the central features of the Fordist labour process. First, instead of an increasing division of labour into specialized tasks, workers are expected to perform a range of jobs. As we pointed out in Chapter 2 this trend towards the increasing division of labour was one of the central tenents of Adam Smith's economic theories and one which has been widely recognized to accurately describe a key feature of evolving industrial organization. Secondly, and perhaps more fundamentally, these innovations in the labour process also reverse an historic tendency for the deskilling of work. The significance of this is illustrated by a central feature of the payments system used in Japanese auto firms where as a general rule wage improvements are directly linked to the acquisition of supplementary skills. The principle behind wage payments are that workers are paid not for what they do, but according to what they can do.

Just-in-Time (JIT) Production

If this Japanese labour process is seen as having had its roots in flexibility, then it follows that once these flexible work-procedures had been implemented it became feasible to reduce inventories substantially and to move to a JIT philosophy. On the other hand, though, it is possible that the true line of causality in the origins of this labour process ran the other way - that is that the primary decision made was to reduce inventories, and the increasing flexibility of production was a necessary consequence of this. Indeed, the manager primarily responsible for steering the JIT philosophy through Toyota in the early 1950s - Ono Taiichi - believed that the central principle behind the system was the necessity to reduce costs by lowering inventories once the Japanese markets for trucks had been lost after the war.8/ (Until the early 1950s most of Japanese vehicle production was of trucks rather than autos). But irrespective of whether it was the desire to reduce inventories or the quest for flexibility which led to the origins of the new labour process, the sustained reduction in these inventories in the Japanese auto industry has been remarkable.

Figure 4.2 (derived from a Toyota training manual written for its foreign subsidiaries) illustrates the central principle behind the JIT philosophy - the elimination of waste. Waste may take a variety of forms - of time, of faulty goods, of machinery, and so on. The problem with the Fordist supply-driven system, argues Toyota, is that inventories mask these various forms of waste. Thus it is the responsibility of management to

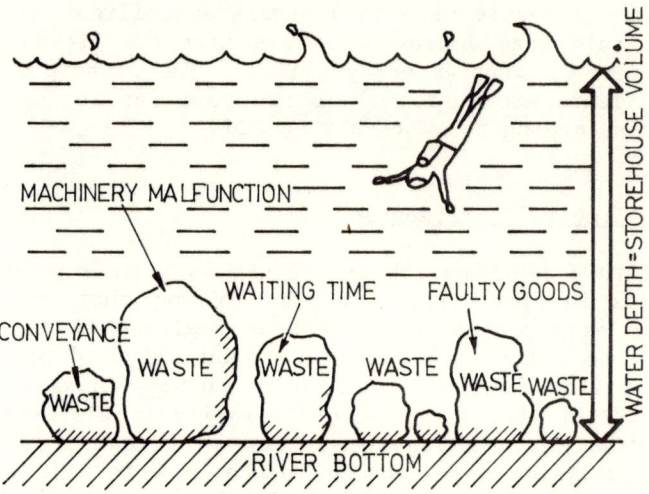

Source: Supplied by Toyota Motor Coporation

Figure 4.2 If the River Is Deep There Is No Bottom in Sight!

systematically drive down inventories so that the defects in the production system can be identified and then rectified. (Inventories are akin, as the Figure shows, to murky water which hides the lurking danger of stones from the innocent diver).

Characteristically, therefore, the production system is "tightened" by being squeezed of inventories until the point of breakdown, at which stage the bottlenecks to production are identified and then tackled.9/ The result has been a very significant reduction in working capital and finished product stocks. Table 4.9 shows the overall comparison between the Japanese and United States auto firms. Inventory turns are the number of times that the average level of inventory - including, until 1980, of finished autos - can be divided into annual turnover;

Table 4.9
Trends in Inventory Turns for United States Auto Assemblers and Toyota, 1973-1984[a]

	1973	1978	1980	1983	1984	1985
Ford	5.3	6.5	9.6	12.2	14.2	16.6
Chrysler	5.6	6.3	6.4	12.6	14.7	19.0
General Motors	5.4	6.7	10.1	11.0	10.3	11.9
American Motors	7.2	6.4	5.8	12.0	15.3	15.5
Toyota				88.6	90.0	

Sources: Adapted from Automotive Industries, April 1985, April 1986.

[a]Post-1980 figures confined to work-in-progress, raw material and supplies; pre-1980 figures include finished products.

clearly the higher the number of inventory turns, the lower the average level of inventory. Two factors are striking in relation to this table. The first is the progress made by the American firms once they got the message of JIT in the late 1970s. The second is the very superior performance of Toyota whose average inventories in 1984 were between six and nine times lower than those of their United States rivals.

Toyota was the pioneer of this system and still performs better than any of its rivals, in Japan or elsewhere. But JIT production is a complex organizational phenomenon. One of the primary features required for successful implementation is the close physical proximity of suppliers. Toyota's solution to this problem has been unique and is probably difficult to replicate to a precise degree. It produces autos in Toyota City. This was set-up in virgin agricultural territory in 1937 and was named Koromo until 1959. Over the years most of Toyota's component suppliers settled on adjacent land and where no suitable infrastructure was in existence, purpose-built roads were constructed to ferry components and raw materials to the plant In the case of its two largest suppliers (both Toyota subsidiaries) deliveries of parts - which are installed in cars within two hours of arrival - are made on an hourly basis. In 1950 Koromo had a population of 30,000 - by 1980 this had risen to around

300,000 of whom 75 percent relied in one way or another on production for Toyota. Ninety-five percent of industrial freight movements in the areas were destined for Toyota.

Nissan had a particular problem in meeting this challenge since the shortage of industrial land around Tokyo - where its plants were located - made such geographical proximity and tightness of inventory supplies more difficult to organize. In early years it tried to respond by automating its way to reduced inventories, but towards the late-1970s it began to realize that this was not the solution. It developed an Action Plate Method (APM) - modeled on Toyota's *Kanban* cards10/ - for controlling in-plant inventories and then made substantial progress in reducing its work-in-progress. This APM scheme was rapidly successful, reducing Toyota's inventory-superiority from a factor of 1.6 in 1979 to 1.4 in 1981. (It subsequently rose again to 1.9 in 1983, almost an historic high in the relative superiority of Toyota's control of inventories compared to Nissan).11/

Other Japanese firms made similar steps after the mid-1970s, illustrated by the case of one of the minor assemblers in Table 4.10. Having reduced the average level of work-in-progress from 4.8 shifts in 1975 to only six hours in 1983 in, this firm has targeted its work-in-progress ratio to fall to 0.01, equivalent to an average of around two hours production requirements. But with an anecdote they illustrated the competitive advantage arising to Toyota from the proximity of its suppliers. In many cases Toyota's largest component suppliers deliver at one-hourly intervals, directly to the production line. This is easy for Toyota whose suppliers were down the road, complained the interviewed firm, but they were more constrained in many cases since about 50 percent of their components and raw materials came from as far away as 30 miles; indeed, a small proportion of their inputs came from over 300 miles. When questioned whether they had ever experienced disruption to production in the context of these "stretched" inventory lines with little buffer stock (see Table 4.10), the group of engineers being interviewed conferred and then "admitted" reluctantly that some years back - about four, they thought - when there had been a particularly bad snow-storm, one of their delivery lorries had got stuck on the motorway and production had been held up for two-to-three hours!

It is difficult to calculate how much of the competitive cost advantage of the Japanese assemblers arose from the reduction in inventories. These cost reductions

Table 4.10
Inventories as a Proportion of Monthly Production, in a Smaller Japanese Auto Firm

Year	Ratio
1975	0.19
1977	0.19
1978	0.07
1979	0.05
1980	0.04
1981	0.03
1982	0.03
1983	0.03

Source: Interviews.

can occur for a number of reasons - much lower storage space, reduced working-capital costs, fewer discarded defects, less labour to handle storage and inventory control, etc. One senior production manager estimated that the savings to his firm since the introduction of JIT had been in the order of 15 percent of production costs.

But, of course, for this system to operate in any meaningful way - especially in the context of the numerous tiers of subcontracting which characterize the Japanese auto industry - it is necessary that not only the assemblers but also the component suppliers and their subcontractors adopt similar policies towards inventories. Although no systematic study has been undertaken of inventories in these various tiers, all of the first and second tier subcontractors whom we visited in Japan had made extensive efforts to move to JIT policies, both within their plants and between their own suppliers and final customers.12/

Zero-defect policies

The function of inventories in the supply-driven labour process is to ensure the continued operation of the plant which should not be allowed to stand-idle because of a faulty component. If necessary faults would be discovered at the end of the process and rectified afterwards. This conflicts fundamentally with the manufacturing philosophy in the Japanese labour process in which not only are inventory lines deliberately stretched to breaking-point, but this is then used to pinpoint areas for technical inputs. Quality is therefore an essential part of both reduced inventories and of technical change.

Though the financial implications of zero inventory are obviously important, the particular significance from our perspective of this specific element of the JIT philosophy derives from the linkage between inventory reduction and the issue of quality. Zero inventory in vehicle production demands zero defects in components for the obvious reason that if externally sourced parts prove defective, there is no recourse to inventory in-house and therefore faulty parts soon result in the stoppage of production. In the JIT system, quality has both an internal and an external dimension involving both quality levels in intra-plant production and in bought-in parts and raw materials.

Since Japanese assemblers source an exceptionally high percentage of their components from external suppliers, they rely fundamentally on suppliers being able to provide them with components of consistent quality. This is ensured in three ways. First, component firms must pass stringent "quality audits" to qualify as a supplier. Where quality problems with existing suppliers arise, firms such as Nissan send teams of quality engineers to assist the suppliers to achieve the desired standard - a procedure that is easiest to follow in relation to suppliers based in Japan both because of their proximity and because of the close working knowledge that the supplier has of the auto producer's procedures and standards. It is not just the assemblers who undertake these quality audits, but also the first and second tier of subcontractors in relation to their own suppliers. Second (as one of the largest component firms described the process in relation to their inputs from the second tier of suppliers), all suppliers face a 100 percent check on quality for the first six months. Depending on their performance, this check is either maintained, modified to a lower level or abolished. Third, and perhaps most importantly, assemblers emphasized to us that they rely on the trust they have built up with their suppliers through long years of association as a guarantee of quality. When suppliers reward this trust with consistent quality, assemblers in turn reward suppliers through a combination of price mechanisms and stable contracts.

These three factors are an important (though not the sole) reason why the assemblers interviewed categorically preferred to source the vast majority of their components from Japan rather than abroad and why components available from developing countries are scarcely ever given consideration.13/ Further and, as we shall see in later Chapters, the quality factor is an important determinant of the sourcing strategy being pursued not only by Japanese firms producing in the United States but also increasingly by their United States and Western European competitors.

Quality also plays a critical role in the functioning of internal JIT and is worth pursuing this further here because it provides an important criterion for our evaluation of the performance of United States and Western European firms in Chapters 5 and 6. Again the issue needs to be viewed via its relationship to the philosophy of zero inventory. (This relationship is captured effectively in Figure 3.1 where the inventory level is equated with the water level in a river). If the level of inventory is high, it obscures hidden problems and gives the illusion that everything is acceptable, when, in fact, it is not. By deliberately "forcing the water level down", i.e. moving to zero inventory, problems are exposed and can be corrected before they cause trouble. All of the Japanese firms interviewed were of the opinion that this type of quality enhancement - that which is internal to the plant - is much easier to transfer abroad than that which is external to the plant or firm.

The link between quality and reducing inventories is well-illustrated by the case of Toyota. In a series of quality recalls by the Japanese government in 1969, Toyota had had the highest rate of problems, accounting for 28 percent of all recalled vehicles.14/ Consequently, in its stamping plant, Toyota emphasized further the switch from the volume production of identical stamped parts via long runs and high inventories (because of the need to maintain high levels of capacity utilization of expensive equipment) to batch production in small lot sizes largely because of its desire to upgrade quality considerations. With the previous mass production approach, if stamped parts proved defective, this meant large numbers of costly parts were defective and there was a consequent reluctance to jettison a significant amount of work-in-progress - when stampings were produced in small lots, defects could be minimized and corrected quickly.

The emphasis on total quality, like inventory reduction, yields significant benefits. For instance, because Japanese auto producers are able to maintain a reliably high level of production quality, fewer inspectors are required - in one case, a Japanese plant producing a transit van whose equivalent was also manufactured by a

United States firm at two sites in Western Europe, required only 15 inspectors per shift compared to 83 and 68 at the Western European plants; similarly in 1980, 80 to 85 percent of cars produced by a Japanese plant came off the assembly line without defects, whereas at the "best" Western European plant of a United States producer each car required the repair of seven to eight defects. This factor accounts for the far fewer numbers of repair bays found in Japanese plants (around 10 on average) compared to the United States plants built in the 1970s and early 1980s (often as high as 72). This in turn reduces fixed investment costs since the elimination of repair bays, like the minimization of inventory storage space, means less equipment and machinery is required and allows the physical size of the plant to be reduced. As a result, Japanese plants are typically half the size of United States and Western European plants producing at the same level of output (see Tables 4.2 and 4.3). And finally, of course, the emphasis on quality feeds through into the final product and is a key factor explaining the attractiveness of Japanese products in overseas markets as well as being a major area of competitiveness in their domestic markets.

It is partly for this reason that the quality circles have become important in Japan, although they serve the subsidiary functions of improving morale and contributing towards incremental technical change (see below). Quality Circles really took-off in Japan in the 1970s. The number of employees involved jumped from just over 100,000 in 1962 to over 1 million in 1978 and 1.5 million in 1984, with an increase in circles from 10,000 to around 100,000 in 1978 and 181,000 in 1984. By 1984 Toyota had 5,850 Quality Circless with 37,515 members and Nissan had 4,004 with 37,389 members.[15]/ There are no general measures of just how substantial the quality of output in these Japanese firms is although the quality of Japanese consumer durables is widely recognized and the reliability of their semiconductor components far exceeds that of the American and Western European producers[16]/. The important point to be stressed here, however, is that quality is not merely one of a series of chosen objectives in Japanese manufacturing. It is endogenous to the new labour process, for without it JIT could not operate and flexibility would be severely hampered.

Giving responsibility back to the detailed worker

A series of features in this new system of production contribute to the need to give responsibility for important decisions to the detailed line-worker. Once a JIT structure is adopted, zero-defect policies must be utilized. This requires the line-worker to be responsible for quality control (QC) rather than the specialized QC department, for if there are any defects the whole line will rapidly grind to a halt. By its nature quality control - and, more important, the rectification of errors - necessitates decision-taking. In addition, giving responsibility to the base of the production hierarchy also flows from flexibility in production since the worker is no longer subservient to the same extent to the moving and unchanging production line.

Of course this is a radical departure from the Fordist system and conflicts fundamentally with the central precept of Taylor that "all possible brain work should be removed from the shop and centered in the planning and laying out department"17/. It finds expression in a variety of features in the Japanese system, of which two are illustrative of the enormous significance of the changes in the labour process. The first example concerns the virtual abolition of the quality control department, with its ancillary "rectification bays", as a specialized sub-unit in production. These are largely absent in most Japanese plants in which worker-control over quality is widespread and often dominates the production ideology in the workplace. The second example concerns the use of the so-called *Andon* lights. Their origins go back to Toyota in 1955 when workers were first given the responsibility of stopping the production line if they noticed defects or if inventories piled up to cover the needs of more than five cars. The *Andon* lights themselves were first introduced in Toyota in 1957. These comprise a series of lights and switches next to every workpoint. One switch and an accompanying light signals that the worker is under pressure. The second light/switch indicates that assistance is required or the production line will grind to a halt. The third and most important switch available at all workpoints is a switch to bring the line to a halt if any error is noted. This, of course, is a decision of fundamental importance in the context of production line operation and represents a significant change over past procedures. In fact, not all Japanese firms have introduced this radical step and Nissan, at least, does not allow workers to stop the production line. They are expected, instead, to tag white stickers to work-in-progress which they deem to be defective.

Worker involvement in technical improvements

It is necessary here to digress briefly into a distinction between different types of technical change. In a recent paper Freeman[18]/ distinguishes between three different variants. The first and most global are the revolutionary technologies (such as steam engines or microelectronics) which are pervasive and which diffuse in clusters. Next come the radical innovations (such as nylon and polyethylene) representing significant changes in process and product. Finally there are the incremental innovations in product and process.

The new paradigm emerging in Japan sees technical change as a _total_ process, encompassing changes in product, production technology and work-organization.[19]/ In the auto industry this is expressed through the rapid introduction of revolutionary and radical technologies (such as those involving the application of electronics and new materials) with which the old Fordist paradigm is finding it difficult to compete. The introduction of these new technologies is forcing the Japanese auto assembly firms into substantially greater levels of R&D. In both Nissan and Toyota's case this has risen to around 4 percent of turnover - which, by comparison with the overall ratio for all manufacturing industry in the United States of around 2 percent, and around 6 percent for the information technology sectors, is a significant level. Between 1962 and 1980 the industry consistently invested more than 20 percent of its gross profit in new equipment and production facilities.[20]/ As we shall see below, this is being backed by a growing investment in R&D in the component sector as well.

These extra resources being put into design and process-engineering departments are most suited to radical innovations involving the application of new machines, the development of new products and the introduction of new manufacturing philosophies. The incremental changes in product, and especially process, ideally belong on the shop floor where line-workers - who come into everyday contact with what takes place in production - are best placed to notice the need and opportunity for simple changes. But the problem with the Fordist paradigm was that it gave no

Table 4.11
Suggestions Submitted by Employees for Improvements in Product and Process at Toyota, 1979-1983.

	Number	Percentage implemented	Suggestion per employee
1960	9,000	39	1.0
1970	40,000	70	2.5
1973	247,000	76	12.2
1976	380,000	83	15.3
1979	575,861	91	13.3
1980	859,039	94	19.2
1981	1,412,565	94	30.5
1982	1,905,642	95	38.8
1983	1,655,858	96	31.8

Source: Information Supplied by Toyota Motor Corporation.

space for this type of shop-floor creativity.

The system which has developed in most Japanese auto factories is in sharp contrast to the Fordist experience and takes a number of forms. First, the general atmosphere is conducive to suggestions, especially with the regular meetings of quality circles. Second, in each plant three or four finished car-bodies are set out for inspection by the workers who are encouraged to stick labels to the vehicles wherever they see faults. And, third, there is a systematic provision of financial rewards (ranging from $2 to $800 in 1984) for suggestions which are implemented.

Table 4.11 shows the record of suggestions and implementations in the Toyota company between 1960 and 1983. The sheer extent of these - over 1.6m in 1983 - is quite mind-boggling in comparison with the virtual non-existence of such schemes in most of the United States and Western European auto firms. In the early 1960s when Toyota was operating the same employee suggestion schemes as its American counterparts, the company averaged around 1 suggestion/employee/p.a., about four times the United States average. By 1982, as can be seen from Table 4.11, the average in Toyota had risen to over 38.

It is true that many of these suggestions may be of a trivial nature and are best seen as a mechanism for maintaining company morale. But this is emphatically not the case for all of them. The really significant factor is that it effectively takes care of many of the incremental technical innovations, leaving the design departments free to concentrate on more fundamental problems. For example, one of the assembly plants pointed out that the installation of various components and sub-assemblies under the cars was a backbreaking task in which the workers were slowed by the inconvenience of working above head-height. One of the suggestions - which seems trivial but is nonetheless important - was to tilt the cars over on a 90° keel. This enabled the workers to work with greater speed and for the production line to move faster. It is for this reason - the endogenization of technical change within the labour process - that Baba observes that the Japanese see the factory as a laboratory.21/

THE TRANSITION TO COMPUTER-INTEGRATED MANUFACTURE

The preceding discussion of the Japanese approach to production organization shows that much of the impressive gains in productivity registered by the Japanese auto industry through the 1960s and 1970s resulted from three factors: the achievement of scale economies, the introduction of a series of related organizational innovations subsumed under JIT, and the incessant improvement of conventional production technology through a stream of incremental technical changes. By emphasizing these aspects, analysts such as Altshuler et al and Schonberger sought to refute the widespread impression in the early 1980s that the Japanese "miracle" was due to the extensive use of sophisticated computer-based automation technology. They argued that the auto industry in Japan as well as in the United States and Western Europe was still in the very early stages of absorbing computer-based technology - and that firms in the latter countries in particular had first to cope with the new organizational innovations pioneered by the Japanese before attempting the widespread introduction of the systemic electronics-based embodied technologies. While we broadly agree with this argument in relation to the dominant trend in the Japanese auto industry in the 1960s and 1970s, we feel that from the perspective of 1987 this conclusion significantly understates the extent to which Japanese auto production plants were, and are, being adapted to exploit the systemic and productivity-enhancing possibilities inherent in computer-based production control and automation.

Therefore in this section, we shall try to illuminate

the nature and implications of this transition from a production system whose critical strength lay in its organizational elements to one where technological factors are becoming increasingly pre-eminent. It is important to bear in mind our earlier observation that there are variations in the strategies adopted by the various Japanese firms. At the one extreme is Toyota which has historically placed little faith in embodied automation technologies - at the other is Nissan with a long term commitment to the introduction of the most advanced embodied automation technologies.

Microelectronics, Flexibility and Mixed Production Lines

As we have seen, flexibility in the Japanese automobile production arose autonomously out of domestic market conditions and through the introduction of JIT production methods. But, in the early 1970s two factors helped the Japanese industry enormously in their export markets. The first was that the nature of Japanese geography and roads had meant that the industry had concentrated on much smaller vehicles than their United States counterparts, so that when world oil prices rose sharply in 1973, the Japanese were ideally placed with a range of fuel-efficient cars. Secondly, rising consumer affluence and the attractiveness of Western European cars in the innovation-starved United States auto market led the buying public to reject the standardized mass produced vehicles manufactured by all major firms in favour of a wider variety of car models suited to more individualized tastes.

If we remind ourselves of the Fordist philosophy ("any color as long as it is black") that dominated United States producers' model strategy in the early 1970s, then the significance of the Japanese approach becomes clear. Japan's auto producers aimed not only to give their customers an enormous range of choice, but ultimately to produce each car to the specification of individual customers. There were many dangers inherent in this strategy, not the least being the potential loss of scale economies in production. So, if mixed production was to be efficient, in addition to the general requirements posed by the JIT philosophy for inventory-reduction, there was the ancillary need to handle a greatly increased variety of parts[22]/ and a significantly more complex pattern of production control. Component ordering and control was therefore an important element of the new production philosophy.

In principle computerized production and inventory control has the potential to enable the fine-tuning of production organization. Yet the system of in-house component ordering and production scheduling utilized in the initial establishment of JIT was initially (and still is in some cases) essentially paper-based. With hindsight it is possible to conclude that in the initial stages of the introduction of this new philosophy of production, the utilization of a sophisticated embodied technology (such as computers) would probably have made the transition less likely since one of its core philosophies - "do it right the first time" - required in the first instance a change in managerial perspectives. Computerization in the early years may have in fact hindered the recognition of this simple and fundamental point. However, whilst recognizing the paper-based origins of the JIT system, it is important to note that the diffusion of JIT frequently coincided with the growing availability of computer-based control systems. Consequently, when some Japanese firms such as Nissan, Mazda and Mitsubishi first adopted the JIT philosophy in 1976 and 1977, they also introduced the use of computers to manage it, albeit initially in a limited fashion. Even Toyota, relatively skeptical of the power of embodied technology to transform production, had installed an IBM calculating machine to handle personnel records as early as 1953, and this was substantially enhanced by major computer acquisitions in 1960, 1963 and 1966.23/ Organizational innovation thus opened the way for the successful introduction of computers.

The switch to mixed production also had important implications for the utilization of electronics-based technologies in the automation of machining and assembly. During the pre-electronics era the Japanese firms (with the relative exception of Nissan) had wherever possible sought to automate these tasks through the use of simple work-saving attachments (such as limit-switches) and general purpose machines, since the hard-automation technologies being utilized by their competitors were too inflexible to cope with mixed production strategies. But as production began to increase and these simple machines began to offer lesser chance of maintaining the increase in productivity, the auto firms began to take advantage of the numerically controlled (NC) tools and first generation industrial robots. These provided the necessary degree of flexibility, maintained productivity-growth and could operate cost-effectively in relatively low batches of production.

The findings of Watanabe (reinforced by our own research presented below) show clearly that the demands for flexibility inherent in JIT and the use of mixed production lines had led auto firms to introduce limited numbers of automation technologies such as NC machine tools in the early 1970s. As the decade progressed innovation began to incorporate industrial robots and flexible transfer machines. However, after a few years, as the push to offer a diversified product range based on mixed production lines began to intensify, and as NC technology matured, the pace of introduction accelerated rapidly, from 1975 for NC machine tools and from 1980 for more advanced types of robots.24/ Between 1975 and 1982, the auto industry utilized between 10 and 15 percent of all NC tools shipped in Japan and by the end of 1982, it was the second largest user, accounting for 23 percent of total NC tools in use (compared to the United States auto industry which by that time accounted for only 4 percent of total NC tools in use).

Table 4.12 demonstrates the intensity of use of new-vintage NC tools in Japanese auto firms compared to the United States. Not only did the Japanese industry - with a lower level of automobile output in the early 1980s than its American counterpart - possess over 60 percent more NC machine tools, but the average age of these machine tools was much lower. Whereas almost half of the American machine tools were more than eight years old, only one-sixth of the Japanese tools were of this age; by contrast over half the Japanese machine tools were less than two years old, compared to only one third in the United States industry.

The picture is roughly the same in relation to industrial robots. Some 200 industrial robots (not just programmable, but of all types) had been produced in Japan by 1968. This rose to more than 124,000 by the end of 1982. Of this, 74 percent were produced in the 1978-1982 period, with the auto industry being only marginally the second largest user of advanced robots over that period, accounting for 32.5 percent of total shipments. Watanabe suggests that by the end of 1983 there were some 4,000 programmable robots in use in the automobile industry, with the five leading producers doubling their use of robots to more than 3,200 between 1979 and 1984.

Watanabe's findings are important in documenting the relationship between the need for flexibility implied by

Table 4.12
United States and Japanese Auto Industry Use of Numerical Control Tools by Age of Machine[a]

	0-2 years		3-7 years		>8 years		Total
	No	%	No	%	No	%	
Japan[b]	3,416	57	1,664	27	937	16	6,017
United States Auto Industry	1,274	34	623	17	1,799	49	3,696

Source: Adapted from Watanabe

[a]For Japan as of 30 Sept 1981; for United States as of end 1983
[b]Figures related to transport machinery sector of which auto industry accounts for 82.6 percent of NC tools used.

the growing spread of mixed production and JIT, and the use of NC tools and industrial robots. However, simply counting numbers misses the crucial point of qualitative differences. Over time the way in which these technologies were used and controlled has altered fundamentally. They moved from being introduced on a stand-alone basis to being increasingly tied into computer-integrated systems of production, or (in terms of our analysis in Chapter 2) from intra-activity to intra-sphere and intersphere automation. Thus, whilst the organizational breakthrough implicit in mixed production and JIT (and responsible for such a large share of Japan's competitive advantage in the 1970s) certainly emerged separately from computer technology, the interaction between them during the 1970s grew slowly at first, but subsequently deepened considerably towards the end of the decade.

We can now turn to our empirical findings to illustrate these points with reference to the two main elements in the new form of production system that will increasingly dominate the automobile industry (and many others) in the years to come - computer-integrated flexible automation and computer-controlled supplier relations and production scheduling.

Electronics and Flexibility in Production

Each of the auto producers interviewed in our survey

had mixed production lines in their assembly plants. As we will discuss later, there are inherent costs involved in the present generation of the technology used on mixed product lines that causes unit costs to be somewhat above those for dedicated lines. Consequently, where possible, producers prefer to use dedicated lines (coupled with JIT and automation) to produce at the current minimum economies of scale of 400,000 units per annum. Nevertheless, most firms are dedicated to maintaining and extending their mixed production capacity. Hence, Nissan's Murayama plant can assemble the Micra/March and Sunny/Sentra as well as the Bluebird (each with a different floor plan); Toyota assembles the Celica, Camry, Vista and Carina on mixed lines at its Tsutsumi plant; Mazda's Hofu plant can handle many varieties of three different floor pans and its Hiroshima plant can assemble six different types of the 323 and Ford cars; and the Mitsubishi plant can assemble the Minica saloon, the Mirage and the Lancer.

The important point about mixed production is that assembling cars with different floor pans imposes severe demands on the control of work-in-progress and precision adjustments to the embodied technologies used. In these plants (and others not visited), flexibility has been greatly enhanced by the use of central- computers to control robots, NC tools and flexible transfer lines. Virtually all the plants use flexible robots and programmable CNC tools to carry out a large and growing percentage of painting, welding and machining. Mitsubishi has 60 percent robotic welding, Nissan has 212 robots for painting and welding at Murayama, Toyota uses 314 robots for welding at Tsutsumi, and so on. In many cases central computers send instructions as to the adjustments necessary for different products, color, etc. and these cases represent in themselves examples of a considerable degree of computer-based flexibility. However, it is in the progressive entry of assembly robots into tasks previously carried out manually where the use of computer control enhances and is indeed becoming increasingly essential to flexibility.

The degree of computer-based assembly flexibility varies considerably and it must be stressed that a large percentage of assembly is even now done manually in Japan. The use of assembly robots by some companies is still quite limited - as in Toyota where robotized assembly is only just being introduced due to the relatively late conversion of the firm's management to a belief in the cost advantages of automated assembly. However, even in Toyota assembly robots are used, while in other companies the process of robotized assembly is much more advanced (though sometimes unevenly spread among plants) and is indicative of future trends.

Nissan appears to have the most clearly focused long term view of their systemic characteristics of the new electronics-based automation technologies. For example, at its Murayama plant it makes extensive use of automatically guided vehicles (AGVs) which autonomously collect and deliver work-in-progress to the assembly line as the parts are needed. In 1984 it was clearly recognized that these AGVs were not cost effective as a separate sub-process, but it was argued that they were an important learning-component for the long-run strategy of systemic automation. Moreover, argued Nissan, when the same line was producing 106,000 variations of three different floorpans, it would be extremely difficult to ever get inventories really low unless the delivery and collection of work-in-progress was coordinated through a centralized computer and executed by individual NC controlled pieces of equipment such as AGVs, NC machine tools and robots. At the same Nissan plant, one line uses 14 robots to apply window sealant, install rear windows and to install seats.25/ In another Nissan plant, Zama, robots do all of the above as well as the sub-assembly and installation of instrument panels. Nissan is also pioneering the use of laser-based inspection systems at its Murayama and Opana plants. Robot mounted laser systems have been installed that are capable of tracking a moving vehicle and scanning the entire painted surface of the car in 1.2 minutes compared to the 45 minutes the job used to take when done manually. The system is able to monitor the size, location and number of surface defects on each car while also providing feedback information to the paint shop.

Mazda's Hofu plant uses robots for a variety of assembly tasks including window sealing and installation and door installation (tasks done manually at its Hiroshima plant). Equally advanced is Mitsubishi which on one line has robotic front and rear window sealing and installation, as well as the flexibly automated unload, weld and installation of instrument panels, robotized front and rear door assembly, and robot assembly of spare wheels - the latter highlighting the importance of computer control since virtually each car has a different specification of tyre.

Implicit in some of the examples given above is the growing use of the techniques of modular assembly (a concept which is spreading rapidly in the United States and Western Europe and which was described in Chapter 3). Basically two innovations are involved. The first is the production by external suppliers of completed sub-assemblies (for example, instrument panels) which had previously been assembled by the auto producer on-site from discrete components. Now these are provided intact by the supplier, delivered JIT to the appropriate point in the final assembly line, and fixed into place by robots or workers with a minimum degree of adjustment. The key point is that very often this involves the integrated design of the car, the component and the installation technique to facilitate the use of robots. A second assembly innovation follows the same principle of redesigning the order of assembly (in line with the use of modular systems) so that the car is in effect assembled from inside out to minimize the need to remove components already installed to allow the fitting of other components.

The Mitsubishi case cited above, where robots are used in computer-synchronized and directed off-line sub-assembly activities (that is, door assembly and spare wheel assembly), is indicative of another notable trend - the movement of flexible automation into areas other than final assembly. Mazda for instance is experimenting with automatic sensing and inspection systems; Nissan relies extensively on computers for achieving flexibility in its press shops where a wide variety of parts (from 12 types of a single van part to 400 different types of wheel housing) need to be stamped and delivered via in-plant JIT.

Automation has even begun to enter the arena of die change where semi-automated Quick-Die-Change (QDC) presses incorporating movable bolsters have begun to be introduced, reducing already low die change times even further. In Toyota, the semi-automated equipment in use on one line allows presses to be changed in only one minute. Figure 4.2 demonstrates the advantages offered by automation even in situations where organizational changes have already proven very effective. Note the sharp reduction (nearly 90 percent) in change-over-time and the increase in the number of shots per hour between 1978 and 1980 on a 500 ton press line following the introduction of a semi-automated QDC press. (In addition to reducing change-over and increasing machine-utilization, the QDCs additionally replace three out of five workers on the old line). This differs from the Toyota example cited above in that it involves die changes in five (rather than one) 500 ton presses simultaneously.

Computer-integrated control of production scheduling and supplier relations

Flexible automation is only one part of the new system of production that is emerging in Japan. The other element is the growing use of computers to control the inter-plant and intra-plant dimensions of JIT. Obviously enough, in a system as tightly organized as JIT, it was always necessary to have centralized control over component ordering and production scheduling to ensure efficient operation. And as noted earlier, while the control system used by Japanese auto firms are in some cases still paper-based, a growing number of firms are switching to computer-to-computer digital communication. Indeed, some firms such as Mazda and Mitsubishi have used computers to manage JIT from the very beginning. However, much more important than the control of JIT by centralized computers is the fact that most of the Japanese companies - especially Nissan - have begun to integrate computer-controlled flexible production automation with computerized JIT management. There are differences of course between companies in the extent of this integration but the trend is clear.

We can best illustrate this by looking closely at one of the most advanced facilities in Japan (in 1984-85) at Nissan's Murayama plant where computers are used to control all parts of the production process. This incorporates flexible automation technologies (as discussed above), production scheduling, components ordering from external suppliers, and in-plant JIT.26/ The starting point for this process comes with the monthly specification of a three month rolling production schedule, which predicts plant output, component requirements and refinements. (Except for engines, these are predictions rather than orders). The next step is the setting of Master Schedule 1, fixed twelve days before the onset of a 10 day production period; Master Schedule 2 fixes daily production of engine and body types; Master Schedule 3 fixes the precise mix of accessories required (for example, mirrors) to specific dealer orders;27/ and Master Schedule 4 giving a specific computer-based code to each car that contains all the relevant information necessary for it to be assembled to the exact specification of the customer.

The unique feature of this system of production control is that it involves extensive and intensive use of computer interfacing between assembly plants and suppliers, between the production plants and the head office host computer, and among the computer-based systems used within the plants themselves. Computers have been used with Master Schedules 1-3 since 1970 - but Master Schedule 4 (the central integrating element in this system) has only been computerized since 1982 - before that it was paper-based.

The Nissan system is known as the Action Plate Method (APM) and it is designed to streamline production of computer-integrated manufacture and produce direct to orders from customers. This system has both an inter-plant and an intra-plant component. The functioning of the interplant component of APM (roughly equivalent to Toyota's Kanban system of JIT) is set out in Table 4.13.

As the table shows, deliveries occur on average on a daily basis (by volume rather than value). Until five years ago, the average was 2-3 days though even then, 50 percent came daily. Nissan believes it is possible to reduce this further and aims to get 50 percent of parts delivered four times per day by 1988.28/ Nissan's management see their ability to strive for this goal being directly linked to their use of computer-based ordering. Perhaps the most significant factor revealed by the table is that computer-based ordering accounts for 90 percent by quantity and 90 percent or more by value of all components used.

This computer-based control system is fully extended to the shop floor (the intra-plant component of APM). At the earliest stage of chassis construction, each car has a metal bar code which defines it in great detail (Master Schedule 4). This is read by laser at different work points and the plant's 216 robots are able to adjust their performance automatically to whatever the scheduled product mix calls for. To support this flexibility, a sophisticated computer-controlled parts scheduling system (delivered in part by AGVs - which are coordinated by the same computer) ensures that exactly the right number and type of components (for example, sub-assemblies, engines, doors and accessories) are delivered as the body reaches each work-point. This system relies upon the automatic tagging of each mixed component pallet with a plastic tag (the "Action Plate") so that when the next work-point begins using the pallet, the tag is returned to source, automatically indicating the need for the next pallet.29/ Production in this system is therefore "pulled" by final customer order, rather than "pushed" as in the earlier Fordist lines.

The critical and integrating function of the computer is clearly apparent from the above description of

Table 4.13
Nissan's Inter-Plant CIM System

Component Types	Delivery Frequency	Quantities	Order Mode
High value and bulky products[a] (e.g. engine and transmission glass moldings and mountings door trim; radiator; air conditioning fuel tanks	3 hrs 3 hrs 3-5 hrs 5 hrs 5-6 hrs	40% by number, greater by value	DNC - direct by plant computer to supplier computer
Less sophisticated, less bulky and less expensive parts[b]	Daily	50% by number	assembler produced computer tape delivered to supplier
"Synchronized" parts (trim, tyres, carpets, seats, etc).	Hourly and two hourly delivery[c]	+5% by volume	paper-based

small sub-assemblies (brackets, etc.)	Twice Daily	+5% by value	paper-based
Small general parts with wide application and low value[d]	5-10 days or as needed	+1% by value	paper-based

Source: Interviews

[a]This DNC system involves ordering two days before delivery, one day before actual use. But production fluctuates and great flexibility is required. The components are largely provided by first-tier suppliers.

[b]Order given six to seven days in advance.

[c]This is necessary since these items are bulky and incur expensive storage costs. These parts are installed within 80 minutes of the car emerging from paint shop.

[d]Supplied by small sub-contractors.

production control at Nissan's Muruyama plant. The other Japanese auto firms that were visited have similarly functioning computer-based systems for controlling different parts of the production process, though none were as fully integrated as the Nissan system. For instance, though the Tsutsumi plant of Toyota followed a similar mode of computer-based production scheduling to Nissan, only 10-20 percent of component orders were made via delivery of computer tape - no DNC ordering was involved at all. In the case of Mazda, they, like Nissan, used computers for component-ordering and had a sophisticated system of automated intra-plant parts-delivery based on laser scanning, but this was in place in only one plant (the other used paper tapes) and controlled the car-specific delivery of only major sub-assemblies and larger parts to the appropriate assembly plant. Thus in Mazda, workers selected these other parts from pallets which are not car-specific but whose delivery was automated. The same was true of Toyota and Mitsubishi where (except for the car-specific delivery of transmissions) each worker had to read a paper printout and select the appropriate part from the larger stock along the line. This involved on-line in-plant stocks of 2-4 hours and meant they have to have as many pallets as the type of cars being produced - a problem not faced by Nissan and imposing a cost on mixed production systems.

In the above discussion, we have necessarily presented an oversimplified picture of the trends currently taking place in process innovation in Japan. It is of course possible to point to many exceptions to this picture. As we mentioned earlier, not many plants exhibit the extensive degree of computerization characteristic of the Nissan plants described above. Toyota's Kamigo Engine plant is an example of this. The plant is impressive in many regards - one of the lines we visited employed only 200 people, producing two types of engine with 50 varieties; each engine takes only 20 hours to assemble and daily output is 1800. But parts are delivered by fork lift truck rather than automatically, while the engines are assembled in a very labour intensive fashion. Toyota, however, is recognized to be lagging with respect to the introduction of CIM.

It would also be a mistake to assume that the Japanese are world leaders in all aspects of computer use. This is definitely not the case in the area of Computer Aided Design (CAD), where Japanese auto firms - though improving fast - are still considerably behind their competitors.

And in the next chapter we will point to examples in the United States and Western Europe where firms are attempting to leapfrog the Japanese in terms of the degree of assembly automation. Moreover, it is also the case that achieving extensive computer integration in production does not automatically mean success in the marketplace. Product design and consumer attractiveness are obviously crucial and in the short run automation can be costly. Witness the case of Nissan and Mitsubishi. Despite the advanced nature of their production systems both have experienced recent difficulties in meeting their target sales and in competing with the market leader - Toyota - in costs. And Mitsubishi, finding it difficult to escape from quota restraints, has had to team up with Hyundai in an attempt to increase its market penetration overseas. By contrast Toyota fares best in the marketplace but is relatively slow at process innovation.

In an interview with an executive of another auto assembler it was suggested that Nissan's Murayama plant was largely experimental and not representative of a general trend. This may have been true of the situation in 1984-85, but we believe this is largely because it, like the other more advanced plants of Mazda and Honda, is one of the newest plants in Japan.30/ And, certainly, Nissan's management did not see the plant as experimental, since not only were they striving to introduce a similar degree of computerization in their other plants, they also regarded Murayama as a prototype for their United Kingdom and United States operations. This suggests to us that Murayama is not an exception but simply the leading edge of a trend that will rapidly diffuse through the rest of the industry.

Thus in the case of Murayama and the other plants discussed, what we are witnessing is a marrying of all the traditional elements of JIT mentioned earlier with computer-integrated production control, declining plant and product scale economies arising from computer-based flexible automation on mixed production lines, and computerized supplier links. The essential point is not simply that computers are used to carry out separate tasks, or that robots will replace all assembly workers - they will not, as many tasks will of necessity remain best carried out by physical rather than machine labour. Rather, it is that the functions already efficiently performed and controlled via analog means are now being integrated into one system.

An interesting feature of this strategy is that it conforms to the discussion of the intra-plant systemic features of CIM described in Chapter 2. (Indeed the schema for automation presented by one of the largest component firms was very similar to the systemic inter-sphere conceptualization presented in Chapter 2). Nissan is especially vigorous here in that they have automated some subprocesses of production (for example, robot installation of seats and the widespread use of AGVs) despite their realization that, as islands of automation, these innovations are not cost-effective. Their real value, Nissan believes, is to be found in the role they play in the generation of control software and as testing grounds for the functioning components of intra- and inter-sphere automation.

COMPONENT SUPPLIERS AND AUTO ASSEMBLERS

The third and final of the three essential elements of the era of systemofacture is the qualitative nature of the relationships between firms who are involved in a vertically integrated chain of production. As we saw in Chapter 2, the social division of labour in the machinofacturing era was one of conflict - firms in the vertical chain of production were adversarial in their relationships with both their suppliers and their customers. Dual-sourcing and arms-length negotiations were the norm and, perhaps most importantly, both product development and production control were performed autonomously by the various firms in the production chain.

All this contrasts very sharply with the relationships which characterize the chain of production in the Japanese auto industry. There are a variety of reasons explaining this market-structure - the components industry was particularly weak in the 1930s and the 1950s (the two crucial decades of the industry's development) and the assemblers were forced to take an active role to stimulate production; external-sourcing (as opposed to the solution adopted by GM in the 1920s) was advantageous because it involved lower wage-payments and minimized the financing problems being experienced by the assemblers; and it reduced the risk to an assembly industry still uncertain of its own long-term viability.

What emerged from this was a Group structure in which individual assemblers were closely incorporated with their captive suppliers. The banks played a quite crucial role in this, beginning with the assemblers themselves. Both of the major auto firms are linked to particular banks -

Toyota's problems in the late 1940s led to its links with the Mitsui Bank and during the 1950s the Mitsui Bank and other banks became its largest shareholders31/; in Nissan's case the largest shareholders were dissolved by the United States administration after the war and by 1984 the four largest shareholders were either banks or life insurance companies.32/ Many of the smaller assemblers also have banks amongst their principal shareholders. But Japanese law limits bank-holdings to around 5 percent of the equity of industrial companies although no limits are placed on cross-equity holdings within a Group. As a consequence each of the major Groups comprise of a series of complex equity inter-relationships with affiliates holding shares in other affiliates of the same Group. Strategic control over the whole operations is however exercised by the assembler itself in a number of ways, including the Subcontractor Groups (see below).

Interwoven with the complex pattern of organizational links is a relatively diverse structure of component producers. There are over 10,000 suppliers employing almost 500,000 people, yet many of these are small producers, much smaller than those in the other major manufacturing countries. Only around 500 of these firms can be classified as primary suppliers (which proximate to the role played by the component firms in the United States and Western Europe). The rest comprise of a series of secondary and tertiary subcontractors, some of whom are very small indeed, perhaps employing less than 25 people. Figure 4.3 - although a little dated, but still representing the general pattern of supplier-assembler relationships - provides a clear view of this structure in the case of the Toyota Company. In 1977 there were only 168 primary suppliers, of whom around 20 percent were small (defined as employing less than 300 workers or having paid-up capital less than ¥100m). Each of these had its own captive secondary subcontractors - most of these were small firms, as is the case for each of the largely-captive tertiary subcontractors. The captive nature of these various tiers of enterprises is important - in 1981 the 310 largest component manufacturers delivered 84 percent of their output to their Group assemblers33/ and predominantly single-sourcing contracts have generally been the norm so far.

This system of integration is characterized by a number of features which are qualitatively different from those of the machinofacturing era. First, as we saw exemplified in the case of Toyota City, proximity to the

Figure 4.3 Division of Labour in the Japanese Auto Industry

Source: Small and Medium Enterprise Agency, MITI (1977)

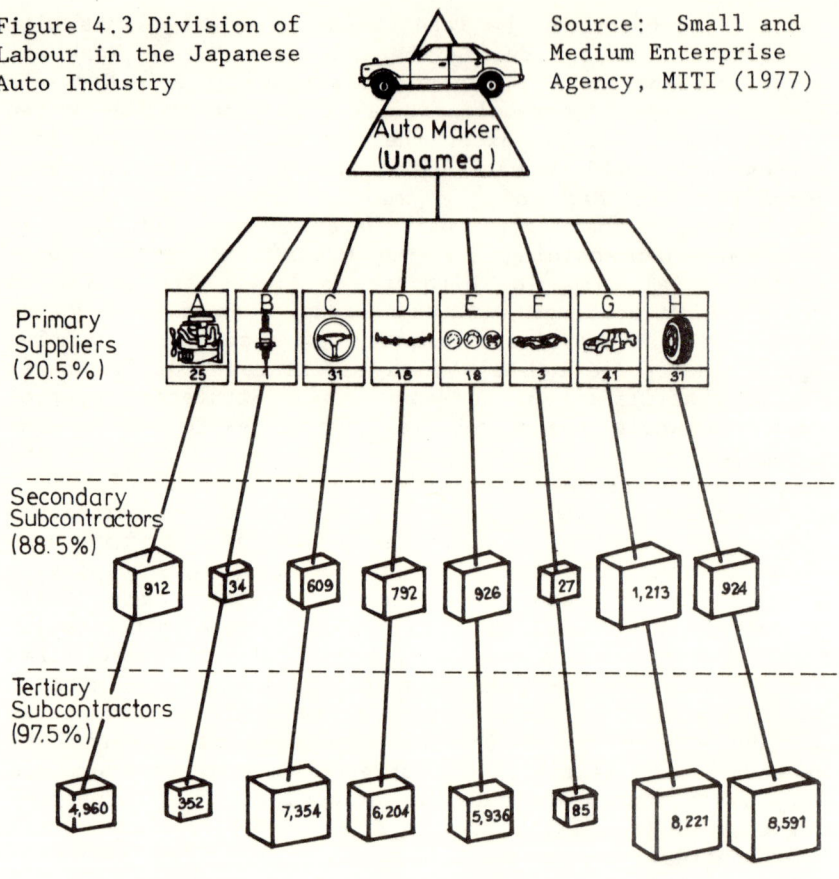

KEY: A - Engine parts
      B - Electrical parts
      C - Driving assy.
      D - Suspension/Brake parts
      E - Meters and Accessories
      F - Chassis assy.
      G - Bodies
      H - Other parts

Notes: The number of companies for 'Primary Suppliers' is real, but those for 'Secondary' and 'Tertiary' subcontractors include possible overlappings. The figures in parentheses for 'Primary Suppliers', 'Secondary' and 'Tertiary' subcontractors show the respective percentages of small and medium-sized businesses to the total in the respective sectors. Small and Medium Enterprise Agency defines a small and medium-sized manufacturing firm as a company which employs less than 300 workers and/or whose paid up capital is not greater than ¥100m.

suppliers is particularly important if JIT production methods are to operate smoothly. Second - and also essential for JIT - the close integration of production scheduling is necessary if inventory levels are to be kept low throughout the chain of production. This involves detailed coordination between firms. Third, the reliability of both quality and delivery are essential if JIT is to operate, so a close bond of trust must be established between the firms in the vertical chain of production. Trust is also key in another sense since, it is characteristic of the assemblers that both car and component design should be coordinated from an early stage. Thus instead of the traditional Western European/United States pattern of component firms developing parts in secrecy and then making the finished products available to the assemblers for incorporation into the final product, both sets of designs proceed iteratively and in tandem. Generally this involves the secondment of design staff from the assemblers to the primary component suppliers and vice versa. Fifth, when quality and other difficulties arise in production, the assemblers will provide (and often insist on) trouble-shooting teams to rectify the problems. The same pattern exists between primary and secondary, and between secondary and tertiary subcontractors. Sixth, the assemblers will often force strategic directions on suppliers or insist on regular reductions in price. Their power to do so partly arises from the long-term nature of these predominantly single-sourcing relationships. And, finally, each of the assemblers has developed a structure for coordinating the long-term strategic orientation of individual members of the Group as a whole. Toyota began this in the late 1930s with a Toyota Subcontractors Discussion Group (20 members), and this was expanded after the war. By 1983 they were grouped into two teams, one with 224 suppliers and the other with 57. All of the other manufacturers have established similar coordinating groups.

It is these features - linked to the complex pattern of inter-affiliate equity holdings - which provide this vertical chain of production with its <u>systemic</u> characteristics. When the system operates tightly, as it does in the case of Toyota, it assumes a quasi-organic character. In this, it is difficult to establish the contribution made by each single element of the chain, with the whole being more than the sum of the parts. The transfer to other countries therefore becomes much more difficult and it is not surprising that of the Japanese auto assemblers it has been Toyota which has been most

Table 4.14
JIT Performance of Japanese component firms

Firms	Product	In-Plant Inventory	Die Change Times	Subcontractors
1	Mufflers	1981 - 7-20 day stock of steel; 1984 - 2 day stock; 1985 - 1 day stock	1981 - 30 mins; 1984 - 15 mins; 4 times per shift	steel from supplier 1 hour away; delivered in 10 ton lots but could provide in 5 ton lots
2	Brake Cylinders	1981 - 7 day stocks of steel; 1984 - 1 day stocks; delivered 4 times/day		50 subcontractors
3	Brake Cylinder; disc and drumbrakes	current average for all inputs is 0.5 days plus 2 days for work-in-progress	1984 - 20 mins; changed 4 - 5 times per day	JIT parts delivery from all subcontractors, equivalent to 60% value added; subcontractor payment by mini computer
4	Variety of minor mechanical	4 days plus work-in progress; 10% improvement	1980 - 30-40 mins 1984 - 10 mins 1985 - 1 min with	150 suppliers; 50% within 10 miles

		and electronics products	annually; finished goods - 0.8-5 days; delivered to customers 1-2 times per hour to Toyota - once per day to Mitsubishi	automatic die changer; dies changed 5-10 times per day	
5	Radiators; fuel tanks; mufflers		1981 - 4-5 days 1984 - 1.5 days	1982 - 40 mins; dies changed once per day; 1984 - 25 mins; dies changed 2 times per day; 1985 - 18 mins	JIT delivery from parts suppliers
6	Brakes		1981 - 3-5 days average for all inputs; 1984 - 1 day down to 1.5 hours	1981 - large press 20-30 mins 1984 - large press 5 mins 1981 - small press 5-6 mins 1984 - small press 1 min die change 10 times per day.	subcontractors located 1.5 to 5 hours away

Source: Interviews

reluctant to venture abroad.

This pattern of supplier/assembler relationships is clearly distinct from that which had evolved in Western Europe and the United States. Nevertheless it is not an unchanging scheme, although whilst it continues to evolve, its systemic nature remains largely undiminished. Currently there are a number of factors which are inducing such changes, and since it is the components sector which is the primary focus of our empirical study, it is worth considering these in greater detail.

Before doing so, however, it is worthwhile to briefly draw attention to a subset of our findings here which demonstrate that the principles and procedures of JIT pervade the whole of the Japanese auto sector. As Table 4.14 shows, Japanese suppliers exhibit the same concern with inventory reduction, minimization of downtime and JIT delivery practices as do the auto firms themselves. Not shown in the table but readily apparent from our interviews, was a consistent concern on the part of the suppliers with maintaining and improving product quality. The firms visited all had somewhat different methods for checking the quality of their own products but the significant point is that most had defect rates of less than one percent. One firm, a producer of air conditioners, had a defect rate of 0.037 percent compared to the equivalent product produced in-house by GM which had a product defect rate of greater than one percent.34/ All the firms in turn expected equally stringent quality standards from their own subcontractors. All of this of course suggests an important lesson for the United States and Western European auto producers: if they are to succeed at JIT, the principles have to be pushed right through the entire supplier network.

STRUCTURE AND CHANGE IN THE JAPANESE COMPONENTS SECTOR

As noted earlier, the close cooperative relationship that has evolved over the years between Japanese auto firms and their component suppliers has been a key element in the overall success of the Japanese auto industry. The networks of organizational and financial ties that bind groups of suppliers to different assemblers have both directly observable and more implicit benefits to both sides. For the assembler, reliable suppliers able to provide consistently high quality and competitively priced parts are essential to the efficient functioning of JIT. Equity involvement with major suppliers not only gives the assembler an important role in influencing the supplier operations and management but also provides valuable insight into the supplier's technological capabilities. Moreover, the ability of the assembler to offer long-term and stable contractual terms gives it the leverage to extract a continuous round of improvements in price and productivity.

The supplier reaps considerable benefits from this arrangement as well. Output, investment and innovation strategies35/ can be planned in an environment where risks are minimized and where the guarantee of high volume sales has allowed the components industry to achieve scale economies. Moreover, the assembler provides a reliable source of managerial and technical assistance as well as offering access to financial support on good terms. This is especially valuable to the second- and third-tier suppliers.

There are, of course, drawbacks to both sides in this relationship. For the auto assemblers, the main disadvantage lies in the implicit "contract" between it and the supplier which constrains its room for manoeuvre during periods when demand is growing slowly or when the supplier is not performing to expected standards. Likewise, the supplier's fortunes are tightly tied to those of its major customer. Should these decline, the supplier cannot easily switch allegiances. Moreover, because of their general single-sourcing relationship, suppliers have often been prevented from developing a broad product range to the detriment of their international competitiveness. Assemblers have also used this dependence to force policies on their suppliers. For example Toyota insists on an annual decline in component prices (usually four-five percent) and Mazda was forcing one of its largest suppliers to adopt CAD and to upgrade its R&D.

Nevertheless, despite these drawbacks, it is clear that the unique mode of assembler-supplier relationship in Japan confers a substantial competitive advantage to the auto industry. It is this fact which has led the United States and Western European auto firms to vigorously pursue a fundamental restructuring of the supplier industry in an attempt to respond to the Japanese threat - and as a result their assembler-supplier relationships are currently in a considerable state of flux. However, though the Japanese components industry is not experiencing a similar degree of disruption,36/ our interviews identified two sets of pressures acting on the industry which are of particular interest to our concerns.

The first relates to the process of internationalization of production currently being pursued by Japanese auto firms in the United States and Western Europe. At one level, these moves - along with the restrictive trading regimes which provoked them - mean that by the end of the decade, domestic demand for components in Japan could be reduced considerably. This will significantly increase the level of domestic competition and force component firms to look to exports. At the same time, the larger Japanese component firms face a different challenge from these same forces - that of moving overseas in conjunction with their major customers. This element is of particular interest since this process will inevitably affect both the level and pattern of demand for offshore components flowing into the United States and Western Europe as well as influencing the international strategies of the component industry in these countries. This is an issue which we take up in much more detail in Chapter 7.

A second set of dynamic forces operating on the Japanese component firms are basically technological in nature. These arise from a combination of pressures - from the auto producers to improve quality, productivity and their product range; from competition between both domestic and foreign suppliers; and from the supply side "push" being generated by the wave of technological advances in electronics and new materials. Consequently, we found a clear trend among Japanese component firms towards an increasing degree of technological intensity in both process and product technology. Since these pressures are indicative of those affecting the components industry more widely (and which therefore can be expected to affect patterns of FDI and offshore sourcing), we shall explore these developments with reference to three issues: the shift towards flexible production automation; new products and increasing R&D intensity; and the implications for scale economies.

Flexible Production Automation

In Chapter 3 we suggested that in virtually every category of component - from generic items such as nuts and bolts produced in vast numbers to more complex engines and transmissions - there appeared to be a trend towards increasing complexity in both product or process technology. Among the component firms interviewed in Japan, we found a good deal of supporting evidence for this argument in the area of process technology. And what is particularly significant is that in a number of the cases, this was occurring in firms producing components which either by virtue of product simplicity or because of the labour-intensive process technology used previously, are arguably suitable for production in DCs.

One such case was that of a company 48 percent owned by Nissan and employing some 4,440 people. 37/ Its main product lines are in bulky, non-mechanical parts such as mufflers, radiators, and air conditioning units. Between 1979 and 1984, labour productivity at this firm grew rapidly - by 10-15 percent per annum - and much of this had been due to the introduction of a variety of flexible automation technologies which have replaced traditional labour-intensive techniques. Thus in the muffler shop (organized on a JIT basis) they have introduced a flexible transfer line and reorganized the assembly process into eight separate cells. On the line, 14 robots for welding and unloading, plus electronic controls for rapid adjustment of machine tool-settings have given the firm the necessary increase in flexibility to handle 30 different products. This move to increased flexibility via automation was essential because of the large variety of constantly changing products produced by the assemblers.

In addition to increased flexibility, the introduction of these new lines has been associated with a twofold increase in labour productivity, product quality has been vastly improved, and JIT performance has been measurably enhanced. 38/ Following this successful transition to electronically-controlled flexible production this firm plans to computerize its in-plant JIT system over the next four years. Hence we see here the same shift to computer-integrated manufacturing and production control as in Nissan, its parent firm.

Similar examples of the use of flexible automation were found among firms producing similar types of components. One firm, a small producer of fueltanks and a subcontractor to Mitsubishi, used a flexible, robotic painting system to paint 20 different types of fueltank on a JIT basis; and though not using robot welders in fueltank assembly, it had installed a 28 fixed-step robotic welder for rear-end assembly. Another company, a producer of dashboard instruments such as speedometers and tachometers, had also recently introduced automation technologies - an automatic die changer (allowing die change times of one minute), a new metal cutting line using six CNC machining centres, and - to partially replace the labour-intensive assembly of speedometers - a flexible assembly line capable of producing 50 different models, with a model changeover every 24 units, at a rate of three units per minute. Labour productivity improvement averaged 12-13 percent between 1975 and 1984, and in the last five, the use of automation technologies has become an increasingly important source of this, accounting for over 40 percent of total productivity improvement. Still another firm, a producer of car doors for Mazda, was set to move into a more extensive use of CAD equipment both for its own product designs and so that it can receive designs directly from Mazda for conversion into digitized NC tool and precision tool instructions.39/

Perhaps the best examples of the growing technological sophistication among component firms comes from two of the largest major suppliers to Toyota, Company A (with 8,000 employees) and Company B (with 27,000 employees). Both these firms have enjoyed a consistent growth in sales (between four and ten percent per annum since 1980), produce large numbers of components (up to 10,000 different types in the case of Company A) and have in place all the expected features of the Japanese system of production (JIT production and delivery, quality control circles, low downtime and high capacity utilization figures, etc.). Though there are differences in their relative strengths, both firms are committed to technological progress through the increasing use of flexible automation and computer-based control on the production side, the growing use of CAD in design, and rising investments in product R&D.

On the production side, both firm's exhibited a strong commitment to automation (which Company B claimed extended as far back as 20 years). In the early years this centered on the use of robots and NC tools in stand-alone applications to take over repetitive tasks and remove unpleasant work. In the last two to three years this pursuit of automation has begun to result in the introduction of flexible manufacturing systems. This is being driven by the need to maintain flexibility in the production of consistently high quality and frequently changing parts. In Table 4.15, we provide some data and information on the use of flexible machining and assembly lines by these firms.

There are a number of important points to make about the flexible manufacturing systems (FMSs)40/ described in the table and about the areas where the companies' views on

Table 4.15
Flexible Manufacturing Systems used by Two Japanese
Component Firms

Firm A - FMS for Brake Assembly at 40,000 units per month

	Old Line	FMS
Capital costs	3 x ¥30m	¥120m[a]
Workers	12	1[b]
Tooling	Same in both lines	
Energy	Same in both lines	
Index of Space	300	100
Number of product types	6	20

Firm B - FMS for Assembly of Speedometers

	Old Line	FMS
Number of lines[c]	3	1
Number of product types[d]	2-3	50
Workers[e]	30+	3
Capitals costs	Y100m	Y300m

Source: Interviews.

[a] Plus development costs associates with team of 4-5 people working 4-5 years
[b] Requires significant increase in maintenance personnel and capabilities
[c] FMS output equivalent to 3 old lines
[d] Adjustment from one model to another is triggered by dummy part inserted into line
[e] No extra maintenance personnel required

flexible automation reinforce each other. First, the differences in capital and labour productivity and output mix between the old and the new FMS lines is striking. Second, both of these firms considered that the primary contribution of the FMS lines had been to improve product quality and to substantially increase product mix flexibility. This was particularly crucial because it allowed them to continue to accommodate the now-continuous demands for product change coming from the assemblers.
Similarly, both of these firms either already had

computer-based production control systems in place or else were introducing them rapidly. They also felt that though first generation FMS lines tended to be expensive, in the future these would result in a reduction in plant-scale economies.41/ Firm A's views were particularly striking in this regard. It was now company policy that all new plants employ less than 1,000 workers (the current average) and be below a certain size limit (100,000 sq m). The ability to do this was based on assumptions about the rapid introduction of FMSs. It is also interesting to note that the intensity of work increases substantially with the use of FMS. Both firms felt that with FMS, they would be required to move to a two-shift day rather than the single-shift productions generally used with traditional labour-intensive lines.42/ This was necessary to maintain a high level of capacity utilization of the more investment-intensive FMS lines.

Firms A and B also exhibit some contrasting features which are worthwhile exploring further. Firm A had as comprehensive an approach to production automation as any of the assembly firms we visited. The FMS described in the table was in fact developed by the firm when it realized that the equipment offered by machinery suppliers was incapable of fulfilling its requirements. This system will soon be extended to all 128 assembly lines producing this product. In addition, the firm plans to extend the use of another FMS used in the assembly of brake-drums which offers three times the capacity of the line replaced, and uses only one worker instead of four. In 1985, seven of these FMSs were introduced, replacing 21 of the old lines. By 1989, the firm plans to expand its use of flexible manufacturing technologies into clutch and transmission assembly as well, thereby automating the assembly of approximately 70 percent of its products in the short space of seven years. The firm has also developed an FMS for machining families of brake parts which it feels is more advanced than anything else in the field since it involves not only automatic turret changes but can also machine both cast iron and aluminum.43/ In interviews, the point was made that their use of FMS gave them a considerable competitive edge over both foreign and Japanese competitors. They claimed that compared to their closest existing foreign competitor (a firm in the Federal Republic of Germany which they had visited), with the full implementation of its plans for the introduction of FMSs it would be able to produce five million components per month with 1,000 workers compared to the 10,000 workers the competitor firm currently required to produce the same level of output. In 1984 they supplied 100 percent of Toyota's needs and 50 percent of Mitsubishi's requirements.

Firm B, though using FMS and a large number of robots (200 in 1984 rising to 500 in 1987), did not in the course of our interviews demonstrate the same comprehensive approach to automation as did Firm A. On the process side, management laid emphasis, as noted above, on the continuing need for automation as a source of competitive strength. For instance, their general policy towards future growth is that sales are expected to increase by 10-20 percent annually with a stable labour force. This suggests a productivity increase of around 10 percent per annum, given inflation and the expectation on the part of its parent firm (Toyota) of a 5-6 percent annual decrease in selling prices. Automation is clearly expected to play a major role - yet unlike Firm A, the introduction of robots had not yet penetrated the assembly area. They also faced a fairly severe shortage of the production-engineering skills needed to design and implement automated production systems.

It needs to be borne in mind, that this trend towards flexible intra-sphere production automation have been preceded by continuous investment in "stand alone", intra-activity automation on the part of the Japanese component industry with a large number of firms shifting to the use of NC and CNC machines in the late 1960s and early 1970s. And as in the case of auto-assemblers, Watanabe's research found that the pace of introduction had increased considerably from the late 1970s onwards. In keeping with our findings, this occurred in response to three major sets of pressures - the need for greater production flexibility, and shorter product life and the demand of meeting the mixed production cycles of the assemblers on a JIT basis (one small supplier of electronics products had had to increase its product range from 1,200 to 2,000 within three years); because of continually growing demands for higher quality products from the assemblers that can only be met through the use of automation techniques; and because of a general expectation that wages would continue to rise relative to capital. This relates not only to the product precision and consistency that can be obtained, but also because NC tools and robots can be easily adapted for use in 100 percent piece-by-piece inspection procedures.[44]/

New Products and Increasing R&D Intensity

Concomitant with the above trends in production technology, the Japanese components firms have in recent years stepped up both the level of R&D investment and the pace and scope of their new product development efforts. One significant motivation for this is that Japanese assemblers now appear to be increasing the pressure on their suppliers to diversify away from total dependence, both on one customer and on auto-related products.

The underlying rationale from the assemblers point of view for urging suppliers to diversify and depart from their historic closeness to individual assemblers is that this induces technological improvement via competition and allows suppliers to reap scale economies more quickly. It also, obviously enough, reduces the burden of the close relationship on the assemblers themselves when the component supplier underperforms and this has been an especially important consideration in the context of the technology-deepening which is currently occurring in the component sector. Thus among the assembler firms interviewed two had adopted a policy of dual-sourcing wherever possible - for instance, one had four suppliers of steel, three airconditioner suppliers, two radiator suppliers, and so on. They argued that this did not undermine the fundamental strengths of single-sourcing in the Japanese system because often the second sources were only allowed a small share of total purchases and this forced their major suppliers to continue their efforts to upgrade their technological strength.45/

We have already mentioned the other major set of pressures operating on component firms - those arising from autonomous developments in new materials and electronics. Obviously these pressures are particularly strong in the electronics area where the powerful drive of the Japanese car firms towards the electronification of the car feeds back immediately to their demand for components. This sort of pressure has led most of the firms we interviewed to conclude that there were now very few "mature" auto components - and that the only way to remain competitive in product technology was by simultaneously increasing R&D and expanding the range of products on offer so that the cost of R&D could be spread out more evenly.

Though no reliable sectoral level data exists for R&D by firm size in the Japanese components industry, at least among the larger firms there has been a growth in R&D investment over time in recent years roughly in line with

Table 4.16
R&D as a Percentage of Sales for Two Large Japanese Component Firms, 1978-1984.

Year	Firm A	Firm B
	% of Sales	% of Sales
1978	4.8	
1979	5.0	2.7
1980	5.4	3.0
1981	5.5	3.2
1982	6.1	3.3
1983	5.9	3.7
1984	na	4.0

Source: Interviews.

that occurring in the vehicle manufacturers. This is borne out by Table 4.16 which shows trends in R&D as a share of sales for two of the largest component firms in Japan, denoted as Firms A and B above.

As the table shows, the share of R&D investment in these two firms has been rising steadily in recent years (and much more quickly than in the past) and both are committed to increasing the absolute and relative levels of R&D - in the case of Firm A the target for 1990 is seven percent and in firm B a doubling to eight percent by the same year. If so, this would put them above the United States Information Technology industry average of around six-seven percent.

This increase in R&D effort was mirrored by an increase in R&D among some of the smaller firms in our sample. Typically R&D in these firms has seldom exceeded 2 percent of sales. But as we shall see, there does appear to be a significant divergence between large and small firms in the proportion of resources being devoted to R&D.

Along with the growth of R&D expenditure, there is an equally important shift in the composition of the R&D effort and in the focus of product development. During the 1970s, much of the R&D among component firms was directed towards meeting United States and Japanese targets on exhaust emissions and in absorbing the effects of major structural and design shifts, such as the move away from rear-wheel to front-wheel drive. This focus has now almost entirely shifted towards accommodating the growing pressure for electronics and new materials. This trend is exemplified in the case of one of Toyota's largest component suppliers. In 1975 their R&D and product engineering staff stood at 2,800 (already large compared to non-Japanese firms), of which only 5.3 percent were electronics engineers. By 1983, this total had grown to 4,300 of which 16.3 percent were electronics engineers. Of the 300 graduates hired annually in recent years, 250 are engineers, amongst whom electronics and physics skills (that is, for work on new materials) are clearly of growing importance, with mechanical skills declining considerably.

As a result the firm's product line now contains a high percentage of electronics-based components. It produces its own LSI and CMOS microprocessors specifically designed for use in the harsh environment of automobiles which involve large temperature variations and vibrations, electrical interference and frequent voltage change and dirty operating conditions. It anticipates that electronics will come to be a key growth sector in the future in auto products where it expects sales to grow from ¥688.9bn in 1983 to ¥1 trillion by 1989. Electronics will lie at the heart of more integrated component systems, including communication between the car and its external environment and "head-up" display systems.46/ In another large firm, more than 1,200 engineers are involved in R&D on what the firm calls "mechatronics" - the development of a component system based on electronics that replace whole families of mechanical components as well as advanced product development in areas such as turbo-chargers and automatic transmissions. Some small firms showed a similar emphasis - in the case of one producer of minor mechanicals, 10 out of 20 product development engineers were working in the electronics area.

The shift to electronics is such that it is now clearly the most well established trend in product technology and is reflected in a simultaneous move towards the incorporation of systems within products (see Chapter 3). However, obviously enough, new product development efforts among the firms in our sample were not limited to this area alone - new materials, in particular, are increasingly the focus of R&D and product development efforts. Ceramics, plastics, new metal alloys and lighter and stronger composite materials were all featured in the development plans of our sample-firms and no doubt prevail among other Japanese firms as well. While the shift to electronics involves both product substitution and a significant degree of new product development, an important characteristic of new material related development is that these are overwhelmingly incorporated into substitution products - a trend that has led many of the firms interview to envision a particularly rapid rate of new material based product substitution towards the end of the decade. For instance, one firm, a producer of radiators and fuel tanks, expected to make a complete shift to the use of plastic and aluminum substitutes by 1988. Others in our sample were moving quickly into the use of composite materials and ceramics to substitute for metal-based engine and suspension components. Not only are these developments a clear indication of growing technological intensity among component firms, but they also underline the point made earlier that product technical change is increasingly moving into categories where developing countries had previously enjoyed both a genuine and a potential comparative advantage. It also will have effects on the nature of the assembly process since once products are molded they can incorporate a number of formerly discrete components and steps in assembly.

Yet another change taking place among Japanese component firms involves diversification from auto products into non-auto products.47/ This trend is still in its early phases and many component firms still depend overwhelmingly on auto related products. However, there are clear signs that Japanese component firms - responding to long term growth in competition on the domestic market and pressures for diversification from assemblers - are looking to non-auto products as a source of growth in the future. Among the examples from our interviews, one firm with a strong tradition in electronics has just entered into an agreement to produce printed circuit boards for a United States firm, Allen Bradley; another has invested heavily in the development of cryogenic coolers for industrial use; while for yet another its most rapidly growing market for all products is that for its automated toilets!

Implications for Plant and Firm-Level Scale Economies

The third set of trends we wish to highlight derive from the impact of the product and process related developments described above on plant and firm-level scale economies.48/ As we noted earlier in this chapter it appears that the product and plant economies of scale in vehicle assembly are declining due to the diffusion of CIM and flexible forms of organization. Our interviews among Japanese components firms added some support for this hypothesis though clearly there are important differences in trend. Not all firms or components are affected in this way. For instance, one of the component firms involved in the production of transmissions estimated the minimum economic scale for a new plant in the United States would be 250,000 units annually and involve an investment of $10m. This would be equivalent to the scale they now produce at in Japan. Another suggested that with the early generations of FMSs, investment costs - and therefore minimum plant size - had risen. However, both also acknowledged that in time these costs would decline.

Overall there was a general agreement among our sample firms that plant scale economies were coming down or were likely to be reduced in the future, particularly as flexible manufacturing technology matured. Here the data presented earlier (in Table 4.15) suggests clearly that for particular product types, FMS reduces plant sizes due to the substantial increase in labour productivity (resulting in fewer workers), lower space requirements and increased product mix capacity. One firm, a producer of mufflers and radiators calculated that in 1979 their plant size was double that of 1984, and produced a smaller volume. In addition their labour productivity has grown at 10-15 percent annually and their product mix has steadily increased - two trends which were only possible due to the introduction of flexible automation technologies. As noted above, Firm A (in Tables 4.15 and 4.16), is pursuing a rigorous policy that all new plants will employ less than 1,000 people and occupy physical space of less than 100,000 sq.m. compared to the current of 1,000+ employees per plant and a 185,000 sq.m. size average. The ability to do this, whilst simultaneously meeting the assemblers requirement of annual price reduction of four-six percent, is conditional upon the firm's plans to introduce flexible manufacturing systems.

For our concerns with FDI and the international division of labour a significant dimension of the scale effect relates to trends in firm-economies of scale. Since one of the sources of these scale economies are rising indirect costs of production (such as R&D) it is possible that the shift towards greater technological intensity have implications for firm size and thus for the type of firm likely to be able to compete internationally in the components industry in the future. Whilst the growing technological intensity is just beginning to pervade the industry it is difficult to draw clear conclusions in this regard.

Nevertheless, our interview results do suggest that this is the case. The growing importance of embodied technology as a determinant of firm-scale emerges very clearly from the evidence presented earlier which showed that component firms are being both pushed and pulled toward greater technological intensity in process and in product technology. Underlying this shift is the increasing importance of investment in R&D, a factor which in our sample stands out as one of the most crucial determinants of competitive success. We see in this growing technological intensity a repetition of the shift taking place within the Japanese auto-industry as a whole from a comparative advantage based on organizational factors to one with a much stronger base in embodied technology.

Within this shift, it also appears that by virtue of their size, capital resources, and closer relationships with final assemblers, the larger component firms are moving into areas of more sophisticated product and process technology where smaller firms are unable to follow. In the process area, this obviously implies a greater intensity of use of stand-alone intra-activity automation technologies as firms size increases (Table 4.17). Watanabe explains the significance of this phenomenon by arguing that automation technologies are not appropriate to activities and products of many small firms.49/ However an alternative explanation (which we believe to be correct) is that this trend in utilization demonstrates that the smaller Japanese firms are often simply not able to handle the demands of automation. They have been able to survive and even prosper in the recent past because of a rapidly expanding world market for Japanese cars and relatively stable process and product technology. Under conditions of slower market growth and the greater pressure from assemblers for the development of new and more complex products, the smaller component firms are likely to suffer adversely.

This conclusion emerges in a range of ways from our empirical results. One of the most graphic illustrations comes when we compare the radically different approaches adapted by a large and a small firm to brake-drum assembly. We have already shown in the discussions relating to Table 4.15, that one large firm interviewed is using a FMS to manufacture brakes requiring 1/12 of the labour, 1/3 of the

Table 4.17
Numerical Control Tools and Robots Installed by Japanese Component Firms, by Firm Size, 1983 (Units, Number of Employees)

	Number of Firms using Equipment	100-299	500-999	1000-4999	Over 5000	Total
NC Machines	20	5	104	289	759	1,156
Robots	21	11	172	270	190	909

Source: Adapted from Watanabe, (1984).

space and able to assemble nearly three times as many products as the traditional process. One the most striking features of this installation is that the brake-drums are assembled in dust-free rooms which workers enter into through air-locks, after having changed their shoes and donned all-white uniforms similar to those worn by workers in the electronics industry.

This situation compares dramatically with that of another much smaller firm where a more labour intensive assembly process is followed, under which work conditions are extremely pressurized and unpleasant, and which closely resembles the conditions recounted in Kamata's graphic description of labour conditions at Toyota in the early 1970s.50/ The use of FMS by this firm is ruled out for a variety of reasons, many of which have to do with scale related constraints on capital and skill availability. As Table 4.18 shows this firm has seen its rate of sales-growth decline significantly in recent years, which would be made more acute if inflation were taken into account. It has also seen a substantial reduction in sales per employee. We attribute both factors to its failure to invest in new embodied production and in product technology. Underpinning the large firm's use of FMS was a management commitment to being at the leading edge of process technology and in the event of the appropriate system not being available, there being also a willingness to commit the resources to underwrite the necessary R&D effort.51/ This option is not open to the smaller firm whose existence we believe, along with that of similar firms, is ultimately in doubt.

The significance of R&D goes beyond the ability to develop process innovation and extends importantly to the product side as well. Here with the current shift to new

Table 4.18
Rate of Growth of Sales per Employee in a Technologically
Laggard Small Japanese Manufacturer of Brakes, 1979 - 1984[a]

	1979/1980	1980/1981	1981/1982	1982/1983	1983/1984
Sales (¥m)	8,192	10,089	9.797	7.976	8,500
Sales 1979=100	100	124.4	119.4	97.4	103.8
No. of Employees	315	344	359	353	340
Employment Level (%) 1979=100	100	109.2	114.0	112.1	108
Sales per Person (¥)	26,005	29,330	27,290	22,595	25,000
Level of Sales per Person 1979=100	100	112.8	104.9	86.9	96.1

Source: Interviews.

[a] Financial year (April to March).

materials and systemic-electronics, product R&D capability is now seen by many of the firms interviewed as crucial to future competitiveness. As we shall see in the next two chapters, the shift to the greater use of externally designed and produced component systems currently taking place in the industry on a global level draws heavily on component firms' R&D capability. Even in relatively straightforward products like brakes where many developing country firms are hoping to succeed as exporters, the integrated nature of new braking systems means that assemblers and suppliers have to be jointly involved in design from an early stage, with the supplier able to carry more of the basic and detailed design burden than ever before. Thus the Japanese assemblers are continually pushing their suppliers to upgrade their technological

Table 4.19
Share of Production Value by Capital Classification of Japanese Auto Parts Firms, 1979-1983 (% of Total Production Sector)

Capital (Unit, million Yen)	1978	1979	1980	1981	1982	1983
0-99.9	10.16	10.10	10.18	10.25	10.35	9.44
100.0-999.9	34.00	32.40	30.00	29.40	27.70	28.50
10000.0-20000.0+	54.60	57.20	59.50	60.10	62.00	62.05

Source: Compiled from Japan Auto Parts Industries Association, Annual Statistics, 1984.

capabilities, especially their investment in R&D. In a number of cases in our sample, assemblers had either abandoned small suppliers, threatened to take over quality-control or placed firms under pressure in other ways because of their failure to upgrade their R&D effort. Large firms are responding - their average annual R&D expenditure has grown to 6 percent of sales in recent years while that of smaller firms has remained around 2.6 percent.

What our research suggests is that the existing implicit "contract" which has hitherto led assemblers and the primary component firms to keep small firms in business may not ultimately be able to protect smaller subcontractors from the growing pressures of increasing technological intensity. This therefore raises the question of whether the small firms will be able to survive in the future. Thus while Watanabe observed that the number of firms with less than 100 employees increased marginally in the last ten years, Table 4.19 (which shows trends in production value by size and by capital classification, a good proxy for technological intensity), demonstrates that the larger firms are clearly growing in significance.

* * *

In this chapter we have tried to do two things. The first was to demonstrate that the Japanese model of production organization is not static, but is evolving rapidly. The ultimate resting place of this process is not yet clear - what is clear however is that the competitive advantages of the organizational breakthroughs of the 1960s and 1970s are being consistently enhanced by an industry wide transition towards CIM. Together with a new pattern of relationships between firms locked in a vertical chain of production we have characterized this as reflecting the transition to a new era of production, systemofacture. Significantly this is being accompanied by a rise in the degree of technological intensity among component firms in which size and the level of innovative effort (in both product and process) are playing a growing role in determining competitiveness.

From the point of view of our concern with the TNC and the NIDL, the significance of these trends within the Japanese domestic industry does not lie in their direct implications on the sourcing decisions of Japanese auto firms for their plants in Japan. Components for these plants, as we shall show in Chapter 7, have always been supplied by Japan-based suppliers and will probably continue to be so in the future. Rather the implications are different and relate to wider, global dimensions. One of the most obvious of these indirect implications is that the evolving Japanese model is setting best-practice standards for the world industry, which if successfully replicated by others, could lead to substantial changes in the pattern and determinants of sourcing and of FDI. Moreover, and as we shall also consider in later chapters, the pressures that are pushing Japanese vehicle builders and component firms towards a more internationalized production base, could in fact lead them into FDI in industrially advanced countries on a scale that was unthinkable only five years ago. We turn now to explore these and other developments in Chapters 5-7.

NOTES

1. It is interesting to note that the head of R&D at Volkswagen/Audi believes that the Western European industry had much more to fear from Japanese manufacturing

technology than from its product technology.

2. This difference in approach is carefully documented in Cusumano (1985).

3. Altshuler et al 1984).

4. Cusumano (1985) p. 186.

5. See and Altshuler et al (1984) and Cusumano (1985) for a discussion of the complexities of this problem.

6. On average and including overtime, between 1965 and 1983, Japanese auto workers worked 10 percent longer than their American equivalents (Cusumano, 1985, p. 198).

7. This table is drawn from Cusumano's detailed study. Altshuler et al (1984) provide much higher estimates of the differences in relative labour-productivity performance between 1970 and 1981, but these are not adjusted to take account of the factors considered in Cusumano's comparison. Altshuler et als' figures also include estimates for the Federal Republic of Germany which show a largely static labour-productivity between 1977 and 1981.

8. See Cusumano (1985) p. 271.

9. This procedure is clearly explained in Schonberger (1982).

10. For a description of the Kanban system see Schonberger (1982) and Cusumano (1985).

11. These latter figures are drawn from Cusumano (1985) p. 301.

12. This may of course be a reflection of the fact that the assemblers who arranged these visits to suppliers tended to allow us to only see the better firms. However, in the course of these visits we also observed component firms who were at the edge of profitability and seemed unlikely to survive in their existing form. This suggests that we saw a biased, rather than an exclusive, sample of firms.

13. The lower price of many components available from Japan vis a vis _all_ other countries is another - a lower price that derives not just from lower unit labour costs but from greater efficiency.

14. Cusumano (1985) p. 335.

15. Figures from Inagami (1984) and Cusumano (1985).

16. By the late 1970s the significance of this had begun to penetrate United States industry. A comparison of breakdowns per rental car in the first 12,000 miles of operation in 1977 showed a rate of 3 to 4 for United States cars, and .55 for Toyotas. Such startling figures were used ideologically by United States management in an attempt to change established procedures. See Wantuck (undated).

17. Taylor (1903) pp. 98-9.
18. Freeman (1984).
19. See Kaplinsky (forthcoming) for a more detailed discussion of the total nature of technical change in the new paradigm.
20. Watanabe (1984).
21. Baba (1985).
22. The Toyota Crown (available in 10,000 varieties) could, for instance, be fitted with 80 different types of fender.
23. Cusumano (1985).
24. By "advanced" we refer to robots with playback, numerical control and/or "intelligent" features rather than the much more numerous manual manipulators, fixed and variable sequence robots.
25. Out of 216 used throughout the plant, and 1500 for Nissan as a whole.
26. A similar system is in operation at their Zama plant.
27. Which are received at the beginning of the planning cycle via computer-to-computer links.
28. Some companies are ahead of Nissan on this count. For instance, the average component delivery rate at Toyota is four times per day; the most frequent deliveries come from Nippondenso who deliver 16 times a day and the least frequent delivery is once per day (though some small components are delivered weekly). Nissan's comparatively poor showing in this area may be linked to the geographical factors discussed above.
29. This is modeled on Toyota's much commented upon "Kanban" system.
30. Honda's Suzuki plant and Subaru's Gumma plant, though not visited, are understood to make even more advanced use of assembly robots than the Mitsubishi or Nissan plants described in this chapter.
31. In 1983 the Mitsui Bank was the largest shareholder (5.1 percent), followed by the Tokai and the Sanwa Banks (each with 5 percent). Next came the Toyota Automatic Loom Works, the original founder of the company with only 4.3 percent.
32. The Industrial Bank (6.1 percent), Dai-Ichi Mutual Life (5.4 percent), Swiss Credit Bank (5.3 percent) and Fuji bank (4 percent).
33. Dodwell (1983).
34. In fact they had just been visited the week before by a representative of a GM component firm who had "boasted" that after a sustained quality-enhancement

campaign, they had just managed to reduce defects to around one percent.

35. For instance, Mitsubishi and Nippon Steel are collabourating closely in R&D work on rust inhibition. This requires Mitsubishi to provide this supplier with early details of their model designs to facilitate Nippon's R&D efforts. In turn Mitsubishi necessarily has to have the confidence that Nippon will not pass on these designs to competitors. It is interesting to note that where Mitsubishi works with foreign suppliers, this confidentiality is formalized in a contract.

36. Because they already enjoy the organizational relationships with the assemblers that are necessary for best-practice.

37. This firm also has two United States subsidiaries involved in the production of air conditioners, and it has exported its product technology to Thailand (radiators), Mexico (mufflers) and Taiwan Province (air conditioners).

38. See Table 4.14 (first entry) for details of their JIT performance and for other firms described in this section.

39. This is behind much current practice in the non-Japanese auto industry. As we have already noted the Japanese industry has been relatively slow to take-up CAD technology. This may be because CAD involves writing as well as numbers and lines. Japanese orthography is particularly difficult, with over 1,800 characters required to read a simple newspaper. It is this which also explains the relatively slow adoption of word-processing in Japan as well as the correspondingly rapid uptake of fax technology (see Kaplinsky 1987)

40. Flexible Manufacturing Systems are considered in the most rudimentary sense, here, to refer to the ability to change production specifications automatically. This does not necessarily imply that all of these systems incorporated reprogrammable CNC machinery at all stages - in some cases machine specifications could be reset with mechanical devices. The general trend however was to incorporate CNC control systems.

41. This view was echoed by another firm in the sample who claimed that where its minimum economies of scale producing mufflers was now 10,000 per month using FMS, five years ago the minimum efficient level of output would have been twice this level.

42. This creates unusual problems for the Japanese industry. When the labour market was tight in the early 1980s the auto industry was forced to make increasing

utilization of female labour. But Japanese law prohibits women working during the night. Thus many firms were forced to utilize single-shift working even though they would have preferred to operate on a dual-shift basis.

43. Developing this system required a team of five engineers and R&D staff working for two years.

44. Watanabe, (1984).

45. This point is also made in Dodwell (1983).

46. Head-up displays - a technology initially developed for fighter aircraft - involve the reflection of important information on to the driver's screen so that the driver does not have to take his/her eyes off the road to read relevant information from the dashboard.

47. See, also, Dodwell (1983).

48. There is considerable confusion surrounding the concept of scale economies in production. Not only do plant-, product- and firm-economies of scale need to be separated, but there is the ancillary difficulty with each of these elements of scale themselves. Is plant size to be measured by physical parameters, by the number of workers, by the volume of production or by its cost? In the discussion which follows all of these various elements of change are considered. See Kaplinsky (1986) for a discussion of these issues and for the sources of these changes in economies of scale.

49. Watanabe (1984).

50. Kamata (1982).

51. In fact, given the long-term commitment to the development of these automation technologies the incremental resources required for this development in brake-drum manufacture were slight, in the order of 4-5 people over 4-5 years.

5

Technological Transformation Among the United States and Western European Motor Vehicle Assemblers

In a seminal study of the United States automobile industry in 1978, Abernathy pointed to what he saw as the major productivity dilemma characterizing the industry at that time.1/ Having adopted a product cycle perspective over the decades which viewed the automobile as a mature product, the industry saw itself as being faced with a trade-off between product instability and process efficiency. The roots of the dilemma lay, as we have seen, in the particular strategies adopted by the United States auto producers, especially in the decades after World War II. Given the logic of this approach, the United States industry was characterized by fierce price competition within the context of product standardization. Whilst the primary focus of technical change was process technology, this too had atrophied and tended to be limited to the fine-tuning of the Fordist supply-driven mass production system. The ideology of much-heralded model changes had in fact degenerated into a series of minor product-differentiating face-lifts. The industry thus believed the economics of mass production to be immutable, and this competitive strategy thus allowed little room for genuine product diversification or major process innovation. This myopia was reinforced by a view (common in the early 1970s) that concentration levels in the industry would continue to rise at the world level leaving only a handful of giants surviving into the 1980s. Explicit in this was an expectation that production would gravitate to low-wage sites in the developing world, mostly controlled by TNCs. Only in components was it conceivable that indigenous firms would also become exporters.

The falsity of this dichotomy was revealed in the 1960s by the international success of the Western European industry which demonstrated that a significant degree of comparative advantage could be built upon a sophisticated and diverse product technology, allied to low-cost process technology and Western Europe's own version of the mass production techniques it had earlier absorbed from the United States. And even as the United States industry began to formulate a partial response to the Western European threat by "downsizing" its model range, the final nails in the coffin of the Fordist labour process began to be hammered home by the rapid Japanese penetration of international markets in the mid-to-late 1970s.

As the full scale of the Japanese threat emerged (within the context of recession and slow growth in demand), United States and Western European auto firms responded in a variety of ways, and a number of strategies have unfolded over the past two decades. The first and still major line of defense adopted (see Chapter 3) was to retreat behind protectionist barriers, at levels reminiscent of the inter-war period. The second short-lived response was the idea of the "world car", a strategy primarily adopted by the United States producers. Its intent was to spread heavy design and development costs by producing virtually the same car in a number of markets. A logical extension of this strategy was to globalize production rather than design and development. This extended the Fordist conception of standardized products to the global level and attempted to attain scale economies in component and vehicle manufacture by locating production wherever unit costs could be minimized. As we shall show, the logical extension of this notion is still being pursued in the present period through the search for low-cost offshore component suppliers and the overseas sourcing of smaller vehicles.

Another, and partial, response has been to concentrate on the opportunities offered by the diffusion of microelectronics into capital goods, a phenomenon which began to offer substantial productivity-gains after the mid-1970s. Most of the Western European and United States producers decided that these new electronics-based automation technologies - together with developments in materials technology - offered significant opportunities for cost reduction and enhanced product competitiveness. As a consequence, there has, since the beginning of this decade, been a rapid acceleration in the pace of process and product technological change underwritten by an enormous surge in new capital investment and R&D expenditure. Where individual firms have not been able to afford the large investments in technology and R&D, joint ventures and other forms of collaboration have been formed with erstwhile rivals.

Subsequently, and most recently, the auto producers appear also to be attempting to introduce a series of organizational changes that are modelled on their perception of the Japanese model. This includes the introduction of JIT and closer relations with suppliers and the use of quality circles and statistical process control (SPC). These organizational changes are being pushed through in conjunction with the technological initiatives noted above. Little attention has been placed so far on a thorough-going absorption of the new labour process described in Chapters 2 and 3.

However, judging from the scale of new technology-related investment, it is clear that the strategy of technological transformation became the core component of the United States and Western European industries' restructuring in the 1980s. Moreover, despite their declared intent of learning from this Japanese schema of organization, some of the major producers are simultaneously pursuing locational policies (premised on the search for price-competitiveness, rather than product innovation) which directly contradict the lessons to be absorbed from the Japanese experience.

Each of these strategies has important implications for the offshore sourcing of components, and therefore for the incorporation of developing countries in the international division of labour. Protectionism - especially when it incorporates local-content legislation - clearly makes such a strategy difficult to pursue. So, too, does the logic of the Japanese model which is premised on low inventories, locational proximity and close interelations between firms. Technological transformation in itself does not relate directly to sourcing-strategies, but insofar as it leads to a significant reduction in the importance of labour as an input into production, it, too, will probably militate against significant offshore sourcing. By contrast the global-sourcing strategy explicitly plans for greater third-world production, both of finished vehicles and of individual components. But if this strategy is associated with a failure of the technological response to stem the tide of Japanese competitiveness then the combined weight of Japanese imports and their drive for (protection-induced) production in the United States and Western Europe could result in a declining market share for domestic producers. This would reduce the extent of their offshore sourcing whatever strategy they adopted, simply because it would reduce their output of automobiles.

The critical technology-related factors that will therefore determine the level and nature of demand for offshore components in both the short and the long term are the scale of new investment being made by vehicle producers; the pace at which these investments are taking place; the time-frame within which their effects on productivity will be felt; the extent to which new machinery substitutes for labour; and perhaps most importantly, the extent to which Western European and United States firms are able to successfully introduce both the technological and the organizational components of systemofacture.

As it is the technological response which has been dominant since the early 1980s, through the rest of this chapter we shall be examining various dimensions of the role that technological change is playing as the central strategy in the restructuring process being pursued by Western European and United States auto producers. In Section 1, we discuss the main trends in both process- and product-related technical change now present in the United States and Western Europe. Section 2 puts flesh to this general picture by focussing briefly on the technological strategies adopted by a few individual producers and putting this in the context of other strategies which are being simultaneously pursued. Section 3 concludes the discussion by speculating on the effect which these technological developments are likely to have on the overall competitiveness of the United States and Western Europe industries.

THE SEARCH FOR A TECHNOLOGICAL SOLUTION
TO DIMINISHING COMPETITIVENESS

The central component of the strategy adopted by the major United States and Western European producers to confront the "Japanese challenge" is the adoption of radically-new process and product technologies. The pervasiveness of this response is illustrated in Figure 5.1 which maps out the levels of technological change in the auto industry. This usefully illustrates a number of important points. First, there are various dimensions to technological change not only in relation to different categories (that is in product, process and materials

185

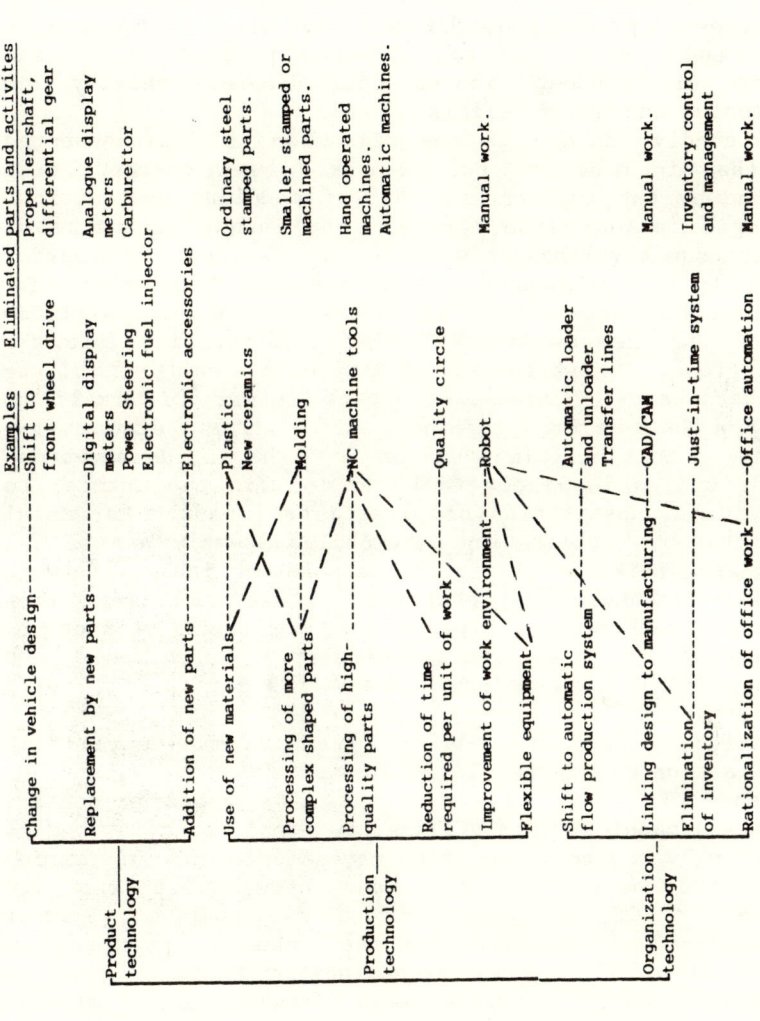

Source: Adapted from Watanabe (1986)

Figure 5.1 Recent Technological Changes in the Japanese Automobile Industry

technology), but in qualitative terms as well. Although there is always a mixture of radical and incremental technological advance occurring simultaneously in most industries, the balance in the auto industry at the present time lies clearly in the direction of radical change.2/ This is to be seen in a rush to increase the level of automation in production, the extensive use of computers in design and overall control and the pursuit of a wide variety of product innovations drawing heavily on electronics and new materials.

Secondly, change in one dimension is interconnected with that in others. For example, a new concept being absorbed by the industry is that of modular construction. Its logic follows from the inherent labour intensity of current assembly lines as well as the growing technological complexity of the product. The essential feature is that instead of a large number of discrete components arriving serially on the assembly line for incorporation into the final product - which is traditionally built from the outside inwards - assembly in the future is likely to involve the mating together of modules drawn from suppliers, thus building the car from the inside outwards. Modular design is likely to be allied (in the future) to the partial substitution of plastic body panels for metal ones, thereby facilitating automobile assembly as well as repair. There is therefore a close linkage between materials technology (plastics), process technology (new assembly techniques), product technology (interiors redesigned to facilitate modular production) and organizational technology (new relationships with suppliers).

Thirdly, as is well-evidenced from Figure 5.1, microelectronics figures large in each of these dimensions of change. It is incorporated in capital goods to control of process machinery, is utilized in final products, and is increasingly central to the management of information within the assembling firm and between it and its suppliers. Of course there are many other types of technological change affecting the industry, particularly in the realm of product technology with such items as continuously variable transmission, dieselization, emission reduction, four-wheel drive, greater fuel efficiency and 'intelligent' navigational systems. But none approaches the pervasiveness of electronics, which is anyway a key enabling technology in each of the aforementioned innovations.

The Scale and Scope of Investments in New Production Technology

Western European and United States motor vehicle producers are in the midst of one of the largest capital investment programs ever undertaken at any time in any industry. Taken together, (and depending on whose estimates you believe) the leading motor vehicle manufacturers in the United States and Western Europe will have spent in excess of $100bn on new plant and equipment in the decade after 1975 when they first began to respond to the Japanese challenge. Scale is not the only significant feature of this investment program for its nature and orientation is fundamentally different from past capital investment expenditure. During the late 1970s, much of the investment in new plant coincided with the need to retool fixed production lines to produce new models and in particular, to accommodate the shift from rear-wheel drive to front-wheel drive. This reflected the dominant post-war trend towards ever greater levels of dedicated automation to produce high volumes of a standard product.

In the current phase of investment - beginning around 1983 - the emphasis has shifted to flexible automation (which given the preoccupation with machinery rather than organization is not the same as flexible production - see Chapter 2). Based around the extensive use of CAD, CNC machine tools, programmable robots, automated material handling systems, automatic testing equipment and, ultimately, FMS it represents not only a major initiative but a fundamental transition from the previous preoccupation with dedicated production. When operating successfully, this technology will not only offer reduced product- and plant- scale economies, but it will also provide manufacturers with the capacity to both produce for niches in the market and to switch models quickly in response to changing demand, at a much lower changeover cost. Even though Japanese producers may be ahead in many areas, there can be little doubt that automation in the Western European and United States assemblers has now transformed many of the stamping, welding, painting and machining operations, and is being extended (albeit at a slower pace) into the assembly of components, sub-assemblies and the final vehicle. Similarly, the advantages of CAD are being aggressively explored to reduce the time taken up in the design/engineering/prototype phase and thus to enhance the designer's capability to seek optimum, cost-effective solutions. In the area of computer-based integration between design and production, it appears as if Western European and United States producers may be equal to, if not somewhat ahead of the Japanese.

In Western Europe the three leading volume-producers - VW, Fiat and Renault - are now each investing annually more than $1bn introducing new production technologies, with Peugeot and RG not far behind. It is estimated that through the 1980s they will have invested well over $50bn. Compared to the United States a proportionately greater share will have been directed to product technology, partly because this is the forte of the Western European industry and partly because the average age of the Western European capital stock was lower than that of the United States producers. However, despite the record levels of investment, it needs to be remembered that the Western European volume car producers have been operating under severe financial constraints as a result of five years of overall net losses and the continuing burden of substantial overcapacity. Though VW and Fiat are now relatively healthy financially (and can thus afford the scale of investment mentioned above), others such as Renault and RG still face difficulties. These, as much as any other factor, are influencing the pace at which they can pursue increased competitiveness through new technology.

But it is in the United States that the largest investments have been made in an almost frenzied response to the loss of market-share by domestic producers. GM's investment program has been averaging $6-7bn per year over the last five years and it plans to increase this to more than $7 bn annually in the future. Ford has been maintaining a $3-4bn annual expenditure rate and though it expects this to dip slightly in the future, even this level will still be well above what they were spending in earlier years. Chrysler, so far financially constrained from pursuing the same scale of investment as the other two giants, has nevertheless, recently announced plan to increase its capital investment program to $1-3bn per year over the next five years. By the end of the decade, therefore, virtually none of the United States industry's 255 domestic plants (including 47 engine and transmission facilities and 89 assembly plants) will have been left untouched in this drive to rebuild, retool and re-equip. Table 5.1. shows this trend clearly. Whereas until the mid-1970s investment had been running at well below $5bn a year, it subsequently rose sharply, exceeding $10bn annually between 1979-1982, falling back slightly in 1983,

Table 5.1
Capital and R & D Expenditures for United States Auto Firms, 1975-1985 ($ billion)

	1975	1976	1977	1978	1979	1980	1981	1982	1983	1984	1975-84
Capital Expenditures	2,156	2,471	4,540	5,766	6,888	7,311	7,761	6,795	5,125	6,980	55,793
Research Development	1,245	1,656	1,890	2,217	3,414	3,418	3,554	3,600	4,034	4,700	29,726
TOTAL	3,401	4,127	6,430	7,983	10,302	10,729	11,315	10,395	9,159	11,680	85,521

Source: Adapted from USITC, 1985

and then moving ahead to reach new record levels of more than $11bn in 1984 and 1985. Also indicated in Table 5.1 is the growing emphasis on R&D. Whereas its share of the total was 35.8 percent for the whole period and 35 percent in 1982, it rose to 44 percent in 1983 and 67 percent in 1984.

All of the projects reflect the same general shift noted in Western Europe towards higher levels of automation, greater utilization of CAD, growing computerized control of in-plant production and increased flexibility. However, unlike Western Europe where final assembly is receiving the greatest share of investment in new technology, there is a roughly equal emphasis in the United States on upgrading metal-working facilities such as stamping plants. The character of the investment that is going into final assembly (still sizable in absolute terms) is, moreover, probably slightly less advanced overall than in Western Europe, both in terms of the range of assembly tasks being automated, and in terms of the degree of computer-integrated production control being introduced. The same is true in the area of flexibility on the final assembly line but as with Western Europe, there is no mixed production equivalent to the Nissan and Mazda factories in Japan described in the previous chapter. Table 5.2 summarises the characteristics of a select set of recent investments in new process technology (including CAD systems) at the plant-level by United States and Western European auto producers.

However, though the United States and Western Europe are reasonably close in terms of state of the art process-technology, because of their greater resources the United States firms tend to engage in more "leading edge" experimentation than the Western European and perhaps even most Japanese firms. We shall review GM's strategy below, but three types of leading edge project common to the industry should be mentioned here. GM and Ford (though not Chrysler) are both pursuing an aggressive takeover/joint venture strategy with regard to high-tech information technologies. In the case of GM's purchase of Electronic Data Systems (EDS) and Hughes these acquisitions reflect a strategy of partial diversification. However, especially in the case of EDS which has a specialized capability in centralizing data bases and linking different electronic devices together, they also feed-in to the grander program of CIM. Not only is this the case for centralizing data bases and inter-machine communication, but it is also planned to facilitate a much more rapid introduction of advanced technologies such as vision and artificial intelligence systems in assembly robots. Some of these recent acquisitions are listed in Table 5.3.

In a drive to enable this transition to CIM, spearheaded by GM but now also including Ford and Chrysler, the United States auto industry is moving rapidly towards the adoption of a standardized protocol for machine-to-machine communication between computer-based devices used on the factory floor, in technical facilities and in offices. This represents two major initiatives. The first - termed Manufacturing-Automation-Protocol (MAP) - focuses on linking individual machines, or groups of machines together and was initiated by GM. The second - Technical Office Protocol (TOP) - results from a collaboration between GM and Boeing (the aerospace manufacturer which is also an intensive generator of information) and relates to the control and transfer of information in the office environment. These moves represent an unusual industry-wide attempt to facilitate computer-based integration and flexibility in the design, machinofacturing and co-ordination spheres (which together represent one of the three central pillars of systemofacture - see Chapter 2). GM was spurred to take action in this direction in the early 1980s after it realized that many of the computer-based systems being installed in its factories, design centres and offices could not communicate with each other from within the same buildings let alone between different locations. The company has used its very considerable purchasing power to force auto industry vendors of computer systems and automation technology to agree to supply their equipment with a MAP and TOP facility.

GM has now been joined in its endorsements of MAP and TOP by almost all of the auto industry and most firms in the the automation and computer industries, both in North America and more recently in Western Europe and Japan. (The United States is currently well ahead of the Japanese and Western European industry in introducing data-handling systems).3/ Though still at an early stage of diffusion, both MAP and TOP are now accepted - at least in principle - by many firms in the industry. And, though there are still mainly technical, organizational and commercial hurdles to be overcome, the industry has now demonstrated a strong commitment to pushing the protocols through as quickly as possible. Once in place, MAP and TOP will play a key role as an integrator of the different elements of systemofacture and provide empirical justification of the shift of the industry to the new systemic technologies.

Table 5.2
Selected Investments in Automation by United States and Western European Component Firms

Company	Product	Type of Automation	Cost	Comments
Ford	Engineer and Transmission for Taurus and Sable	Extensive flexible machining; LAN with 650 linked devices; AGVs for parts delivery; computer monitoring of production and quality parts delivery.	$700m	No repair bays. Daily JIT parts delivery. Modular assembly.
Chrysler	Chrysler Le Baron and Dodge Lancer	101 robots for welding, sealing, painting, material handling, urethane and hot melt glue applications; 162 laser vision inspection machines. Extensive computer monitoring of production via 600 data capture devices, CAD/CAM	$325	75% of suppliers within 400 miles. 70% of daily delivery on JIT basis.
GM	Oldsmobile Toronado and Cadillac Elderado	Robogate system (80 welds performed by 10 robots at 48 second cycle time); 2,000 programmable devices including 260 robots; 50 AGVs; laser vision inspection	$600m	JIT delivery on 7 hour basis is planned. Repairs done on line so no repair bays.

GM Canada	aluminium radiators		$45m
	suspension systems	All involving the use of extensive automation.	$23.7m
	stamping		$230m
	truck assembly		$550m
	car assembly		$220m
Volkswagen	Golf II	250 robots for select and fit of battery, bumpers, fanbelt, wheels, engine and interior assembly. Computerized production and inventory control. Electronic scanner for automated part delivery via AGVs. Off-line automated assembly of 14 sub-systems.	$385m on plant: $770m on design and production engineering.

Source: Interviews and Trade Journals

Table 5.3
GM and Ford Affiliated Leading-Edge Companies

GM			
Applied Intelligent Systems Inc	Ann Arbor, Mich.	Machine Vision	12.6% for under $5m. Warrants for additional 17.4% by 1989. R&D funding not released.
Automatix Inc	Billerica, Mass.	Machine Vision	Option for 5% at $10 per share or the market price, whichever is lower, for $3.7m investment. Option for an additional 10%. R&D funding of 9.8m.
Diffracto Ltd	Windsor, Ont.	Machine Vision	15% for $5.6m. Warrants for an additional 15% for $6m. R&D funding of $7.5m.
GMF Robotics	Troy, Mich.	Robots Machine Vision	Joint venture of GM and Fanuc Ltd. Initial investment of $5m from each.
Robotic Vision Systems Inc	Hauppage, N.Y.	Machine Vision	18% for $8.9million. Warrants for an additional 12% for $10.9m. R&D funding of $3.9m.

Teknowledge Inc	Palo Alto, Cal.	Expert Systems	$4.05m for 11%. R&D funding.
View Engineering	Simi Valley, Cal.	Machine Vision	20% for undisclosed amount. R&D funding
Ford			
American Robot Corp	Pittsburg, Pa.	Machine Vision, Robots, Computer-Integrated Manufacturing	$20m investment for an estimated 15% in equity and for R&D funding.
Carnegie Group Inc	Pittsburg, Pa.	Expert Systems	$14m for 10% in equity, development contracts and technology agreements.
Inference Corp	Los Angeles Cal.	Expert Systems	$14m for 10% in equity, development contracts and technology agreements.
Measurex Corp	Cupertino Cal.	Computer-Integrated	No equity stake, $7.2m for three years in software development. $3.8m in pilot program hardware toward joint computer integrated manufacturing systems for Ford Body and Assembly Operations
Synthetic Visions	Ann Arbor, Mich.	Machine Vision	$3.8m for 17%

Source: *Automotive News*, February 1986. Reprinted by permission.

A third leading-edge strategy which the big three United States firms all have in common are the so called "clean sheet" projects by which they intend to launch an entirely new range of small compact cars that will be directly competitive with the Japanese. Termed Saturn in the case of GM, Alpha for Ford and Liberty for Chrysler, the key features of these projects are that the cars will be domestically produced on greenfield sites in highly integrated plants that allegedly will incorporate leading-edge process and product technologies. The aims of these projects are twofold. The first is to provide a specific project-focus within which the companies can explore leading-edge process and product technology for use on a wider scale. The second is to allow United States firms to recapture the small car segment of the market by means of technological leapfrogging. None of these plants will be in substantive production until the end of the decade so it is too early to judge their merits. However, given the intense interest these projects have generated, we report our research findings in relation to GM's Saturn project in more detail in the next section.

Despite the fact that United States firms all seem to be moving in more or less the same direction *vis a vis* new technology, there are differences in strategy and emphasis. Chrysler, by virtue of its more limited resources, has been forced to be more conservative in its plans. In particular, it has not been able to pursue a vigorous investment program in the area of stamping where it was only able to invest $120m in new stamping technology in 1986, equivalent to re-equipping only 20 percent of its capacity. Interestingly though, this has not prevented the company from achieving the best performance in terms of improving productivity. Nevertheless, the company has (as noted earlier) announced plans to re-equip all existing plants with best-practice process technology by 1990 and indeed in the hype characteristic of the industry, the company claims that by 1988 the Chrysler Assembly Division will be "the most sophisticated car producing entity in the world".4/ Since Chrysler outsources a much higher level of components (70 percent on average) than either GM or Ford, the company may well be able to approach this objective because it will be able to concentrate its investment on the core areas of final assembly and stamping to a much greater extent than its two competitors who have to support investment programs in their larger numbers of in-house component firms.5/

Ford, as also noted above, has a considerable program

of investment in new technology. For example, the company invested $1.2bn in new tools and facilities to build a new engine and transmission for its Taurus and Sable lines. In addition, it is in the middle of re-equipping all 15 of its stamping lines, but because the average cost per line is about $50 - 200m, this is a slow process. For instance, only three lines were refurbished in 1984. However, it has ordered ten FMS lines for its United States and Western European drive-train plants, but since achieving flexibility via FMS is expensive, these systems will only be used for work on higher priced models.

Perhaps more notable, Ford has coupled its investment program with a strong commitment to a new manufacturing philosophy that is explicitly modelled on the lessons it claims to be learning from the Japanese. In the early 1980s it adopted a global "after Japan" (AJ) corporate policy. Recent analysis has suggested that Ford is much further advanced in this regard than other United States firms.6/ The evidence for this comes from various dimensions. For instance, Ford's quality ratings have improved significantly in recent years due to its adoption of Japanese concerns with total quality and defect prevention; on the quality side, overall improvement in terms of the percentage of cases that come off the line with what is known in the trade as "first time" quality is up from 60 to 90 percent in three years. This means fewer repairs, much smaller reworking bays in the plant and lower maintenance costs during the car's life. The company's pursuit of a strategy emphasising defect prevention via the extensive use of SPC techniques and preventive maintenance has allowed all final inspection to be eliminated from some of its plants. This emphasis on quality is working through to the productivity side as well where assembly productivity rose by 35 percent between 1982 and 1984. The company's Wayne assembly plant is considered to be one of the most efficient in the United States, able to assemble a Ranger pickup with 50 percent fewer person-hours than GM takes to make a similar product. Most of these gains have not been accounted for by automation, but by improvements in organization, schedule-stability, inventory reduction, higher capacity utilization, shorter die change times and greater use of JIT methods. JIT is similarly used at the Lima engine plant described above where it has also virtually eliminated repair bays with the company adopting the Japanese approach of relying on zero defect components and being prepared to completely shut down the line if repairs are needed. Indeed Ford is acknowledged to be well ahead of GM and Chrysler in terms of the introduction of JIT within the plants.

GM, of course, stands in a category on its own since the distinctive feature of its strategy is that it has the financial resources at its disposal to seemingly do everything coterminously - an aspect which has led some commentators to suggest that this is because it does not actually have a strategy, but is only throwing money at the problems it faces. This may be true. Nevertheless, the sheer scale, tempo and scope of GM's investment program is such that it will have an inordinate impact throughout the sector and therefore it deserves a more detailed discussion - one that we undertake below for it and two other firms.

Product Innovation: From External
Pressure to Internal Momentum

During the 1970s, the major impetus for product innovation in the motor vehicle industry arose from the external operating environment. The impact of the two energy price rises and the rapid imposition of air-quality mandates meant that the industry was quickly forced to bring into production a variety of product innovations that had actually been on the shelf for some time - diesels-engines, catalytic converters, fuel injection, turbo chargers, high strength steels, aerodynamic bodies, front wheel drive, and many others.[7]

Though these external pressures for product change are still an important influence in the process of product technical change, two other factors have become equally, if not more, important in the 1980s. The first is the fierce competition that now exist in the final market which no longer - as in earlier days - centers around price, but also incorporates product considerations. The second is the supply-side pressure created by the rapid pace of technical change in new technologies such as electronics and new materials.

Indeed it is the interaction of all three of these variables that explains much of the pattern and orientation of current and future product innovation in the motor vehicle industry. Both externally derived pressure to improve safety emission standards and fuel efficiency and competitive market conditions are inducing auto firms in Western Europe and the United States to focus their competitive efforts on the introduction of electronic engine and drive train management systems and to increase their R&D on the use of new, highly durable, but light-weight materials, such as aluminium, plastics, ceramics and composite material in the engine, car body and frame. Similarly, fierce Japanese competition is forcing the pace on the introduction of a bewildering variety of electronics-based product changes (though many of these are nothing more than superfluous gadgetry) as well as the search for productivity improvements via new assembly techniques based around new design concepts and the use of large scale molded structures in order to reduce labour input in final assembly.

The use of electronics in the product is spreading rapidly and in the course of its diffusion is extensively transforming the vehicle itself. The United States market for automotive electronics (excluding entertainment systems) is expected to be $6-8 bn in 1986 rising to $12 bn by 1990. Most of this production of electronics is done in-house by GM, Ford and Chrysler, with GM's Delco Electronics alone producing 250,000 integrated circuits per day. Volkswagen consider that electronics is the fastest-growing area of innovation. It currently accounts for 12-14 percent of manufacturing costs and Volkswagen estimate that this will rise to 25 percent by 1990. In 1985 Japanese cars used ten times the number of electronic components than in 1980.

A good deal of growth in electronics consumption to date has been taken up by the introduction of microprocessor based powertrain control systems. These applications range from electronic ignition systems where only a decade after the first versions were introduced in the mid 1970s they are now used in nine out of ten United States autos and nearly as widely in Western Europe. They are also incorporated in fuel-injection systems (up from 13 percent of cars in 1982 to 38 percent in 1986), in cruise control systems (now available on 51 percent of all cars in the United States) and in increasingly sophisticated and comprehensive computer-based on-board engine control systems like Ford's EBC-IV system. This processes one million engine control commands/sec as well as diagnosing faults and controlling transmission generation. The diffusion of electronics has now spread beyond engine control into the control of other core operating and electrical systems such as the transmission, suspension, brakes, steering, diagnostics and maintenance, windscreen wipers, heating/air conditioning and instrument panels, as well as into a range of non-essential electronic devices such as electronic key locks, digital clocks, on-board navigational systems, head-up display units, memory systems for seat settings and seat belts, sophisticated environmental control systems and safety oriented communication systems.8/

Available evidence suggests that the introduction of new material based product innovations, while moving fairly quickly, is not quite as advanced as electronics. Some materials such as engineering plastics and resins are being brought into use rapidly, with plastic-use per car expected to rise 30 percent over the next five years (from 200 lbs/car to 300 lbs/car) and an increase of around 120 percent expected with engineering resins over the same period (from 25 lbs/car to 60 lbs/car). Already plastics based materials are used on a wide range of products and components - body panels (GM's Fiero), bumpers (Ford's Scorpio, Aerostar, Taurus, Escort and Sable; as well as in cars by GM, Chrysler, Peugeot and Fiat); wheel rims (Saab and RG); hoods, decks, side and rear doors (Chrysler, Peugeot and Fiat) and in a variety of exterior and interior trim. Expectations are that this diffusion will continue in the future, picking up pace in the 1990's - for instance 50 percent of fenders on all United States cars are expected to be plastic by 1995.9/ Similarly the 1990s are expected to see major advances in the use of composites for molded panels and even in the chassis. The use of aluminium for body frames (with plastic panels attached by adhesive)10/ is being explored as is the widespread use of ceramics, carbon fibres, aluminium, high performance plastics and other materials in engines and other components.

Precisely what this means in terms of the rate of substitution of new materials for steel and other traditional materials is unclear. Volkswagen estimate that the steel-plate content per car will fall 17 percent in Japan and 13 percent in the United States and Western Europe between 1985 and 1990. However, these figures are largely speculative. Nevertheless, despite this uncertainty, it is expected that fundamental changes in body frame and panel technology are likely to come. When they do, they will be accompanied by a restructuring of the traditional manufacturing processes which has evolved through the use of steel in car and which has led to the development of discrete subprocesses in stamping, die making and final assembly. One in-house study by GM has estimated that about 10,000 workers in these operations could be replaced by a molding operation employing about 500 workers and using only four robots.11/

SELECTED COMPANY CASE STUDIES

Although the above overview is useful in outlining the broad directions of the process of technological restructuring now underway in the United States and Western Europe, it is too aggregate to allow us to illustrate some of the key points that are of particular importance to our argument. Thus in this section we shall draw on our empirical research to present case studies of the technological strategy being pursued by three final vehicle assemblers - the Rover Group (RG), Fiat and GM. They have been selected because in different ways each represents an alternative strategic response to the Japanese challenge.

Rover Group: the Ideology of Systemofacture; the Reality of Technological Dependence

As noted earlier, one major dimension of the restructuring response by United States and Western European auto assemblers has been to establish some form of relationship with their erstwhile Japanese competitors. These have been of two types - the first involving straightforward purchasing or cross marketing arrangements designed simply to fill gaps in the model line-up; the second, less common but more significant arrangement, has been attempted by United States/Western European firms to "learn" from the Japanese through involvement in joint production arrangements such as NUMMI (the GM/Toyota Joint Venture) or the recently announced VW/Nissan deal. One of the longest running of these has been RG's link with Honda, involving the joint design and production of a new model range called the 800 Series in the United Kingdom (Sterling in the United States) and the Honda Legend in Japan.

In the midst of British Leyland's (RG's predecessor) crisis in the mid 1970s which saw employment and output levels decline dramatically as a result of a collapse in market share, RG took the crucial decision that if the company were to have a long term future, it would have to assimilate Japanese industrial production methods. RG were anxious to distance themselves from what they saw as the American approach which had typically been to focus on the adoption of isolated parts of the Japanese model such as quality circles or inventory-reduction with relatively no real understanding of how they fit into the overall structure. Instead RG set out to achieve a thorough-going and comprehensive assimilation of the Japanese system of production. This perspective was one of the underlying reasons why RG began its relationship with Honda in 1979. This perspective also meant that RG was quick to learn that it could not simply slavishly imitate a method of production organization that had taken 20 years to perfect and which exhibited many features specific to Japanese culture. The system had to be comprehensively assimilated, but - it was argued - in a way which suited the particular circumstances of RG in the United Kingdom. What is striking is that though RG management recognized the crucial role of organization as the key to Japanese success, it has consciously pursued a policy that has sought to use technological advance as a driving and guiding force to achieve the necessary organizational change.12/

Thus, in the course of moving to JIT organization in production, RG has embarked on a program of robotization. The company believed that to ensure that these technologies are used at peak efficiency, it is necessary to organize production on a JIT basis. By 1986 over 200 robots had been installed and RG plans to continue introducing them rapidly through the rest of this decade, particularly in the areas of trim and final assembly. Other elements of new electronically-controlled equipment were also introduced. Examples of this include the use of low pressure casting technology on the M16 engine cylinder-heads (to achieve greater accuracy, higher consistency, and minimum waste); the use of precision metal forming techniques in place of forging to minimize machining, reduce waste and improve quality; the use of AGV's to connect computer-controlled machining centres in order to maintain JIT; and the introduction of FMS mixed engine assembly lines developed for production of both its aluminium 1.6 and 2.0 liter overhead camshaft engines as well as the engine for the 800 Series. Flexibility is present in both in different ways - the 1.6 and 2.0 liter engines require very different assembly techniques carried out on the same line; the 800 Series engine is expected also to be produced in a number of different versions but at a level of minimum efficient output of only 150,000 units per year, which is less than one-third of the previously estimated minimum scale of 500,000 units per year. The flexibility built into both lines also means that future engine designs can be produced without the need for extensive prototype testing or expensive retooling.

Equally as significant is the connection RG has made between the principle of designing for ease of manufacture and the pursuit of computer-integrated engineering (CIE). RG is pursuing the objective of carrying out all aspects of car manufacture, from design to production, on the basis of a common language and data-base that allows an integrated data flow from start to finish. So far more than $17 million has been spent on 200 CIE work stations at its Cowley plant, and substantial parts of the 800 Series product and component design and tooling (powertrain, chasis and suspension) were carried out on this system. This allowed tool designs and manufacturing costs to be reduced by 30 percent with spin-offs arising in other areas as well, allowing RG to cut time for its recent new model launches. By using a common data-bank, the integrity of the overall product and its components is ensured while at the same time facilitating close interactions in production engineering to improve manufacturing efficiency.

Finally, RG has also taken on board the importance of developing long-term relationships with suppliers in which design is seen as an interactive and collabourative, rather than an arms-length and confrontational process. In the most recent period it has opted for a system of "preferred suppliers", reducing the number of suppliers from 1,200 to 700. The aim, in the words of RG's Managing Director, is to

> give suppliers confidence in the future, confidence to press ahead with research and development, new investment and the introduction of advanced technology13/

This represents the ideology of RG strategy - an attempt to learn new organizational methods from Japan and to mate these together with the introduction of new electronics-based capital goods. Together with a complementary commitment to changing the relationship which it has with suppliers, RG has adopted the philosophy of the three central pillars of systemofacture. But these intentions have been blunted by three major obstacles. First, RG's suppliers - especially the United Kingdom-based ones - have seldom been up to the challenge. For example, in the early 1980s two of the United Kingdom's largest automotive electronic firms - Lucas and Smith Industries - teamed-up to provide a capability to manufacture dashboard instruments in Wales. The quality and design of these products were so poor, however, that RG terminated the contract in early 1987 and moved instead to a Japanese firm (Aisin Seiki) who were Honda's supplier and who agreed to build a plant in the United Kingdom.

The second major obstacle confronting RG has been the inability of its senior executives to pass the message down through its various tiers of management. Much of this had been weaned on the worst form of confrontational management in the late 1970s and seemed unable to absorb the central feature of the Japanese labour process that a new form of management/labour relations was required. Instead of absorbing the emphasis on quality of its Japanese collabourator, Honda, RG management maintained the Fordist supply-driven mentality designed to churn production out at any cost. The consequence was a collapse in market-share in 1985-1987, partly due to the quality problems being experienced by its products, especially the newly-launched Montego range. The new Sterling - launched with great optimism in the United States in 1987 - provoked very critical comments on build-quality.14/ Similarly, Honda had to establish a separate "rework" facility in Swindon - some distance from the RG plants which assembled its vehicles - to rectify the various errors built into its vehicles by RG. (Rework facilities, as we saw in Chapter 4, are anathema to the Japanese assemblers). Another indication of the difficulty which RG was experiencing with its managerial cadre - as well as that of some of its suppliers - related to its conception of JIT production. For some plants this meant establishing a special warehouse which fed the assembly plants on a quasi-JIT basis; the warehouses themselves, though, kept a large stock of parts on a "just-in-case" basis!

The third obstacle which prevented RG from translating the ideology of systemofacture into practice related to its source of funding, and the perspectives which this embodied. As we saw in Chapter 4, the Japanese firms are able to plan product and process development on a long-term basis, in Toyota and Nissans' case, spanning five decades. RG has found itself in a very different situation. By the time it awoke to its underlying problems in the late 1970s, it was already incurring substantial losses - $289m in 1979, $1,213m in 1980 and $1,045m in 1981. The British stock market is notoriously short-sighted, so it offered no viable route to restructuring. Instead recourse was made to the State, with RG effectively becoming nationalized. The problem here was the election of a government committed not only to minimizing the costs to the exchequer, but also to a highly confrontational style of management-labour relations. In these circumstances, the transition from machinofacture to systemofacture was virtually ruled out, except over the long-run (if, indeed, RG could survive that long).

Instead, RG fell into the arms of Honda. Honda was a late entrant to the Western European market and, given the nature of the export limitations which had been reached with the Japanese producers, it found itself with a small market share. In addition, at the point of this collaboration, Honda was itself weak in precisely the one area where the RG had developed strengths - the design of up-market, medium-sized cars. Thus, from Honda's point of view collaboration with RG offered a number of attractions - the ability to absorb design-skills, the possibility of building a long-term presence in Western Europe either by subcontracting production to an established producer or (more likely) by becoming a producer itself. RG had no alternative. It needed a short-term filler for a market-niche (the Ballade, marketed as a Rover), it was anxious to learn Japanese manufacturing techniques and it was financially too strapped to fund the development of the new products which it required.

The first collaboration (that is, excluding RG's contract to assemble the Ballade) was for the Series 800/Legend. Characteristically, although both firms worked to the same time-scale, the Legend was launched fully one year before its British alternative. Moreover, the 800 Series rapidly developed a reputation of faulty quality, whereas the Legend maintained Honda's previous exemplary standards. Subsequently a collabourative agreement was reached to develop a new medium-sized (by Western European, not United States standards) auto code-named the AR8, due out in 1989. But most significantly, in 1987 Honda (having acquired a large greenfield site for unexplained reasons a few years earlier) announced that it would begin manufacturing 70,000 engines a year for the new AR8 (and other?) cars. At the same time - as mentioned above - RG jettisoned two of its largest and longest-lived component suppliers in favour of one of Honda's Japanese suppliers. Thus, although RG's recent attempts have been guided by a clear-sighted perspective on the transition to systemofacture, and although it has made substantial improvements in productivity (which doubled in less than five years)15/, the balance of judgement must be that it has retreated into technological dependency on Honda, and has made only slow progress in moving to encompass the organizational and labour process innovations pioneered by the Japanese.

The Evolution of a 'Technology Strategy' at Fiat

Of all the non-Japanese volume manufacturers Fiat has perhaps been the most successful in restructuring itself over the past decade. This was done in response to three major sets of problem that beset the company in the 1970s - a disastrous attempt to globalize production that involved new assembly investments in Brazil and other countries (of which only Brazil now remains), a weak product portfolio and a decade of labour unrest during which trade unions were able to confront company power and to limit the intensification of work within the old machinofacturing labour process. The result was that during the late 1970s Fiat experienced a dramatic drop in output (25 percent decline in three years), productivity and competitiveness, accompanied by a rise in total employment through the end of 1980.

The company responded to each of these pressures in turn. It began by shifting course in its global strategy, withdrawing from all overseas production except for Brazil, with a particularly significant and acrimonious departure from Spain, its largest overseas subsidiary.16/ It also involved a withdrawal from marketing in the United States.17/ The second step saw a major confrontation with the trade union which was won by Fiat. This was followed by a dramatic and rapid reduction in the labour force, beginning in the late 1970s. In the five years between 1979 and 1983 total employment at Fiat was reduced by nearly 50 percent. But as RG - which had taken similar action - had found, on its own these two measures were not adequate. So, to this Fiat added a combination of product innovations and sweeping technological and organizational changes. What is notable about Fiat's approach to technological innovation is that through the 1970s, the company initiated a number of pilot technological interventions with the threefold objective of increasing production flexibility, reorganizing work in response to trade union demands and consciously "learning" how to use automation technology. This provided the basis on which the company has proceeded to push flexible automation farther into engine and final assembly than perhaps any other vehicle manufacturer in Western Europe and the United States. It is for this reason that we focus on Fiat's technological innovations rather than on their successful introduction of new products which were well-received in the Western European market.

This process has moved through three stages. During

the 1970s, robots were introduced on a piecemeal basis primarily for ergonomic reasons in response to trade union pressure. The introduction of the much publicized Robogate system[18]/ marked the first attempt at flexible automation - robots did almost all the holding and welding and AGV's brought body parts to fixed workstations for assembly. The line was computer-controlled which allowed for flexibility in body types that could be handled via computer control of parts delivery and robot performance. Labour productivity was increased by 45 percent and the skill profile of the remaining workers on the line changed dramatically from the standard predominance of assembly workers to a majority of maintenance personnel.

The second stage came with the introduction of the Asynchronous Engine Assembly Line (LAM) in 1981 to assemble the RITMO engine series. Again, computer-controlled AGV's delivered parts to four automatic transfer lines and to ten computer-directed work stations, where, due to the immaturity of assembly-automation, LAM engine assembly remained labour intensive. The benefits for the company of LAM were significant - rejection rates for finished engines were cut by 50 percent and 20 percent fewer workers produced almost 50 percent more engines. Most importantly, the line had great flexibility due to the extensive computer control of parts delivery and workstations operation, as occurred in the Nissan plants described in Chapter 4. This means that output rates were no longer geared to the most complex unit being produced and gave the plant the capability to handle 110 different versions of the RITMO motor.

The third and most significant phase of Fiat's automation trajectory came with the FIRE engine production facility at Termoli. The FIRE (fully integrated robotized engine) line represents Fiat's biggest push yet into flexible automation. The objectives of the FIRE engine project (spawned by a now defunct collaboration between Fiat and Peugeot) were to design a new class of engine in a way that would cut its weight significantly, reduce component numbers (from 6-700 to 4-500), and most importantly would greatly simplify assembly to allow the highest possible degree of flexible automation. The results (shown in Table 5.4) have been dramatic. What the table also shows is that Fiat also undertook a massive training exercise for the plants' 950 employees at a cost of $21m that was designed to give workers both a mix of higher skills and to ensure that only the most co-operative, adaptive, and youngest workers were employed.

Table 5.4
Fiat's FIRE Engine Assembly Plant, Termoli, Italy.

Description

Cost	-	$371m ($50m for development; $300m plant and equipment; $21 training)
Employees	-	950
Output	-	462,000 annually rising to 572,000 if needed. (Able to achieve increase with only 80 additional workers)
Product	-	3 cyl 6500cc; 4 cyl 850 cc; 4 cyl 999 cc; 4 cyl 1.3 liter
Robots	-	56 Robots; 92 programmable handlers
Computers	-	103 (27 testing; 45 diagnosis; 12 stores; 7 assembly line; 9 engine testing; 3 overall production control)

Comparison with LAM Engine Plant at Mirafiori

	FIRE	LAM
Degree of Automation	90%	26%
Automated Stations	78	30
Manual Stations	2	15
Computer Dialogue Parts on Main Assembly Line	16	2
Machine Time[a]	46.5 mins	114.4 mins
Assembly Time	61 mins	171 mins

Source: Interviews; Gooding, 1985.

[a]FIRE compared to 903cc engine for Fiat 127

While FIRE was under development, Fiat continually upgraded the level of automation on both the LAM and the Robogate systems. For instance, at the STRADA plant an additional 100 robots have been introduced into various assembly applications including the use of visual robots to bolt hinges to doors and install them automatically. And through these developments, Fiat's machinery-supplying subsidiary Comau developed an expertize in CIM that has led to extensive sales to auto assemblers in other countries. Overall, Fiat's investment in new technology and new model development and R&D was equivalent to $8.5bn between 1980 -

1986. The individual gains in productivity deriving from this have been significant as shown above - and for the company as a whole productivity has increased from 14.8 cars per worker per year to 25-28 in 1986. This has meant a very significant increase in both competitiveness and profitability. Nor has Fiat relaxed the pace of advance and two other areas are currently receiving attention as future avenues for change. The first involves a very considerable investment introducing new materials in product, specifically in relation to the greater use of plastics. It is recognized that in the long-term this is likely to have considerable implications for the organization of assembly, a view similar to that of GM. The second major area of future change involves a long-term commitment to restructuring supplier relations along JIT lines; we return to this development in the following chapter.

GM: Doing Everything as a Substitute for Choice

With a turnover which exceeds $100bn, GM possesses options which are open to few of its competitors. Most importantly, it has the possibility of exploring a large number of strategic avenues simultaneously. Of course, this is not necessarily an advantage because unlike the Fiat experience which has just been recounted, this strategy of doing everything can easily collapse into a failure to make the hard choice between exclusive options. We will recount in later chapters how GM's declaration of "absorbing the Japanese experience" is wholly contradictory to its simultaneous policy of offshore sourcing. But in this chapter we will concentrate on the major thrust of GM's response to the Japanese challenge - the development of a technological counterattack. In this GM invested around $60bn between 1978 and 1986, only to find its United States market-share fall from over 48 percent in 1978 to less than 40 percent in 1986, and that its 1986 profits (at $2.9bn on sales of $103bn) were lower than those of Ford (profits of $3.3bn on only two-thirds of GM's sales), the first time this has happened since Ford's heyday in 1924.

The spur to GM's headlong pursuit of a technological solution to its problems was the realization in the late 1970s of its near complete inability to compete with the Japanese. Between 1973 and 1980, GM's market share in the United States crashed from 51.5 percent to just over 44 percent; labour-productivity was virtually stagnant (see

Chapter 4); its quality ratings were among the lowest in the industry; and finally, the company endured a collapse in profits in the early 1980s, both globally and domestically. In response to this series of setbacks, GM management committed itself to the most fundamental restructuring of its operations and manufacturing philosophy since the Sloan revolution. The objective, as stated by management, was to take the maximum advantage of new technology and to make the company fully competitive with Japan and others across the whole model range on a global scale through the 1990s and into the next century.

As we have already indicated GM's strategy is multifaceted and appears to encompass every aspect of the company's operations. For instance there has been a major reorganization of United States operations to improve managerial efficiency. This has involved shuffling five divisions, involving 47 assembly and stamping plants and 300,000 employees into two mega-divisions - Buick-Olds-Cadillac (BOC), which was expected to concentrate on larger cars, and Chevrolet-Pontiac-Canada (CPC) for smaller autos. In the course of this reorganization, some 20,000-30,000 middle level managers have been "squeezed out" in an attempt to peel away unnecessary layers of management of the company. Another element of the company's strategy already mentioned (and examined in more detail later) is its offshore-sourcing activities involving a dramatic rise in both whole-vehicle and component imports. Still another element which we examine in Chapter 6 is a major change in supplier relations including the introduction of inter-plant JIT.

Amidst all this there can be little doubt, however, that GM has decided to mount its most determined challenge to the Japanese in the technological sphere. Technology is playing a role in the company's restructuring efforts on a scale not really found in any other company. 19/ This is borne out by the size of its recent and planned investment programs. Between 1979 and 1983, GM's capital expenditure totalled more than $33bn - three times the rate of investment of the previous four year period, with a further $27bn between 1983 and 1986. For instance in the short space of six months in 1985, GM's new Chevrolet-Pontiac-Cadillac division announced over $3.5bn worth of investment intended to completely redesign and re-equip 10 of its 16 assembly plants. As might be expected, these investments do incorporate a substantial slice of state-of-the-art automation particularly in stamping, welding and machinery and to a certain extent in final assembly - though much of this is fixed rather than flexible automation.

But in addition to these attempts to retool existing plants, GM's investment program also incorporates a variety of other initiatives that are better classified as "leading- edge projects". We have already mentioned some of these such as its acquisition of small, specialized high technology companies, the Saturn project (reviewed later) and its commitments to MAP and TOP. Another which has attracted a lot of attention is its recent costly acquisition of Electronic Data Systems ($2.1bn)[20]/ and Hughes Aircraft ($5bn). While creating possibilities for diversifying out of its long term reliance on automobiles into information systems and defense electronics,[21]/ it was believed that these acquisitions would also strengthen the company's electronics and information technology capabilities. The Hughes acquisition is very recent and therefore no plans have yet been announced as to how the they will be integrated into GM's operation. In relation to EDS however, it is clear that the company is intent on exploiting EDS's capabilities to the fullest in its restructuring process. Like MAP and TOP on an industry-wide level, EDS is an essential component of GM's move towards CIM. Not only is EDS involved in automating GM's paperwork, it is playing a key role in the MAP initiative, in devising computer systems for Saturn, in developing computer-based management and production systems for other plants, and even in setting up a satellite-based communication system linking all of GM's worldwide operations, including its massive dealer network.

Given the scale of the financial resources at GM's disposal[22]/ it is not surprising that its investment program in leading edge technology includes virtually every type of project undertaken by all of its competitors. It is not possible to review all of these so we will instead highlight three very different programs that are indicative of the strategy being pursued by the company.

<u>GM Research: R&D into Advanced Computer-Based Automation Systems</u>. Within the GM Technical Center there is an advanced computer research group known as GM Research which serves as the company's think tank with regard to the future use of automated systems in design, engineering and manufacturing. This group's recent projects range from developing computer models of materials performance to the use of artificial intelligence in areas such as machine vision, natural language processing and systems. The group interfaces on some projects with the new high-technology acquisitions mentioned earlier, but they are a separate

entity whose work is not likely to be supplanted by these acquisitions including that of EDS. Some of the most advanced projects currently being developed by GM Research are detailed in Table 5.5 and as can be seen, the end objectives of these projects will affect all stages of vehicle design and manufacture. Beyond that, the table demonstrates the pervasive ability of computer technology to be harnessed in every sphere of production activity.

<u>Factories of the Future</u>. The company has three Factory of the Future (FOF) projects that are exploring areas beyond the current state-of-the-art in flexible automation and represent one strand of the company's strategy to leapfrog the Japanese. The objective of the FOF projects are to integrate three concepts of computer-based control that are now present (if at all) only as isolated systems in operating production plants - computer-integrated manufacturing (CIM), computer-integrated engineering (CIE), and computer aided design/computer aided manufacture (CAD/CAM). The aim behind this interaction is to create an environment and production system within which continuous advances in design, assembly and materials use can be accommodated and absorbed without the need for retooling.

One of the FOF projects is based in a pilot plant at the Saginaw Steering Gear manufacturing facility. This single line plant will manufacture five different types of front drive axles. CAD has been used for plant design, product design and tool design, and via a CAD/CAM link, will direct the operation of the 60 manufacturing cells that will carry out all machining and (robotized) assembly operations. Computer-controlled AGV's will deliver parts from an automated storage and parts retrieval system. This comprehensively computerized facility is intended to eventually operate around-the-clock, seven days per week in a paper-less mode with no direct labour. The cost of this FOF is $55 million. This is roughly double the cost of setting up a conventional plant to produce the same product and is an indication of GM's willingness (and ability) to invest considerable sums of money in a learning process which it hopes will eventually be widely diffused not only in machining operation but in auto assembly as well.

<u>Saturn: GM's response to the Japanese small car invasion</u>. The Saturn project is the most well-publicized element of GM's strategy to recover its competitiveness in the small car segment from Japan by technological leapfrogging. Saturn was originally promoted as being an entirely new concept that would fully integrate leading-

Table 5.5
Advanced Computer Projects at General Motors Research Facility

Project	Objective/Project
1. RoboTeach	Replace human 'teachers' of robots with off-line robot programming system. Essential with complicated assembly techniques.
2. AutoColor	CAD package to allow designers to sketch 3-D color shaded automative shapes. Allows aesthetic check without clay models.
3. MultiMatch	Computer vision system to allow robots to perform 100 million visual imaging calculations per second. Will greatly increase variety of tasks robots can perform.
4. Advanced Computer	Allows prediction of vehicle structural behaviour during crash.
5. GM Form	Advanced computer graphics software to simulate formability of sheet metal. Eliminates extensive tryout and redesign process.
6. AutoChip	Design tool for IC design.

Source: Adapted from Rowand, 1985.

edge product, process, material and organizational technologies and allow GM to defeat the Japanese at their own game. The Chairman saw it as "the key to GM's long-term competitiveness". The cost of the project is $5bn and Saturn has been set up as a completely separate entity (the first such marque for 50 years) with its own dealer network and an entirely new manufacturing facility currently being built at a cost of $3.5bn in Tennessee (close to the Nissan plant) and far away from both the company's and the UAW's traditional mid-western base of operations. It was to include two final assembly lines, engine and transition assembly plants, stamping plant, foundry, and major component sub-assembly plants and was rated to produce 4-500,000 cars a year. Though details are being kept closely guarded the key technological and organizational characteristics of Saturn are set out in Table 5.6. As in the case of RG, GM's plans incorporate the three central features of systemofacture - new flexible labour processes, the widespread application of CIM and more organic links with suppliers.

There are two major points to be made about the implications of the Saturn project. First, there is

Table 5.6
The Main Features of the Saturn Project

Design and Materials
- 100 percent CAD design of car and components;
- use of the "space frame" design ((first used in Pontiac Fiero) allowing inter-changeable body panels made of plastic or aluminium;
- 100 percent design-for-assembly with car broken down into 20-30 sub-systems;
- extensive use of electronics in the car;
- an entirely new engine (45-60 mpg) transmission, and braking system
- full on-line access to designs by suppliers

Process
- fully modular assembly (from inside out) of off-line prepared sub-assemblies;
- 100 percent CAE;
- maximum degree of CAD/CAM machining and assembly control;
- fully automated in-plant parts delivery to assembly point via overhead rail and AGV vehicles;
- electronic AGV guidance system linked to flexible assembly and 100 percent parts and in-line sequencing;
- JIT production to customers order;

Organisational
- 100 percent JIT suppliers delivery direct to final assembly;
- close supplier location within "Saturn City" complex;
- extensive supplier involvement in sub-assembly component design and manufacture to minimise on-site assembly;
- full electronic link to suppliers for ordering and scheduling;
- paperless management, marketing and manufacturing systems;
- zero inventory;
- 100 percent single sourced;
- maximum degree of local sourcing;
- Japanese-style labour relations with lifetime employment and no-strike clauses and elimination of craft distinctions.

Source: Interviews

speculation about senior management's real motives underlying the design of Saturn's organizational structure and proposed pattern of labour relations. By seeking to establish a completely separate entity empowered to negotiate a host of new and much more flexible agreements with suppliers, dealers and the UAW, some observers view Saturn as the forerunner of a plan to build an entirely "new" GM, freed from the institutional constraints that have caused it to be such a high cost and inefficient producer. (An alternative consideration is that GM chose to set up the plant close to Nissan's previously non-unionized plant; this either meant that GM, too, would be free of a union-agreement or that, more likely, Nissan would be forced into a recognition of the UAW). Even if these speculations prove to be groundless, the philosophy underlying the Saturn mode of organization does suggest that the company may nevertheless be seeking to put into place some of the lessons it has allegedly learned in this area from the Japanese in general and from initiatives such as the NUMMI experiment, and is thus a forerunner of what will happen in other plants. Secondly, though the above outline of the known technological characteristics of Saturn all suggest "leading-edge", perhaps the most intriguing fact about the project is the way in which the industry's perceptions of its uniqueness has changed. Where once it was expected to break entirely new ground in product and process technology, some observers now suggest that it will simply be the leading edge of old technology - and that it will basically be a conventional vehicle built in a highly automated but also relatively conventional plant.23/

Indeed, following public speculation, the Saturn Project's president conceded that "its probably less automation than the original concept".24/ Moreover, there are fears that if Saturn's production is concentrated on only one standard model produced in very large numbers (originally planned to be 500,000 units but subsequently downgraded to only half this capacity) it will not be able to compete with the Japanese strategy of producing a large variety of different cars in smaller volumes (often all on the same line). One cynic from another company suggested that every ten years or so, GM announced plans that it was about to revolutionize the car business and sweep all its competitors away - this had been the case in 1960 with the Corvair, in 1970 with the Chevrolet Vega, and in 1980 with the X cars. Each of these ventures had failed miserably and with Saturn scheduled for a 1990 debut, the timing for another colossal failure seemed just about right! Since the plant is only now being built only time will tell if the project is able to live up to its advanced billing either as a success or a failure.

WILL THE TECHNOLOGICAL SOLUTION WORK?

In the introduction to this chapter we raised the question of whether or not the current rush of the United States and Western European industry into new technology was going to be sufficient to close the competitive gap with the Japanese. As we noted earlier this is an important consideration for our analysis because of the implications this holds for component sourcing and investment location decisions. The data presented earlier in Chapter 4 comparing industry, firm and plant productivity levels between different plants and companies in Japan, the United States and Western Europe suggests that at least up to the end of 1984, the productivity differential in favor of the Japanese was substantial. Prior to the late 1986-early 1987 devaluation of the dollar it was estimated that the Japanese cost advantages on their imports into the United States was $2,100 for subcompact cars, $2,300 for compact cars, $3,100 for mid-size models and a $4,000 gap for sports cars.25/

This was not particularly welcome news for the United States auto industry given the huge investments which had been made in new technology and the expectations it had engendered about its technological rebirth. To compound their troubles, the first reports of the new Japanese plants in the United States suggest that the Japanese have lost little of the cost advantages they enjoyed as importers. Both Nissan and Honda's United States plants are apparently maintaining at least a $1,000 - $2,000 cost advantage over cars built at United States owned plants.26/ The significance of this is clear since one of the main explanations offered by United States firms for the Japanese cost advantages on imports were that these advantages were largely based on favorable foreign exchange rates and lower foreign wages. And while it is true that the wages paid by Japanese producers in the United States are slightly lower than those of their domestically-owned competitors, it seems certain that much higher productivity is responsible for most of the cost advantages they currently enjoy. Even more worrying for the United States is the fact that the Japanese firms are really only part of their way through effecting a complete transfer of their system of production to the United States. (We take up this point in Chapter 7.)

Similarly, the United States and some Western European auto firms seem also to be falling behind in product innovation. Whereas it was confidently expected that the United States and Western Europe would continue for some time to possess a strong lead in product technology over the Japanese, there are growing signs that this may no longer be the case. Altschuler et al cited evidence that showed Japanese car firms overtaking other firms in the number of patents they were taking out in the United States. Assuming that the number of patents were a good proxy for the level of innovative effort, they argued that by virtue of their patenting behavior, Japanese firms appeared to be much more innovative in recent years than either of their two groups of major competitors.27/ Some of the results are given in Table 5.7 and suggest that while United States firms are frequently shown to have a research "presence" in most areas of innovation, the Japanese (and to a certain extent the Western Europeans) are ahead, being engaged either in prototype or full scale production. Given these trends it is clear that whatever competitive gains the United States and Western European firms believe they have made, they still have considerable ground to make up.

In addition to falling behind in product innovation, a wide variety of obstacles have been encountered in the course of assemblers efforts to introduce new production technology. Some of these are typical of any industry trying to introduce information technologies rapidly· A few examples are illustrative here. The much-vaunted Buick-City complex in Flint, Michigan cost $400m to refurbish. However robotic windscreen installers (fairly common in Western Europe and Japan) failed to work, generally dropping the screen on to the front seat; GM thus had to withdraw them and substitute labour for the task. In a second example, one large United States assembler purchased 84 robots for use in assembly of a new line of cars but was never able to use them because they were overspecified. In a third case many assemblers in the early 1980s discovered that most of the computers in had installed were unable to "talk" to each other - a situation that has prompted the United States car makers in particular to pursue the MAP initiative (discussed earlier) to ensure computer compatibility. Other problems arise because of the immaturity of some of the new product

Table 5.7
Comparison of Product Development Efforts by United States, Western European and Japanese Assemblers.

Product	Japan	Western Europe	United States
Direct injection diesels	In production	Pre-production prototype	Testing of research vehicle
Ceramic diesel engine	Hotplug and plug in production	Prototype under development	R&D only
Ultra-lean burn engines	Pre-production prototype engine		R&D only
Variable displacement	In production; and prototype	Testing and research vehicle	No activity
Discrete gear transmissions	In production by 2 firms	Prototype	No activity
Continuous variable transmissions	In production	Prototype pending production	R&D
Advanced aerodynamic car	Production	Production	Prototype

Source: Adapted from Kahn, 1986.

technology based on microelectronics. For instance, reliability problems plagued early microelectronics-based products because the harsh operating environment found in cars had never before encountered by the electronics industry. These problems have largely been solved but others remain - such as the continued high cost of sensors and actuators that are essential in systems where electronics meets the physical environment.

By far the greatest problems on the technological front though, seems to arise because firms are simply trying to move much more quickly than their absorptive capacity will allow. Thus there is evidence that a number of new plants, touted as being showcases for automation have experienced severe difficulties in trying to reach planned production capacity on schedule because of problems with automation. This was the case of VW's efforts in its new Hall 54 where as noted earlier the level of fixed automation involving assembly robots is among the highest in Western Europe. Start-up problems connected with automation lasted much longer than expected. The same has been true of GM's Ellesmere plant in the United Kingdom. Designed to produce the Astra with a high level of automation and computer control, hardware and particularly software related problems delayed the plant from reaching full capacity for almost a year.

Most recently, attention has been drawn to the plight of United States-based assemblers. Not only have they encountered substantial problems with their automation plans, but their difficulties have also attracted a good deal of public scrutiny and media interest. Ford's new Aerostar van scheduled to be built in a highly automated facility in St. Louis, was seven months late coming off the line in 1985 due to a combination of incompatible computers (from 24 different suppliers) which were too sophisticated to be used by workers even after months of retraining; mismatches between design and the capabilities of automation technology; and the failure to get very expensive pieces of machinery to work cost-effectively (like an unused robot vision and laser inspection system and a multimillion dollar computer system to monitor machine functions and trouble spots in the manufacturing process).

Similar problems plague GM, of which the most widely reported have occurred at Buick City where nine months after opening, only 45 cars per hour were being built instead of the planned 75. At GM's Hamtramck plant, automated at a cost in excess of $500 million to produce luxury cars in the $20-30,000 range, eight months after opening, production is at less than half the planned level with almost all of the difficulties being blamed on the fact that too much automation was introduced far too quickly.28/ Problems in achieving the scheduled output rate have thrown the planned JIT system into disarray - where originally between 400-450 trucks were due to unload material daily, components are now having to be warehoused on site, and delivery frequency cut back to weekly or longer.

There are two ways of interpreting these problems. One is to see them as being an inevitable part of the learning process that was always likely to accompany the introduction of new technology on such a scale. In this case, the answer is simply to slow down the rate of introduction of automation to bring it more into line with absorptive capacity. GM, for instance, has now been forced to do this not only in Buick City and Hamtramck but in relation to its GM10 new model program - and no doubt other assemblers have had to rein in their plans similarly. This argument is currently being made by senior management (among the assemblers) who admit to having been unrealistic in their initial expectations about their absorptive capacity, but who now claim that they are moving quickly down the learning-curve and will not repeat those mistakes in the future. These managers appear to genuinely believe that the teething problem being encountered now with new technology will become much less problematic over time.

This of course may be true. But it is also possible that the technological problems cited above stem directly from failures at the managerial and organizational level and will therefore never be resolved unless drastic changes occur in these spheres first. In short the critics argue that the social organization of production has got to be put into place first before the technology's potential can be fulfilled:

> New technologies haven't made any massive improvement in the auto industry productivity ... so far they have turned out to be more show than substance. Automakers could make bigger gains by scrapping outmoded work rules, managing their work force better and handling their parts inventories more efficiently.... The goal of all the technology push has been to get rid of hourly workers. GM (for instance) thought in terms of automation rather than replacing the current system with a better system. 29/

A good example of this tendency to see the role of automation solely in terms of using technology to solve a non-technical problem comes from Western Europe at VW's Hall 54 plant at Wolfsburg. While fixed automation successfully squeezed out much direct labour (accounting for the elimination of about 1,000 jobs), the indirect labour required to keep the plant running is still very high. The net result is that unit costs have not really reduced substantially, design and assembly inflexibility is introduced due to the fixed nature of the automation, and the production process is vulnerable to stoppage in the event of automated equipment failure. 30/ Considering the evidence from Japanese plants, given earlier in Chapter 4, the most striking feature this revealed was how little indirect labour is used in Japan compared to the still very considerable number of such workers to be found in United States and Western European plants. Thus if automation is introduced without reorganizing production in order to eliminate indirect workers, the net gains in terms of total factor productivity are unlikely to be very great. A good number of industry analysts reviewing the evidence (from Hall 54 and elsewhere) suggest that for all their efforts at introducing automation, United States and Western European firms have so far not yet tackled the problems of how to reduce indirect labour, largely because of their failure to move to multi-tasking and multi-skilling labour practices (see Chapters 2 and 4). In addition much of the flexibility in the Japanese plants arose from organizational and worker flexibility. This we termed flexible production and distinguished from the approach - exemplified in the above discussion of the United States industry - of flexible automation.

One interesting development has been the attempt by some firms (notably RG and GM) to engage in joint ventures with Japanese firms in order to "learn" Japanese methods of production first hand. These are only two of a larger set of ongoing attempts by Western European and United States firms to revitalize domestic competitiveness by having a direct transfusion of Japanese methods of design, organization and management. Altogether there are now seven such collaborations, some involving the creation of a new entity and others allowing for different degrees of interaction between established firms. The distinguishing feature of them all is that the Japanese are in effect "conducting clinics in organizational best practice for the benefit of their venture partners".31/ The seven collaborations involve the following firms:

    Alfa/Romeo/Nissan (ARNA)
    General Motors/Toyota (NUMMI)
    Chrysler/Mitsubishi Motors (Diamond Star)
    Honda/RG
    Nissan/Volkswagen
    Daimler Benz/Mitsubishi Motors
    Ford/Mazda

The Alfa Romeo/Nissan collaboration proved to be a commercial disaster. The initial plan had been to produce around 60,000 annually of the Alfa versions of the Nissan Cherry; yet between 1983 and mid-1986 (when production was halted) only around 50,000 had been produced in total. Fiat, who acquired Alfa Romeo in 1987, rapidly quashed Nissan's attempts to buy the ARNA plant as a bridgehead for production in Italy. Of the other collaborations, only the Honda/RG and the NUMMI joint venture between Toyota and GM have been in operation long enough to get any sense of whether there has been a successful transfer of Japanese best practice.

The Honda/RG collaboration (which we reviewed above) has not yet generated sufficient concrete productivity and quality figures to carry out any analysis, although we did point to the problems which RG was experiencing in matching Honda's quality- and inventory-standards. In the case of NUMMI, Toyota agreed to take over full managerial responsibility for setting up production of a Corolla variant at a GM plant closed in 1982. The deal is that Toyota runs the plant and in the course of it GM is allowed reasonably good access so that its managers can absorb first-hand the Toyota approach. The operation of the plant itself is such a remarkable success that it is now rated as one of the most efficient plants in the United States.32/ But it is not at all clear if GM management has been able to absorb the important managerial and organizational lessons from Toyota. It has not been easy for the traditional GM managers to assimilate the new practices within the Freemont plant. But it is proving even more difficult to transfer the lessons learned to GM's 30 car and truck assembly plants in the United States quickly enough to offset the enormous competitive advantages enjoyed by the Japanese. The prospects according to some observers are not especially good.33/ Thus the long-term success of NUMMI as a learning vehicle for GM is still open, as is this issue in relation to the other joint ventures.

Similar question marks can be raised about the other efforts being undertaken to introduce organizational innovation within established plants. Take for example improvements in the quality area. All commentators agree that quality standards have improved significantly among United States and Western European car manufacturers and all of them have made "improved quality" a centerpiece of their competitive response to Japan. That such a commitment seems to be working its way through to improved productivity is apparent from the evidence we cited earlier in the case of Ford. And as we shall see in the next chapter, the assemblers' commitment to quality is being vigorously pushed in the area of supplier relations.

Moreover, all assemblers have aggressively pursued the introduction of techniques such as SPC, and rigorously computerized testing of final vehicles, components and engines.

Yet since the central focus of most of the efforts to improve quality is on fault detection rather than fault prevention (as is the case in Japan), this suggests that United States and Western European firms have perhaps not yet absorbed the competitive significance of the Japanese concern with "total quality" built into the product from the start. Thus while there have been considerable gains in introducing SPC into day to day operations, one of the more sceptical United States assembly-managers argued that "the industry has often failed completely to integrate quality resources as part of corporate planning".34/

Such a perception is further reinforced by other observations made during our interviews. For instance, United States firms in particular frequently emphasized the considerable investments being made in very expensive sophisticated, computer-controlled testing equipment to check for faults in the final product, including especially the engine. Yet in most Japanese plants, managers are so sure of the quality of their product that cars are dispatched from final assembly to the distribution network with minimal testing. A firm like Honda does not even "hot test" its engines after final installation.35/ Yet GM spends millions on computerized testing equipment to do just that; and its managers resolutely believe that the use of this equipment will ensure better quality products, when in fact all it will do is improve detection levels and require even more cars to be sent back to the line for rectification!

Similar points could be made about the introduction of JIT (an issue we take up in more detail in the next chapter) where at one level we are presented with a public commitment to JIT by senior managers, yet as we saw in Chapter 4, the movement to JIT on an industry level is still slow and the gap with the Japanese remains enormous. Moreover, other anomalies continue to exist in this area such as managers of assembly plants that are allegedly operating on a JIT basis either refusing to accept JIT deliveries from suppliers or forcing suppliers to warehouse several weeks supply of components but then allowing the components to be delivered on a "JIT" basis from there! This is a phenomena we discovered in both the United States and Western Europe. Similarly, whereas we placed considerable emphasis on the significance of Japanese quick-die-change techniques as an example of how organization is tied to productivity (see Chapter 4), our interviews in Western Europe and United States consistently failed to turn up average die-change and stamping times that matched those achieved by the Japanese (Table 5.8). It could be argued that these points suggest that even though senior management is convinced of (and is publicly committed to) the need for fundamental organizational change, these viewpoints are not yet shared by middle-level and plant level management who continue to operate within the conventional mass production organizational paradigm.

Another, more cynical, interpretation of the difficulties firms are encountering in restructuring themselves is that management is seizing upon a particular perception of Japanese organizational change because they offer an additional set of weapons in their struggle to break down the control of organized labour on the one hand and, on the other to bring even more pressure to bear on the supplier network. (We shall explore these points in relation to the supplier network in the next chapter).

Despite company efforts to publicize their desire for better working relations with their labour force, conditions in some companies hardly seem to have changed at all from the adversarial character of past decades. Thus we find very considerable antagonism between labour and management centering around the introduction of organizational innovations such as quality circles and employee participation programs. Most companies have introduced these in one form or another - in GM they are called Quality of Work Life (QWL) programs and Employer Participation Groups (EPG) and in Ford they are called the Employee Involvement Program (EI). Considerable efforts have been made by companies to get unions to accept quality circles. Indeed some Ford managers argued to us that the long term survival of the company depends vitally on company-wide endorsements of its EI program at all levels - a commitment which Ford claims has been forthcoming in the United States (but not in Western Europe) and was responsible for its excellent no-strike record in the United States between 1980-1985.

Yet in many cases, there is still a very conspicuous degree of tension between labour and management over the underlying objectives of quality circles. While management argues that quality circles are a mechanism that will not only improve working conditions but also better the companies' overall competitiveness, some elements of organized labour tend to see these moves as part of a

Table 5.8
Die Change Performance in Selected United States and Western European Assemblers.

	1980	1983	1985
United States 1			
Line A	4 hrs	4 hrs	3 hrs
Line B	8 hrs	5 hrs	2.5 hrs
Line C	4 hrs	2 hrs	30 mins
United States 2			
Line A	6 hrs	5 hrs	3 hrs
Line B	4 hrs		90 mins
Western Europe 1	6 hrs	3 hrs	10-15 mins

Source: Interviews.

concerted management strategy to break the power of the trade unions ... [it] eats away at the power of the unions [since the] main point is to convince workers that their security and future are tied to the success of the company, or plant or department, instead of to their union.36/

A recent survey suggests that there is evidence that supports the views of labour on this point. Membership of quality circles was optional at first, but is now mandatory. Their introduction appears invariably to be associated with work speed-ups and the only ideas adopted by management were those which eliminated jobs. SPC has been used to get workers to monitor themselves and to identify "slackers". This has lead to increased competition between workers and the elimination of jobs.37/

There have also been reports that the collaboration of the UAW in GM's plans for new style labour contracts in ventures such as Buick City or Saturn was less than voluntary. In the case of Buick City, the early 1980's found unemployment running at 23 percent in Flint, Michigan where Buick City is now located. When GM proposed the plans for Buick City, these were initially opposed by the unions and Flint City Council. GM then threatened to close down all of its plants in Flint and not surprisingly both the unions and the City council then agreed to GM's terms. The willingness of the UAW to accommodate attempts by GM to extend these new principles into NUMMI, Saturn and now the Van Nuys assembly plant in California was possibly granted under the same sort of pressure. In the case of the Van Nuys agreement where the team-concept method of working has been approved, the big stick was the threat to close down the plant in 1990.38/

* * *

We have seen, thus, that the most significant response of the United States and Western European industries to the Japanese challenge was to innovate to competitiveness. More than $120bn of investment was involved, and nowhere was this more significant that in the case of GM. Yet the evidence suggests that these attempts were not entirely successful. Progress was made, but not only were Japanese levels of competitiveness not attained, but the major Western producers found themselves up against a moving target. Belatedly the recognition dawned that embodied technological innovation alone was an inadequate response; a change in labour process, in philosophy and organization was also required.39/ One particular aspect of organization which is key is in the area of external relations between the supply network and the final assemblers. It is to this that we now turn our attention.

NOTES

    1. Abernathy (1978).
    2. Radical technical change is defined as in Chapter 2 to incorporate changes in product and process which do not emerge directly out of incremental changes.
    3. In mid 1986 the World Federation of MAP User Groups (representing all users in any industry) had 715 members from the United States, 170 from Western Europe, 144 from Canada and 140 from Japan.
    4. Callahan, (1985).
    5. What is most significant about Chrysler from our perspective is that partly because of this constraint on investment, the company is aggressively pursuing offshore

costs. This is an issue to which we will be returning in Chapter 7.

6. McElroy, (1984).

7. See Altshuler et al (1984) for a discussion of these innovations.

8. See Crisp (1986) and Garner (1983) for a review of these developments.

9. Automotive News, 20 January 1986.

10. GM, Ford, Chrysler, RG and Audi all have major R&D projects underway in these areas and expect to move into commercial production in the 1990s.

11. McCosh, (1985).

12. Snowdon, (1986).

13. Financial Times, 30 March 1987.

14. Financial Times, 30 September 1987.

15. Snowdon (1986).

16. The major point of conflict was that after Fiat's withdrawal from Spain, Seat - its erstwhile Spanish partner - began to market the Ibiza throughout Western Europe. Fiat attempted to block this by arguing that the Ibiza was very closely modelled on one of its own products, the Ritmo, but lost its case in the Western European Court.

17. Having consolidated its position in Western Europe and Brazil, in 1986-7 Fiat found itself posed with the problem of handling the collapse of the independent Alfa Romeo marque (which, as one of its dying acts, had formed a rather unsuccessful collaboration with Nissan). Ford, with only a small market-presence in Italy was anxious to take-over Alfa, a step which Fiat opposed for obvious reasons, since it had a dominant position in Italy, with a market-share of 44.7 percent in 1986. As a consequence Fiat acquired Alfa Romeo, with the declared intention of making it into a thriving up-market product. As part of this strategy Fiat plans to re-enter the United States market by marketing Alfa there.

18. In fact there have been two generations of the Robogate System. Both were deigned for flexible production but only the latter, more flexible one utilized AGVs.

19. For instance the company says it plans to have 20,000 robots in place by 1990 and it has formed a joint-venture with Fanuc of Japan to help it achieve these objectives. GM-Fanuc is now the leading robot maker in the world.

20. In addition to acquiring EDS and its technological capabilities, GM found it had also acquired a Board member, Ross Perot, who was highly critical of GM's bureaucratic layers of management. To stifle this criticism GM had to

buy Perot out - at a cost of a further $700m.

21. The ultimate protected market for a company unable to compete in an open domestic market for cars.

22. Even after the $5bn acquisition of Hughes in 1985 it still had close to $6bn in cash assets.

23. Much more advanced product technology is expected from the new range of GM80 cars scheduled to be introduced in 1989, a year before the Saturn launch. Moreover GM is actually spending a good deal more (in the region of $10bn) on its multi-plant launch of the GM10 series planned for 1988.

24. Business Week, 16 March 1987.

25. Zoia (1986).

26. Ealey (1986).

27. A more recent study (cited by Kahn, 1985) which compared the relative innovative performance of the three groups of firms, confirmed this trend.

28. It included a fully computerized paint facility capable of switching between 19 colors which encountered continuous problems; an automated wheel- and tire-installation system (currently utilized in a number of Japanese plants - see Chapter 4) that is not expected to be used ever because of doubts about its economic and technical viability; and a fleet of over one hundred AGVs that remain idle waiting to be phased in once computerized production scheduling problems can be sorted out! (Knebs, 1986; Nasi, 1986).

29. Nag (1986) pp. 1-2.

30. Griffith (1985).

31. Womack (1986a) p. 5.

32. ibid

33. ibid

34. Interview.

35. It is instructive here to refer back to the discussion in Chapter 4 where we observed the general relative reluctance of Toyota to introduce advanced automation technologies. At its relatively labour-intensive and technologically-conventional engine plant in Toyota City, all engines continue to be "hot-tested", that is, run for a time to ensure that no defects have been built-in.

36. TIE (1985) pp. 16-17.

37. GM Worker's Voice, p. 2.

38. Delcrenzo (1986).

39. But full recognition of the change in labour process has not yet been fully absorbed and little has permeated through to the shopfloor.

6

The Restructuring of Assembler-Supplier Relations and the Growth of Technological Intensity in the United States and Western European Components Industry

As we have seen in previous chapters, the auto assembly industry in Western Europe and the United States has been undergoing a painful period of recovery over the past decade, the results of which cannot yet be determined clearly. But this restructuring is not confined to the assemblers and is now also being experienced in the components industry. However, whereas the process is relatively well advanced amongst the assemblers, the full force of change has only just begun to be felt by the supplier firms. Beginning in the early 1980s a period of severe rationalization began in both the United States and Western European component industries, involving both the closure of a number of firms (many of them in the small to medium sized category)1/ and a shedding of labour by those remaining. This rationalization was linked to the substantial downturn in demand in the early 1980s and is not yet complete. Although many of the firms that have survived are among the strongest and are therefore better equipped to withstand competitive pressures, the process of rationalization is not over.

A significant element in this change emanates from the auto assemblers and is being transmitted through the many conduits that link the two sectors. Thus component firms are being forced to respond to an entirely new set of performance criteria established by the assemblers. The reasons for this are that the assemblers recognize that the eventual outcome of their own restructuring efforts will be strongly influenced by the extent to which complementary changes can be introduced successfully into the network of supply. This inevitably creates many problems, both for the suppliers and the assemblers.

The components industry also faces pressures that are

independent of the demands of the assemblers, although they are in many respects similar in nature. For instance suppliers in Western Europe and the United States also face the prospect of increased competition in their domestic market, coming primarily from inward investments by Japanese suppliers. But it also arises from the potential threat posed by DC competitors. Moreover they also are confronted by the same technology-push forces affecting the assembler-industry, as well as a much more competitive international market. On balance though, the process of restructuring that we document below is more a response to the actual and perceived pressures imposed by assemblers than to these other inducements to technical change.

An important distinction has to be drawn between the current experience of the components industry in the United States and Western Europe and that of Japan. While in all three industries we find evidence of growing technological intensity (with its own set of implications for DC sourcing and investment patterns), it is only in the United States and Western European cases that we see dramatic change in assembler-supplier relations. The reason for this is clear since, as we saw in Chapter 4, the Japanese industry had already forced through these changes over the past three decades. But it is significant because previously it was the weak links between assemblers and suppliers in Western Europe that partly accounted for their poor competitiveness. Moreover, particularly in the United States, it was also these weak links that created the opportunity - and indeed the necessity - of sourcing components from DCs.

As with developments affecting the assemblers, the main trends of the transformation currently passing through the components industry are reasonably clear, involving each of the three central pillars of systemofacture identified in Chapter 2 - in the labour process, in the adoption of electronics-based technologies and in changing supplier-assembler relationships. Because of the fundamental nature of these changes there can be little doubt that we are witnessing a period of marked change within the components industry that will ultimately have major implications for its structure and for its global division of labour. However, while these modes of restructuring are similar to those occurring in the assembly sector, the process of change is not only less well advanced overall in components, it is also much more uneven across product categories, companies and particularly countries. While this may not be surprising given the scale and heterogeneous nature of the components industry, it does make the final outcome more difficult to predict in terms of our central concerns with FDI and offshore sourcing.

At the end of the last chapter, in common with many industry-analysts, we concluded that technological change alone could not be a panacea for the ills of the industry and that organizational change would also have to take place if restructuring was going to result in a more competitive United States and Western European industry. Belatedly, the assemblers have come to recognize this fact, although their primary thrust remains on the technological front. In contrast it was striking that our interviews among component firms revealed that it was precisely within the organizational area where they felt most pressure for change from the assemblers. This was particularly true in the United States where virtually every aspect of the assembler-supplier relationship seems to be in a state of flux and destined to move in a direction quite different from that of the past.

The old system was one in which component suppliers and assemblers were involved in an adversarial relationship. Multi-sourcing was the general pattern, design-secrets were zealously guarded and plants were physically distant, sometimes spread across continents. However, in an environment in which JIT organization should ultimately be paramount, in which rapidly evolving process and product technologies are closely interrelated and in which technology is increasingly complex, this assembler-supplier relationship is anachronistic. Instead, design secrets have to be shared, involving a relationship of trust; R&D efforts have to be spread, partly because of the overall complexity of the process; quality standards have to be achieved reliably; and plants have to be proximate. All this should ideally put an end to the previously adversarial relationship and new, more cooperative and long-term relationships will have to be forged, as has become the general rule in Japan. But this is proving to be no easy task as both assemblers and suppliers are finding it difficult to overcome the ingrained practices of earlier years. Moreover, the process of organizational change needs to be viewed from a long time-perspective, having taken some three decades to develop in Japan. And, as in the case of the assemblers, it is precisely these uncertainties about the length and breadth of this transition phase that gives rise to contradictory trends in the sourcing of components, with apparently contradictory-policies - JIT and offshore-sourcing being pursued simultaneously.

However, despite this preoccupation with a change in organizational links with suppliers, a second major manifestation of the restructuring process is also to be found in the growing technological sophistication of the automobile components industry. As in the case of the assembly industry, this is leading to a fundamental change in its nature, with the likelihood of particularly severe effects on industry-concentration.

In what follows we consider five major issues in the development of the components sector which are central to our concern with the incorporation of the developing world in the global division of labour. In Section 1, we examine the growing complexity of the supplier selection process and the new role of quality as a key selection-criterion. Section 2 discusses the changing contractual relationship between assembler and suppliers, whilst Section 3 considers the nature and implications of the new set of design relationships that are emerging. The diffusion and impact of JIT practices on suppliers is explored in Section 4 and Section 5 presents evidence on technological development within the supplier sector itself.

COMPLEXITY IN PRODUCT PURCHASING: THE GROWING IMPORTANCE OF QUALITY

Historically, purchasing criteria were relatively straightforward for bought-in components. Provided suppliers could demonstrate a minimum level of product technology, production competence and financial support, they were allowed to bid for contracts. The final selection of the supplier was based largely on price and an ability to deliver without interruption. To protect against such interruptions, it was common to reach agreement with more than one supplier. But the dominant characteristic of the assembler-supplier relationships was the single-minded pursuit by purchasing agents of the lowest possible prices, often accompanied by last-minute switchovers to alternative suppliers who were able to shave only a few cents off prices.

However, there is widespread recognition within the industry that the assemblers have begun to alter their attitudes towards component-purchasing. As a result this has become considerably more complex and multi-faceted. The single-minded concern with price and delivery -

characteristic of earlier years - has been downgraded and there is now a much greater emphasis on both quality- and technology-related criteria in determining supplier selection. This shift seems to be occurring in both Western Europe and the United States, and is is illustrated in Figure 6.1 which charts the change in assembler criteria for selecting suppliers (as perceived by the suppliers). What it shows is the sharp decline in the relative importance of short-term price compared to characteristics such as quality, delivery performance and manufacturing and engineering competence. Particularly striking is the dramatic increase in the importance of the quality variable. From a point in the mid 1970s, where quality was among the least important determinants of supplier selection, this criteria has now assumed primary importance.

This concern with quality began as a perfunctory response when the assemblers became aware they were were losing market share to higher quality Japanese vehicles.2/ However, it now appears to have both broadened and deepened as the relationship between competitiveness and quality has become more widely appreciated. Assemblers have let it be known that they no longer wish to have to inspect for quality at all - if the supplier cannot guarantee perfect quality then there is no contract. In short, quality is no longer one of the criteria on which an assembler will judge a supplier's bid - if the quality is not up to standard, suppliers are unlikely to even be allowed to bid. It thus becomes one of the entry tickets in the race for supply contracts - without it, suppliers are not even allowed to the starting line.

Pressure by the assemblers for increased quality manifests itself in various ways. Most assemblers have established some type of quality-verification program as a means of weeding out suppliers unable to meet their standards. These are minimum "entry ticket" standards and are much higher than in previous years. Chrysler, for instance, has set up a measurement system to monitor suppliers and sends teams of quality-assurance people to do field surveillance on component-quality before shipment. Beyond that, assemblers have also established programs like Ford's QI award (similar to the Deming Award in Japan) which must be attained before firms can qualify for long-term, single sourced contracts. Through this Ford has come to be judged to be among the most severe judges of quality in the industry. One of the companies in our sample, a United Kingdom supplier of foundry-based components, had

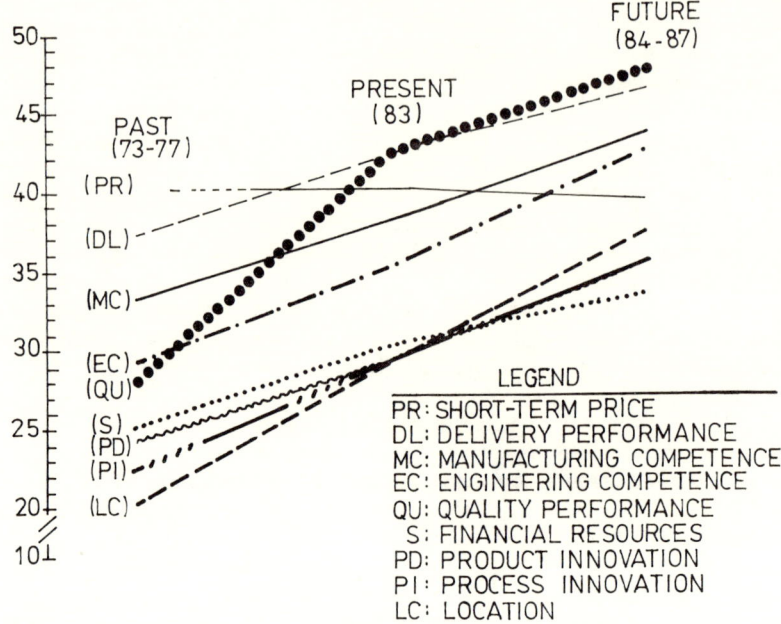

Source: R. E. Cole et al, <u>Participants Report on a Survey of the North American Automotive Supply Industry</u> (Industrial Technology Institute, University of Michigan, 1985). Reprinted by permission.

Figure 6.1 Trends in Perceived Assembler Criteria for Selecting Suppliers

failed to meet these standards set by Ford and had never been able to redeem itself. It would be prepared now "to gladly accept any rigour enforced upon us". In the United States, Ford claimed that this pressure to increase component quality had led to a reduction of 60 percent in the repair of autos arising from outsourced components.

In the early 1980s, Fiat and RG in Western Europe also both set quality guidelines that all suppliers had to meet by the end of 1985 or else contracts were to be cancelled. Fiat introduced two methods of quality verification. The first was subjective as Fiat engineers visited suppliers' production lines to rate quality levels and compare these with competitors; in the second method they asked independent quality auditors to check components for quality, and Fiat estimated that by 1985 its overall component quality was 30 percent better than in 1983. However Fiat still ranked its own components suppliers at a far lower level than Japanese firms.

As we noted in the previous chapter, a key quality control technique being pushed by assemblers is the use of Statistical Process Control (SPC). All the United States assemblers interviewed had set up training programs to instruct suppliers in the use of the technique. Chrysler, for instance, trained more than 50 smaller suppliers in SPC in two-week seminars, provided them with manuals for their workers and then monitored and supervized their actions to make sure the suppliers implemented the technique. For Ford, the requirement to use SPC is absolute. All firms must have SPC in place by 1990 or they will not be allowed to bid. The company has invested significant resources in training about 40 percent of its suppliers in the use of SPC and feels that the rest will have introduced it well before the 1990 deadline.

A narrow focus on quality which is confined to SPC may, as we noted in Chapter 2, reflect a misperception about the role of quality in competitiveness on the part of the industry. However, there are signs that at least as far as suppliers are concerned, assembler concerns with quality now appear to go well beyond the use of SPC and extend into pressures to improve procedures and engineering standards, and to introduce cost controls and other devices. One supplier stated that the pressures it faced from assemblers on quality were such that

> in all of our plants throughout the world [32 plants in 10 countries], this company has been so involved over the last three years with scrambling to meet new quality standards that we have been unable to devote real attention to anything else.

Given these sorts of pressures, it is not surprising that the newfound concern of assemblers with quality has caused considerable problems within the supplying industry as firms have struggled to respond. Indeed many of those who did not respond or take the quality criterion seriously, saw their contracts cancelled and some have subsequently gone bankrupt. This has particularly been the case in the United Kingdom and the United States. For instance RG's shift on quality in the early 1980s is widely believed to have led to the demise of a large number of supplying firms. In the United States, when the upswing in demand for cars began in 1984, many assemblers found that so many suppliers had gone bankrupt and so many more were unable to meet new quality standards that several plants were forced to close periodically, and model introductions were delayed because the suppliers that remained were unable to maintain the supply of quality components.

Among the firms that have survived, there is still considerable rancour over what they perceive as unfair pressure by assemblers for both quality improvement and price reduction. When quality first became an issue, suppliers were looking for signs that the assemblers would allow the traditional trade-off between price and quality. However, contrary to the declared intent of the assemblers to sacrifice price for quality, such a trade-off was not permitted to occur and the pressure to push prices even lower remains. Thus most suppliers in Western Europe and the United States believe that price is still the crucial selection variable for the assembler, no matter what is said publicly by senior management. They point out, however, that while the aggressive pursuit of low prices was always seen as the route to promotion for purchasing personnel, the current generation of "ambitious" engineers are in charge of both price and quality verification procedures. As suppliers see it, they are thus forced to absorb the worst of both worlds.

There can be little doubt that assemblers have increased pressure on both fronts. Many have taken a cue from the Japanese and are demanding annual price reductions from their suppliers. (But unlike the Western European and United States component firms, the Japanese suppliers have long absorbed the obsession with quality and consequently are not having to devote their full resources to these two issues simultaneously). The complaints made to us by the suppliers, corroborated by statements made by the assemblers to suppliers and in the press, are quite clear in this regard.3/ However it is a misperception of the current situation to see this as evidence that price alone remains the only consideration of the assemblers. One indication of the heightened importance of quality to assemblers, and the more complex purchasing decisions that result from this, is the fact that in all the big three United States assemblers, purchasing has now been centralized. Responsibility for these decisions have been moved from the plant-level to higher levels of management where more complex evaluation techniques can be used. This shift coincides with interview statements made on the long term importance of quality and of the assemblers' intention to stick to these standards.

The basic implication for the industry of this pervasive trend towards higher quality components is that quality is likely to become a driving force behind productivity improvements and cost reductions. But this is only likely to happen if the other elements of organizational change called for in the transition to systemofacture are also implemented. This is certainly the lesson of the Japanese experience as we described in Chapter 3 - the pursuit of quality, though a distinct concern, is closely allied to the pursuit of minimum inventory, greater flexibility in production and work, and so on. Whether or not the United States and Western European industry has learned this part of the lesson fully is not yet clear. But what is clear is that an emphasis on quality has been established and that it is one of the key factors of the new mode of assembler-supplier relations that is currently evolving. As we shall see in Chapter 7, this has important implications for offshore-sourcing and FDI.

RESTRUCTURING CONTRACTUAL RELATIONS

The contrast between Japanese and United States/Western European assembler supplier relations is probably strongest in the area of contractual relationships. In the case of Japan, the well known features of single-sourcing[4]/ and long-term contracts are agreed and implemented in an atmosphere of mutual trust and reliability. They are clearly crucial features that underlie the efficient functioning of the Japanese mode of production organization. In the United States and Western Europe, contractual relations have traditionally been conflict-ridden with contracts deliberately kept short-term and many components procured on a multi-sourcing basis. This allowed assemblers to impose price as the near-sole determinant of competition and to maintain control over technology and thereby reduce their dependence on what they perceived to be unreliable partners.

As with quality, United States and Western European firms now appear to have recognized the need to change the basis of their relationship. This shift in the nature of assembler-supplier contractual relations has three dimensions - a movement away from short-term contracts towards those with a longer term time horizon, often involving much larger volumes thnn previously; a decline in multi-sourcing and a rise in the degree of single-sourcing, accompanied by a variety of new forms of relationships; and, directly as a result of these moves, a deliberate overall reduction in the total number of different suppliers being contracted by assemblers. Along with the changing quality/price emphasis described above, these altered contractual relations represent the most thoroughgoing organizational change the industry has yet seen since Sloan's reforms in GM in the early 1920s.

Since assembler strategies in these areas are still evolving it is a little difficult to judge the overall degree of progress. The movement to single-sourcing is perhaps most pronounced, with the United States firms all announcing these policies six-to-seven years ago, but not really making any reasonable gains until the last two-to-three years. As a result there is still a long way to go to meet the objectives of one hundred percent single-sourcing that have been publicly announced for projects such as Saturn and Buick City. Overall in the United States, GM appears to have advanced furthest and claims to have established single-sourcing relationships with about 40 percent of their 3,500 suppliers overall, with even higher figures claimed for individual components. For instance, chassis components for the CPC divisions of GM are 97 percent single-sourced, precisely the reverse of the situation 10 years ago. The trend is now reasonably well established in the two other major United States assemblers, with Ford being closest to GM.

The situation is different in Western Europe where there already were a large number of single-sourcing arrangements, either because there was only one national supplier of a part (for example, Associated Products for clutches in the United Kingdom), or because of already existing equity relationships between the assembler and supplier, as in the case of Fiat Componenti and Fiat. Nevertheless the assemblers are pushing hard in their drive to increase the extent of single-sourcing. Peugeot, for instance, has embarked on a well-publicized plan of shifting from dual-sourcing to single-sourcing and by late 1985 had realized about 40 percent of its goal. Fiat has announced similar plans. In 1987 RG introduced a system of "designated suppliers" (see Chapter 5). Its aim is to go as far towards full single sourcing as possible, although there can of course be different suppliers for the same component to different cars. For instance the alloy wheels for both the Maestro and the Metro are single-sourced, but from different suppliers.

Once again, as in the price/quality trade-off, suppliers tend to be sceptical about the true commitment of assemblers to single-sourcing, citing the fact that there has always been a very considerable degree of single-sourcing, particularly where the component supplier enjoyed a clear technological edge. The same scepticism is voiced in relation to the equally well-publicized shift that assemblers are making in awarding multi-year, high-volume deals rather than the traditional single-year contracts. As in the case of single-sourcing many of the senior management among the assemblers have openly committed themselves to establishing multi-year contracts with their supplier. For instance, GM claims that such contracts now cover about 30 percent of component supply. But as in the move toward single-sourcing, the introduction of multi-year contracts is moving slowly.5/

The long years of continual price pressure from the assemblers and the numerous examples given to us (and cited in the literature) of assembler unreliability and untrustworthiness, all suggest that the scepticism of suppliers may be well-founded. Two of these examples can be quoted, both drawn from the United States. One large supplier had, on the go-ahead from an assembler, built a new plant to produce a particular part, yet found that the assembler had then awarded the contract to an in-house supplier. Similarly, another firm which had invested a considerable amount in R&D to develop a new product innovation, claimed that after they had passed on the designs to the assembler, it had in turn given the designs to a Latin American firm to which it had awarded the contract because it could produce the part cheaper than the original innovator.

The above are typical of the evidence given by suppliers to back up their scepticism about the seriousness of assembler commitment to single-sourcing and long-term contracts. Yet the assemblers responded to this scepticism by reiterating their long-term commitment to push single-sourcing to the limit. One of them observed that even though some suppliers may still be seeing requests for arms-length tenders, this was "anachronistic and will die out". On the basis of our own interviews we are convinced that senior management among the assemblers are committed to these changes not just for their own sake, but because they appreciate that any attempt to move to just-in-time production, or to fully embrace the notion of modular design by shifting the locus of the innovative effort onto component suppliers, simply could not survive under the old

Table 6.1
Selected Examples of New Ford-Supplier Contracts in the United States, 1985

Supplier	Product	Value ($m)	Terms
Eaton-Clark	engine components; transmission	285	5 years; single sourced
Rockwell	rear axles	350	5 years; single sourced
Allied	airbrake air		5 years; single sourced
Borg-Warner	diesel-engine clutches		5 years; single sourced
Spicer	drivelines	750	5 years; single sourced
Sifco	front axles		5 years; single sourced
Dana	front and rear axles, clutches and frame assembly	2,000	10 years; single sourced

Source: Interviews

regime of multi-sourcing and cut-throat pricing competition. Table 6.1 gives some examples of the nature of the new type of contractual relationships being forged.

Therefore, both in the United States and in Western Europe, changing contractual relations are accompanied by assembler-imposed shifts in other dimensions of the assembler-supplier relationship. Interestingly, these other shifts are most pronounced in the area of supplier involvement in the component design and innovation process

- an important aspect of technological restructuring. One of the three United States assemblers reviewed practices in other sectors and decided to restructure its supplier relations by providing only broad specifications and letting the supplier fill in the design-detail. It was hoped that as a result it would ultimately obtain the part at a mutually agreed price and output level.

Another Western European assembler refers to its suppliers with whom it is developing a new type of long term relationship as "Preferred Suppliers" (a strategy also recently adopted by RG) and has a contractual link which formally recognizes this status. The main components of this relationship are specified as

- agreement to full collaboration in future process and product technological development;
- supplier accepts full design-responsibility and is therefore incorporated into the assembler design process;
- supplier guarantees of quality and performance standards along with supplier approval of assembly techniques involving use of the part;
- supplier agreement to performance standards set by and periodically audited by the assembler;
- agreement covering faulty parts, and mechanisms to settle disputes over this;
- integrated link of supplier via CIE into assembler procedures and database; and
- agreement on scheduling and delivery.

This latter example illustrates the widening base of interaction and joint effort that is created by prior agreement in single-sourcing and long-term contracts between the assembler and supplier.6/ Thus there is evidence that assemblers are indeed <u>seeking</u> to tackle organizational matters in their relations with suppliers as a prelude to technological restructuring. With the industry going through a period of rapid technological change in car design and components, long term single-sourced contracts allow assemblers to make demands that suppliers take on more of the R&D and engineering function, yet at the same time give suppliers a degree of security that ostensibly makes it easier for them to make the necessary financial commitments to meet these new demands. These commitments would almost certainly not be made if short term contracts were in place. Assemblers thus appear to recognize that their own best interests are met by having a local supplier network that enjoys long term viability. And of course suppliers are equally expected to be attracted by the prospects of long term stability among their customers that the supply of quality components will help ensure.

That at least is how the evolving relationships tends to be portrayed by management in the assembly firms. In reality though, this picture of mutual benefit belies the fact that the assemblers still enjoy very considerable power *vis-a-vis* suppliers. The assemblers (particularly in the United States) see the agreement of long-term single-sourced contracts as being a guarantee that the suppliers would deliver annual price reductions as well as other improvements. For example, the Vice-President of Procurement of a United States assembler responded that

> We'll be supervising suppliers directly and are on an aggressive campaign to reduce parts and materials costs. The emphasis today is on cost containment, productivity and the shipment of superb quality parts from suppliers. If a supplier achieves a long term relationship with us we ought to expect that he do things better each year. He shouldn't be coming in each year, asking 'How much can I raise the price?" It can't be; we expect price <u>reductions</u> ... We basically would like to have all of our suppliers do what the oriental (sic) people do - offset their labour costs with increased productivity.

GM's approach to this issue is no less delicate. In letters sent to suppliers announcing the new terms on which GM was prepared to consider long term contractual relationships, it argued that once a supplier achieved this status, it (GM) would expect a five percent price reduction per year through productivity gains and quality improvements and GM was "challenging" suppliers to develop other cost reduction programs through design, material changes and so on. The first year savings could be kept by the supplier but after that these had to be passed on to GM, a move "which will further reinforce our mutually respective competitive position in the world market place". The letter concludes in a similar tone - "Please indicate your acceptance by manually signing below and returning the [tearaway] attachment to this office by March 30, 1984" - a date only two weeks after the letter was <u>sent</u>!

This letter from GM is illuminating for two reasons. First it suggests a tough line from the assemblers towards

Table 6.2
Current and Estimated Reductions in Numbers of Auto Parts Suppliers 1980-1990 (Units)

	1980	1985	1990
United States 1	3,200	2,600	1,300
United States 2	4,000	3,500	1,800
United States 3	1,600	1,300-1,400	700-400
Western Europe 1	1,300	850	700
Western Europe 2	3,000	3,000	2,000
United States Supplier 1	600	400	300
United States Supplier 2	90	75	40

Source: Interviews

the suppliers. But second, and perhaps more significantly, it raises the question of how clearly GM has heard the message from Japan. There, the experience is one of a long-term relationship involving trust and discussion - a tear-off slip requiring agreement within two weeks hardly embodies the "new spirit" which is supposed to be governing the relationship between the assemblers and suppliers. The tone of this circular was repeated in an interview with another United States supplier in which considerable scepticism was raised by the assembler concerning the adequacy of its suppliers' responses to these developments - "only 20 percent of the effort required". And where this particular assembler is insisting on clear evidence of cost reduction and productivity-improving investment, they find that some suppliers either do not believe them, claiming they are already competitive (which they are not) or that they can not afford the new investment. This assembler no longer cared to wait and in fact was already in the process of closing down relationships with such suppliers, preparing to cancel a long standing arrangement with one firm that they "knew would cause the closure of the plant and the loss of 5,000 jobs".

Unfortunately for the suppliers, it is this power on the part of the assemblers to withdraw contracts, that makes the current process of restructuring contractual relationships (which appears in principle to offer salvation to the supplier industry) one that has in practice led to significant cuts in the number of suppliers. Table 6.2 lays out past, current and projected levels of the numbers of supplier used by some of the major assemblers in the United States and Western Europe and shows the substantial declines in supplier numbers (and indirectly) in employment in the supplier industry. One estimate given to us in our interviews was that in both the United States and Western Europe it was likely that the number of component firms would be cut by at least another 20 percent by 1990.

RESTRUCTURING THE DESIGN RELATIONSHIP

In the past, assembler-supplier interactions in the area of design have been circumscribed by the adversarial nature of their arm's-length contractual relationship. Assemblers took upon themselves the responsibility for the design and assembly of the majority of components and component systems. This involved breaking-down each sub-system within the vehicle into its component parts, developing full specifications for each part, submitting the specifications for tender to a variety of suppliers, and then assembling the sub-systems in-house using the components provided by the suppliers. Design was thus a very closely guarded process, undertaken entirely in-house. The objective of this strategy was to ensure assembler control over the technology incorporated in the vehicle in order to reduce the potential market power of the suppliers who might otherwise be able to develop systems expertise and thereby increase their relative power over price-determination. Obviously, the assembler was not always able to impose this relationship for all components or systems, but for the most part the assembler was extremely reluctant to cede control over component design to suppliers.

As in other dimensions of the assembler-supplier relationship, the nature of this interaction at the design interface is beginning to undergo a series of fundamental alterations. The manager of a leading Western European assembler has argued that the benefit derived from their system of integrated planning, design and engineering on productivity and quality was the single most important dimension of the competitive advantages built up by the Japanese in the 1970s.7/ As this aspect of the Japanese model has become more clearly understood, United States and Western European assemblers have begun to take steps to assimilate what is for them an entirely new and alien component-design philosophy. As we shall see, some assemblers have grasped the implications much more fully than others and their approaches to implementation differ dramatically, as does the degree to which they have tackled the problem. Those that are in the process of doing so have found that it requires pervasive organizational and technological changes to established practice. And as we shall see in the following chapter, we believe that the trends now emerging in the design sphere will be among the most important determinants of the future international competitiveness of DC component firms.

These changes which are taking place are occurring at different levels and dimensions. Some are largely internal to the assembler. We have already mentioned one of the most important of these - the move towards off-line sub-assembly. The basic philosophy here is straightforward. In order to streamline final assembly and to reduce the labour content in assembly (which is still relatively un-automated), the aim is now to assemble larger systems off-line and to route these to the final assembly point for installation as a system, rather than have individual components brought together and installed on the final assembly line itself. This approach has implications both for component design (which is expected to facilitate off-line assembly) as well as for the systems/vehicle interface (to allow easy installation in the final assembly stage). A good example of this has recently been adopted in Western Europe by a United States TNC in relation to the installation of the "cockpit" of a new model of passenger car it is assembling in the United Kingdom and the Federal Republic of Germany. The "cockpit" which includes instrument-panel, steering-column, pedal-assemblies, controls for heating and ventilating, and the radio is assembled off-line and tested on computer diagnostic equipment before being installed. Installation takes place through the door-opening and is accomplished simply by fixing twelve bolts and plugging in the wiring harness to the main loom. This eliminates the need for assembly workers to be on their backs on the car floor to install dash components while the vehicle is moving.[8]/

This example demonstrates the benefit at the final assembly stage from this approach. But it is also important to note that such changes have downstream implications for the suppliers. Suppliers responsible for different components of the cockpit repeatedly emphasized that this reorientation of assembly-philosophy had forced them to redesign many of their products. Moreover, the notion of designing for ease of assembly is pervasive and does not stop at the final assembly stage. Indeed, we found numerous examples where the supplier firm had redesigned a component in order to make its own assembly process more efficient. One of these involved a supplier who had initially installed a relatively labour intensive line producing emission control valves in early 1984, staffed by 13 people to assemble one million units/year, with a 12 second cycle time. One of its major customers increased the order to two million/year but wanted the whole component redesigned to allow easier final installation in the vehicle. The supplier was able to redesign the component but found it could not meet the demand for two million units/year cost-effectively by simply duplicating the existing line, and was thus forced to automate the production line using assembly robots. However they soon found that the robot could not assemble the existing product since it had originally been designed for manual assembly. Thus the supplier was forced to undertake an additional product-redesign to allow automated assembly in its own plant so that it could provide a component that could be automatically installed at the final assembly stage. This illustrates the complex and iterative nature of the response which was required.

This shift towards a "design for ease of assembly" philosophy on the part of the assemblers has even more fundamental implications for suppliers than those highlighted above. These arise out of the attempts by assemblers to introduce "modular design" concepts. As a consequence where vehicle builders used to exert tight control over component design and assembly, they are becoming increasingly willing to cede responsibility for this set of activities to suppliers. Thus a new division of design responsibilities is emerging.

The assembler and vehicle designer now approach the task of vehicle design by seeing it as composed of a series of interrelated sub-systems. Only, instead of doing all the design tasks for all components, they now concentrate on (the increasingly complex task) of overall vehicle design and on specifying the broad functions of interface specifications for the different vehicle systems. These "black box" specifications are then turned over to the supplier who now has responsibility for detailed system and component design as well as being responsible for the production of the finished system (and its component parts), and obviously for delivery of these to the assembler. The change in approach is captured in this interview quote:

> at the present time, X does all the design work and passes these drawings on to the suppliers. However, in the future, with simple as well as with more complex sub-assemblies, X will increasingly ask the suppliers to develop the product, with X only defining shape, appearance and functions. The technical solutions will be those of the suppliers.9/

Under these arrangements the vehicle manufacturers can be seen to be moving to system level assembly and integration. In the words of one assembler interviewed: "We no longer wish to deal with individual component suppliers but rather to concentrate our efforts on developing the best possible working relationship with suppliers of systems". To give only one example of this approach in practice, one United States supplier of seats related to us how previously it had had to bid on the basis of assembler specifications and to separately produce and deliver individual elements of the car seat - seat backs, cushions, seat frames, pads, springs, fixtures, seatbelts and other minor components. These were then put together during final assembly and the complete seat installed by the vehicle builder. Very often, the supplier would not win contracts for all the seat components because the assembler's design and purchasing strategy meant that it was seeking the cheapest, multi-sourced components. But now, in the last three contracts that the supplier had bid for, it had been asked to tender for the supply of the entire fully-assembled seat and been given a great degree of latitude in the design and assembly area. As a result it was estimated that its unit production costs would decline by nearly 20 percent. In another example of this new willingness on the part of the assemblers to accept supplier design input, a design-engineer for a brakes-supplier said that the assemblers were now accepting 90 percent of their suggestions for improvement in both product and final assembly - a situation he had never encountered in 30 years in the industry. A third example was that of a supplier of instrument panels who in its most recent contract was required for the first time ever - to design the panel, contract the suppliers of plastic-moldings and the various meters, ensure zero-defect quality, assemble the parts into a system and deliver these as one system to the final assembly plant on a JIT basis.

This movement towards modular design and the devolution of system responsibility to suppliers is prevalent in both the United States and Western Europe, though obviously there are differences in emphasis and in the degree of progress being made towards implementation. Interviews with one French assembler turned up very little effort to foster new design relationships with suppliers, while some United Kingdom suppliers were openly sceptical about the assemblers' commitment to this practice because of its implications in the words of one senior manager "for their monopoly buying power in the market". Interestingly, in the case of one United States assembler, we were told in the United States that the company was fully committed to the design-for-manufacture approach and in both its North American and Western European operations "are relying increasingly on the capabilities of our suppliers to provide product design and self certified quality". However, one United Kingdom manufacturer of springs argued that the same assembler was "frightened" of design-for-manufacture and would not accept any changes it had suggested. Similarly, a major European supplier observed that it appeared that whilst purchasing departments in the assemblers were in the forefront of pushing for new design relationships, the design engineers did not seem nearly as keen to pursue the new strategy.

Despite these occasional "counter-examples" the sense emerging from our interviews was that there was a definite and clearcut - albeit slow-moving - shift towards this new approach on the part of the assemblers. And the pace of change will undoubtedly increase over the rest of the decade in line with the introduction of new model ranges since most of the progressive trends emerging in the United States were drawn from the very recent and ongoing experiences of suppliers dealing with GM and Ford in relation to the Saturn, Buick City, GM10, Alpha, Sable and Taurus model ranges.

The trend towards modular design has a number of important implications. For this shift to work at all requires a new form of contractual and working relationship between assemblers and suppliers. This explains (and was cited as the prime reason for) the big-push on the part of assemblers towards long-term/single-sourced contracts. This new relationship has different (and sometimes contradictory) dimensions as described by one United States firm as follows:

The in-house name for these new relationships are

Integrated System Suppliers, and Value Managed Relationships and their fundamental feature is a long term stable relationship, with the supplier taking over the bulk of engineering R&D for the relevant system.

Under this, the supplier gets a five-year contract at a greatly increased volume and a guaranteed chance to bid against other firms at the end of the period. However the assembler retains considerable power - for instance it gets access to detailed process-data, marketing rights to the design and even has a <u>contractual escape clause</u> allowing a switch to another supplier should a better or cheaper product be offered. This assembler firm in particular had so far only established a few of these relationships but was looking to increase the number substantially in the near future.

This overall trend is more or less in line with what we found at other firms. However what was particularly interesting was that this assembler was prepared to push the concept even further in different areas. For example, it was exploring the possibility of having engineers from component-firms work alongside its own engineers, conceivably even setting up offices inside its plants (an idea mentioned in another interview as a possible mode of operation for Saturn). However it expected objections to arise from its own engineers because this implied a shift towards relying on external expertise. In another area this assembler expected that these new long-term relationships might result in joint ventures - and indeed it was already engaged in developing a joint-venture with a component-supplier producing trim and fittings in the United States, Japan and Western Europe. A Western European firm also moving towards long-term contracts of this sort had explicitly allocated funds to help support the greater R&D effort they were calling for from the suppliers. They were prepared to support 50 percent of R&D costs if the product was unique to the assembler and would second its own engineers to work with the component firms' engineers if requested. In another example, one United Kingdom firm operating under a long term contract collaborated closely with a United States-owned Western European assembler in financing the development of an anti-locking braking system. However this willingness by an assembler to assist its supplier in financing the transition to the era of systems-design and supply was not a common finding.

Another consequence of these trends (which we take up in more detail below) is that these moves by the assemblers are effectively forcing a shift towards greater technological-intensity on the part of the suppliers. The assemblers and suppliers now expect that the suppliers should shoulder a far higher burden of product engineering efforts than in the past. This implies not only more R&D on the part of the suppliers, but development work of a different sort as well - away from work on individual components towards systems-engineering. All the suppliers we interviewed expressed their willingness to make this transition, though some assemblers often had doubts as to whether the supplier could actually deliver on these claims. Nevertheless, the Western European component-suppliers were particularly enthusiastic about these trends since it reinforced their natural comparative advantage. One company supported this view with an example of a new product it developed using its own computer-simulation model which the assembler was unable to replicate because it had neither the relevant simulation expertise or the product-technology.

From the perspective of the assemblers there are often also good cost-savings arising from this transition. One assembler suggested that by shifting the component engineering burden to the supplier, the assembler would save on unit engineering costs since the costs of in-house component engineering by the assembler was usually two-to-three times that of the component firm (because of the latter's specialization). Similarly, other assemblers also expected to make substantial savings by being able to close down those parts of their internal managerial system which had been involved in particular aspects of their relationships with suppliers. In interviews with two United States assemblers it was pointed out that once the product design and supplier rationalization process was completed, they expected to see drastic reductions in central headquarters' management and engineering personnel - those being made redundant by these changes were expected to reach as much as 50 percent of staff in the relevant departments.

Along with increasing R&D, there are other manifestations of growing technological intensity that we shall explore below. These include an increase in the number of joint ventures being struck between component firms with the express purpose of sharing development costs and gaining access to advanced technology, and the rapid spread of computer-based linkages between assemblers and suppliers, not only in the increasingly common area of parts ordering and scheduling, but also in the use of shared data bases and integrated CAD linkages.

A further feature of this trend towards greater system-integration is largely technological in nature. Not surprisingly, new product technologies involving both microelectronics and new materials are playing an increasing role as a facilitator towards systemic technical change. We shall explore this in more detail below but the point is obvious. Developments involving both microelectronics and new materials (such as plastics) are almost inevitably going to lead in the direction of different sub-systems rather than merely substituting incremental redesigns of existing products. This trend has obvious strategic implications for suppliers of those components likely to be replaced or eliminated entirely, and also for assembler-supplier relations. Because of the need for close tolerances and finely fitting interfaces at the system level, the development of the new product technology often requires close interaction early on in the design stage between assembler and supplier. Major suppliers seem to have targeted this area as one where they can use their greater product specific expertise to develop new technology-based sub-systems, and then subsequently to enter into joint development agreements with vehicle makers so as to adapt these new concepts to the individual assembler's requirements. This is what happened in relation to the anti-lock braking system developed jointly by a United Kingdom firm and a United States TNC assembler in Western Europe where electronics was the key to this new braking system. In the United States an electronics firm is pursuing a similar joint product development scheme with two United States assemblers to introduce computer-controlled, fibre-optic-based multiplex wiring system in volume cars. And in Italy and France component firms are working very closely with assemblers in utilizing plastics in rear-doors, front-ends, and dashboards where numerous individual components will be replaced by single molded pieces.

The final implication of this shift towards modular design and system integration we wish to emphasize relates to the determinants of competitiveness and industry structure. This too has different dimensions. There was a consensus among the supplier firms that the ongoing shift towards systems supply would continue and would become dominant in the industry. This implied that the ability of a component firm to supply systems would become, as in the case of quality, a <u>minimum</u> criteria for competing nationally and internationally. The assemblers would really only be looking to firms with this system capability to enter into long-term relationships - without it they would not even be "allowed" to compete.

A clear example of how systems capabilities are becoming crucial to competitiveness and component markets comes from the competitive strategy of a United States manufacturer of brakes and wheels. As the trends towards system-supply became apparent in 1983-1984, this firm developed a strategy that allowed it to offer a complete wheel assembly and manufacturing installation capability to the assembler. This involved the provision of a new brake system (engineered and manufactured in a new facility to assembler requirements), the installation of these brakes into the wheels, the design of an easy installation interface between the wheel/brake unit and the vehicle, wheel painting to required colours on a completely flexible basis and JIT delivery to the point of final assembly. This system offered the assembler a unique off-site produced sub-assembly that was not available from any other brake manufacturer and was also in keeping with the assembler's objective to go for flexible JIT in smaller plants. The firm has won two long-term contracts on the basis of this strategy - one of these to supply Saturn and the other to supply a Japanese assembler in the United States. Similar examples of both trends were given to us by producers of dashboards (some details already mentioned), ignition-systems, entertainment-systems, window and door operating systems, and seats. In the case of the seat manufacturer, it has just built a new $12.5m plant to assemble complete seats and deliver these to a final assembly plant 14 miles away within 108 minutes of the order being placed. For the first time, this plant will have all structural, metal, foam and trim operations under one roof in order to facilitate the JIT assembly and delivery of completed seats.

There are a number of important capabilities that are inherent in this new requirement to compete on the basis of a system design and production capability. These include the need to master new product technology in electronics and new materials, the ability to handle interactive CAD communication with the assembler and the ability to sustain a rapid rate of product innovation. The reduction in product-life is such that many of the suppliers interviewed reported that their entire product range had had to be replaced in the last five years, often by entirely new products exhibiting much higher levels of integration and technical complexity.

All of these variables are obviously interrelated and just as obviously do not necessarily exist in all component categories. Nevertheless the implication of their collective presence is that the current process of pervasive change in assembler-supplier design relationships is substantially increasing both the technological and the organizational barriers to entry in the component industry. Consequently they reinforce the new locational tendencies we have emphasized in other chapters and suggest that unless suppliers (whether from industrially-advanced or developing countries) are able to develop close organizational, technological and geographical relations with assemblers along the lines described above, it is unlikely they will be able to compete in the future.

THE TREND TOWARDS JUST-IN-TIME

The principle of JIT in production organization has been discussed extensively in Chapters 2 and 4, in which we distinguished between intra- and inter-plant inventory reduction. (The progress of intra-plant JIT was considered in Chapter 4, in which the Japanese firms were compared with North American and Western European assemblers). But as we noted, JIT is much more than an inventory minimization system. With its emphasis on flexibility, minimal waste, minimal downtime and small batch production it is rapidly becoming the new organizing principle in assembly industries in the 1990s and beyond in much the same way that the Fordist principle of just-in-case inventories dominated not only the auto industry but most other assembly-based industries in the machinofacturing era. In specific relation to the auto industry and in particular to the component sector, it is no longer a question of whether, but rather when JIT will become an industry-wide practice.

There is little doubt that the message of JIT has at the very least been heard throughout the industry. Whether or not it is being implemented with the same enthusiasm is quite a different matter, especially in Western Europe. In both the United Kingdom and France, though the national assemblers have become fully aware of the importance of JIT, it had not assumed a high priority at the time this research was being undertaken. Many rationalizations were offered as to why it could not be achieved in these particular situations, including the argument by one that while all Japanese plants were located on sites with a flat terrain, their leading production plant was in a very hilly location! But even if arguments such as this do hold some validity, these only refer to inter-plant, and not intra-plant JIT. Of the Western European assemblers, Fiat appeared to have the strongest commitment and a relatively clear policy (in keeping with the clarity of its overall strategy outlined in Chapter 5). The company is striving to achieve limited JIT on a company wide basis, moving to weekly deliveries by 1988 compared to monthly deliveries in 1985. Their 24 main suppliers - many of whom are affiliates of Fiat - are reported to be cooperative. Already, by 1985, 70 percent of suppliers (by volume) were in the Turin region, with the average distance being only 30 kilometers. Fiat's average inventory level in 1985 was eight days in 1985 and although they had plans to reduce this to two days by 1988, senior management thought that an average level of five days was a more realistic expectation.

In the United States, the situation is markedly different. Statements by firm and industry spokespeople, trade journals, industry shows, and press reports are replete with references concerning the necessity to adopt JIT. In early 1985 <u>Automotive Industries</u> observed that

> You can get an argument on almost any subject in the American auto industry. But a few things are almost universally agreed on. One is that Just in Time production is probably going to do more to make the US auto industry competitive than any other single thing.10/

Referring to the speed with which JIT is being adopted, the article goes on to cite the views of a leading expert on United States JIT

> Progress has been made toward JIT production... in terms of actual implementation it only amounts to 2-3% overall ... but if you look at the attitude changes and what's planned for the near future, we're probably 30-40% along the way [with] most of the work still to be done ... but if you take a very broad view of JIT - meaning the disciplined approach of shipping just the required amount at just the required time and just the required parts - it should go 100% over time.11/

Unfortunately, it is virtually impossible to judge the rate of diffusion of JIT through the various tiers of the industry. In terms of the big three assembler firms, we have already discussed some of the problems involved in their efforts to introduce internal JIT (Chapter 4). In terms of external JIT relations with suppliers, every company has a JIT program in place and virtually every plant has some JIT delivery; but overall progress is difficult to chart. At our interviews in Ford, GM and Chrysler for instance, it was claimed that virtually all engine and assembly plants had some form of JIT but this applied to only around ten percent of all bought-in components.

Most of the attention in the press has focused on experiments at GM's Buick City plant and in its Oldsmobile division as well as in Chrysler's Sterling Heights' plant. Given the problems discussed in the last section of Chapter 5 in relation to the introduction of automation technology, it is difficult to judge the long term feasibility of the program for JIT laid out at Buick City and summarized in Table 6.3, since it has not yet been fully implemented. However the plans do give an indication of GM's approach. GM has had more demonstrable success with their JIT program in the Oldsmobile division, which unlike that proposed for Buick City is already fully under way. The JIT program at Oldsmobile depends on immediate electronic communication between the Division and 70 principal suppliers. These 70 provide 700-800 parts and between them account for 85 percent of parts needed for GM20 cars. Deliveries are on average made on a daily basis to the Division's plants participating in the program, with many parts being delivered twice daily. Overall, after two years of effort, the program was about 70 percent implemented by 1986.

While the situation is uncertain vis-à-vis the assembler's overall JIT position, the picture is much clearer when viewed from the supplier's perspective. They recognize that the pressure to move to JIT is perceived as likely to be sustained. The ability to deliver JIT, like the provision of enhanced levels of quality and the supply of component systems, is expected in the future to become a minimum criterion for tendering. This perception was being translated into reality with every component-supplier we interviewed in the United States already moving towards implementing JIT delivery to their customers. Table 6.4 provides information on various dimensions of JIT adopted by our sample of United States firms.

Implicit in this data are the significant number of

Table 6.3
Targets for JIT at Buick City - mid 1986.

The following features are particularly significant:

Supplier location. It is planned that 80%+ of parts will come from suppliers within a 100 mile radius and 99% within 300 miles. So far, though, only 53% of parts come from within 100 miles. Fourteen new suppliers are building new plants to supply on a JIT basis. Special snow-clearance teams established to keep roads clear in winter.

Inventory level and delivery frequency. Inventory levels will be reduced from 10 days to 8 hours on average. Full JIT delivery aimed for with an optimum of one hour. So far only 20% delivered truly JIT with remainder stocked in warehouse. 100% returnable component containers will be used and dozens of truck carriers normally used to move parts will be reduced to only five.

Synchronized supply of stamping to assembly. No production of stamping to stock as in previous Buick plants; rather as needed car-specific pressing and delivery from adjacent stamping facility. New quick Die Change fender presses allow 1.1 minute die change on 2 fender press.a

Flexible automation. Moderate use of assembly robots but extensive automation elsewhere, e.g. rapid-change robotized painting system handles 25 colours. Changeover time of 9 seconds.

Zero defect strategy. Suppliers expected to deliver perfect quality. Receiving dock inspection for quality has been eliminated. Reduction of repair bays from 72 to 10. Repair bays within line, rather than off-line.

Limited modular assembly. Some major sub-assemblies assembled off-line but synchronized with final assembly line. Doors fitted after interior assembly. Computer control of component delivery limited major sub-assemblies.

Overall space minimization. Planned output rate of 75/hour but assembled in 1.5 million square feet facility which is half the size of traditional plants.

Electronics, combined with shift to systems is hurting small suppliers who specialize in providing mechanical sensors and actuators to larger systems suppliers. These devices and parts are found everywhere in the car - to sense wheel speed, control foot pedals, gear movements, brake systems, etc. All the surfacr mounting look the same but the control mechanisms are being completely transformed. This trend is simultaneously leading to reductions in total number of suppliers and a change in supplier-contractor preferences towards firms able to deal with demands of electronic control systems and interfaces.

Source: Interviews

---

[a]Before the Buick City concept, Buick fenders were handled 22 times before installation and had to travel 8,000 feet from stamping plant to assembly plant. With new Buick City layout, fenders are now handled only 6 times and travel only 140 feet.

Table 6.4
Select Examples of JIT Practices Adopted by United States and Western European Component Firms

Company	Product	Work in Progress	Inventory	Through-put	Delivery	Set Up	Other
1	Machined Parts	50% reduction down to 40 days	120 days			Reduced from 3hrs to 20 secs	
2	Trans-mission	438 cases down to 40 cases with increase in shipments	Reduced by 72%	1 week to 2 hours			25% saving in floor space
3	Machined Parts	80% reduction	98% reduction	10-8 days down to 28 mins	Twice daily from monthly		
4	Shafts	22-23 days down to 9 days	60% reduction	1-18 days down to 2 hours	From weekly to daily		Greatly improved reaction time
5	Cams	20 days down to 5 days	40% reduction	Increased by 200%			
6	Brake	70% reduction	down to 3 days		16 plants supplied on 1-2 day basis		

7	Clutches	80% reduction	down to 1 week	150% improvement	8 plants on daily basis	Overall machinery time reduced by 80%
8	Transmission	40% reduction	down from 30 days to 1 week	12 days to 2 days	30% of output delivered 2 day average. Expected to increase to 60% by 1990	Expect to build 3 new plants to deliver JIT
9	Rivets		Down to ½ day	50% improvement	Hourly	Reduced by 80%	1/3 unit price reduction possible due to savings
10	Seats	down from 3 weeks to 2 days	1 month down to 1 day	180% improvement	4 plants delivered JIT. Daily to GM1; 25 mins to GM2; 2 hrs to Nissan 2 hrs to Ford.	4 new plants built to deliver JIT

Source: Interviews

firms who either have already built geographically proximate facilities to final assembly or are prepared to do so - by one estimate 40 percent of United States component suppliers are considering relocation to facilitate JIT delivery to their customers.12/ In addition to this, a number of component firms had no plans to relocate for JIT because they already had plants sufficiently close to existing assemblers to meet their JIT requirements without new investment. There seems little doubt, therefore - at least on the basis of the induced investment response of component firms to site new plants near installations such as Saturn and Buick City as well as the Honda and Nissan facilities - that not only are the suppliers willing to move, but that the assemblers fully expect them to do so. Indeed, three of the firms listed in Table 6.4 emphasized that their willingness to build new plants close to final assembly and to subsequently supply on a JIT basis was responsible for their winning contracts. By contrast, one of the firms interviewed had recently lost a contract because it was not able to guarantee JIT delivery, partly because of locational factors.13/ Another significant feature emerging from this table is that the movement towards JIT supply is apparent across firms operating in all types of product category. However it is difficult to judge how realistic is the expectation of one of our respondents that, by 1990, 90 percent of component firms will be supplying more than 75 percent of their output on a JIT basis. Despite the fact that one firm expected that within 12 months it would already be at more than 60 percent JIT, we doubt that these levels of performance can be realized.

There are three general points which emerge from our research on the adoption of JIT among United States and Western European component suppliers. The first is that there are still many problems to overcome before the sector can be considered as having adopted JIT procedures effectively. Many of the strategic plans for JIT remain just that - strategic plans. In many cases the management which is aware of the problem has found difficulty in translating its message not just to the shop-floor, but also to the Board. Moreover, there are still firms (or at least key individuals within firms) who see JIT solely as a technique for forcing their suppliers to shoulder more of the costs of holding inventory. More evidence of misunderstanding arises in relation to another commonly-cited problem involving the growing use by suppliers of warehouses located close-by assembly plants from which the suppliers can then deliver on a JIT basis. We found numerous cases of this and indeed were given examples that showed that despite public commitment to JIT on the part of senior company staff, some plant managers still implicitly expected suppliers to maintain buffer stocks (of up to one month) at such warehouses in case of a shortfall in supplier delivery. Some analysts have interpreted this as evidence that the industry's understanding of and commitment to JIT is fundamentally flawed. This is a possibility, but more likely the use of warehouses by suppliers not close enough to secure daily deliveries on a JIT basis is seen by both assemblers and suppliers as an acceptable interim solution in what is, after all, a period of transition. Over time therefore we see this phenomenon fading in importance as JIT procedures become firmly established in the industry.

A second general conclusion which can be drawn from our research concerning JIT relates to the attempt by the United States industry to facilitate JIT through infrastructural initiatives. One of these is an industry-wide initiative called the Automotive Industry Action Group (AIAG) - a non-profit group established in 1981, involving financial contributions and the secondment of staff from both assemblers and suppliers. The AIAG mandate is to tackle a whole range of problems collectively that are inhibiting the industry's progress towards adopting new best-practice systems of organization and production. The AIAG operates through a series of working groups specializing in particular topics. These act both as an educational force and as a catalyst for change in the industry through holding seminars, disseminating material and video tapes, training programs, conducting surveys and developing industry standards. The AIAG has so far established six working groups concerned with the following activities:

- <u>Communication and Electronic Data Interchange.</u> Working to develop standardized electronic data transmission formats for the huge volume of information that the industry currently exchanges via paper.
- <u>Bar Coding</u>. Working to develop industry standards for the use of bar codes and other forms of labels to denote the contents of component-containers. These codes will contain production details for cars in assembly and sub-assemblies to facilitate automated assembly and JIT delivery and to identify any type of

product at any stage in its use or manufacture.
- <u>Company Coding</u>. Working to define specifications for an industry-wide company coding system, thus making it possible to denote by code the name and geographical location of a company or company division.
- <u>Just-In-Time</u>. Working to promote awareness and diffusion of JIT techniques. Extensive involvement of staff in servicing, training exercises and technical assistance.
- <u>Returnable Containers</u>. Working to promote the use of returnable containers designed for Just-In-Time shipments and to establish national guidelines for trucking and shipping.
- <u>Schedule Stabilization</u>. This group researches and disseminates information on methods of improving schedule stability and manufacturing flexibility.

The scale of AIAG activities is still small, and despite the drumbeating in industry literature, its impact so far can still only be considered marginal. Nonetheless, the collective nature of this effort in an industry notorious for the intense character of its competition is an illuminating insight into the restructuring process that is currently underway in the United States.

A second industry-wide initiative that is being pursued by the assemblers is their rapid push to establish electronic link-ups with their suppliers. These linkages are expected to serve two purposes. The first relates to the exchange of information regarding component ordering, shipping-notices, build-programs, material-releases, invoicing, and so on. All the United States and some of the Western European assemblers have been setting up systems to deal with these information flows for some time now. The need for these links using computer-to-computer communication is obvious and we have already seen the benefits accruing to Nissan in Japan from such a system, especially in relation to JIT (Chapter 4). An internal GM survey estimated that there are approximately 50 or so different paper-based forms through which assemblers exchange information with their suppliers. Multiply this in the case of GM's 26 divisions, 3,500 suppliers and thousands upon thousands of different parts and it seems surprising that they have ever been able to communicate with each other. It is partly to "clean-up" this messy set of procedures that GM acquired Electronic Data Systems (Chapter 5).

It is for this reason perhaps that, particularly in

the United States, assemblers have adopted a perspective that sees the attainment of an on-line computer-based link-up with suppliers as being a key feature of the new relationships which are being forged. Thus firms like GM and Ford (as well as RG, Fiat and Volkswagen to a lesser extent in Western Europe) have in the last few years placed an increasing degree of pressure on their suppliers to get "on-line" - and with compatible computer systems - as quickly as possible. In the United States, AIAG is playing an increasingly important role in facilitating this process. Certainly GM and Ford felt, by the end of 1984, that they were sufficiently far-advanced in this with their major suppliers that they could set deadlines during 1985-1986 by which the rest of their supplier network were expected to be on-line. It is illuminating to note that they did this in the dictatorial fashion of old. GM sent one of its vintage letters threatening that suppliers had to be on-line by a certain date or else face the consequences. Ford called together a meeting of all of its smaller suppliers and, in the words of one participant, "knocked our heads together", stating that by the end of 1986 they all had to be hooked into the Ford computer network or risk losing contracts. The fashion in which this was done again raises questions about whether the assemblers really have adopted a more co-operative Japanese-style approach in their dealing with suppliers or if they are, as their critics claim, assuming that a technological solution is the answer to their problem.

Western European companies interviewed were well aware of the possibilities of electronic link-up in this area and some have already moved quite far along this route. RG, for instance, has been working closely with its 350 major suppliers and many of its smaller supply companies to set up a similar system and are even willing to subsidize the purchase of the computer system if necessary. On the other hand some firms such as Peugeot and Renault have little or no computer links with their suppliers, though systems are under development. Nevertheless despite the slower progress in Western Europe, the trend towards electronic link-ups in area of component ordering, scheduling and purchasing is well established.

This is not yet so in the second area of electronic link-up which relates specifically to the design stage. Obviously enough, the desirability of achieving such a link is clear to all concerned. And again many assemblers appear to see an inseparable linkage between shared design data bases and the success of the new long term design relationships between assemblers and suppliers. And there seems little doubt that in time, on-line access to each other's design data-bases and indeed even interactive joint design will be widespread. However the current reality is that events are moving slowly in this area and few truly successful design-links have been established between suppliers and assemblers. One of the major sources of difficulties is incompatibility between CAD systems. Within both assemblers and suppliers there has been a great proliferation of different systems. As a result it is not surprising to find six or seven different systems in the same assembler, and even two or three different ones in the same division. All of these might in addition be different from those used by the suppliers. All the United States assemblers and some of the Western Europeans (again RG stands out in this regard)14/ are working very hard to overcome these problems individually and collectively through the establishment of company-and industry-wide standards and protocols (for example the MAP, TOPS and IGIS initiatives).15/ However, it is widely recognized that there is still a long way to go to achieve fully operational interfirm computer-based interaction in the design sphere - estimates ranging between five-to-ten years or even longer were frequently made in our interviews.

A final conclusion to be drawn from our research on JIT is that as a general rule most component firms thought it unlikely that they would be able to achieve levels of inventory reduction commonly found in Japan. This conclusion is aptly summed up by the views of one of the managing directors of a United Kingdom components firm

> It is worth noting that for many of our components the average stockholding ten years ago was two months at the assemblers and two months at our premises. In theory this could be cut down to two days or even one day. However, it is worth remembering that in Japan component suppliers are situated a mile from assemblers ... In the UK this geographic proximity is not possible and will therefore always inhibit the full implementation of JIT concepts. We believe that in Japan the production line dries up after one shift if there is a breakdown in component deliveries. Clearly we could not operate on such a slender margin of safety in the UK

In addition to this progress by the major component firms in providing output on a JIT basis to the assemblers, the industry faces the additional problem of diffusing this system beyond the assembler-supplier level to also incorporate sub-contractors. In Chapter 4 we observed that in Japan, JIT was pervasive at all levels of the supply system and that if the United States and Western European industries were to remain competitive then their adoption of the new principles of organization would have to be similarly pervasive. Our research findings suggest that in the United States at least, many major component-firms are in the process of restructuring their relations with their own suppliers. Many of the same steps described above are being followed - the introduction of new contractual relations, a new emphasis on quality, setting up electronic links on scheduling and so on. But there was no evidence of collaboration with their own suppliers in design. Although less progress seems to have been made on JIT, the process of change is slowly percolating through the supplier industry. Indeed some of the major suppliers felt they were doing rather better than the assemblers in restructuring supplier relations. Nevertheless there are still many problems to be overcome in the course of the component-firms forcing the rigours of JIT down through their own supplier network. For instance one United Kingdom producer of springs argued that while it was prepared to give JIT delivery and quality guarantees to assemblers, its suppliers were often not prepared to do so. It faced particular problems with its steel supplier to whom it is really only a very small customer. Thus the Managing Director of the company claimed that when he tried "to pass on the JIT performance criteria demanded by the assembler to his steel supplier, these were met with a mixture of abuse and ridicule." So far we can only conclude that below the topmost levels of suppliers, the structure of the supply network has not yet been fundamentally altered. When these changes are forthcoming, this is likely to have a significant impact on global sourcing (Chapter 7), but as yet the process is only just beginning.

TECHNOLOGICAL CHANGE IN THE COMPONENTS SECTOR

As the discussion in the earlier sections indicates, United States and Western European suppliers are preoccupied with responding to the new demands being thrust upon them by the assemblers and by their own efforts to address internal organizational and managerial reforms.

But, in addition to these dynamic forces the industry is also having to cope with a series of technological innovations whose roots are exogenous to the components industry. Because many component firms have traditionally operated with a low level of product and process technology, utilizing well-tried materials and focussing primarily on meeting assemblers' price demands, this poses a particularly difficult transition for them. However, as we argued in Chapter 3 (and will demonstrate further below), this passive attitude to technological innovation is no longer viable. Thus greater technological intensity and complexity is inevitable in the industry. Moreover, market-structure seems certain to change since high technology requires large outlays of R&D which provides the basis for firm economies of scale.

Consequently, concentration in the industry is growing rapidly, but is taking a variety of forms. In some cases the spreading of technological costs involves the linking of equity with competitors. In other cases it is leading to an array of technological collaborations as well as cooperation in development and production in other countries (to spread costs over greater sales). FDI - another way of spreading heavy indirect R&D costs - is also another possible outcome of these trends towards change in the industry. All of these developments in the components sector mirror those realized in the late 1970s and early 1980s by the assemblers.

We shall review these developments below and assess their implications for our major concern with FDI and offshore-sourcing in the following chapter. However, before engaging in this discussion it is important to bear in mind that while the components industry in Western Europe, the United States and Japan manifest similar technological trends, there are important differences in the context within which these innovations are occurring. The clearest difference is that while Japanese firms are able to concentrate on technological matters, United States and Western European firms are having to respond to both organizational and technological change. Similarly, conditions governing performance differ significantly between Western Europe and the United States. In Western Europe - with the possible exception of the United Kingdom - it appears that assemblers in France, Italy and the Federal Republic of Germany have yet to submit the components' industry to the same kind of pressure to restructure as have their United States counterparts. This is partly because Western European assemblers operate in more protected markets and are not yet facing the same scale of competition as are the Americans. Another factor contributing to the difference between the United States and Western Europe is that United States component firms themselves face a very substantial competitive threat from foreign firms. These are of two types - the first comes from the impending invasion of Japanese component firms seeking to invest directly in the United States and the other is from an increase in imports from low-wage countries, in some cases nurtured by the offshore-sourcing strategies of United States assemblers. And finally, the severe pressure that United States assemblers are now under from the Japanese in their domestic markets is beginning to alarm United States suppliers who face the possibility of a decline in demand from the Big Three and significant barriers to sales to Japanese auto firms, both with respect to the domestic and foreign operations. This specific set of circumstances is provoking United States component firms into responses that are particularly important for our concerns. The first (which we explore in the final chapter) is to increase the level of their offshore activity both to reap short-run cost-cutting gains and to establish themselves in developing markets that might hold some potential for the future. The second (discussed below) is to pursue the formation of joint ventures, particularly with their erstwhile Japanese competitors.

The Predominance of Product Change

At a time when so much technology-related activity is occurring in the components industry, it is difficult to pinpoint specific trends as being dominant. Nevertheless, our interviews suggested that developments relating to product technology were among the most important factors to which component firms were having to respond. Assemblers are insisting on higher quality, better performance and a wider product-mix. This translates into demands for the suppliers to move further into the use of electronics and new materials and to increase the systemic nature of their products. Simultaneously, foreign competition is increasing and is expected to become even fiercer. Thus domestic component firms are under pressure to match these new entrants in performance and quality, as well as on price. Among the many developments occurring in this area in the United States and Western European component sector, three stand out as being particularly important for our concerns.

Growing R&D and design intensity. The quickening pace of product change forced through by the car assemblers requires component firms to step up the level of R&D effort. This is essential if the component firms are to be able to cope with the demands of developing new product technologies beyond their experience as well as being able to meet the need to supply sub-systems instead of individual components. This has a number of implications. First as in the case of Japan (Chapter 4), new R&D staff are increasingly concentrated among electronics and new materials specialists. Of 250 R&D staff employed by one United States firm, nearly 40 percent were electronics engineers, while 50 percent of new R&D staff employed by a United Kingdom engine parts firm had either an electronics or new materials background. Second, there has been a steady (albeit slow) increase in R&D investment, as shown by Table 6.5, for a select group of larger TNC component firms. As the table shows these firms are all consistently above the industry average of 3.1 percent in 1982. And, third, there is a growing divergence in R&D expenditure between firms providing systems (7.6 percent of sales in R&D) and those providing individual components in the traditional fashion where R&D expenditure is below 3 percent of sales.[16]/

It is clear from the activity of these six large United States-based component firms - all TNCs - that proportionate spending on R&D grew sharply in the early 1980s, sometimes even trebling in a period of three years. Of this, product R&D was consuming on average more than 60 percent of all R&D expenditure in our sample firms. In addition to increasing levels of R&D, management has sought to integrate product R&D and production engineering more closely, with many firms taking steps to effect a smooth flow of ideas and communication between staff in all departments and to create in the words of one senior executive, "a technological hot house". This growth was viewed as an essential feature of future competitive strategy that is necessary to allow component firms "to avoid being squeezed by low cost imports from the Third World on the one hand and high value added products from Japan on the other".[17]/ Interestingly, this movement towards greater R&D efforts is reflected across a wide variety of product categories. Just as interesting is the fact that in firms where R&D was not rising (and there were a number) there was generally a strong difference in perspective between R&D and design engineers, and senior

Table 6.5
Trends in R&D Expenditure for Selected United States Component Suppliers, 1979-1984

	R&D as % of Sales					
Year	Firms 1	2	3	4	5	6
1979	2.9			1.6		
1980	3.3			2.0		
1981	3.4	2.8		2.3	3.2	
1982	3.4	3.0		2.4	3.3	2.6
1983	3.8	3.3	2.5	-	4.0	2.8
1984	4.0	3.5	2.7	2.8	4.5	6.0
1985		3.6	3.2	5.2	6.6	

Source: Interviews

management "who still believe that the only key to competitive success is to make the products fast, cheap and in volume".18/ One of the engineers interviewed had worked for another firm forced out of business in the last two years because it had failed to undertake the R&D required to keep up with fender product technology. Moreover, a recent survey of suppliers' attitudes to R&D suggested that the current predominance of large firms in the R&D league table was not due to smaller firms indifference to the importance of R&D, but more to the lack of resources on the part of the smaller firms.19/

Mirroring this overall shift in the United States components sector, there are also moves towards greater R&D in the Western European industry. Table 6.6 details the level of R&D support (and number of projects) provided by Fiat, one of Western Europe's largest volume producers to its suppliers between 1981 and 1984. Other examples of this trend are the considerable financial assistance being given by Peugeot to the development of strong national suppliers in brakes, electronic components and transmissions. Almost all of these interventions by the assemblers are designed primarily to upgrade product quality, although clearly there will be derived implications for deepening production technology as well.

Another reflection of the growing R&D effort in product technology is a change in the pattern of diffusion of CAD among component firms. Whereas in the early 1980s

Table 6.6
Support for Component Suppliers' R&D by FIAT, 1981-1984

Year	Cost (Lire bn)	No. of Agreements
1981	7.5	34
1982	9.0	38
1983	11.5	41
1984	15.0	48

Source: Interviews

the use of CAD was primarily confined to the largest component firms, smaller-sized firms are now also having to invest in this key enabling technology in order to survive. The reasons for doing this are largely to meet assembler demands to upgrade product designs, to provide a broader product-mix, to be able to adjust to rapid product change, to incorporate the principles of design-for-manufacture and to be more (and earlier) involved in systems design.[20]/

Thus we found that a sample of firms (composed of producers of small engine components, minor mechanical and bulky non-mechanical parts) with a combined total of 200 plants in 32 countries had spent more than $300 million on CAD systems for their United States plants in the last 3 years.[21]/ They found that the greatest advantages lay in the flexibility of shorter lead times offered by CAD systems as opposed to improvements in the productivity of design engineers.[22]/ And most of the remaining firms had plans either to change their existing system or purchase new equipment to allow themselves to be linked on-line to their principle customers.[23]/ Another response confirming the above trend came from two producers (of brakes and exterior fittings) who reported that the internal pressure to move into CAD was strongest from manufacturing rather than design engineers.[24]/

What stood out particularly in our interviews was the pervasive impact of electronics in the realm of product development. New or redesigned products incorporating electronics (and often pulling along complementary innovations) were by far the most prevalent of all changes identified, with many of these incorporating a shift to systems. Most of the firms interviewed believed that electronics had revolutionized their component-mix causing them either to completely redesign their entire product range over the past five years or to predict that this would occur within the coming five years. The main dimensions of the effect of electronics on product technology are given in Table 6.7.

A further trend in product development relates to the impact of these developments in product technology on smaller firms who are finding that they are no longer able to count on their product-mix remaining stable and therefore have to be prepared to continually explore ways of widening and/or deepening their product mix. In the case of a United Kingdom spring supplier, the firm perceived a threat to its established markets not from individual producers of springs but from new trends in modular engine and suspension systems. Its response was to focus on a particular niche, specializing in a suspension spring for very large vehicles where the engineering/physics problem of spring-design are amplified. To do this, the firm developed computer skills in the production engineering and R&D areas to develop new products and in the process opened up valuable new business opportunities.

In addition to this trend towards niche-specialization there is often also a simultaneous trend towards diversification. One Western European supplier invested $10m in upgrading its product and production technology in its main product (water pumps) and invested a similar sum in the development of a new type of shock absorber (containing 25 percent fewer parts than previous designs and possessing a degree of variability that allows them to be adapted to different vehicles). The inducement to change was similar - a fairly dramatic change in the market for its existing product mix forced it to explore other areas and it fully expects to be forced into further changes in the future.

This shift towards greater specialization and deeper technological intensity is widely reflected across the industry among the more dynamic firms. They see it as essential to their survival - and essential to that of the assemblers who are increasingly reliant upon the technological expertise of the independent parts supplier.

Trends in Production Technology

Like the assemblers the component industry is investing heavily in new production technology, though of course the scale of such investments is much lower and has been constrained by the severity of competitive pressures and the recession in the auto sector in the early 1980s. Nevertheless the commitment to the introduction of new production technology in the components sector is pervasive. In their survey of a representative sample of nearly 300 firms, Cole et al found that 88 percent of all United States component firms had major capital investment program underway or planned.25/ In all of the firms we interviewed there was evidence of considerable activity in this area. The type of investments being undertaken was broad and, needless to say, most of these involved microelectronics-based automation of one form or another, ranging from the installation of fixed automation in machinery, stamping, and assembly, through computer-controlled inspection systems and a growing number of flexible installations. Unlike the assemblers, we did not find much evidence of absorption problems on the part of suppliers. This suggests that for a variety of reasons, they are taking a more measured approach to the introduction of new technology with most firms concentrating on incremental moves into new technology and relatively fewer attempting massive and ambitious investments in state-of-the-art or factory-of-the-future installations.26/

Within this overall shift towards growing technological intensity in the production sphere, a number of important dimensions can be pointed out. First, automation (and particularly flexible automation) is expensive, and many component suppliers are constrained by a shortage of capital. For example, one United States supplier had already installed 160 assembly robots in various plants plus four new synchronous assembly lines in a clutch plant (serving Chrysler on a JIT basis) at a cost of $10m. Their plans called for an immediate doubling of robot use, and the installation of another 40 new automated assembly lines, but these have had to be delayed because of capital constraints. This is similar to the patterns in the United Kingdom where more modest investments have taken place but which the firms would have preferred to increase had the resources been available. The problem of capital availability was cited by Cole et al to explain the greater concentration of large United States component firm investing in new production technology compared to small firms.27/

Tied to capital availability is the question of absorptive capacity. Large firms also tended to have much more scope for experimenting with new production technology than smaller firms in terms of the depth of their engineering and managerial skills, and the existence of multi-plant/multi-line set-ups where risky technical change could be introduced without endangering the firm's viability. Overall the implication is that the diffusion of automation technology is currently being slowed by a combination of difficult macro conditions and growing firm-economies associated with its purchase and use.

Secondly, a slightly different perspective on this problem comes from an interview with a large United States components firm concerning its efforts to improve productivity in its stamping lines. The firm felt that it had made good progress in the last two years in reducing die change times via organizational innovations - these had been cut by 20 percent. However, as Table 6.7 shows, when it compared itself to a Japanese firm with which it has an affiliation, the gap was still enormous. Its planned response to this was to pursue a joint organization/technology strategy where further organizational change is linked to new investment. Thus in 1985 it was expected to spend $22.5m on new stamping technology. However, its expectation is that to replace all of its lines and to reorganize production flow and introduce JIT will require $300m and take 10 years. The reason for this is that their stamping equipment is of varying age, condition and configuration. Thus, they argue, incremental improvement is not really possible and whole lines will have to be replaced simultaneously. This firm was well aware that the Japanese presented a moving target, but they believed that at least the target was clear and that it could be achieved if only they could raise their investment to the necessary level.

Thirdly, in product categories where annual volumes are high and where firms believe that dedicated automation is still possible (for example in semiconductor automation or windscreen manufacture), firms are moving rapidly into fixed automation and dedicated lines and away from the labour-intensive but still dedicated transfer lines that currently dominate the industry.

However, both within firms and between firms the extent of this progress in enhancing production technology varies widely. The result of this is a tendency towards incremental innovation within existing plants rather than radical attempts at automation in new plants (for example Factory-of-the-Future projects). The costs and benefits of this incremental shift towards fixed automation are

Table 6.7
Die Change Times for United States and Japanese Component Affiliates on Comparable Press, 1981-1985[a]

	Japanese	United States
1981	40 minutes	8 hrs
1982	20 minutes	8 hrs
1983	9 minutes	6.2 hrs
1984	7.2 minutes	5.8 hrs
1985	5 minutes	5 hrs

Source: Interviews

[a] Comparisons made by United States firm for identical 15 station, 15- ton press for stamping transmission housings.

revealed very well by the case of one large United States components firm. It is the most profitable automotive division of a $13bn turnover conglomerate. Auto parts accounted for sales of $2.5bn in 1984 and involved 40,000 employees in 87 plants, and 23 engineering and R&D centers in 15 countries. Between 1971 and 1984 it had introduced six different assembly lines to produce the same basic product in a single plant. Output had risen in this plant from 600,000 units a year to over 3 million and labour productivity had increased by a factor of six. The first robots had been introduced in 1982 and by 1984 there were a total of 14 in operation. The chief engineer who had been responsible for this automation program (which will cost $20.3m by end-1986) made the following points. The program has been judged an overall success and involves the most extensive use of assembly automation in the whole company; it is also one of the most profitable plants; the sixfold gain in labour-productivity is obviously significant and constitutes the main rationale underlying the investments; via further improvement in assembly automation, they expect to eliminate a further 50 percent of the remaining direct production workers; and once the program is completed, the configuration of the line in terms of robots and material movement will be replicated throughout the company.

From the engineer's perspective and from that of the Board of Directors, this effort can legitimately be interpreted as a great success. However the firm's efforts can be seen in a less positive light for a number of reasons. First, it has opted for fixed automation rather than looking for more automated flexibility. The lines are all dedicated - hence introducing a new product on an existing line will require either a dismantling and/or major reconfiguration of the line, reprogramming of the stored program process controller in the robots and even the possible abandonment of some equipment. Hence what appears to be an impressive proliferation of increasingly automated lines in the plant is vitiated by static product technology, which has seen only relatively minor design variations over these 13 years. Secondly, even though maintenance has been eased and down-times shortened, changeover times to accommodate relatively slight product variations are still relatively high - up to 8 hours in some cases. (In another firm in a similar situation, changeover times to a new product family on a new dedicated line using fixed automation took one week, with this being sometimes necessary as often as once a month). Thirdly, the emphasis on the elimination of direct labour (although there remained high numbers of indirect labour, which constituted 60 percent of the total in 1984) as the principle objective of innovation suggests that this firm is still operating in the old paradigm, and sees automation predominantly as a means of eliminating directly productive labour. This, of course, as was noted earlier, is a perspective shared by many Western European and United States auto assemblers, and is one that contrasts with the philosophy of the Japanese in which job and skill flexibility has eroded many of the traditional distinctions between direct and indirect labour.

The experience of this firm is not always replicated in the case of other United States and Western European component suppliers, especially where output volumes are relatively low (as is the case in many product categories in the sector). Some of these firms are in the process of introducing more flexible assembly and machinery lines. While these are not always as flexible as their Japanese counterparts, they do differ significantly from the fixed automation lines described above. Some examples drawn from our interviews are given below in Table 6.8. The broad range of benefits arising from these flexible systems is impressive, as is the scope of the product mix that they allow. What is notable about these examples is that in almost every case the flexible installations are the first to be attempted within each company. In most cases more installations are planned (six-to-eight in Firm A for instance) and the firms involved have been keen not to

Table 6.8
Flexible Manufacturing Lines Installed by Four United States Component Firms

	Firm A Old line	Firm A FMS	Firm B Old line	Firm B FMS	Firm C Old line	Firm C FMS	Firm D Old line	Firm D FMS
Product	Compressor		Air conditioner and compressor		Brakeshoes		Transmission parts	
Number of Lines	4	1	3	1	2	1	15	4
Capital costs	$2.5m	$12m	$300–$8000,000 each	$8–10m	NA	$2m	NA	$36m
Workers	24	4	16	2	5/line per line	1	15/line	2 direct 5 indirect
Number of product types	1/line	10	NA	86 different parts	2	6	NA	NA
Output	75% increase		30% increase		46% increase		47% increase	
Comment			35 person years of software R&D required				cycle time improved by 60%	

Source: Interviews
NA: Not available

repeat mistakes of first generation FMS users in other sectors.28/ Almost all of these projects reported teething problems, none suggested these lines were profitable as yet, and most of the firms found they were forced to undertake a considerable degree of in-house engineering because the new, flexible automation technologies are still under development. These are significant obstacles to diffusion but nevertheless are indicative of an industry in the early stages of learning. Thus even if the number of FMSs being introduced are still very low, the trend toward a greater rate of diffusion over time seems well established.

A number of smaller component firms interviewed achieved a rapid expansion of sales and a growth in market-share following investments in advanced production technology. One of these in the United States was a seat manufacturer that had switched to a "high tech" strategy involving heavy investment in product R&D and new flexible automation, tied to willingness to deliver JIT. It saw its sales revenue grow from $170m in 1981 to $450m in 1984 and expected it to nearly double again by 1988 as new flexible JIT plants now under construction came on stream. A similar story can be told concerning a small rivet producer which subcontracted production from a much larger component firm we interviewed, providing 30 percent of its rivet-requirements. This firm was established by one person who was committed to using fully flexible automation (and guaranteed JIT delivery of high quality rivets) and was competing with much larger rivet producers. The firm is competitive on all aspects - delivery, price and quality - and larger users are prepared to provide as much business as the firm can handle.

TECHNOLOGICAL AND ORGANIZATIONAL LEARNING VIA JOINT VENTURES

While joint ventures have traditionally been a feature of the auto components industry, they have primarily been undertaken to either share production capacity or to allow for the cross-marketing of complimentary products. When component firms sought to acquire technology in the 1960s and 1970s, they sometimes entered into joint ventures, but more usually resorted to licensing. However in recent years there has been what can only be described as an avalanche of joint ventures between component firms in different countries (approximately 100 between 1983 and mid-1986). It appears that United States component firms have been particularly aggressive in this regard. The objectives of these joint ventures are twofold and differ substantially from earlier experiences.

First, component firms are finding it necessary to increase sales to provide for a larger revenue base over which these increased capital and R&D expenditures can be spread. One answer is to find a partner with complementary products and in different markets. This is the rationale behind recent joint ventures between Dana-Spicer in the United States and ZF in the Federal Republic of Germany, and between Eaton in the United States and Iveco in Italy. Secondly, there is a clear trend towards joint ventures between United States and Western European firms on the one hand, and Japanese component firms on the other. Indeed such joint ventures (still far more numerous in the United States industry than in Western Europe) predominate in the current spate of agreements. Thus we find that TI silencers of the United Kingdom has set up a 50:50 joint venture with Nihon Radiators to produce brake and fuel tubes in the United Kingdom; Hoover Universal has joint ventures with both Ikeda and Takechi to produce seats and headlinings in the United Kingdom and the United States; Kanto Seiki has joined with NP Echo to produce instrument panels and plastic bumpers in the United Kingdom; Nihon Radiator and Harrison Radiator have teamed-up to produce air compressors and airconditioning units in the United States; Ikebana and Delco Marine have joined to produce brake components in the United States.29/

The reasons for the Japan bias should be self-evident from earlier discussion. United States and Western European component firms are being pressed to upgrade both their organizational capacity and their technological capabilities rapidly, with the pressure being especially severe on the Americans. At the present time, Japanese component firms are recognized as often having a superior capability in both areas and United States firms in particular are seeking to absorb this technology via joint ventures. Another factor determining the choice of this path of action is that through it, these firms might be able to head off any direct competition with the Japanese in domestic markets - competition which the Western European and Americans operating in many product categories would find it difficult to defeat. This is particularly the case with supplying to Japanese auto assemblers operating in the United States or United Kingdom whom domestic component firms are keen to supply. One recent study observes that on the first exposure, domestic firms are confident they can supply Japanese firms simply because they supply Ford, Chrysler and GM and deliver 1 percent defects, but in the case for instance of Honda (United States) many firms have been turned down because 1 percent defect rate is simply not good enough to meet the standards of Japanese assemblers.30/

Hence United States and United Kingdom firms keen to meet these new demands are looking to "learn" via joint ventures with the Japanese. In many senses this seems a positive strategic response but the situation facing many United States and Western European component firms is not easy. As we shall see in the last chapter, the objective of Japanese component firms operating in the United States or United Kingdom is not only to supply Japanese assembly plants operating in those countries but also to satisfy the needs of domestic auto assemblers. The domestic component producers know this, and fear that despite the new form of assembler-supplier relations being forged, domestic assemblers are as likely to switch their sourcing to the wholly-owned Japanese subsidiaries as they are to switch from wholly-locally owned to joint venture production. Thus the reality for the Western component firms is that if they do not or cannot absorb Japanese standards of best practice in organization, quality and technology:

> it is likely that these ventures will become the method for industry exit for American firms through a gradual process [whereby] the automotive operations [of the United States firm] contract [and] the joint venture reverts to the Japanese partner. The US may end up with a competitive component industry but under the aegis of Nippondenso, Stanley Electric and Nihon Radiator rather than Shellar, Gloke and Delco.31/

Among our interviewees, most firms were optimistic they could learn via joint ventures but recognized that the organizational changes were more difficult to absorb than the technological dimensions. For example, one very large firm producing transmissions with a long-running technology-sharing arrangement pointed out it was learning "an awful lot of common sense about production". Yet, after a number of years, if a comparison was made in terms of units produced per person-hour, its United States plants were competitive with those of its Japanese partners only if direct labour alone was counted. Virtually the same point was made by a firm involved in a joint venture to produce air-conditioning units, but this time in relation to quality rather than indirect labour use. The United States firm felt that despite many years of experience producing these units, when it initially compared quality with its Japanese joint venture partners, the management was "astounded at the appalling standards of our own products - standards which still have to be raised by an order of magnitude". So, it is yet unclear whether joint ventures between Japanese and United States (or Western European) component firms will act as a Trojan Horse or as a source of salvation.

* * *

Following the initial response to the Japanese challenge in which the Western European and United States assemblers unsuccessfully attempted to automate their way to competitiveness, belated attention was given to absorbing the lessons emerging from Japan concerning the relationship between assemblers and suppliers. At an ideological level most of these assemblers seem to have absorbed the necessity of restructuring these inter-firm relationships. In practice, though, the follow-through was uneven, varying between firms, countries and types of components. Nevertheless the first substantial steps have been made and this will clearly have important long-term implications for the nature and location of the global components sector. This is of course of great significance to the insertion of the developing world in the international division of labour in this industry and it is to this subject which we now turn. Are the assemblers likely to source their components from low-cost developing countries? Are the component suppliers likely to site export-oriented production platforms in these poor countries? Are TNCs likely to dominate the components sector in the same way that they straddle assembly?

Before we turn to this discussion it is important to overview the broad progress made by the industry in making the transition from machinofacture to systemofacture. As we saw in Chapter 2, this involves important changes in three major areas - in the type of embodied technology utilised; in the nature of inter-firm relationships; and in the labour process which is utilized. As we have seen in Chapters 5 and 6, the non-Japanese industry has made some progress in the first two of these. However there is little evidence that it has yet absorbed the necessity of restructuring the labour process and, moroever, when this realization does dawn fully there will remain the question of transferability. As we shall see in the final chapter there are reasons to suppose that the absorption of these new work practices may prove to be even more difficult for the non-Japanese industry than the introduction of new systemic embodied technologies, and the transition to a new pattern of interfirm relationships. It is this which suggests a particular opportunity for developing countries at this point of transition in global industrial history.

NOTES

1. Over the 1980-83 period, the rate of failure of small United States component firms was 50 percent greater than that of large United States firms. The United Kingdom industry has seen a particularly severe decimation of its activities.
2. Thus RG spokesman in the early 1980s repeatedly stressed that the loss of market share they experienced was due to the low quality of bought-in United Kingdom components (Smith, 1983).
3. Assemblers have emphasized repeatedly in recent years that they expect annual price reductions to become a permanent feature of life for suppliers. In one joint-interview with the purchasing managers of a Western European producer, we asked what was the most important criteria for supplier selection. All three staff present replied in unison - "price!".
4. It should not be thought that all contracts in Japan are single-sourced, nor that the situation is unchanging. In recent years there has been a tendency to widen the scope of dual-sourcing, with the second firm producing only a small proportion of total requirements (see Chapter 7). The point of this is to sharpen competitive pressures amongst suppliers, particularly with respect to product innovation. It remains, however, a relatively insignificant phenomenon by comparison with the procedure in the United States and Western Europe.
5. Cole et al (1986) surveyed suppliers perspectives of how fast assemblers were pressing to introduce organizational changes such as single-sourcing and multi-year contracts and found that at least in the supplier's

view, the movement towards both of these objectives was fairly slow.

6. Though this assembler still comes in for considerable criticism from its suppliers for the heavy-handed nature of its negotiating tactics.

7. Snowden (1986).

8. Mullins (1985).

9. Technical Director, Western European Motor Vehicle Firm.

10. Callahan (1985).

11. ibid.

12. Cole et al (1986).

13. Yet its Japanese affiliate - with whom United States management is in close contact - had introduced JIT in 1977.

14. RG estimates that by 1990 or earlier, their 100 core suppliers will be fully integrated via CAD, with a second tier linked through some form of translation network, and a third tier who would never be linked at all. A very large United States firm pointed out that in three years it had got eight of its 19 divisions on-line to its major customers via CAD, and hoped to have the remaining 11 divisions on line within another three years.

15. The MAP and TOPS initiatives are discussed in Chapter 5. IGIS is a system being developed by various CAD vendors to enable the portability of software and the interchange of design and drafting data.

16. Cole et al (1986).

17. Interview, R&D Manager of United States components firm.

18. Interview, R&D Manager of United States components firm.

19. Cole et al (1985).

20. These various competitive benefits - together with the difficulties of achieving them - are analyzed in Kaplinsky (1982).

21. To give an example, a large producer of engine parts and transmission system had spent $24m since 1983 so far on installing two mainframe computers and 22 workstations in one division, and 40 terminals in production control divisions. It expected to spend another $10m in 1986. All the terminals were used for design work and very few were integrated into CAD/CAM procedures.

22. Not that these improvements in labour-productivity were absent. Two firms who had kept a record of this observed productivity improvements on detailed design on the order of 5:1 and 3.5:1 - results consistent with the

earlier findings by Kaplinsky (1982).

23. One United Kingdom firm was a heavy (and early) user of CAD but unfortunately invested in a McDonnell-Douglas system that was not expandable or compatible to either Ford or RG, its two largest customers. So they have to scrap it and to invest in new and compatible equipment.

24. One French firm reported that CAD allowed it to overcome serious redesign problems with parts not fitting properly or assembly being made more difficult. In one case CAD-based part redesigns facilitated assembly improvements which allowed output to be increased from 1.4m units/year with six people to 2m units/year with seven people.

25. Cole et al (1985).

26. See also Cole et al (1985) for supporting evidence.

27. ibid.

28. One production R&D engineer pointed out that few of the FMS plants he knew about were profitable as yet and many had encountered major running-in problems - for example the highly publicized FMS installed by GE for the production of railway engines has to be shutdown every day to allow cleaning out. The engineer argued that such problems virtually negate the advantages provided by this first generation FMS but are surmountable in that many of these problems are design faults that can be corrected in future rounds of investment. The problem - as he acknowledged - is that there is a discernible learning curve such that the ultimate benefits are difficult to realize without a preparatory round of cost-ineffective investments.

29. See Womack (1986a) for a listing of recent United States-Japanese joint ventures.

30. Berry (1986).

31. Womack (1986a) p. 23.

7

Systemofacture, Investment Location and Off-Shore Sourcing

Our principle research objective has been to analyze the determinants of investment location and international sourcing by TNCs operating in the automobile and auto components sectors, and to utilize the insights derived from this investigation to draw more general conclusions about the changing overall pattern of these phenomena. In executing these tasks, the research had first to document the changing characteristics of best-practice production. In Chapter 2 we argued that these trends pointed towards the emergence of a new mode of best-practice production organization that will ultimately render current systems obsolete and uncompetitive, and characterized this as the transition between machinofacture and systemofacture. We hypothesized that in this new era we would witness a process of global restructuring of industry which would substantially alter the economics and politics of location and thus change the nature of global competition.

In our view, the information presented in Chapters 4-6 confirms that such a process of transformation is underway in the auto industry, involving a shift from the Fordist mode of mass production towards new best-practice standards defined by what we call systemofacture. This involves changes in the labour process, in the dominant technology utilized and in the nature of inter-plant and inter-firm relationships. The evidence to support this conclusion is strong. The reasons why virtually all of the major actors in the United States and Western European industry are now engaged in what is almost a frenzy of adaptation to the new best-practice are also clear. They are - as shown in Chapters 4, 5 and 6 - clearly unable to match the competitive threat from Japanese auto producers. Without the protection afforded by state intervention in trading relations in the sector in the early 1980s, many volume auto producers would already have been forced either to abandon production or to retreat into specialist product niches.

By the mid 1980s, Western auto firms have come to recognize that the respite they enjoyed earlier in the decade cannot endure. In part this is because state intervention is often porous. But more substantively, it has led to a significant inward flow of Japanese investment in new auto production facilities in the major IAC markets. Thus the major auto assemblers have little choice but to attempt to effect, in the shortest possible time, a technological and organizational metamorphosis so pervasive that it would normally take decades in the life of an industry. As Chapters 5 and 6 demonstrated, the assemblers are striving to respond on at least two of the three major fronts. First they are harnessing advanced manufacturing technologies to an extent hitherto probably unmatched by any other industry. Secondly they are trying to come to grips with an organizational reorientation towards inter-firm relationships which requires abandoning the principles by which production in the industry has been organized for more than 50 years. And, finally, they are only fumbling their way towards the adoption of new, flexible labour processes. Given the scale and scope of effort involved, it is unsuprising that the transformation is proceeding slowly and unevenly across companies and countries. Indeed, so fundamental are the changes required that some of the major actors in the industry - previously in a seemingly unassailable position - may in fact be unable to survive in their present form.

Despite these qualifications, our research confirms that the broad movement of the auto industry towards systemofacture is firmly established. The implications for the components industry of these developments are profound. Because they are essentially dependent on the decisions, strategies and ultimate success or failure of the assemblers, all component firms now find that they, too, are having to cope with unprecedented demands for change in established practices. This comes after a period of severe rationalization, so that the consequences of having to comply with these additional demands has meant that many firms - particularly the smaller - have succumbed in recent years.

Those firms that have survived have experienced a fundamental alteration in the determinants of competitiveness in the industry and face the prospects of requiring significantly increased financial and human resources if they are to stay the course in the future. The inter-firm organizational requirements of the new mode of assembly - proximate location of production, JIT delivery, enhanced product quality, greater design inputs and flexibility in supply - dictate that component suppliers be prepared to undertake the necessary changes to meet these requirements, if necessary by investing in the establishment of flexible production facilities close to the point of final assembly.

It is our wider concern with the incorporation of the DCs in the international division of labour in manufacturing that has drawn our attention to the components sector. This is because a TNC strategy of global sourcing of individual components - especially from low-wage cost DCs - was believed by many not only to be the evolving pattern in the auto sector, but to be paradigmatic for many other industries. Therefore any change in the nature of this sourcing-dynamic clearly has important implications, both for the overall pattern of FDI and for the future of a particular type of export-oriented industrialization in the developing world.

Our attention therefore turns to the locational response of both the non-Japanese auto assemblers and their component suppliers to the new competitive environment. The discussion which follows will take the following form. In Section 1 we consider the underlying locational logic of systemofacture, backed by evidence from the Western European, United States and Japanese industries. This is then contrasted in Section 2 with a discussion of the evolving short-term competitive dynamics which are affecting sourcing decisions, especially in the United States. It contrasts two major strategic responses, distinguishing between the strategies adopted respectively by the "winners" and the "losers". The chapter concludes by drawing together the implications of these trends for component-exports by developing countries.

THE LOCATIONAL LOGIC OF SYSTEMOFACTURE IN AUTOMOBILE COMPONENTS

The long term locational logic of the new era of production which is evolving - and for which detailed descriptions have been drawn in earlier chapters - can be stated very simply. In the context of new best-practice production systems, the location of production in low-wage economies for export either of whole autos or of the major components therein is an unlikely outcome of the restructuring process. Both the organizational and technological characteristics of the new system clearly militate against off-shore sourcing. The organizational restructuring seem particularly important. Its various aspects - such as the need for mutual collaboration based on trust and familiarity, assembler reliance on supplier quality-assurance, closer design-interaction and (most importantly) proximate location for flexible and JIT supply - all demand that suppliers and assemblers are close in time and space.1/ This trend away from foreign-sourcing is reinforced by the technological dimensions of the new order and is currently being played out in the auto industry. Labour-saving flexible automation in production technology and greater design-intensity and flexibility in new product technology also reduce some of the advantages of low-wage unskilled labour. Moreover, the transition to modular-design and the increasing utilization of electronics and new materials are likely to prove equally problematic for DCs, largely because they facilitate the labour-saving automation of assembly. The final of the three pillars of systemofacture - that is the changes in labour process - in itself provides less of an impetus away from the DCs since it is arguable that the introduction of these new work-practices is more difficult in those IACs with a legacy of Fordist work-attitudes. We will return to this latter issue in the final chapter, but merely observe here that while it _is_ an issue of significance, it is likely to be outweighed in the short-to-medium run by the locational logic of the new inter-firm relationships and the introduction of the new technologies.

These views are backed by two sorts of evidence from our interviews. The first comes from United States and Western European assemblers and suppliers asked to speculate on the long term future of component supply from, and export-oriented FDI in low-wage, DC economies. In the United States, the response was consistently that in virtually all but a few component categories, high volume offshore-sourcing of auto components within a JIT context was very unlikely. One assembler was

> not optimistic about the developing countries as major component suppliers since labour costs are being reduced through automation, scales of output are coming down bringing with them less need for savings

on process related costs, and product changes related to modular design philosophy are increasing the need for complexity and close links.

These conditions, it was argued, would be extremely difficult to fulfill in developing countries. Another assembler qualified this view slightly by saying that only Mexico, Brazil and the Republic of Korea were likely to be represented in the long-term future, and even then this would only be on the basis of a joint-venture with TNC suppliers. This firm foresaw that

> there is no longer any possibility that we will actively search out low cost suppliers in countries such as Thailand or Colombia as they would not be able to meet our company's demand for cost, quality and technology.

Quality and design factors were also mentioned frequently by United States suppliers - one firm captured this common sentiment by stating that

> it is simply not possible to establish quality control on Third World component suppliers to levels sufficient to meet the demands of JIT. We estimate that the quality of most Third World countries at 10-40 percent below US and West Germany, and at 50 percent plus below Japan, except where a TNC subsidiary is involved,

while another argued that

> most of the southward movement of the component industry has come to a stop. Now, the trend towards design-integration works against offshore-sourcing for new components. Design is a process requiring close attention and is extremely difficult to do across 6,000 miles of ocean. We tried it but now have all our R&D facilities close to production with production in turn close to final assembly.

The Western European reaction to the long-term was similar, if a little more circumspect. While most felt, as the United States firms did, there were differences. One assembler believed that the Asians NICs were unlikely competitors as suppliers of original equipment but could become a significant source in the parts aftermarket in five-to-eight years. For another assembler (one of the largest volume producers in Western Europe), the only offshore-sourcing

> are a few parts that are simple to make, with process technology from a European firm and where quality can be guaranteed such as horns, safety belts and cushions. Even this small amount will probably decline in the light of JIT - though the aftermarket will remain strong.

Interestingly, United Kingdom assemblers and component firm were the most optimistic (or fearful) of the long-term threat of developing country competitors in a JIT future. Their general feeling was that while right now these sources of supply were only suitable to meet the demands of the aftermarket, in five years time this could change as TNC component firms and the foreign car assemblers were dragging local components firms up to scratch - a process that could easily spill over into exports. This confirmed the view of others in the United Kingdom who saw that the outward flow of technology from developed country suppliers would ultimately create a new variety of competitors in the DCs.

Whilst all this "evidence" is of course speculative, it is possible to corroborate our judgement of the long-term locational logic of the new form of production by referring to the experience of Japan, since its industry has been practicing this "new" philosophy for 20 years. The evidence on the attractiveness of offshore-sourced components to Japanese assemblers is uniform and pervasive. Left to market forces alone, Japanese assemblers simply do not feel compelled to search for component supply <u>anywhere</u> offshore; one of its largest assemblers believed that this was because

> the best and cheapest components are available within Japan, and can be provided under the strictest and most severe delivery criteria

This preference is demonstrated in Table 7.1 which shows the insignificant fraction of component demand met from imports (on a total domestic production base of $24.4bn in 1984). The share has always been extremely low and the slight increase in recent years has had less to do with the search for low-wage sources than with political factors. Most notable here are the rising pressure from

Table 7.1
Imports of Auto Components from Non-OECD countries into Japan, 1981-1984 ($'000s)

	1981	1982	1983	1984
Imports from				
World	106,637	113,052	148,832	1291,867
(as % of domestic production)	(.0046)	(.0053)	(.0053)	(.0079)
Non-OECD countries	102,139	8,048	10,478	21,038
(as % of domestic production	(.00045)	(.00038)	(.00046)	(.00086)

Source: Compiled from OECD Statistic Series B, Imports of Commodities: 1981-1985; JAPIA, 1984.

the United States and Western Europe on the Japanese to open their markets to imported cars and components and the foreign-exchange-balancing policies[2]/ of some countries where Japanese auto firms have assembly plants such as Mexico (from where Nissan imports engines), Australia (aluminum castings imported by Nissan) and the Philippines (air conditioners imported by Toyota). Apart from these trends, which are expected to increase slowly over time, none of the Japanese firms interviewed could see any economic grounds or any criteria by which significant quantities of components would be sourced from DCs, even from the Asian region where Japanese firms are heavily involved in production activities. The organizational logic of JIT and the technological features of systemofacture and new product trends do not allow, or require, offshore-sourcing into Japan.

These views are derived from interviews and purchasing policies in operation at a period when the exchange rate was around 225 Yen to the dollar. But by mid 1987 the dollar had sunk to less than 150 Yen and some press-speculation suggested that this would be reflected in greater Japanese component-sourcing from DCs, especially from Taiwan Province and the Republic of Korea. There are two dimensions to this problem - offshore-sourcing to meet the needs of the Japanese market, and offshore-sourcing to meet the needs of foreign markets. Insofar as the former is concerned we have to set two factors against the locational logic of systemofacture. The first is the above-mentioned foreign-exchange balancing policies of some countries which may force the Japanese producers to import some components. But these are only likely to be drawn from the largest markets such as Mexico, Brazil and Taiwan Province since in the smaller markets of other potential producers (such as Malaysia, India and the Philippines), the potential sales are not adequate to justify the adoption of such a policy. The second qualifying factor is that Mitsubishi - disadvantaged in the United States and Western European markets by its late arrival - has adopted a joint-venture strategy in two countries, the Republic of Korea and Malaysia. In both cases - and especially in Malaysia where it has most control over its affiliate - it is possible that Mitsubishi may strive to achieve scale economies by sourcing some of the components required to meet demand in Japan. But in our view, both of these cases are likely to be of marginal significance in meeting the demand for autos in Japan.

Meeting the demand for autos in foreign markets poses additional problems for DC sourcing by the Japanese assemblers. In Chapter 3 we observed a rapidly growing trend towards protectionism in all of the major markets. This has two important implications for offshore-sourcing. First, to an increasing extent these Japanese investments are encountering a climate in which the degree of local content is becoming increasingly contentious.3/ The pressures are mounting against the so-called "screwdriver operations" by which most components are imported from Japan and merely assembled in the final market.4/ - for example, both Renault and Ford Europe have called for a minimum local-content of 80 percent.5/ In the United States similar pressures began to emerge when it was recognized that imports of components from Japan rose from $480m in 1980 to $2.8bn in 1984, and this was before the major Japanese assembly plants had come on stream. This protectionism has widened from an initial preoccupation with Japanese-sourced components and now includes those from the NICs. In April 1986 the United States lifted tariff-exemption status from $3.2bn (out of a total of $13.3bn) of automobile and components imports from the major NICs, with a particularly severe effect on Mexico (affecting imports of wiring harnesses, seats and other parts worth $973m), Brazil ($261m), Taiwan Province ($188m) and the Republic of Korea ($181m).6/ This was followed with further actions specifically against component imports in January 1987.7/ Secondly, we have already observed that proximate location is essential for the smooth-operation of JIT schedules and there is a clear financial cost in sourcing components for assembly to foreign markets from third countries.8/

All of this is reflected in a significant new phase emerging in the Japanese industry's development. The initial steps towards the foreign assembly of autos is now being complemented by the foreign-manufacture of components for these autos. As we have seen, this has occurred for two reasons - because it fits the logic of JIT production and because of increasing protectionism against "screwdriver operations". For example, by the end of 1984, Mazda - which had not yet formally committed itself to a North American assembly plant - was exploring joint-ventures with over 100 United States component manufacturers. Thirty-nine Japanese affiliated component plants started operations in the United States during 1982-85 and a study undertaken for the United States embassy in Tokyo in mid 1986 confirmed that over 300 additional Japanese component firms were about to move into the United States.9/ Similarly, a number of Japanese component firms have begun to establish themselves - independently or through joint-ventures - to feed the Nissan and Honda manufacturing facilities in the United Kingdom.10/ As we saw in Chapter 5, in one case this will also involve supplies to RG, displacing those of its largest traditional supplier. These trends are not confined to the Japanese. Hyundai - the Republic of Korean producer forced by protectionist pressures to assemble autos in Canada - will be sourcing tyres, windshields, air conditioners and spark-plugs from United States component suppliers and, already by 1986, was sourcing more components from Canada than all the Japanese producers combined.11/

A final potential locational dimension of the Japanese industry's strategy is the possibility of sourcing fully-assembled autos from DC sites to IAC markets. Only Mitsubishi is marginally involved in such a strategy, partly through its joint-venture with Hyundai (where it has little influence over strategy) and in Malaysia (where the financial difficulties encountered by its joint-venture with the state-backed Proton car are inducing some marginal exports). However Mitsubishi considers these prospects slight and also plans to manufacture autos in the United States in collaboration with Chrysler. Nevertheless, this option cannot be ruled out entirely given the significant appreciation of the Yen in recent years; it is however unlikely.

Since the Japanese competitive success in operating JIT and the other elements of systemofacture is beyond question, these arguments confirm our more speculative estimation of the long-term sourcing strategies of restructured United States and Western European firms. Taken together, the organizational and technological features of the new production systems represent a fundamental shift in the determinants of international location that work directly against the low-wage comparative advantage that the developing world currently relies on to secure a presence in the international motor vehicle and components market.

SHORT-TERM COMPETITIVE DYNAMICS IN THE ASSEMBLY INDUSTRY

Over the longer term, the logic of the transition to systemofacture thus implies a significant reduction in both export-oriented FDI and offshore-sourcing by TNC auto and component firms. Yet, as we have seen in earlier chapters, there is some way to go before the United States and Western European firms make a successful transition to the new order. Moreover, the inherently political nature of the events determining this transition (both on the shopfloor and in the wider political sphere) suggests that there is no easily predictable - or indeed even single - pattern which will unfold. Therefore, in addition to these imperatives of long-run location, it is also important to focus on a shorter time-horizon in which the major non-Japanese producers attempt to cope with more immediate competitive dynamics. In particular we have to explain why one of the principle features of the first half of the 1980's has been a sharp <u>rise</u> in the volume and value of components and whole vehicle exports originating from DCs and destined for the United States and Western Europe, often tied to TNC activity. Moreover it is also necessary to explain why this pattern of export growth is expected to increase steadily through the rest of the decade before it tails-off in the predicted manner.

To do this we need to remind ourselves of the characteristics of the post-1979 competitive dynamic in the world motor industry. (We have already described these conditions at some length in Chapters 3 to 6). The central feature is that the United States/Western European duopoly in the global industry that emerged during the post war decades after the 1950's and 1960's was decisively confronted during the 1970's by successive waves of competitively priced, highly diversified products of consistent quality exported from Japan. These products quickly captured significant market-share in virtually every market targeted. At first this onslaught provoked a comprehensive protectionist response from the West, which while providing some respite for domestic producers (and a very profitable one at that for United States assemblers) did little to address the underlying structural weaknesses of the industry. To tackle this task, the industry has embarked on the process of fundamental restructuring that is detailed in Chapters 5 and 6.

Yet, through this early phase, Japanese assemblers had a clear preference to continue producing in Japan and to export completely-assembled autos to other markets. This reticence to consider FDI was due precisely to their fears that they could not replicate their system in different countries, with the weakness of the foreign components sector seen as being a particular problem that would be difficult to overcome. However, despite these preferences, protectionist responses to the beleaguered plight of national capital and organized labour in the West nevertheless provoked a second Japanese invasion. This time the invasion was not of finished products but of Japanese capital, technology and social organization incorporated in a wave of FDI, initially in the United States but subsequently likely to reach Western Europe at some time in the near future.

The scale of this onslaught is almost breathtaking. Twelve Japanese-owned or managed assembly plants in North America are already operating, in construction, or have been announced. When completed, these will add up to more than 2m units of capacity at a direct investment cost of $5bn. The key question in the minds of many (including the Japanese themselves) is whether or not Japanese assemblers in the United States (and Western Europe) could replicate the system of social organization and productive efficiency on which their export success rested.

If the recent spate of reports, both published and unpublished prove correct, it appears that the answer to this question is a qualified yes. Qualified in the sense that while their performance far exceeds that of the existing United States producers, in terms of the functioning of the whole production system itself (that is, including the manufacture and delivery of components), its efficiency remains some way behind that in Japan. Two of the three functioning Japanese-owned or managed assembly plants in the United States - the Honda plant at Marysville, Ohio and, the NUMMI joint venture in California - are now reckoned to be the best and most efficient assembly plants in North America, producing superior quality products in a more varied mix, with productivity at least two times that of established American facilities.12/ Some of the features of the Japanese plants in the US are presented in Table 7.2. It is important to bear in mind that with the exception of a unique and highly automated stamping, welding and painting line in the Honda plant, the process machinery used (particularly in the assembly stage) is relatively conventional and not nearly as automated as in the most modern plants of the United States assemblers such as those of GM in Hamtramck or Buick City.13/

In addition to the efficiency of these new assembly plants, Japanese component firms operating in the United States have also begun to better the performance of their American-owned rivals. A large share of these investments entail the Japanese in some sort of joint-venture with local firms. Some of these have been actively encouraged by the Japanese assemblers operating in the United States because of their concern with the poor quality and performance standards of the American suppliers.14/ The significance of this process is that even those United States suppliers who do not have a Japanese joint venture partner will, if they wish to keep their business with the assemblers, have to increasingly act and perform like Japanese suppliers in terms of their production organization, delivery performance and quality levels. Otherwise even United States car producers are likely to turn to Japanese-based components suppliers for their needs. Indeed Japanese parts suppliers have shown themselves easily able to meet the American assemblers' criteria of 15 percent minimum cost savings for outsourcing with many of the parts being available for some 30-40 percent below comparable products manufactured in the United States. Whether they will be able to duplicate these savings in their United States plants is still unclear, but on the basis of the experience of the Japanese assemblers, we think this likely.15/ In the long term therefore, it is possible that it may be the Japanese themselves who will force through the restructuring of the United States auto components industry.

What is occurring in the United States industry is thus highly significant and almost impressive in scale.

Table 7.2
Performance Comparisons of Honda and Toyota United States Assembly Plants with GM and AMC, 1985

	Toyota/NUMMI[a]	GM Fremont[b]
Product[c]	Chevy Nova/Corolla	"A" body cars
Annual Output	200,000	330,000
Employment	2,500[d]	7,100
Cars per worker per year	80	46

	Honda, Marysville, Ohio	AMC, Toledo, Ohio
Product	Accord, Civic, Prelude Accura Legend, Intergra	Jeep (2 models)
Daily Output	875	750
Employment	2,432	5,400[e]
Size	1.7m sq. ft.	5.4m sq. ft.
Die Change Time	8 mins	60 hrs
Finish Units Inventory	8 days	70 days
Component Delivery	3 hourly average	2 weekly average
Absenteeism	1%	7%

Source: Adapted from Merwin, 1986 and Womack, 1968a

[a] NUMMI is Toyota joint venture with GM. All management is by Toyota staff
[b] NUMMI operates in former GM Fremont plant - closed in 1983
[c] Products are roughly similar
[d] Includes stamping operation not carried out at Fremont
[e] 3,000 workers laid off by AMC since September 1985
[f] Dies changed 3-4 times per day

In the space of eight years the Japanese will have built up an auto industry in North America which is twice the size of the United Kingdom and Brazilian industries and four times that of Mexico. The combination of direct exports from Japan and the output of the United States plants means that by 1990 the Japanese assemblers are likely to account for around half of the total United States market.

This fundamental restructuring of the industry (particularly in the United States, although there are also some echoes emerging in Western Europe) ultimately has a significant impact upon the incorporation of DC producers in the global industry. This is the case both for indigenously-owned firms and TNC affiliates exporting from these countries. In both cases the growing dominance of Japanese assemblers and component suppliers in the United States market seems likely to sharply reduce United States component imports from low-wage economies. But, aside from their attempts to restructure their domestic operations in the image of the Japanese model, have the United States TNCs also aped the Japanese TNCs by setting their sights against offshore-sourcing?

The answer is that whatever the long-term locational logic of systemofacture, the United States TNCs are simultaneously increasing their offshore-sourcing of components, including from low-wage economies. Fearful that they would not be able to reduce costs quickly enough in the short run, all United States assemblers have since the late 1970's and early 1980's been exploring a variety of conduits and mechanisms to source both finished units and components from offshore suppliers. Though there are a large number of arrangements both underway and planned, these break down into three categories.

The first involves the import of finished vehicles and components from Japan. In an apparent implicit acceptance of Japanese supremacy, the Big Three - lead, as often, by GM - have now all concluded deals with both affiliated and unaffiliated companies that will bring sub-compact cars to the United States from Japan. The near-total reliance on Japanese firms as a source of supply for these vehicles reflects the abandonment by the United States assemblers of this rapidly growing segment of the market to the Japanese, and inevitably raises questions about the long term viability of projects such as Saturn, Alpha and Liberty. Whole vehicle imports have been complemented by a growing range of powertrain imports, coupled with a long list of production parts such as starter motors, alternators, clutches, engine parts, hollow stabilizers, balljoints,

Table 7.3
Current and Planned Imports of Vehicles by United States Assemblers from Japan, Republic of Korea, Brazil, Taiwan Province and Mexico

Assembler	Partner	Product	Scale (p.a.)	Date
GM	Isuzu (Japan)	Subcompact	30,000	1986
GM	Suzuki (Japan)	Subcompact	17,000	1987
GM	Daewoo (Republic of Korea)	Subcompact	70-80,000	1987
GM	GM Mexico	K cars	20,000	1986
GM	GM Mexico	Sport Truck	10,000	
GM	GM Mexico	Heavy Goods Vehicles	(NI)	1987
GM	GM Mexico	J Cars	(NI)	1987
GM	GM Mexico	Subcompact	(NI)	
Ford	Mazda (Mexico)	Subcompact	70-80,000	1987
Ford	Lioho (Taiwan Province)	Subcompact	40,000	1989
Ford	Kia (Republic of Korea)	Subcompact	20,000	1988
Ford	Ford (Brazil)	Compact	20,000	1986
Chrysler	Mitsubishi (Japan)	Subcompact	130,000	1987
Chrysler	Chrysler (Mexico)	Mini Van/K cars	12,000-1,000,000	1988
Chrysler	Chrysler (Mexico)	J cars	48,000	1986

Source: Interviews

NI = No information

stampings and electronic engine control devices. Table 7.3 provides a select list of these import arrangements.

The second category of imports relates to import of whole vehicles from affiliated firms in the Republic of Korea, Brazil and Mexico and, again, largely reflects the United States firms' inability to compete head-on with the Japanese in the compact and subcompact categories. In part these steps reflect the impact of trade restrictions placed on imports of Japanese vehicles and allow the United States assemblers to circumvent these restrictions (which they, of course, were instrumental in introducing in the first place!). Once again GM is the major actor via its joint venture deal with Daewoo to import a new small-car produced in the Republic of Korea starting in 1987. But both Ford and Chrysler are not far behind. Ford is sourcing small-cars from a second Republic of Korean supplier, Kia, and partly through its links with Mazda, from Taiwan Province, Mexico and Brazil as well. Chrysler, so far frozen out of the Republic of Korea, plans to import "J-cars" from its Mexican plant after a $500m investment program to bring it up to state-of-the-art. Details of these arrangements are also given in Table 7.3 and, as can readily be seen from the scale of these activities, they are significant both in terms of the implication for the countries involved and in terms of domestic production in the United States.16/ It is not surprising, therefore, that organized labour in the United States has begun to focus on these imports in a new round of protectionist calls.

The third short-term response by the United States industry is to search for cost-reductions in final vehicles by sourcing components offshore. As we have seen this lead them first to Japan. But now, increasingly, they have begun to purchase from low-wage countries in Asia and Latin America, especially following the revaluation of the Yen in 1986-7. While these efforts at component-sourcing have been concentrated on arm's-length deals with independent suppliers, there now appears to be a marked tendency towards FDI and the setting-up of joint-ventures or wholly owned subsidiaries, coupled with the diverting of output of existing plants originally established to produce for the domestic market. Ford and GM have been the most diligent searchers for low-wage sites, being responsible either directly or indirectly for the setting up of 30 component plants in Mexico's Maquiladora export-processing zone between 1980 and 1985. They have now been joined by Chrysler who in 1986 announced major plans for offshore-component production and purchasing in the Republic of

Korea, Brazil and Mexico.17/ The GM/Daewoo deal in the Republic of Korea is of particular interest in highlighting the new trend towards offshore joint-ventures in low-wage sites and is similar (though on a greater scale) to those being attempted by Ford and Chrysler in the Republic of Korea and Brazil. While the leading element is an agreement to jointly produce a small car especially created for export to North America, (at a combined investment cost of $464m) the most interesting aspect is that GM has also induced its different component and assembly divisions (as well as persuading independent United States suppliers) to undertake a variety of joint venture component agreements that involve virtually the whole range of components needed to build entire car bodies, as well as engines, transmissions, electrical systems, brakes, steering, and ancillary parts. These ventures are meant to be at world-scale volume and involve extensive transfer of design and process technology.18/

The United States assemblers claim that they are aware that by entering into this arrangement they may be creating a new competitor, but they believe it will take some time before this happens. By then they expect to have moved on to a higher degree of competitiveness, and in the interim see their Republic of Korean and Taiwan Province ventures as a cheap source of small autos which they can import into the United States to compete against the Japanese. But there are also other reasons for such moves. In many countries foreign-exchange-balancing and other policies have forced United States TNCs to export in order to maintain access to domestic markets. Engines, transmissions and - more recently - whole unit imports from Brazil and Mexico have been particularly stimulated by this factor. Most recently the Brazilian government has been successful in persuading the largely United States- and Western European-owned industry to agree to over $2bn of exports within the next three years in exchange for liberalizing domestic pricing controls. And, finally, the United States TNCs - with markets all over the world - have calculated that even if new trade restrictions prevent them from bringing these autos into the United States, they will either be able to feed the domestic markets where they are produced or sell low-priced autos to third-country markets.

As Table 7.4 makes evident, the combined effect of the strategies reviewed above has been a sharp rise in the level of component imports coming to the United States from developing countries, a rise that most forecasters are expecting will continue through the 1990s. This

Table 7.4
United States Trade in Motor Vehicle Parts and Accessories, 1980-84 (in thousands of dollars; exports f.a.s. value, imports Customs value basis)

	1980 $	1981 $	1982 $	1983 $	1984 $	% change 1980-84
Overall Trade Balance						
Total Exports	9,307,157	11,261,660	10,641,745	11,045,088	13,836,741	48.6
Total Imports	9,025,010	8,447,409	9,112,226	12,597,206	17,057,142	89.0
Trade Balance	282,147	2,814,251	1,529,519	-1,552,118	-3,220,401	1,241.4
Major Import Suppliers 1980-84						
Canada	3,379,057	3,896,053	4,524,980	6,568,970	8,707,872	61.1
Japan	2,828,725	1,821,699	1,822,344	2,112,954	2,727,198	-3.0
Mexico	310,339	418,957	648,003	1,207,665	1,533,390	80.0
Germany, Federal Republic of	797,327	586,035	506,679	631,396	863,222	7.6
Brazil	222,706	247,426	310,457	424,085	603,129	63.5
France	453,734	390,211	294,501	323,594	461,239	1.6
United Kingdom	299,852	260,871	189,526	232,457	362,317	17.2
Korea, Republic of	120,313	163,625	189,234	254,088	339,315	64.5
Taiwan Province	110,084	118,120	133,820	248,446	329,602	66.6
Italy	140,098	147,523	123,524	130,708	104,332	23.9

Source: Adapted from United States International Trade Commission, unpublished data. Cited in JEI, 1985.

complements a similar trend in imports of complete autos. These forecasts are fueled by a consistent round of announcements and plans from the assemblers in recent years that outsourcing would continue to rise. A Delphi study[19]/ based on responses from 130 vehicle manufacturers and 328 parts suppliers showed that the very large majority of these firms expected the percentage of total imported original equipment parts (from all sources) to increase by five-to-six percent annually through 1995. The expectation was that the import of components would rise from 15-18 percent of completed vehicles in 1985 to 23 percent in 1990 and 29 percent by 1995. Further, it was predicted that by 1995, 20-25 percent of imported parts would be produced in foreign plants owned by United States vehicle assemblers and another 15 percent produced offshore by independent United States parts suppliers. Among the parts expected to be dominant in these figures were drivetrains, engines and modular subassemblies (most notably instrument panels and suspension systems).[20]/

Conditions governing the short-term offshore-sourcing behavior of Western European firms in recent times differ markedly from those in the United States. With the possible exception of Volkswagen and RG, all the volume car producers in Western Europe source only a small fraction of their components in the developing world, about 1.2 percent of all component imports into the EEC come from non-OECD sources including countries in Latin America, the Far East (but not Japan), Africa, and Eastern Europe. The share of DC sourced components in the United Kingdom is marginally higher but still small - 3.2 percent in 1984 (£65.9m) and 3 percent in 1985 (£75.1m).[21]/

A typical example of the range of products imported is given in Table 7.5 that shows that these are based on the price advantages of offshore production in relatively simple products. And while imports from some countries have been have been rising slowly, (such as the Republic of Korea and Taiwan Province), none of the volume Western European producers have any plans to substantially increase the level of offshore component-sourcing into their domestic market in the short-term future. The situation is slightly different in the case of finished units. Though the volume Western European producers do have a fairly extensive network of overseas holding and production facilities based in DCs, these facilities are used primarily either for domestic assembly or for the limited export of vehicles and/or CKD kits to other developing countries.

Table 7.5
Examples of Outsourced Products by Western European Volume Producer, 1985[a]

Product	Country Sourced	Price Advantage Over Domestic Product (percentage)
Jacks	Morocco	25
Horns	Morocco	18
Coils	Yugoslavia	20
Cushions	Yugoslavia	15-20
Flat Glass	Czechoslovakia	8
Safety Belts	Morocco	8
Aluminium Castings	Yugoslavia	Marginal

Source: Interviews

[a] Most of these parts imported as part of buy-back arrangements on FDI and used in the replacement-parts market.

There are some exceptions and these mostly center around the strategies of Volkswagen and Fiat. In 1984-1985, Fiat imported about 30,000 units of its 127 engines and another 60,000 commercial vehicles from its Brazilian operations but these figures declined in 1986, partly because Brazilian government subsidies to exports (valued at around 27 percent of total fob price) were reduced. By 1986 the only significant purchase from Fiat's Brazilian subsidiary was of diesel engines, a policy designed to help the subsidiary meet its breakeven output levels of 300,000 units annually in Brazil. Fiat has set itself clearly against a policy of outsourcing, except where this is forced by a buy-back policy, as occurs in North Africa and Eastern Europe. However in these cases Fiat prefers to destine these parts to the after-market rather than to prejudice the quality of its new autos. Volkswagen has announced planned exports of $1bn worth of components and vehicles from its Brazilian plant by 1989 (compared to $350m in 1985) mostly to the United States, Latin America and Africa. In addition there may be an export destination for the increased output expected to come from its recently expanded Mexican plant. In the case of both Volkswagen and

Fiat (as well as for Renault facilities in Mexico) these exports are based almost totally on the strength of government subsidies or as a consequence of foreign-exchange-balancing policies and are not due to low wage based cost competitiveness of production in these countries.

Therefore, by and large, Western Europe's auto assemblers are not being forced to resort to offshore-sourcing as a means of shoring up their short-term competitiveness via the import of lower cost components and finished units. There are three reasons for this. First, and most importantly, the effective quotas in almost all Western European countries limiting imports from Japanese vehicles has meant that Western Europeans are under less immediate pressure from this quarter than are the Americans. Secondly, Western European domestic assemblers have traditionally relied far less on offshore-outsourcing than the Americans, preferring to source nationally as a matter of priority and looking to Western Europe only for those items not available nationally. As mentioned earlier in Chapter 6, with the exception of the United Kingdom, the supplier network has developed with much closer links to assemblers and in the past has also operated at much higher levels of efficiency and quality than their American counterparts. Finally, even though the industry is relatively well-protected from non-Western European imports, there is fierce competition within Western Europe. This has forced suppliers to continually upgrade their process and product technology and caused a large competitive gap to open between themselves and the American component industry. Thus one traditionally finds relatively little outsourcing outside of national companies - overall only 7 percent of the components in the French industry come from outside of France, with most of this from Western Europe. The same figure applies for the Italians, even lower for the Federal Republic of Germany, and around 17 percent for the United Kingdom (almost all from Western Europe, and incorporated in autos assembled by GM, Ford and Peugeot).

Overall, however, our impression is that when these minimal existing offshore-imports of components are combined with the evolving recognition of the long term-logic of systemofacture, substantial resort to offshore-sourcing is ruled out as an option in Western Europe, even in the short run. The one proviso we would make, however, is that this perception may well change if Japanese FDI in Western Europe assumes the same proportions as in the

United States.

Two Strategies Contrasted

In trying to understand the apparent contradiction between the long-term locational logic of systemofacture and the short-term reality of offshore-sourcing by some assemblers, it is helpful to distinguish between two sets of strategies - those of the "winners" and those of the "losers". Whilst this analysis is pursued in relation to the assembly industry, its ultimate impact is to be found in the components sector, since one of the major differences between these two strategic approaches involves their attitude towards global sourcing and the NIDL. It should be borne in mind, though, that especially with respect to the larger corporations in the "losing" category, these strategic responses merely represent central tendencies. They are clearly not exclusive of the pursuit of others amongst the range of potential alternatives, a response which is particularly apparent for GM.

<u>The Winners</u>. The strategy of the winners is quite clear. New product development is of central importance, but is allied to a "zero-defect" philosophy and low cost production. The optimal package available - proximating to our analysis of systemofacture in Chapter 2 - involves the adoption of computer integrated manufacturing technologies within the context of just-in-time manufacture, and labour processes which permit flexible and high quality production. The "tightness" which this system requires for optimization in general favours the location of assembly at the home base, and because of the nature of JIT organization, this means component-sourcing is from the immediate locale. The second-best winner strategy arises from the need to adjust to protectionist pressures in the final market and involves the running of the same system near the final market. The location of part of the system in low-wage DC locales exporting components to be assembled in third country markets is the option favoured least by the winners.

As should be clear by now, the primary example of this strategy is the Japanese industry. As we have argued, the overriding objective of all these producers is to produce in Japan for export to the major markets. Their second-best solution is to move assembly - and later an increasing fraction of component-sourcing - to the final market to overcome the pressures of protectionism. This is currently the strategy being pursued by all the major and medium-sized firms with respect to the United States, and in the case of Nissan, Honda (and potentially Toyota) with respect to Western Europe. A non-Japanese example is that of Fiat, which following its abortive attempt to globalize in the 1970s, undertook a shake-out of large numbers of the labour force in the late 1970s and the regeneration of product technology in the early 1980s. Fiat is now growing in competitive strength, a process that has been accompanied by a strategic decision over the past decade to retreat from production in all other locales, with the exception of Brazil where the domestic market is the major objective. It also involves a reluctance to source components offshore, and instead the component sector is being reorganized in Japanese-fashion and encouraged to locate in the immediate vicinity of the final assembly plants. The third-best solution - locating the production of complete vehicles (rather than of individual components) in developing countries for export to advanced countries - is being pursued by only one of these firms, Mitsubishi,22/ via its relationship with the ambitious Republic of Korean firm Hyundai, and conceivably in the future with its Malaysian joint venture. However it, too, is now entering production in North America with a planned joint venture with Chrysler. Mitsubishi recognizes the similarities with the colour TV industry in which the ability to utilize DC production sites to evade trade barriers is at best only likely to be a temporary phenomenon.23/

The Losers. The losers are those firms which show the least ability to make a successful transition to systemofacture in sufficient time to withstand the competitive onslaught from the Japanese and other producers. An important element of their response centers around a primary concern with global-sourcing as a way of meeting the intensifying pressures of competition. In the extreme case this involves the complete manufacture of the automobile abroad, representing a retreat from manufacture into marketing. But less extreme alternatives are available including the offshore purchasing of core components - such as the engine and transmission or electronic control systems. Yet particularly when this involves production by a non-affiliate, the consequence tends to be the loss of ability to master the fundamentals of product technology. This process of subcontracting production continues down the line of component complexity, with the lower the degree of technological content, the less damaging this strategy in the long run.

There are numerous examples of the adoption of this type of strategy being pursued by United States firms. At the one extreme is the recent decision by GM and Ford to give up the production of small cars and to buy them in from Japan and the Republic of Korea. The simultaneous development of the Saturn and Alpha projects would suggest that the inherent danger of this losing strategy is at least partially acknowledged. The subcontracting of core technology can be illustrated by the experience which almost beset Chrysler during its restructuring in the early 1980s. When it was forced to obtain government guarantees on loans, the United States government attempted to force Chrysler to buy-in a large proportion of its engines from Japan. Although it resisted this major commitment, Chrysler - a long-term struggler in the United States - did contract to buy some engines from Peugeot, a deal which was subsequently terminated prematurely. In a similar fashion, RG - probably the most significant "loser" in the recent period - has come to source an increasing proportion of its core technology from Japan (engines and gearboxes) and from the Federal Republic of Germany (gearboxes). The other end of this losing strategy is currently being pursued by each of the major United States assemblers involving the purchase of components from the Republic of Korea, Mexico and Brazil. The results of this strategy is likely to be a loss of long-term technological capability and probably also the establishment by developing country firms of production sites in the IAC markets.

This contrast between the winning and losing firms represents a form of "ideal type" analysis which of course obscures the fact that many firms simultaneously pursue confused, mixed and even conflicting strategies. Toyota and RG probably represent two ends of the spectrum, with the older United States TNCs situated somewhere in-between. An example of the adoption of confused and even contradictory policies is that package adopted by GM which has chosen to cover the whole spectrum. These include extensive offshore-purchasing via its joint-venture with Daewoo in the Republic of Korea, the introduction of radically new technology in its Saturn plant and the transition to new work-practices and organizational forms in Buick City. The question is what happens when such policies conflict? In these circumstances, which way does GM fall? Perhaps one recent straw is the problem GM confronted with its United States Delco subsidiary in late 1986. In an attempt to move towards systemofacture, GM reorganized its Delco subsidiary to produce sensors and other electronics components on a JIT, single-sourcing basis for all of its 35 assembly plants in North America. Having achieved satisfactory progress, GM then began to search-round for new ways of cutting costs and, based upon relative wage-rates, decided that there was a (short-run) cost advantage in having these same components manufactured in Mexico. This was a direct negation of one of the central pillars of the Japanese system - long-run stability, trust between suppliers and assemblers and security of employment for the workers. Thus GM was simultaneously pursuing contradictory policies. The result was that the 7,700 Delco workers involved (who stood to lose 900 jobs as a result of this relocation of production) went on strike and because of its single-sourcing JIT relationship to GM, all the 35 assembly-plants ground to a halt within days, forcing GM to lay-off 37,000 employees. Faced with this situation, GM had no alternative but to retract its decision to move production of the sensors to Mexico. But what lesson it has learned - that is, whether to merely be more judicious about relocating production or to learn from the Japanese experience more carefully - is unclear; only time will tell. But whichever response does follow will be very illuminating in helping to determine whether GM is likely to adopt a "winning" or "losing" strategy in the future.

This distinction between winning and losing strategies - buttressed by the caveats we shall make in the following discussion - sets the general context for our conclusions regarding global location in the components sector. Global sourcing is a major strategy of some - but not all - of the major assemblers and components firms. We would argue, however, that it is an option chosen by the losers. Moreover, it is an option likely to become increasingly irrelevant as economic crisis at the centre of the world economy endures and as protectionist and in some case local content policies become increasingly prevalent.

COMPONENT SUPPLIERS, OFFSHORE-SOURCING AND FDI

The differences that emerge from the above discussion regarding the offshore-sourcing strategies of United States and Western European assemblers is closely paralleled in the supply industry. Historically, component firm who have entered some form of production arrangement in DC locations (via FDI, joint-ventures or licensing) have done so with the main objective of servicing the local market, which almost always consisted of the subsidiaries of TNC auto assemblers. In many cases component production was set up at the specific request of the assembler itself, keen to bring with it suppliers with whom it had a well-established relationship. Alternatively, the assembler would encourage the suppliers to find a local partner suitable for either a joint venture or as a licensee.24/ Thus around every TNC auto assembly activity in DC countries of any significant market size, one sees clusters either of TNC component firms or of local firms with foreign equity or having extensive foreign technological links.

This has meant that in countries such as Argentina, Brazil, Mexico, South Africa and Venezuela, foreign component firms - while not necessarily numerically dominant - account for a lion's share of the market. This trend is most pronounced in Latin America but can be detected in other countries as well, such as India, the Philippines and Malaysia. Thus in the mid-1970's 52 out of the leading 100 suppliers in Brazil had foreign equity participation, and half the local parts purchased by Volkswagen, Volvo and Ford came from foreign-owned firms or Brazilian companies with heavy technological dependence on foreign firms. In Argentina, 50 supplier firms accounted for 75 percent of sales, and the majority of these had TNC participation, while in Mexico, 45 percent of the market for parts in the late 1970s was met by firms with extensive foreign involvement.25/ Thus the same companies are likely to be involved side by side in the main markets throughout the world, including DCs. A comparison of subsidiaries of the 15 largest TNC component firms in our sample shows that on average these companies overlap with each other in over 50 percent of their developing world locations.

Another pattern (typical of other industries) is that while product technology used by wholly-owned subsidiaries or joint-ventures in DCs was until the late 1970's of relatively recent vintage, production technology was frequently somewhat behind in terms of the degree of automation used. The reasons are obvious - the latest product technology must be incorporated in the final product unless the TNC is willing to have a wide spectrum of product vintages in production (which, with the possible exception of the Volkswagen Beetle, they are not), whereas in the case of production technology there is generally a much greater degree of choice. This is particularly the case for labour-intensive technologies which are inherently more flexible that the pre-electronic automated lines (see

Chapter 2). There are numerous exceptions to this patterns, of course, as for example in the establishment by one Western European firm of a sophisticated sintering line for the production of connecting rods in Mexico, and the production of crankshafts on "a very hi-tech line" in Brazil by a United States firm. In our interviews, about equal weight was given to the argument that the most advanced technology was deliberately held back for commercial reasons, as it was to the argument that such technology could not be transferred because of the limited absorptive capacity of the firm and the sector.26/ (Neither of these viewpoints can of course be verified through interviews with headquarters staff alone).

Thus we have a fairly typical pattern of United States and Western European TNC component firm involvement in the DCs, with a dominant bias toward servicing (and if possible dominating) the local market with production facilities primarily put in place in the late 1960's and early 1970's, at the height of the mass production paradigm. However, our interviews revealed some definite shifts in this pattern in recent years. As we mentioned above this reflects the same global pressures affecting the assembler firms.

Western European firms. Among European TNC component firms - with the possible exception of some United Kingdom firms - there appears to be little interest in setting up new offshore productions sites in search of low wage labour to provide an export platform for sales back to their domestic market. But there is, however, a tendency towards independent expansion by component firms into foreign markets in search of market-position. This includes the upgrading of existing plants, the formation of new joint-ventures as mentioned earlier, and new outward investment. This expansion is currently targeted not only on other Western European countries and the United States but also Brazil, Malaysia and the Republic of Korea. Mexico is consistently by-passed in these investment-programs (unless the assemblers force such investments) because of its economic difficulties, whilst in recent years a great deal of interest has arisen concerning investment prospects in China and India. In only a few cases did we find that Western European firms were exploring the possibility of using offshore sites as export platforms; where this was the case, the exports would be destined for the United States. Examples of this steady expansion of Western European firms into the developing world (almost exclusively to produce for the local market) were a new joint-venture by a United Kingdom firm to produce pistons in the Republic of Korea; the recent take-over of a domestic transmission producer in Brazil by a Federal Republic of Germany firm; and the establishment of a subsidiary by a French components firm in Brazil for the production of radiators.

The driving force behind these moves are twofold. The first - as mentioned in Chapter 6 - is the need to expand sales on a global basis to help offset the rising capital and R&D costs necessary to remain competitive. The second is the feeling expressed by a number of companies that the changing patterns of assembler-supplier relations (with early involvement in design) means that foreign companies had to have a much stronger local presence if they want to capture contracts in the new era. Although this is clearly the case for expansion into IAC markets, it also appears to be occurring in DCs. Thus location in developing countries to export components is, broadly-speaking, not a strategy favoured by the Western European components industry.

<u>United States firms</u>. The current situation with regards to United States TNCs in the component sector and their offshore activities is markedly different. These firms are now facing a barrage of strong and sometimes contradictory forces with regard to their production and investment strategies - powerful pressure from assemblers to reduce prices in the short run, a rapidly growing threat from inward Japanese investment, low-cost imports from DCs and, at the same time, the necessity of ensuring the transition towards introducing systemofacture in their own operations.

Through the 1970's most of the United States TNCs' operating in foreign markets focused on expanding their market share. But our interviews revealed that three distinct trends have been emerging since the early 1980s. The first is basically an extension of past trends and is similar to the strategy adopted by the Western European component suppliers. This involves new or expansionary investment in countries with large domestic markets, largely to meet the needs of these markets. However, almost always this has been accompanied by an expansion of exports from these facilities, either arising from extra capacity deliberately built into the new plants (typically the Republic of Korean situation) or from surplus capacity due to the downturn in domestic demand (commonly the case of Brazil and Mexico). The existence of a well-established infrastructure and skilled and low-cost labour (one-eighth to one-tenth of United States wage-costs) often makes short-run production for export from existing facilities very profitable. Brazil stands out in this respect.

The second trend - closely linked to the above - is a very considerable wave of investment solely for the purpose of export. In the late 1970's this was almost entirely concentrated in Mexico, and now to a more limited extent in the Republic of Korea and Taiwan Province. These investments, either take the form of wholly owned subsidiaries or joint-ventures, and their primary objective is take advantage of lower wage rates and, in countries such as Mexico and Brazil, of government subsidies. In the latter part of the 1970's and the early years of this decade, there was a rush by United States firms to Mexico to set up labour-intensive assembly plants in and outside of the special Maquiladora's zones near the United States border. Between 1980 and 1982, 170 component firms (most, but not all, from the United States) invested $1.6 bn dollars in the expansion or creation of new facilities to assemble products such as wire harnesses, trim, electronic products, switches and solenoids, circuit-boards and seatbelts.27/ More recently, the locus for this type of investment has shifted from Mexico to the Republic of Korea, with its higher skilled and lower paid labour force providing a significant advantage over locations like Mexico. In this new round, joint-ventures are the favored form of investment and a large number of United States firms have set up heavily export-oriented facilities in the Republic of Korea in recent years. More are planned for the future. Whereas in 1980 Japanese firms held the lead over the United States and Western Europe in terms of joint-ventures with Republic of Korean firms (Japan had 11, the United States two and Western Europe four), the balance has shifted somewhat in favour of the latter countries in recent years, with United States and Western European joint-ventures getting close to the Japanese total but with all joint-ventures rapidly growing in number.28/ Table 7.6 gives details of some of these export-oriented joint-ventures between United States and Republic of Korean firms, many of which are of recent origin.

The final and most recent trend we can observe in the locational decisions of United States TNCs in the components-sector is perhaps the most important from our perspective. Our interviews and other anecdotal evidence suggest that, increasingly, component firms are either postponing or cancelling plans to go offshore. In other cases, suppliers explicitly recognized the short-term nature of some of their investments. The reason for this

Table 7.6
Select Joint Ventures by United States Firms in Republic of Korea, Mexico and Brazil, 1984-87

US Company	Partner	Product	Scale	Date
Allied Automotive	Allied (Mexico)	brakes; chassis parts		1984
Blackstone Corp	Samsung Radiator (Republic of Korea) Nihon Radiator (Japan)	radiators	300,000 units	1987
Delco Marine (US)	Harrison Radiator (Republic of Korea)	radiators and airconditioners		1987
Delco Remy (GM)	Daewoo Precision (Republic of Korea)	starter motors, alternators, ignitions distributors	$60m investment	1987
Detroit Deisel Allison	Bancosomex (Mexico)	engines		1986
Dyna Corp	Ishina Gasket (Mexico/Japan)	gaskets		1986
Fisher Body	GM (Mexico)	cut and sew seat covers		1987
Fisher Guide (GM)	Korea Steel Chemical	plastic bumpers	$20m investment	1987

Ford	Mando Machinery	radiators	450,000 units	1987
GM	GM de Mexico (Tamaulipas plant)	steering wheels, instrument panels		1986
Kelsey Hayes	Kelsey Hayes (Mexico)	brakeshoes		1985
Libby-Cwen Ford	Hankuk Glass (Republic of Korea)	auto glass	500-800,000 units ($43m investment)	1986
Saginaw Steering Gear (GM)	Daewoo Precision (Republic of Korea)	steering and drive axles	$30m investment	1987 1987
Sifco Industries	Fortajana, SA (Brazil)	transmissions shafts and connecting rods	$10m investment	1986
Smith Co.	Asia Motor (Republic of Korea)	chassis parts		1987
Rockwell International	Randon, SA (Brazil)	brakes	60,000	1987
TRW Inc.	Kia Industries Co. (Republic of Korea)	steering gears, ball joints, linkages		1987

Source: Interviews, Trade Journals

important transition in strategy is that the component firms are coming to recognize the necessity of siting their production plants near the major assembly plants of their largest customers.

The numbers of such cases that have come to our attention is not overwhelming, perhaps six-to-eight actual decisions not to go offshore and another six-to-ten where the factors have been explicitly considered with regard to past, current or future plans. Yet when added to the broad consensus among suppliers about future trends (as reported earlier in this chapter) this constitutes evidence that the long-term logic of systemofacture is already beginning to assert itself in certain segments of the supply industry. Indeed there appears to be a consensus among industry analysts with whom we have conferred that in a few years time, the movement towards export-oriented offshore investments will have virtually come to a halt.

This shift is most noticeable among firms who have offshore plants committed to assembly activities which are inherently labour-intensive in nature, as in the manufacture of wire harnesses, the sewing of seat covers, and the assembly of electronics products - just those sectors which were predicted to grow in importance in the perspectives offered by NIDL school of FDI (Chapter 1). The experience of one firm (one of the largest captive offshore manufacturers of wire harnesses) graphically reveals the choices the industry faces. This firm has a large number of plants in the soutn of the United States and in Mexico , virtually all of which are committed to the assembly of wire harnesses and related products. So far, technical change has not eroded the competitiveness of its offshore- assembly activities (estimated at 60-70 percent of the total) but this is changing significantly. Technically there are still problems to be solved in the manufacture of reliable electronic multi-switching devices if wire harnesses are to be replaced. Ultimately however, these problems will be mastered - almost certainly within five years. Once this happens the advantage of low wages is reduced and $1bn worth of DC exports may be severely affected. The problem now is what to do in the interim. Management and the engineering staff in the firm and in its parent are divided over the strategy for the next few years. The engineers believe they are close to commercially viable technical solutions - what is required is for an assembler to come down hard in favour of replacing wire harnesses. The parent-company engineers are pushing fast for this decision and want the suppliers to speed-up R&D. By contrast the subsidiary's management believe this would be premature while there is still "money to be made" through offshore-sourcing. But they are well aware that if another competitor solves the technical problem and innovates first, they might lose out on a very considerable market since they expect that "the purchasing agents in [the parent firm] would drop us like hot rocks if we cannot guarantee delivery [of the new product] at the right time, price and quantity". Demand is high enough now for them to consider expansion in Mexico - but instead it looks as though they will try to meet this extra demand for conventional wire harnesses from Taiwan Province, and think strategically about a major push into the new product technology in 1987-1988. However, in 1986 much of this strategic thinking was made irrelevant by the removal of trade preferences on wire-harness imports from Mexico (see Chapter 6). Thus the changing politics of location are likely to lead to a relocation irrespective of these changes in the costs of location.

Almost the exact parallel arises in relation to the choices faced by an independent firm involved in the production of seats. They, like other independent and captive suppliers such as the Fisher-Body Division of GM, had established cut-and-sew operators in Mexico in the early 1980's to take advantage of the disparity in wage rates in a labour intensive product - $23/hr in United States plants compared to $1.50/hr in Mexican plants. However, faced with recent decisions revolving around the supply of seats to new Japanese- and United States-owned assembly facilities in the United States (as well as the removal of trade preferences - see Chapter 6) they opted to build these close to the assembly plants to deliver JIT. They did this for four reasons. First, to get the business that was only available if they could supply on a JIT basis, which they could not from Mexico; second, because of modularity requirements in design and delivery of the seat; third, because new CAD/CAM laser-cutting technology reduces pre-assembly labour input considerably and should make it possible to adopt automated sewing techniques now used by the Japanese; and, finally, because in at least one of the new plants they hope also to introduce new material technology that will allow them to use molded seats and do without sewn-seats altogether. Another very large firm closed down its offshore-assembly of car entertainment systems in the Republic of Korea in 1985 because advances in microelectronic components and assembly automation made it cost effective to produce in the United States.

It is possible to review this trend by component firms to withdraw from offshore-sourcing in terms of the categorization of components offered in Chapter 3. There we distinguished between five sets - generic components (such as nuts and bolts), bulky non-mechanical parts (such as mufflers and glass), trim and wiring, electro-mechanical and systems components (such as wiper motors, ignition systems and brakes) and core technologies (engines, gearboxes and transmissions). Most sourcing from developing countries has traditionally been of generic components and wiring, with the most recent wave of investments going into electro-mechanical components and engine-assembly.

Our reading of technological developments suggests that a new wave of automation is likely to be seen in the assembly phases,29/ adversely affecting wiring, engine and electro-mechanical component exports from DCs. The imperatives of flexible production also suggest that proximate location will be important for all types of components except for the generic ones. This leaves the prospect of the continued offshore-sourcing only of the generic components (market-access conditions permitting) but with some possibility that systemic sub-assemblies may be derived from the developing world if indigenous producers develop some unique technological expertise. But as in the case of fully-assembled autos, all this is contingent upon the openness of markets and it may be that the import of components into the major markets becomes increasingly problematic for political, rather than economic or technical reasons.30/

Given that the auto industry is in the process of transition from the era of machinofacture to systemofacture the pace and present scale of this movement is difficult to judge. So, too, is it difficult to balance the trend towards relocation against the simultaneous increase in the opportunities opening up for offshore exports of components. What we will now endeavour to do, however, is try and evaluate the implication of these seemingly contradictory developments for the incorporation of DCs in the international division of labour in the industry, perhaps through the activities of TNCs.

IS THERE A FUTURE FOR DEVELOPING COUNTRY COMPONENT EXPORTS?

The long-term implications of the transition to systemofacture by the auto assemblers are clear for component exports from the developing world. The successful implementers of the new production paradigm have little interest in sourcing from developing countries. And whilst the less-successful assemblers have come to place increasing reliance on sourcing both autos and components from low-wage economies, they are finding it extremely difficult to maintain their competitiveness in their own markets. Thus either they make the transition to systemofacture (in which case they will reduce their imports from DCs) or they will be unable to survive (in which case there will also be reduced imports from developing countries).

The same trends are being acted out in the components sector where a combination of economic and political factors are forcing the major firms to rethink their sourcing strategies. Whilst this reevaluation is still only occurring at the margin, the trends do appear to be clear. Moreover, it is the United States firms who have developed most reliance on these imports of components and it is in the United States (with its extraordinary and unsustainable balance of payments deficit - see Chapter 1) that the protectionist lobby is becoming most apparent.

From the perspective of DCs these developments are not particularly attractive. Many of them have achieved substantial industrial progress on the basis of exporting parts and components for global consumption across a wide range of sectors. A number of the most industrially advanced of these countries - NICs such as the Republic of Korea, Taiwan Province, Mexico and Brazil - have specifically targeted the auto sector as one of the primary areas for future manufactured exports. These plans must now be open to question.

Most clearly this throws renewed focus on the role to be played by TNCs in the developing world, since given their domination of production in the auto sector, it will be the changing locational policies of these global firms which will be most evident in these poorer economies. This changing pattern of TNC locational decisions may be reflected more in a changing geographical orientation of their exports than in their disappearance. Regional policies may become of growing importance as is increasingly the case in Latin America. There, Ford and Volkswagen have merged their operations in Brazil and Argentina, involving 15 assembly plants capable of producing almost one million vehicles a year. This in part follows a more general pattern of collaboration between auto TNCs in these two countries. But if our research into the locational decisions of the major Western European, United States and Japanese assemblers and component-suppliers is to be believed, the prospects of even sustaining the existing levels of exports to the IACs must be an open question.

So what can be the response of the DCs? If our earlier analysis is correct, then there can be little prospect of relying on the TNCs to export components, except perhaps on a regional basis. From the perspective of the TNCs there is little left of the global comparative advantage provided by low wages aside from the production of generic components, for the assembly of more complex items is becoming increasingly capital-intensive and this reduces the attractiveness of locating in these countries. This is evident from Table 7.7 which shows that even in the late 1970s the very much lower wage-costs in the developing world were of relatively small importance when a complete engine only involved (in best-practice production) 3.5 person-hours of work.

In these circumstances the prospect of significant component exports from DCs will probably be contingent upon the development of specific technological capabilities by indigenously-owned firms. But, as we saw in Chapter 6, the component-sector is becoming increasingly technology-intensive and the financial and technological barriers to entry are growing. This suggests that short of a very substantial commitment of resources - of the sort made in the electronics industry in the Republic of Korea - these indigenous firms may find the development of this technological capability difficult to achieve.

But more generally the auto industry in these developing countries is faced by the same imperative as the IAC industry of making the transition from machinofacture to systemofacture. The key to this is to transfer Japanese best-practice organizational technology to the domestic industry in much the same way as it is now occurring in the United States and Western Europe. One possible route to achieving this is through the direct involvement of Japanese firms in joint-ventures with locally-owned firms, a strategy successfully pursued by Hyundai which short-circuited years of learning via its collaboration with Mitsubishi.31/ If successfully pursued, the resource costs are likely to be relatively limited - yet the potential gains to the industry and the economy could be enormous. It is these gains, and the possible externalities that could arise if the new organizational principles could be applied in other sectors, that make this option attractive.

Table 7.7
Labour Costs for Engine Machining and Assembly

	United States	Japan
Direct Labour Hours per Engine	7.0	3.5
Hourly Labour Cost (1979)	$19.3	$10.86
Direct Labour Cost per Engine	$135.10	$38.01

Source: W.B. Johnston (1981). Reprinted by permission of IMT, Cambridge, Massachusetts, MIT.

True, in terms of national control of the assembly industry, these countries might only be trading one master for another but they would arguably be getting a much better deal, particularly if the restructuring process that followed was to work back through the suppliers network.

Why should the Japanese be prepared to play this role? In general Japanese firms are thought to be fairly reticent investors in DCs, particularly in relation to the transfer of technology. There are however a number of factors at work which suggest that they may become more amenable to developing a larger developing world presence in the auto sector. First, in the past, Japanese TNCs have been reluctant to enter into the larger developing country markets where Western TNCs are already present because of the high costs of entry and what they perceive as fierce competition between established producers. Yet now, with the emerging success of their United States initiatives, they may believe that these larger peripheral markets might be conquered in the same manner. Second, they already possess limited-assembly plants for commercial vehicles and autos (for example, Toyota in Venezuela and Brazil) and in some cases also for motor cycles. Indeed in some cases they possess full manufacturing facility as in the case of Nissan in Mexico and, to a more limited extent Suzuki in India, and Mitsubishi in Malaysia. Presumably, given the right package of incentives these existing operations could be expanded towards a greater degree of integration, provided the supply of quality inputs could be established.

Thirdly, it does appear that the Japanese are in fact beginning to show more active interest in bolstering their activity in these markets. Thus Nissan in Mexico has a major investment program underway, backed up by the surprisingly rapid entry of Japanese component firms into joint-ventures to support this expansion and to provide export to the United States; Toyota and Nissan are engaged in negotiations over the establishment of substantial manufacturing operations in Taiwan Province and Malaysia; Honda is apparently considering the possibility of entering the Brazilian market. And, finally, as all assemblers do, the Japanese recognize that the most rapidly growing markets for autos in the future are likely to be in the DCs (see Chapter 3).

Thus one set of feasible strategies may be to rely on the Japanese auto assemblers to locate plants domestically, perhaps in some cases supplanting the established TNC assemblers, particularly those from the United States. To some extent (as we shall see in the final chapter) this policy becomes more feasible than before for developing countries with smaller markets since the greater flexibility embodied in the new assembly-philosophy goes some way to undermine the scale economies of the mass-production paradigm. Once these new, progressive assemblers are installed, the task should be to put significant resources - with appropriate matching policies - into the development of a local components industry. The long-term aim of this should be that these firms will develop a globally-competitive technological capability which seems likely to be the only weapon which will be powerful enough to maintain access to IAC markets. The costs and risks of such a strategy are significant and will clearly not be appropriate for all developing countries, for our major conclusion is a somewhat pessimistic one.

Such a strategy would require detailed policies to support it. These may rely on enhanced competition in the domestic market in return for trade-balancing, product-rationalization and export market access (where possible). Further, policy-makers would have to provide supportive measures to facilitate technology transfer and to encourage local R&D and engineering work, as well as implementing coercive policies that would impose improved efficiency and quality standards on the components industry. These governments might be able to exploit the current situation and take advantage of Japanese aspirations and the global weakness of Western TNCs to effect a radical transformation of their motor vehicle industry in a way that would rekindle its potential as a source of industrial dynamism. Such a strategy would be complicated and difficult to achieve, requiring as it does a whole new pattern of behavior by all of the actors involved. But in the absence of such bold moves, the window of opportunity for achieving fundamental change in a positive direction may soon pass.

Moreover, there is a distinct possibility that United States TNCs with their profits dropping precipitously at home and market share declining on an international level due to the Japanese advance, may either withdraw altogether from these markets or seek increasingly massive government concessions which the governments might be forced to accept (as in the case of Mexico) because of the crucial position of the domestic industry in the national economy.

Implementing such a strategy is of course likely to be fraught with difficulties, and not only because of the political sensitivity of manoeuvring the Western TNCs out of their entrenched position in the automobile industry, whilst still maintaining favorable trading relations with their governments. Other problems include the question of whether Japanese organizational and work-practices can actually be transferred to the NICs. Also, policy-makers in those countries might have to abandon their long-practiced strategies of offering permanent protection to local suppliers and in imposing often unrealistic local-content requirements. In addition the experience of those firms and countries which have dealt with Japanese FDI (even those in the IACs) is that the Japanese have been particularly reluctant - even by the standards of other TNCs - to effect the substantial transfer of technology.

* * *

The evolving locational pattern of the automobile sector - particularly with respect to the production of components - is thus becoming clear. The successful firms are, for a variety of reasons, moving assembly to the final market and are being followed in this by the component-suppliers. The less-successful firms - particularly the United States TNCs - are in the short-run moving production to low-wage developing economies. But either they will be able to make the transition to the new order of production and match the behavior and efficiency of the industry-leaders, or they will be unable to withstand the pressures of competition. Either way, the prospect for DC exports of components and autos seems somewhat gloomy.

Since the automobile industry is the world's largest industrial sector, these developments in themselves are thus likely to be of considerable importance to industrial strategy-formulation in developing countries. But their impact may either be exacerbated or mitigated, depending upon whether similar events are occurring in other sectors.

In the final chapter we will address the wider implications of the sectoral developments which we have observed. We shall also consider the question of whether the new era of production - systemofacture - is likely to be more easily implemented in developing countries or in the old industrial heartland of North America and Western Europe. Together, these two sets of discussion will help determine not only the future trajectory of developing country industrial development, but also the place of the TNCs in this industrial future.

NOTES

1. This factor transcends technological and spatial considerations. Many component-suppliers and assemblers felt that cultural/national affinity would become an even more crucial determinant of supplier selection as those new relationships became the norm. A French assembler argued that "if we were dependent upon Bosch [of the Federal Republic of Germany] or Aisan Seiki [of Japan] for a crucial component, we would always be concerned that in an emergency we would be faced with the possibility of disrupted supply if that firm's major national customer had also a crisis that demanded attention". Whether the same logic holds true for foreign subsidiaries of the component firm producing in the assemblers domestic market remains to be seen.

2. In which imports of components and vehicles have to be balanced with equivalent exports. Obviously such policies are only attractive in countries with large domestic markets such as Brazil and Mexico.

3. These pressures are not unique to Japanese investments in the auto sector and are being found across a wide range of industries.

4. Utilizing such a strategy and adding-in profit and overheads it is relatively easy to show a local value-added content of sixty percent. Under existing rules-of-origin definitions this is enough to qualify as "domestic production" in most countries (probably except Japan!), including the EEC.

5. Financial Times, 24 September 1986.

6. Automotive News, April 7 1986.

7. Automotive News, 8 December 1986 and April 7 1987.

8. An interesting observation on the lack of confidence by the Japanese assemblers that they could successfully transfer their work practices to the United States was that most of them observed that given the existence of protectionism over final products alone, they would prefer to continue sourcing components from Japan. They argued that with careful organization and carefully located assembly plants they could effectively replicate the JIT system utilized in Japan, except for the extra two weeks required while the components were in transit at sea. The only factor inhibiting the adoption of such a strategy was the recognition that given the underlying balance of payments problems of the United States, local-content would inevitably become an increasingly important concern.

9. Financial Times 16 September, 1986.
10. More than ten by mid 1986.
11. Automotive News, 8 December 1986.
12. Womack (1986a).
13. In light of this, it is interesting to note the views of Roger Smith, GM Chairman, cited in a 1985 interview. Smith seemed almost eager for the confrontation. "GM can't match Japanese costs in Japan, but if the Japanese really try to build new empires in the US that means a new ball game, on a level playing field. It's a game we think GM could win. When they start doing the castings and engines and transmissions here in the US- oh, come on in - then we'll give them a different story". Stavro (1985) p. 54.

14. The Japanese plants in the United States have - to a greater or lesser extent - attempted to purchase from local firms. In 1985-1985, Honda purchased roughly $200m a year from 40 United States suppliers; Nissan had 88 local suppliers with purchases of $114m and NUMMI expected to have 20 by the time it reached full capacity (JEI, 1985).

15. Although there is less evidence than for the assembly plants, our interviews with Japanese component firms operating in the United States indicates clearly that they are pushing to introduce their own methods and standards. For instance one producer of radiators, mufflers and air conditioners has two United States joint-ventures' plants where both internal JIT and quality controls have been successfully introduced, though still not yet at Japanese standards. Inventory levels have been reduced from 20 days to 10 days in 6 months, and wastage reduced from 4-5 percent to less than 1 percent (in Japan the levels are 2 days and 0.01 percent respectively).

16. An indication of how significant an impact the

expansion of auto exports can have on an economy - even a large one - can be gleaned from the experience of the Republic of Korea in 1986. In that year the country produced its first trade surplus since the end of the war, totaling $4.6bn. Of this about $2.8bn was due to lower energy prices, $400m to lower debt-charges and the remainder to an increase in non-traditional exports, of which the export-surge of autos was the most significant component. The macro-economic consequences of this were substantial, including talks being held with the IMF about the revaluation of the Republic of Koreas' currency.

17. Chrysler announced plans to increase component imports from Brazil from $30m in 1985 to $100m in 1986 and to import $700m worth of parts from Mexico in the five years to 1990 years. Roughly similar imports of components are planned from the Republic of Korea.

18. Womack (1986a).

19. Delphi studies involve guesstimates by industry leaders and knowledgeable observers of likely future trends.

20. The Delphi study was undertaken by Arthur Anderson and Co and is cited in Krebs (1985).

21. Calculated from SMMT (1986).

22. Though recently both Toyota and Nissan have been showing strong interest in limited local production of autos in Taiwan Province and Malaysia, some of which may be exported to IAC markets in an attempt to circumvent trade barriers.

23. The similarity between these developments and the experience of the United States colour TV industry (Baba, 1985; Sciberas, 1977) is striking. Faced with competition by high quality imports from Japan in the early 1970s, the United States firms chose to compete on price and did so by shipping out production to low efficiency-wage developing economies. Their Japanese rivals chose instead to concentrate on a combination of automation, JIT organization and product improvement. They not only swept up the United States market, but the transfer of production abroad by the United States firms provided the opportunity to DC firms to absorb the technology and compete themselves - a mere decade later - in the United States. A familiar sequel to this comparative story is that once these Republic of Korean and Taiwan Province firms were able to compete, they too found themselves blocked by protectionist pressures and were forced to locate production near the final markets.

24. Often the decision to produce abroad was forced

upon the supplier by the assembler. One European firm who had recently established a plant in Mexico at Ford's "request" (that is, insistence) made it clear that if they had a choice they perhaps would have preferred not to be in Mexico, but "when Ford says jump, you jump".

25. All figures from O'Brien and Aleu (1984).

26. There is anecdotal evidence from the literature to support another common feature of disproportionate TNC involvement trade. Unger (1985) shows for Mexico how only two foreign firms accounted for 85 percent of component exports (of a total of 571.7m pesos) while other foreign firms accounted for 95 percent of a total import bill of 923.2m pesos.

27. Winter (1985)

28. So far, Japanese firms retain a much larger lead as a source of technical assistance for Republic of Korean component firms. As of 1984, there were 58 licensing agreements between Japanese and Republic of Korean firms compared to only 28 for all other countries.

29. Some of the Japanese assemblers - notably Nissan and Honda - see this as a major area for technological progress. Honda believes that two-thirds of its assembly labour-force would be displaced between 1986 and 1990 (verbal communication, Dan Jones).

30. We can give two recent examples (glass and steel wheels) that are indicative of the trend towards protectionism against components. In the case of glass, two United States firms, Ford and Libby Owens, who had established joint-ventures in Mexico to export auto glass to the United States were found by the United States International Trade Commission (ITC) to have been receiving "unfair" export subsidies from the Mexican government. In relation to steel wheels, the Wheel and Brake Division of a United States TNC has appealed to the ITC that Brazilian steel wheel manufacturers were dumping their output in the United States. It is interesting that one of the Brazilian manufacturers accused of dumping steel wheels on the United States market is in fact the subsidiary of another United States TNC, Rockwell International. The company bringing the suit does not source in Brazil - but is an active exporter from other Latin American markets.

31. In earlier years this was also a tactic utilized by Mazda in learning from Ford.

8

TNCs and the New International Division of Labour in the Era of Systemofacture

In attempting to explain the insertion of the developing world in the international division of labour in manufacturing we have covered a wide terrain. In Chapter 2 we began with an historical account of the transition in the sixteenth-century from handicraft production in the home and small craft-workshops to manufacture in the first factories. Although these factories saw a progressive division of labour, they remained small in scale, producing a heterogeneous bundle of products predominantly for the local market. This "industrial revolution" was largely confined to Western Europe because it was there that the social relations were most appropriate for the development of these first factories, with non-agricultural production in other countries continuing to be met by artisanal and handicraft labour. International integration in manufactures in any meaningful sense was thus slight, even though Ricardo's theory of international specialization in cloth and wine production between England and Portugal was developed within this period of manufacture.

The era of manufacture ran into difficulties over the next two centuries. Because the process of production depended upon the dexterity of the individual worker, with the intensity of his/her supervision and the efficiency within which labour-tasks were divided and allocated, there was a limit to the growth in labour-productivity. These limits were overcome increasingly rapidly in the last quarter of the eighteenth century when the first true "machines" were introduced, marking the transition from the era of manufacture to that of machinofacture. The introduction of these machines - in which the process of production was determined by the productivity of the machine rather than the individual laborer - provided scope for the gradual spread of industrialization throughout the world. Their introduction was complemented by the development of an appropriate pattern of work and production organization. This is best understood in terms of the gradual evolution of six features of what we have called the machinofacturing labour process (and which others refer to as the Fordist labour process)

The first saw the increasing division of tasks. This was followed by the separation of skilled from unskilled tasks and the employment of the cheapest available source of labour for the unskilled elements (women and children in nineteenth century Europe). The inherent variability of skilled labour provided the impetus for the third stage of this labour process, that is, the progressive mechanization of skilled tasks. Nevertheless, despite this substitution of machinery for labour, the control of factory workers was becoming increasingly difficult as the scale of these factories continued to grow - hence the significance of the fourth phase of this labour process, the introduction of Taylorist methods of control. Henry Ford's innovation of the moving production line linked to special-purpose machinery and standardized products - with heavy inventories acting as a buffer "just-in-case" anything should interrupt this supply-driven system - marks the fifth element of this labour process. But it was only after the development of cheaper forms of transport and the globalization of markets during the 1960s that the final stage of this labour process - the New International Division of Labour (NIDL) - was able to emerge, particularly in sectors such as clothing, electronics and automobiles. In this, all of the previous five stages of the labour process were extended on a world-scale. "World-factories", comprising of highly-divided tasks being undertaken for subsequent incorporation in global products, began to penetrate developing countries where cheap-labour (often women) became the basis for comparative advantage. At the height of this supply-driven machinofacturing era, the mass production of standardized products in which price was the major determinant of competition came to be the dominant paradigm. And some developing countries - NICs - came to fill an important role in this global division of labour.

During the 1970s many of the contradictions inherent in this era of machinofacturing production came to a head. Not only did productivity-growth slow, but it became increasingly uneven. Conflict in the workplace became endemic, which was not entirely surprising given the alienation which flowed from increasingly divided tasks and the tensions which inevitably rose from the systematic application of Taylorist control over work. And, partly because of the unevenness of technical change and partly because of its very nature, the level of unemployment rose steadily and became difficult to reduce. International economic tensions grew and protection - dormant in the IACs since the 1930s - began to adversely affect the growth of world trade and to threaten the export-led growth which had been associated with industrialization in many developing countries.

It is in Japan - relatively untrammeled by the social history of machinofacture - that a new era has begun to emerge. Its final shape is naturally unclear, partly because it is not preordained and partly because no era remains static. Yet its central features are evident, and we have identified these as comprising of three pillars. The first involves the adoption of a new flexible labour process in which the past tendencies towards the increasing division of tasks, the deskilling of work and the removal of control over production from the worker are reversed. The second relates to the development of new systemic relationships between plants and firms, and the third involves the adoption of systemic, computer integrated manufacturing technologies. In contrast to machinofacture, the basis of competition in the new era is not on the lowest-price of standardized products, but is increasingly determined by product innovation and quality. We have referred to this new era as that of systemofacture.1/

These developments are not unique to Japan; nor is it likely that the "new order" will be identical in other countries. For example, in Italy it is similarly reflected in the development of a new, flexible labour process and the rapid diffusion of electronics-based automation technologies.2/ But the pattern of inter-firm relationships which has evolved is less of the Japanese-style dominant-large-and-subordinate-subcontractor type and more about collaboration between equivalent small and medium sized firms. Similarly the new labour processes which are beginning to be developed in Western firms - notably by Ford in the auto industry3/ - will inevitably show significant variations. The important feature which they all display, however, is a decisive break with the past.

The brunt of our analysis of the automobile industry in Chapters 3-7 has been to show how the geographical sourcing of components and autos differs between these two eras of machinofacture and systemofacture. The early phase saw a transition towards a global strategy, in which the developing countries assumed a progressively more important role. But in systemofacture - in which the economics of location are very different - such a globalized form of production is sub-optimal. Moreover, the gradual emergence of protectionism in the major markets and the labour-saving nature of technical change have meant that production is more likely to occur near the point of the final market than at the site of least-cost.4/

We believe from our analysis of emerging trends in the automobile industry that these conclusions can be validated for that sector's future operations. But how generalizable is this picture? This final chapter will address this issue. In Section 1 we consider the problem of transferring the Japanese system of production to other countries; this is key to later discussion of the future prospects for industrialization in the developing world. Section 2 addresses the sectoral generalizability of our conclusions and considers some factors which will affect the extent to which the changing global location in the auto sector is likely to be mirrored in other branches of industry. This is followed in Section 3 by a consideration of the likely implications of these events for the nature and extent of continued industrial progress in the developing countries. The chapter concludes with a discussion of the likely consequences for the continued dominance of global production by the TNC.

THE TRANSFERABILITY OF THE JAPANESE SYSTEM OF PRODUCTION

The striking absolute and relative advance of the Japanese economy in the post WW2 period has made it a model for international emulation. Yet, despite its reputation, the performance of the Japanese economy has not been uniformly superior across sectors and its international presence is not disproportionately large.5/ But what makes Japanese economic prowess so noticeable is its sectoral concentration, probably most evident in automobiles, consumer electronics, semiconductor memories and machine tools. Nevertheless, despite this uneven performance, there can be little doubt that when Japanese industry and the state target a particular sector for future concentration, they tend to achieve their goals. In these circumstances their performance is setting the standard for others to emulate.

Historically, in the latter-machinofacturing era, this was a role performed by the United States economy, and by the auto sector in particular. Although the moving production line, the standardization of products and the interchangeability of parts were not pioneered by Henry Ford it was he who made them into a paradigm for other sectors to emulate.6/ In the same way, current events in the Japanese auto and electronics sectors are setting the standards not just for other countries, but also for other sectors. As we illustrated in Chapter 4 the superiority of performance by the Japanese auto industry is evident in relation to each of the three pillars of systemofacture which we have identified - the adoption of systemic CIM technologies, the development of systemic inter-plant and inter-firm relationships and the introduction of a different and flexible labour process. But are these transferable to other environments? And if there are difficulties in making this transfer, is the Japanese experience to be explained by cultural or by political factors, or by a combination of the two? This will obviously affect our judgement as to the extent to which the new era of production can be transferred and to what sorts of enterprises, sectors and countries. It is instructive here to consider each of these three pillars of systemofacture in turn.

The Adoption of CIM in other Countries

In our discussion of CIM we have pointed to two important characteristics. The first (considered in Chapter 2) is the systemic nature of electronics-based technologies, reflecting the pervasive use of digital-logic in control systems and the convergence occurring between information-processing and information-transmitting technologies. Whereas previous vintages of automation technologies had generally confined productivity gains within individual processes or spheres of production,7/ the introduction of these new electronics-based automation technologies concentrates the productivity-gains at the level of system-implementation. These systemic productivity-gains are currently being reaped predominantly within each of the three spheres of production, but the cutting-edge of technological progress is focused on the reaping of inter-sphere gains, as in the introduction of CAD/CAM and the introduction of centralized data-bases for a single plant or firm.

There is much evidence - including from the auto sector (see Chapters 4 and 5) - that although the leading edge of technological development is often to be found in Northern Europe and the United States, it is in Japan that the most pervasive productivity-gains are being realized. In a narrow technological sense there is no reason why this technology cannot be transferred to other economic environments, as long as the various elements of the electronic jig-saw are in place so that advantage can be taken of the synergistic qualities of this new technology. It is here that it is possible to see particular difficulties arising for developing countries. This is because the relationship between labour and capital costs in the IACs is such that the adoption of many elements of this electronic jig-saw (such as word processors) is justified on cost grounds even though in other activities the new electronics technologies (such as CNC machine tools) are primarily introduced for reasons of product quality or the reduction of lead-time in innovation. Yet in DCs the factor-price ratio is such that there is little justification for introducing those elements of the electronic jig-saw which are not essentially being adopted for reasons of product quality. Thus it is not that the capturing of these systemic gains in developing countries is technically infeasible, but more that it is likely to be hampered by the less-pervasive introduction of the various elements of electronics technology in these low-wage countries.

Another important technological element here concerns the investment in the infrastructure required to take advantage of synergies between different electronically-controlled equipment. That which facilitates communication within enterprises (local area networks) can be looked-after by individual firms, but the transfer of information between establishments and firms requires social investments in new communications technologies such as fibre-optics (in the short run) and digital networks such as Integrated Services Digital Network (ISDN) in the longer-run. The Japanese have probably made the most significant investments in these new digital highways and quite clearly have the most articulated long-term strategy. But in general it is in the IACs rather than the DCs that the most thorough-going investments in this technological infrastructure are being made. On the other hand, the IACs have a long history of investment in now-antiquated electro-mechanical and analogue telecommunications technology and possibly have a greater legacy to overcome than developing countries.

The second relevant feature of the new electronics-based automation technologies which we observed (in Chapter 6) was that unless prior changes had been made in the labour process and factory organization, many of the benefits arising from the introduction of these technologies were difficult to capture. The case is most graphically illustrated in the first attempts by the United States and some Western European assemblers to cope with Japanese competition. In less than a decade they invested nearly $100bn in advanced manufacturing technology, but because they had failed to make prior changes in organization and the labour process, much of this investment was wasted. Yet, in Japan where the introduction of the new CIM technologies was preceded by organizational and labour process change, the full systemic benefits of these technologies are being captured. In this case the problem of transfer is one which affects the IACs more than the DCs since it is in those countries with a long industrial past that there remains a potentially stultifying heritage of machinofacturing practices to overcome.

Nevertheless, despite these potential difficulties, it is unlikely that the obstacles to the widespread adoption of CIM technologies will be substantial, even if the full benefits will be difficult to capture without simultaneous or prior changes in the labour process and the organization of production. This is in fact evidenced by the performance of some non-Japanese firms. For example, in the auto sector, Fiat is the most prominent, having proceeded very rapidly down the path of flexible automation. (In this it contrasts with both Volkswagen and IBM, both of whom have at various key stages made heavy investments in inflexible automation).8/ Benetton, the Italian garments firm, is another important example which we will discuss later.

The transfer of new inter-plant
and inter-firm relationships

In Chapter 4 we observed the organic relationships which have developed between component suppliers and auto assemblers in Japan, and in Chapter 6 we provided evidence of the difficulties which the non-Japanese auto industry was having in replicating them. As opposed to the arms-length and confrontational relationships which characterized the era of machinofacture, the new pattern displays a much greater degree of closeness and integration in strategic planning, design and production. Locational proximity - relating to the characteristics of just-in-time (JIT) production - is another key component of these relationships and it is this which suggests that the dominant locational form of investment will be that which involves the clustering of linked enterprises and plants (which is of course very different to the "world factories" of latter-day machinofacture). This new pattern of interrelationships is not confined to the auto industry and is becoming increasingly pervasive, particularly as the concept of JIT filters through firm strategies. It has become especially prevalent in the electronics industry, where both IBM and Xerox have made substantial moves towards single-sourcing and JIT production.9/ Thus to some considerable extent the new pattern is clearly transferable.

And, yet, there are problems. In Chapter 6 we illustrated how the absorption of the new ideology about inter-firm relationships was not always matched by the actual policies being introduced by firms. In one case a plea for a "new, cooperative relationship" was accompanied by a tear-off reply-slip which had to be returned to signify acceptance within two weeks! This is an attitudinal problem which may not always be easy to overcome, and in this sense it would suggest that countries and companies with a long history of machinofacturing production are more likely to encounter difficulties in absorption than are new entrants. What it also suggests - a conclusion confirmed by the Japanese auto firms who were considering their investments in the United States in 1984 - is that the redefinition of intra-plant and intra-firm relationships is much easier to achieve than those between plants and especially between firms. The Japanese auto firms were confident that they could get intra-firm JIT in the United States and Western Europe to approach Japanese levels, but they were much less confident of their ability to similarly restructure inter-firm inventory relationships.

The implications of this are complex for the process of transfer. On the one hand the prior existence of a supplier network is possibly an important component of future success in the development of new inter-firm relationships. On the other hand, the ingrained attitudes amongst both suppliers and assemblers may militate against this success; moreover, there is some evidence that in countries where no supplier networks exist, these can be created.10/ To compound the issue, firm-size may also have a bearing on the extent to which these new inter-firm relationships can be forged. Large, integrated firms hold the potential to restructure these relationships internally, without having to create or reeducate arms-length suppliers. To be set against this is the relatively greater difficulties which large organizations seem to have in restructuring their managerial paradigms, as is most clearly evidenced by the recent experience of GM which has been struggling for some time (and with little success) to reduce its various complicated tiers of management.

The transfer of the Japanese labour process

It is worth bearing in mind the important caveats made in Chapters 2 and 4 concerning the "Japanese labour process". In actual fact there is no single model of work-organization throughout Japanese industry, and even though its auto industry is moving along a common trajectory in the development of new work-practices there remain important differences between firms in both philosophy and practice. Nevertheless, when compared with the dominant labour processes utilized in other countries, there is a remarkable and distinctive common pattern which is emerging throughout the auto sector and increasingly also in other sectors of the Japanese economy. These characteristics were sketched out in detail in earlier chapters and the question which exercises our attention in this final chapter is whether they can be easily transferred to other operating environments.

One measure of the difficulties which are entailed can be illustrated by the phenomenon of the *Andon* lights and switches used by Toyota in many of their lines. These not only give the capability to each line-worker of bringing the whole line to a halt if an error is noted, but it is also <u>expected</u> that they will utilize this power when appropriate. Those familiar with the quality of the Fordist labour process will appreciate just how revolutionary is this break with traditional practice.11/ But what is perhaps equally striking about this practice of Toyota is that despite being subjected to the most extreme work-pressures, the workforce only uses this power to bring production to a halt in the interests of the firm, rather than to alleviate the backbreaking pace of work.

The ability of the Japanese firms to maintain control over this "autonomy" which has been given back to the workers requires some explanation. In Chapter 2 we distinguished between two central features of control over work. The first was that of "exterior conditioning", by which management carefully monitors and controls the pace and nature of work; the eight functional tiers of management introduced by Taylor and refined thereafter represent the systematization of this. There have also been some important institutional developments which reinforce these shopfloor controls, including the whole infrastructure of industrial relations. The second feature of control is much less tangible and was described in Chapter 2 as "interior determination", the mind-set of workers which is such that although they are provided with the capability to stop a backbreaking task, this power is only exercised in the interests of management.12/

In explaining the fact that Japanese management seems able to give an important measure of control back to its workforce without having to worry that this control would be exercised against corporate interests, it is possible to point to three general areas of explanation. These are the pattern of industrial relations which have developed in Japan, the possibility that there are cultural explanations for this behaviour and developments in the ideological sphere. Let us consider each briefly in turn.

One of the most important developments in the history of the Japanese automobile industry took place in the first half of the 1950s. It involved the virtual destruction of an independent trade union, first at Nissan and then at other Japanese firms.13/ This set the scene not just for the initial Taylorist intensification of work (graphically described in Kamata's account of working at Toyota in the early 1970s), but also for a second important feature of the Japanese system of industrial relations, namely the development of compliant company-unions. Although these tame company-unions were initially an important instrument for maintaining control over work, it also provided a significant element of institutional support for the new labour process. As we saw in Chapter 4 one of the central features of this labour process is the reversal of the historic trend towards the increasing fragmentation of tasks and the polarization of skills in work. (In the era of machinofacture this division of labour had led to the development of craft-unions). The company-unions have become an important adjunct to task- and skill-flexibility in work, avoiding the problem of inter-union demarcation disputes.

These brief examples of the functions of company-unions in providing institutional support for the new flexible labour process are no more than illustrative of a general observation. The implication which follows from this is that transferring the new labour process to other environments might well fall foul of the legacy of industrial relations inherited from the era of machinofacture. To some extent this is a problem which can be resolved through negotiation, but it naturally also has an important political dimension since industrial relations do not emerge through careful thought and purposive action alone, but also after a long history of struggle. They are not easily reformed, so in this sense the transferability of the new labour process may well be easier to "greenfield" pastures than to established areas of industrial activity. It is largely for this reason that the IACs have seen a drift of industrial concentration, from the "snowbelt to the sunbelt" in the United States and from the North to the South in the United Kingdom.14/ But it is also possibly for this reason that the developing world may well be a more fertile terrain for the introduction of systemofacture.

The second potential factor affecting the process of interior determination is the cultural element. It is often argued that there are unique features common to confucian culture - notably the "group ethic" and the supposed absence of inter-personal conflict - which somehow underwrite the workability of the Japanese labour process. These cultural characteristics of confucianism are contrasted with the supposed "individuality" of Western culture which is said to be reflected in the combative industrial relations of machinofacture. An example of this type of argument is to be found in Dore's recounting of decision-making in Japanese and United States enterprises.15/ Dore observes the cultural dimensions of decision-making in the two countries. In general, Japanese firms make decisions on a consensual basis and this slows down the procedure significantly.16/ By contrast in United States firms the executive decision is authoritarian and generally very rapid. However, despite the rapidity of this decision-taking process in the United States, implementation is slow because the key intra-corporate battles have still to be fought, whereas in Japanese firms, the consensual process ensures that implementation is almost instantaneous. Another example can be given from Kamata's reluctance to use the *Andon* switches because of social pressures from his workmates.17/ Some argue that deference to group-legitimization (a "shame-culture") as opposed to individual responsibility (a "guilt-culture") represents a fundamental cultural divide.

By its nature this is an extremely difficult argument to pursue. How is it possible to move beyond assertion and to document these behavioural factors in a meaningful manner? Are observed differences to be explained by genuinely "cultural" factors - which suggests a very long evolution of behaviour - or do they reflect a more recent process of "social engineering"? And, if the latter holds, can these patterns be replicated elsewhere? Are the differences in behaviour to be explained by factors of political economy? For example, Dore's introduction to Kamata's account of the Toyota labour process in the early 1970s suggests that it is partially explained by the continuation of feudal patterns of behaviour.18/

Emerging from this general discussion of "cultural" factors is the suggestion that to some extent the determination of behaviour can be explained in terms of the creation of specific ideologies. Broadly speaking, ideology can be distinguished from culture by its purposive nature. It involves a set of ideas (affecting behaviour) which are specifically and consciously fashioned. Thus Kamata's recounting of Toyota's attempts to control worker-action through a manifold structure of interventions in social and personal life, as well as work life, reflect the conscious construction of an ideology about work. Similarly, IBM's much-vaunted corporate culture reflects a similar ideological process. The consequence of these distinctions is that whilst the cultural determinants of behaviour may be difficult to transfer, the ideological elements are much easier to replicate.

But the problems in reaching any useful conclusions on the overall transferability of the Japanese labour process remain. Not only is there a clear process of interaction between the domains of culture and ideology, but when is a culture a culture? For a heavily-populated country, Japan is characterized by a unique degree of cultural homogeneity, but are there similarities with other confucian cultures? And if there are, and if these similarities are relevant to the process of interior determination, then there may be limits to the degree of transferability of the new labour process.

The emphasis here is on the word "degree". For the fact is that many elements of this labour process - specifically the trends towards multi-tasking, multi-skilling and single-union status - are becoming increasingly widespread in the older IACs. We do not yet have evidence that this is occurring in the developing world, but there is no particular reason why this should not be the case. But how extensively can these practices be transferred? And, especially important, to what extent can enterprises outside of Japan give back an important measure of control over work to the workforce without this being exercised in ways which management consider to be deleterious to productivity? And, finally, are there reasons to believe that these factors underlying the process of interior determination are adversely affected by the legacy of inherited industrial behaviour? If so, it may well be that the finer characteristics of this Japanese labour process are more-easily transferred to virgin territory, to the "greenfield sites" of developing economies. These important questions await an answer, partly because this is an under-researched area of inquiry and partly because the process of transfer is so relatively recent.

THE SECTORAL GENERALIZATION OF SYSTEMOFACTURE

The analysis in previous chapters was confined to the automobile industry. The fact that it remains the single largest branch of global industry suggests that the conclusions which we drew cannot be ignored, even if the observed phenomena are confined to this sector. They are likely to affect a very large number of workers and firms, not just those in the components sector but also those involved in the provision of the infrastructure for the "motorized society". Yet our wider interests transcend the auto industry itself and in fact we have used its experience to suggest a transition between eras of industrial organization. But to draw this wider conclusion it is necessary to have some sense of generalization, for although the auto sector has long been seen as paradigmatic for other sectors, it obviously has particular features.

Since we are concerned with the insertion of the developing countries in the global division of labour in manufacturing our primary focus in this study has been to consider the locational implications of the transition to systemofacture. At various stages we have distinguished between the changing nature of both the "politics" and "economics" of location and this is a useful distinction to use in considering the sectoral generalization of our conclusions.

The effect of changes in the politics of location on the sectoral transition to systemofacture

Since the origins of the modern industrial world in the mid-sixteenth century, there have been important fluctuations in the free-flow of commodities. In the early mercantilist period, although trade was inhibited by political limits to the flow of commodities, the technological factors underlying international industrial specialization (notably the relative absence of scale economies in production) were relatively unimportant. But as technology progressed, scale economies grew and specialization became increasingly important. As the nineteenth century progressed, so did the extension of this international specialization and competition, leading ultimately to conflict over market access, and the subsequent slide into WW1. During the Great Depression of the 1930s, market access was problematic, in the auto industry (Chapter 3) and elsewhere, with much of global commercial trade falling during WW2.

As we saw in Chapter 2, this protectionist interlude was followed by the "Golden Age" between 1950 and the early 1970s. It saw a period of unparalleled global economic expansion, affecting not only the IACs but also the developing countries. But perhaps more significantly, it was also a period of unprecedented international integration, facilitated by the construction of an open international trading environment through a series of tariff-reducing initiatives by GATT. As we saw, this liberal economic trading order began to break down in the late 1970s with a proliferation of voluntary export restraints, orderly marketing agreements and other types of non-tariff barriers.

This re-emergence of protectionism is key to our projected view of international specialization in the era of systemofacture. We have shown (and will discuss further below) how the new era involves a very different pattern of location between assemblers and suppliers, with geographical proximity and systemic interdependence becoming crucial to competitiveness. But, on their own, these technological developments say nothing about the <u>international</u> distribution of economic activity since there is no reason why these clusters of production should not be located in the Japan or even the DCs, exporting output to the IACs. Our reason for suggesting that - at least in the short- to medium-run - they will be located in the IACs follows from the changing politics of location, the reemergence of protectionism. This is forcing the assembly stage of production to the final market, and in so doing, also leads to the relocation of the subsidiary component-manufacturing stages of the cycle of production. This process is clearly exemplified for Japan's Sony Corporation. One of the most international of Japanese firms (with 70 percent of its total $8 bn sales abroad in 1986) it is being forced to establish production plants in consumer markets. By 1990 it expects foreign-production to have risen from the 1986 level of 20 percent to 35-40 percent of total sales. As the head of its corporate planning division remarked,

> Globalising production is a positive development, but the key reasons for it are negative. From a cost point of view, it would be most economic to concentrate production in one plant and have Japan as factory for the world. But other countries would never accept it.19/

As was shown in earlier chapters, the emergence of protectionism is clearly apparent in the auto sector. But are we to expect that similar protectionist phenomena will appear uniformly across all sectors? The answer is clearly in the negative. But if this is so, is it possible to anticipate in which sectors the new protectionism will surface? Of course this is by no means easy, partly because there are so many factors which go into the determination of specific protectionist measures. These inevitably lead not only to sectoral variations, but also to national ones. Nevertheless, despite all these caveats, it is likely that the extent to which protectionism reappears across sectors will be significantly affected by three major factors.

The first of these concerns those industries which are considered to be of strategic importance. This may either be because they are so large (as in the case of the auto industry) that many governments feel that international location cannot be left to market forces. Their intervention may either take the form of direct quotas (as utilized in the auto sector by the United States, Italy and France) or through a type of quasi-protection involving the subsidization of local firms (as the French and United Kingdom Governments have done for Renault and RG, both of which may arguably have fallen to the onslaught of imports had the state not provided regular injections of cash, through both loans and equity). But another type of strategic industry is that which is considered to be at the leading edge of technology. The most readily apparent set of sectors evident here are those associated with the production and utilization of electronics. This is not confined to Japan, the Republic of Korea and Brazil (all of whom have a track-record of supporting emerging technologies) but now also includes Western Europe and the United States who are moving to both protect and subsidize these leading sectors. In the United States case anti-dumping actions have been taken against the Japanese producers to inhibit them from their well-practiced predatory-pricing strategies. But in 1987 earlier attempts to subsidize the industry were consolidated with a $1bn state-subsidized Sematech initiative designed to assist United States semiconductor firms back to the leading edge of technology.

The second factor determining the sectoral incidence of protectionism is likely to affect precisely the opposite sort of industries to the capital- and technology-intensive strategic sectors discussed above. It relates to the traditional labour-intensive industries in the IACs which, partly because of their labour-intensity, have come to be threatened by imports sourced from countries with lower wages. The most notable examples are the textiles, garments and shoe industries, but it also includes the basic steel industry and much of the capital-goods sector where traditional technology has often been labour-intensive. The particular susceptibility of these industries to protectionist pressure follows directly from three factors. In the first place their labour-intensity means that import-penetration has a highly visible consequence, all the more so during periods of high unemployment. Second, many of these industries are regionally concentrated, so that the political pressures which result from labour-displacement are easily translated into political pressure, much more so than the diffuse general increase in consumer welfare which arises from the availability of low-cost imports. And, third, much of the countervailing employment-creation in new industries tends to occur in other regions, partly because (as we have seen) the innovating firms prefer to establish production in regions which are relatively free from trade unions and workpractices developed in the machinofacturing era.

The final factor affecting the sectoral incidence of protectionism relates to the presence of TNCs in the chain of international production. Where international firms are particularly involved in foreign production and trade, they are relatively more likely to withstand the protectionist pressures exerted on their domestic governments. Thus, in the case of the auto and electronic sectors, most of the largest United States producers have come to rely almost exclusively on foreign supplies for some components; and in many cases production has been subcontracted to foreign-based producers rather than to the foreign subsidiaries of these TNCs.20/ Protection has only belatedly appeared in these sectors. However, where domestically-owned TNCs are not involved in the chain of production there are fewer and less-powerful vested interests opposing the clamour for protection. This is particularly evident in the shoe and garments sectors where although some domestically-owned firms have organized a global chain of production, many of the imports into the IACs come from indigenously-owned Republic of Korean, Hong Kong, Taiwan Province and Chinese producers.

Trying to make sense of this sectorally-uneven incidence of protectionism it is thus possible to conclude that the pressures are most likely to be felt in sectors which (either by virtue of their size or technological content) are considered strategic, in sectors which involve labour-intensive production and in sectors where few domestic firms have international operations. In some cases these three categories overlap and reinforce each other (as in garments and shoes), whilst in other cases they tend to be exclusive (for example, locally-owned electronics TNCs who source some of their components from abroad). But it should not be thought that these factors will alone determine the incidence of protection. They are merely contributory to the relative timing of protection which, as a general phenomenon, is most likely to be affected by the rate of unemployment and the extent and persistence of the trade deficit.

For these reasons, protectionist pressures may well abate as the differentials in productivity between countries and regions are eroded over time. In these circumstances there may well be a greater degree of international integration, as occurred in the post Bretton-Woods period until the middle on the 1970s. For this to occur the new order of systemofacture - which will quite likely take different forms in different environments - will have to have diffused widely through competing nations.

Technological factors affecting the economics of location

There are two sets of technological factors which have an effect on the economics of location, and thus are important determinants of the international division of labour in industry. The first of these concerns changes in economies of scale, and the second arises from the degree of inter- and intra-industry links in the chain of production. But before we can consider the detailed interactions between these factors, it is first necessary to categorize some important technological factors which define sectoral boundaries.

Figure 8.1 pulls together two sets of distinctions which are commonly found in the literature on industrial sociology and production engineering. The first of these relates to the scale of production, with the major cleavages arising between unit (one-off), small-batch and mass production. The second involves the distinction between industries which produce discrete (or "integral") products - that is, those products produced as individual, separate items - and those which produce dimensional products which are measured in terms of volume, capacity and weight.

The interaction between the homogeneity of markets and the type of industry provides the basis for scale economies, and thus for the existence of the "world factories" of machinofacture and the TNC. But the concept of "scale economies" is not quite as simple as it often seems, and it is helpful to distinguish three major dimensions of scale - of product, of plant and of firm. The existence of scale economies in product provides scope for the "world car" (see Chapter 3); plant scale economies suggest the "world factory" and firm scale economies underwrite the TNC. If the transition to systemofacture is associated with a reduction in these scale economies, then its associated pattern of globalization will change. The issue we now consider is whether it is possible to identify sectoral determinants of changing scale economies.

So what factors are responsible for scale economies in each of these three dimensions of scale? The first, and most obvious, is the perspective of management. As Piore and Sabel document,[21]/ the mass production paradigm - with its machinofacturing focus on the production of price-sensitive standardized products - became dominant in the late nineteenth century, and until recently has underlain the strategic perspective of most corporate managers. They

347

Woodward's classification	Nature of activity	Production engineering classification
A. Intergral Parts		
Unit and small batch production	Production of units to customer requirement	Jobbing ('Unit production')
	Production of prototypes	
	Fabrication of large equipment in stages	
	Production of small batches to customer's orders	Batch
Large mass production	Production of large batches	Batch
	Mass production	Mass
B. Dimensional products		
Process Production	Intermittent production in multi-product plant	Batch
	Continuous flow production in single product plant	Mass

Figure 8.1 Scale in Production

came to believe that mass production would inevitably become standard in all products and sectors, and planned accordingly. This has given an impetus to both product and plant economies of scale.

A second factor underwriting the growth of scale economies follows from the engineering principles involved in many of the dimensional industries, particularly those which involve chemical processes. The necessity to control these chemical processes requires the utilization of enclosed containers, but the geometry of volume is such that increases in internal capacity do not occur in the same relation as changes in external surface - in fact, the relationship between these changes in surface and volume is around 0.6. Over the years plant engineers have come to develop a rule of thumb that as they double plant capacity, so capital costs have only tended to increase by about two-thirds, and they have come to dub this as the "0.6 rule". Here we can see a clear technological dynamic towards plant economies of scale in the chemical process industries; it also suggests that the very small firms will also be excluded. But these technological factors do not generally extend to product economies of scale, since many of these process plants can produce a number of different products. They also do not necessarily underwrite the growth of the TNC (with production facilities in a number of countries), although they may influence the degree of international trade.

A third factor providing an impetus to scale economies is specific to the discrete products industries, producing individual units of output. Here the switch from the production of one specification of commodity to another requires the resetting of machinery, commonly known as "downtime" in industry. Production has to be stopped and individual machines have to be adjusted to produce different sizes and shapes. Not only does this downtime lead to the loss of output, but the manual resetting of machinery-specifications frequently leads to the initial spoilage of output.[22]/ Although, as we saw in earlier chapters, the extent of this downtime can be significantly affected by the organization of production, there are nevertheless inherent technological factors which suggest that, all other things being equal, it is best to keep machines running for as long as possible, to "dedicate" them to a particular task. This provides an impetus for both product and plant economies of scale, with the ultimate logic being to specialize production and to transport the final output to distant consumers if the local market is not large enough to ensure the take-up of the whole production of a particular plant and product.

A fourth factor underlying the growth of scale economies has particular implications for firm-size and relates to the indirect costs of production. These are costs which are not directly incurred in production - they thus exclude machinery, labour, raw materials, intermediate components, land and utilities such as energy and water. Indirect costs comprise of activities which lie in the background of actual production and whilst they are not generally used-up in production, if they are not sustained at some general level then the enterprise as a whole will not be able to function competitively. Historically, four sets of indirect costs have stood out in importance. The first is R&D such as that involved in long-run product improvement and development, and this clearly varies in importance between sectors. The second item of indirect costs is management, not so much detailed line-management (which is a direct cost of production) but more the overall strategic planning activities of senior management. Third is the function of raw material and component acquisition and the fourth relates to sales and marketing. All of these indirect costs provide the impetus to firm economies of scale, although as we shall see, this is not necessarily the case and alternatives do exist for the spreading of indirect costs of production between firms.

The "economies of mass resources" are another factor underwriting the growth of firm scale economies. These include a variety of advantages of size which make life easier for the very large firms. A number of examples illustrate their scope - the ability of a large firm to obtain concessionary finance; the provision of guarantees for large tranches of borrowed funds; concessionary prices obtained for inputs as a consequence of the bargaining strength of world-wide sourcing. All these factors - whose import first became evident in the mid-nineteenth century with the development of the "national firm" in the United States - provide a powerful impetus for the domination of large-scale firms in production, but as with the case of indirect costs of production, there are other ways of obtaining access to these economies of massed resources which do not necessarily imply the inevitability of the TNC.

The final factor underlying the growth of scale economies is the existence of large and homogeneous markets. This was crucial in the development of the mass production paradigm in the United States in the nineteenth century, and it was largely for this reason (as we argued in Chapter 2) that the machinofacturing era was forged in North America rather than Western Europe. Clearly, unless the savings arising from dedicated production are so substantial that they dwarf the costs of inventories and transport, then the existence of large and proximate markets is essential for the consumption of standardized output.

The consequence of these six sets of factors was that since the beginning of the machinofacturing era (and probably even before that) there was a consistent tendency for scale economies to grow along all three of these dimensions of scale. Product runs became longer (as in the "world car"), plant sizes grew (the "world factory") and the TNC came to dominate production throughout the globe.23/ The consequences for this are illustrated in Figure 8.2 in relation to small-batch and large-batch discrete products industries and in the continuous process industries. Only in two sets of sectors did these scale economies not grow - those in which demand was necessarily heterogeneous (such as capital goods, some building materials and income-inelastic craft-based consumer goods) and those in which the limp materials in production provided severe obstacles to mechanization (notably garments and leather products).

But with the transition to systemofacture, many of these factors underwriting the growth of scale economies have begun to change radically. In some cases the consequences are to reduce the pressures to the growth in scale. This arises from four sets of developments. First, managerial perspectives have begun to change (as illustrated extensively in earlier chapters) and markets have become much more discriminating. Second, product innovation and quality have increased in relative importance compared to price, particularly in the IACs and the NICs, and this has undercut the standardized-product mentality of Fordism. Third the reorientation of the labour process has significantly cut the extent of downtime during machinery changes - we have documented this extensively for the auto industry, but this is becoming an increasingly widespread phenomenon in other sectors. And, finally, the introduction of electronically-controlled machinery has cut the guesswork out of much of machinery-setting. Instead of the approximate accuracy of manual-setting, the electronic-controls allow for much greater precision and thus much of the wasted production characteristic of product changeover is reduced.24/ But

Dimensions of Scale	Product		Plant		Firm	
Era of production	Machino-facture	Systemo-facture	Machino-facture	Systemo-facture	Machino-facture	Systemo-facture
Small batch Discrete	static	static	static	rising	static	rising
Large batch Discrete	growing	falling	growing	falling	growing	uncertain
Continuous Process	growing	falling	growing	falling	growing	uncertain

Figure 8.2 Changes in the Three Dimensions of Scale in the Transition from the Mass Machinofacture to Systemofacture*

*These are 'ideal types', representing central tendencies. There will obviously be variations, reflecting sectoral specificities, differences in corporate strategy and some differences between countries.

the two other determinants of scale remain unaltered - process industries are becoming more flexible in their output (thus reducing product economies of scale), but continue to rely on large-plants. And the indirect costs of production - <u>especially the R&D component</u> - continue to rise. We documented this extensively for the auto assembly and components industries in earlier chapters, but this phenomenon applies across the board and is perhaps one of the most significant features of modern industry.

Figure 8.2 contrasts these central tendencies in both machinofacture and systemofacture. In machinofacture there was a consistent tendency for scale economies to grow in most industries (excluding some of the capital goods and limp-fabric industries) and across all dimensions of scale. It was this which led most observers to conflate all three dimensions under the simple heading of "growing scale economies in production". However in systemofacture we are seeing something of a divergence. In the small batch industries which were previously impossible to automate, the new flexible electronics-based machinery is providing the impetus for a growth in plant and firm size - the future of many independently-owned small jobshops is threatened. In the large-batch discrete products industries both product and plant economies are falling - firm size also tends to be growing, but as we shall argue below, this is not necessarily the case. And in the continuous process industries a similar pattern is occurring. Thus not only is there something of a reversal in the historic patterns characteristic of machinofacture, but there is no longer a simultaneity in the trajectory of the three dimensions of scale.

Another technological factor affecting the economics of location arises directly from the transition from just-in-case to just-in-time inventories. JIT makes particular sense when a great many components are involved in assembly. When a product is either molded or cast in a single or limited number of operations, or when it comprises of a small number of parts, then the advantage of inventory reduction is largely confined to the final product itself. In these cases there is likely to be a less-significant imperative to locate production in proximate enterprises or near to the final market. The greater the degree of complexity in production - "roundaboutness" as it is sometimes called - the greater the likelihood that the locational patterns which we are observing will prevail.

All of these patterns have been illustrated in the

case of the auto assembly and components sectors discussed in earlier chapters. What we have done here is to provide some schema for understanding the generalization of these trends to other sectors. The undermining of some dimensions of scale in these industries not only has implications for the continued growth of the TNC (a subject to which we shall return later) but also thus affects the economics of location. If large plants and large product-runs are no longer the rule, then there will be a reduced imperative to international specialization in production. Moreover, because of the growth of entry-barriers to markets (the changing politics of location) the prospects for DCs becoming increasingly integrated in the international division of labour in industry are, we believe, limited.25/

To illustrate that this is a process not confined to the auto industry it is instructive to briefly consider the emergence of the Italian garments firm Benetton over the past two decades. Benetton has moved rapidly to the three central pillars of systemofacture - it is highly flexible, makes extensive use of the CIM production technologies and has a radically different structural relationship with its suppliers. Its activities are confined to strategic planning, design, pre-assembly grading and cutting, warehousing and distribution.

Benetton has installed a number of key electronically-controlled items of equipment. Design, grading and cutting occurs through the use of CAD/CAM terminals, allowing rapid response to changing fashions, savings of labour costs and optimal use of material.26/ Dye-composition and mixing is undertaken by electronically-controlled mixers which ensure a large range of consistent colors. The warehousing is highly automated and flexible. Before the final products are automatically retrieved and delivered to the lorries, the labelling and price-tags are made out in the language and currency of the country in which they will be sold. Each of the more than 4,000 Benetton shops in 57 countries (mostly in Western Europe, North America and Japan) are fitted with electronic-point-of-sale (EPOS) terminals which automatically communicate the pattern of sales to Benetton's head office. This enables the firm to finely judge marginal changes in market tastes and to adjust production accordingly. The assembly of the final garments (and the knitting of the cloth) is subcontracted to over 200 local, independently-owned firms which deliver on a JIT basis.27/

As a result of this strategy, Benetton has become the

fastest-growing garments firm in Western Europe. Its sales rose from L55m in 1978 to L623m in 1984, L850m in 1985 and L1,079bn in 1986 (a rise of 22.7 percent between 1985 and 1986. The proportion of output exported has expanded consistently, rising from 55 percent in 1985 to 61 percent in 1986). But its strategy is not unique and at least two Hong Kong garments firms transferred production to automated plants in the United Kingdom in 1985.28/ In part they did so because of their fears of protectionism, but the necessity of being close to rapidly-changing markets was an even more persuasive factor. Here it is instructive to quote the views of the Chairman of the British Clothing Industry Association

> Changes in the fashion industry and the high street are giving Britain's clothing industry an unrivaled opportunity to stem the tide of imports...[T]he old pattern of two fashion seasons with the shops bringing in spring and summer goods in February, and replacing them with winter goods in mid-August, is disappearing...Retailers want to change their displays frequently and instead of placing huge orders twice a year they are placing smaller ones more often. [They] now want to be able to place smaller orders and get a very quick delivery date.29/

In addition to these developments in the garments industry, the growth of protectionism against Japanese imports into the United States and Western Europe, coupled with the rapid appreciation of the Yen, is forcing many of these Japanese firms to move production from their home-bases (the site of least-cost) to the final markets. Thus the President of one on Japan's major opto-electronics, fine chemicals and electronics companies - Konishiroku - explains a recent shift in policy

> Until now the optimum location has been in Japan. But with the changing times and the changing international situation our basic policy has also changed so that now we intend to focus more closely on our customers, the end users of our products. In other words, to site our plants where we have the greatest number of end users.

This change in the locational strategy - mirrored not only by the auto firms described in earlier chapters, but by a host of other Japanese firms - carries in its wake a train of components suppliers. In part this is because of the hostility to "screwdriver operations" in the final markets, and in part due to the inherent logic of JIT. Thus Brother Industries - a large Japanese manufacturer of sewing machines, consumer goods and office equipment - has been forced to move a significant proportion of production from its Japanese plants. Local sourcing in its United Kingdom typewriter factory began at 40 percent, short of the EEC target of 45.5 percent. Brother plans to increase this progressively to 50 percent, and thereafter to 60 percent, but claims it is experiencing problems in obtaining components of adequate quality.30/

The signs are beginning to emerge that these locational strategies of Japanese and Western European firms are finding an echo in the United States. General Electric (GE) has decided to produce colour TVs domestically rather than to import them from Japan. Another firm, Innovative Controls, relocated the production of outdoor light fixtures from Taiwan Province to a highly automated factory in Houston. And IBM makes printers which it previously imported in a North Carolina state-of-the-art factory. Although there are a variety of particular reasons for these locational decisions, they are subsumed by our analysis of the transition from machinofacture to systemofacture. For, as a senior management consultant observed, "People are realizing that stuff out on the sea for six weeks has to be counted as material tied up in inventories".31/

THE IMPLICATIONS FOR CONTINUED INDUSTRIALIZATION IN THE DEVELOPING COUNTRIES

Our analysis of the auto industry suggests that the location of production is likely to become increasingly market-oriented. It is helpful here to relate this conclusion back to the initial discussion in Chapter 1. There we observed that the bulk of FDI was of an horizontal nature, producing similar products in different countries. Although some FDI was vertical and sequential (involving successive stages of value-added in different countries), a significant component in the 1970s appeared to be towards disarticulated FDI, in which the manufacture of individual components - or sub-stages of components - occurred in different countries. The expectations of many observers was that this disarticulated component of FDI in the auto sector (as well as the clothing and electronics sectors) would grow in relative size, along with a continued surge in export-oriented industrialization in developing countries. Our conclusions - involving the increasing market-orientation of FDI - clearly contradict this expectation of the early 1980s.

If it is true, then the role played by developing countries in the international division of labour in the automobile sector will largely be confined to the domestic and regional markets. We have little expectation that, as a general process, they will become increasingly integrated into production for global markets and think it likely that even their existing limited global role will be under threat. In this chapter we have also suggested that similar trends are likely to emerge in other sectors, enabling us to draw more general conclusions regarding the broader pattern of the international division of labour in industry. Other than in some of the process-industries and those industries in which product-complexity is low (and thus where other than the cost of carrying inventories of final products there are no great technical imperatives to relocate production near the final market), we have concluded that the pattern of the auto industry is likely to be replicated in other sectors. So the implications for a deepening of the present trend towards export-oriented industrialization in the developing countries does not look too promising.

But this surely cannot be interpreted as suggesting the demise of developing country industrialization or, indeed, in inhibiting a different pattern of export-oriented industrialization. That process has much too great a momentum to be written-off and many developing countries now possess dynamic industrial sectors and substantial technological capability. What is more likely, though, is that developing countries may well experience a change in industrial orientation and it is worth briefly considering the likely direction of these changes during the transition to systemofacture. Before doing so, however, it is best to bear in mind the heterogeneity of the developing world. Some DCs - especially the four South East Asian NICs (Hong Kong, Singapore, Republic of Korea and Taiwan Province) - hardly qualify as developing countries anymore and have significant segments of their industrial sectors which are at the leading edge of IAC technology. Other DCs such as Brazil, India, Argentina and Mexico have a long tradition of Fordist production and may well be able to make a natural progression to incorporate some elements of systemofacture. But there remain other countries - particularly in sub-saharan Africa - where there is little history of machinofacturing production and where the transition to systemofacture may well depend upon the ability to jump stages of industrial history (if that is indeed feasible).

In considering the potential for industrialization in these countries it is perhaps best to begin with the prospects for systemofacture in these economies. We have already considered some of these issues earlier in this chapter, with the general conclusion that insofar as the adoption of the systemofacturing labour process was determined by social attitudes, it is possible that "greenfield" sites in developing countries were more favorable than those in the IACs where attitudes may have become set in the mold of machinofacture. Moreover, to the extent that there are cultural underpinnings to the Japanese labour process - an uncertain conclusion - it is possible that other Asian developing countries with similar cultural patterns might be able to adopt the new labour process more successfully than the "individualistic cultures" of the west. To be set against this, there were a number of factors, ranging from the pervasive diffusion of electronically-controlled equipment to the more rapid introduction of suitable infrastructure, that suggested a more rapid uptake of systemofacture in the older IACs.

There is as yet not much evidence whether developing-country firms have managed to adopt any or all of the three central tenets of systemofacture. In a recent contribution, Sabel has argued that some Latin American firms have adapted to their place in the machinofacturing era in a way which suggests that they are well-placed to make the transition, almost as if they were proto-systemofacture enterprises./ Briefly, his argument is that the origins of the global crisis in the 1970s forced these firms to experiment with new forms of production which were at variance with the mass production, Fordist model which they had targeted to develop. In particular the small size of their markets made it difficult for them to specialize in the production of standardized commodities and this led to a policy of adaptation. As a result,

> the Latin American firms following this strategy are systematically different from comparable firms in the advanced countries. Whereas the latter organize operations sequentially on the model of the assembly line or continuous process technology,...the former are organized as a collection of semi-autonomous shops

under one roof. Each shop specializes in a particular manufacturing operation or the production of a certain family of parts; similar machines or clusters of machines will thus be grouped together, rather than dispersed in sequences defined by the steps required to build a particular product.33/

Although they suffer from an inability to subcontract production to other small firms - due to the generally poor state of the surrounding industrial base - Sabel argues that based upon the experience of Singapore, it is possible to create a network of suppliers. Moreover, the poorly-understood informal sector in many of these countries includes within it a number of flexible enterprises which also fit the mold of the future.

At this early stage in the evolution of systemofacture, there is no way of confirming Sabel's speculations. It is possible that these Latin American and many South East Asian firms do indeed lend themselves to a rapid transformation, although it is important to note that Sabel's preoccupation remains with the phenomenon of flexibility which, as we saw in Chapter 2, only covers a part of the required transformation to systemofacture. He offers little evidence of the adoption of the new electronics-based automation technologies nor of the organic and systemic integration between firms and plants. Nevertheless it would be fair to conclude on the basis of some of the Asian NIC experiences and those of the Latin American firms to which Sabel refers, that there is no necessary reason why they are unable to make the transition, and a number of reasons why they should be able to do so successfully.

If so, a number of conclusions follow with respect to their future industrial performance. In the first place the orientation of industrialization will have to be directed to the domestic or the regional rather than the global market. In part this is because of changes in the economics of location, but it also reflects the growing incidence of protectionism which we expect to be maintained over the next five to ten years (unless unevenness in productivity-growth is reduced). But, secondly, as a consequence of the reduction in plant and product scale economies (see Figure 8.2), there is a more favorable prospect of meeting domestic needs without incurring the excessive cost penalties which often meant that machinofacturing enterprises operated with substantial excess capacity. An illustration from the auto sector is helpful here. With traditional Fordist lines, a plant needed to produce approximately 250,000 cars of the same type to get to the bottom of the cost curve and the cost penalty for falling significantly below this figure was substantial. Thus, in the context of limited domestic markets which seldom allowed for the consumption of so many of the same size of car, developing-country assembly plants were faced with the prospect of either exporting large numbers of the same car or running at high cost. Now, the new generation of auto plants not only produce at lower levels of scale than this (Chapter 3), but they are also capable of producing a number of different variants of car (Chapter 4). An understanding of the principles underlying this reduction in scale economies (Chapters 4 and 8) make it clear that this same phenomenon can equally apply to many other sectors, particularly those producing discrete products in large batches.

A third implication for future industrial strategy in the DCs relates to the efficacy of protective policies. This has been a subject of hot debate in recent years with the hegemonic view (reflecting the wider trend towards market-oriented policies in some of the IACs and multilateral aid agencies) being that the attempts by DCs to protect and subsidize their industries were inimical to industrial "efficiency" (generally only considered in a static framework) and growth. What we have learned from the experience of the United States in the auto sector is that in the new context of systemofacture, the introduction of protectionist controls over final assembly is often on its own enough to also draw the subsidiary component supplying firms to feed the assembly plants on a JIT basis. Similar conclusions of course apply to developing countries, particularly in the context of the reduction in product and plant economies of scale and this suggests a renewed and progressive role for appropriately specified protectionist policies.

The diffusion of systemofacture has particular implications for a narrow range of developing economies, of which Mexico is the most notable example. Their proximate location next to a large IAC market means that it is quite possible that they can be successfully incorporated into the JIT scheduling of production in the final markets. The weeks long delay in shipping from Singapore to the United States stands in sharp contrast to the few days (and in some cases few hours) required to transport components from a Mexican plant to a final assembler in the United States, particularly if it is located in the South or South West.

Although there are not many developing countries which are "fortunate" enough to be so close to the United States,34/ what this highlights is the growing importance of regional markets. In Chapter 1 we pointed to the fragility of the liberal trading order in the context of high unemployment and significant balance of trade deficits in many IACs. Some observers have drawn the conclusion from this that the global trading order which developed in the latter days of machinofacture is likely to collapse, and that it will be replaced by a series of major trading blocs. These will allow unbalanced intra-bloc trade, but will require balanced inter-bloc trade. One notable observer foresees the emergence of three major trading blocs - the Yen-zone, the dollar-zone and the Deutchmark-zone.35/ Which developing countries become incorporated in which bloc is obviously of considerable importance to their future industrial strategies and to the development of regional specializations. But it also suggests that these factors may not lead to the complete demise of export-oriented industrialization, but to its reorientation. Regional trading may become an increasingly important phenomenon in the decades to come, even if not in the structural forms suggested by Eatwell and Thurow.36/

Perhaps one reflection of these trends towards regionalization and collaboration is to be found in the case of the Brazilian and Argentinian automobile sectors. There, VW and Ford (in competition in all other global markets) have merged their product-portfolios and production facilities within a regional firm called Autolatina. In doing so they not only hope to maximise integration and scale economies, but also (no doubt) their political "clout" in operating environments which they often perceive to be hostile to automobile production.

And, finally, an area of indeterminacy for these industrial policies - a subject which we will consider in greater detail below - concerns the reliance which they will have to place on TNCs for their technologies. The context is one of a general and sustained increase in technological intensity which opens wider the gap between best-practice and average production efficiency. Under some circumstances the increase in indirect costs of production arising out of greater technological intensity also reinforces the movement towards firm economies of scale, and thus the market-power of TNCs. The question is whether this is likely to undermine the trend which emerged during the 1970s of developing countries limiting the presence of - and sometimes even excluding - TNCs operating in their economies.

TNCS IN THE ERA OF SYSTEMOFACTURE

The dominance of the world's economy by a limited number of large TNCs was noted in Chapter 1. Three hundred and fifty firms dominate industrial production and the world's largest TNC - General Motors - has an annual turnover (just over $40bn in 1986) which exceeds the Gross Domestic Product of all developing countries except for Brazil, China, India and Mexico. To varying extents these TNCs account for a significant share of industrial production in most economies, especially in the IACs. In developing countries there is more variability in their dominance over production, with their presence being particularly pronounced in sub-saharan Africa, Brazil, Mexico, and Singapore.

The growth to prominence of these TNCs has been a phenomenon of the past century, especially in the decades after WW2. It is in this same period that the era of machinofacture grew to maturity and in which its dominant labour process - Fordism - extended on a global scale to find expression in the NIDL. But as machinofacture passes into decline and as the NIDL is whittled away by changes in both the economics and politics of global location, it is naturally of interest to determine whether the dominant institutional expression of these phenomena will experience an analogous demise. The TNC - or rather that (minor) part of FDI which was oriented to the pursuit of a NIDL strategy - is clearly an important area of concern here. Once again - as with the case of many other phenomena which we have been discussing - there is a large measure of uncertainty involved, partly because no particular result is pre-ordained and partly because the era of systemofacture is still in its formative years. Nevertheless it is possible to identify a number of important factors which will have a bearing on the issue.

It is probably best to begin by briefly recounting the central factors inducing the pervasive increase in scale since the mid-nineteenth century. Earlier we identified six such factors - the belief by management and engineers that large scale was more efficient, the "0.6 rule" characteristic of many process industries, the downtime and spoiled output arising from product changeovers in the discrete products industries, the growth of indirect costs of production (especially R&D), the "economies of massed resources" and the existence of homogeneous markets. As the transition to systemofacture progresses, many of these factors are experiencing significant changes. Managers are no longer so convinced of the dominance of large scale production, markets are more diversified, and electronics-based automation technologies and changed work practices reduce machine changeover time. Other features - such as the economies of massed resources, the growth of indirect costs and the inherent scale economies in process industries - endure.

These observations induced us to distinguish between three dimensions of scale - in product, in plant and in firm. We observed in Figure 8.2 that in many sectors traditionally characterized by mass production, plant and product scale economies are beginning to decline whilst they are simultaneously beginning to increase in other sectors traditionally associated with small-batch production. But we were left uncertain as to the implications which these changes hold for the direction of firm scale economies, and hence for the continued dominance of global industrial production by the TNCs. Insofar as firm scale economies are determined by the growth of indirect production costs - which is becoming particularly marked as the technological component of production increases - we can expect that there will remain significant pressures towards the global concentration of ownership which provides a mechanism for spreading indirect costs over a large range of output (even though this may involve production in smaller factories of more diversified products). Similarly, the benefits arising from massed resources - notably the bargaining power over suppliers and the access to finance - also show no sign of decline.

For all these reasons it is tempting to conclude that we are likely to see a continuation of historic trends towards concentration. But before reaching hasty conclusions it is worth bearing in mind three major caveats. The first has particular implications for United States and Western European firms, rather than their Japanese counterparts. On past experience it would seem that the very large firms - encumbered by substantial layers of bureaucratic middle-management - have sometimes not proved to be as innovative as their smaller counterparts. As we saw in previous chapters this phenomenon is especially evident in the case of GM, which seems to be finding enormous difficulty in cutting out these bureaucratic layers of middle management.

We have to be careful about interpreting the data here

since although it is true that many of the most successful high-tech innovations took place in start-up firms, many of these have either grown into transnationals or have been taken over by TNCs.37/ Moreover the Japanese *Sogu Shoshu* are seemingly immune from the trade-off between innovation and size and some of the major Western European firms such as Siemens and Philips and (until very recently) IBM have been able to come to terms with the disadvantages of size. Nevertheless there remains at least a suspicion that large firms lose their innovatory spark and that, consequently, this may be a factor inhibiting the continued growth of TNCs. Having said so, it remains the fact that large Japanese firms seem to be less adversely affected by their size and, moreover, are relatively poorly represented in international production when compared to their United States and Western European rivals. It may well be, therefore, that the slowdown in the growth-rate of TNCs applies disproportionately to the firms from the "old industrial center".

The second major factor suggesting that the growth of the TNC is not inexorable relates to alternative ways of spreading the indirect costs of production. Here there are a number of alternatives to the TNC. In Chapters 4 and 6 we showed how the Japanese auto component firms were increasingly striking joint-venture alliances with their United States and Western European counterparts as a way of avoiding the impact of growing indirect research and development costs. Another mechanism which can be an alternative to generating a larger spectrum of technological capabilities and which has been utilized in the electronics industry is to allow different firms to specialize, and then to swap technology. The final way of spreading these indirect costs is to collaborate with small competitors in a variety of indirect production activities. This is a phenomenon which has become evident in recent years in parts of Italy in the industrial districts of the "Third Italy".38/ Here the various small enterprises join together to provide a number of common services such as design intelligence, marketing and basic research.39/

Piore and Sabel build on the examples of the Third Italy and the Baden-Wuerttemberg region in the Federal Republic of Germany to suggest that we are on the edge of a "second industrial divide" where, as in the nineteenth century, the possibility exists of taking two alternative directions - the route of mass production or that of craft-based flexible specialization. There is no doubting the attractiveness of this as a policy option, especially for small countries or for particular regions in large countries. Yet the history of industrial capitalism has been one of centralization and unevenness and it remains to be shown that these same unequalizing tendencies will not grow to dominance in these new industrial districts as the years progress.

The third caveat which should be borne in mind when considering the "inexorable rise to dominance" of the TNC is the political and technological pressure underlying the rise of locally-owned firms in developing countries. The political force of this momentum is often underestimated by observers in the IACs, not least in the auto industry. The MIT study of the Future of the Automobile - a classic of the mid-eighties40/ - held out little prospect for the Republic of Korea's industry. Yet barely three years after the MIT study was published, the Republic of Korean industry was on the threshold of producing one million autos a year. Similarly, it was common in the early 1980s to dismiss the nascent electronics industries of Hong Kong, Republic of Korea and Taiwan Province, yet few now could doubt their sustainability. And the doubts now being cast on the wisdom of Brazilian policies on informatics - in which foreign TNCs are effectively excluded from large segments of the market - suggest that the underestimation of these technological and political capabilities in DCs is a continuing phenomenon. If these locally-owned firms continue to grow in size and capability, this, too, may set limits on the extension of the TNC, especially in the developing economies.41/

So we are left with a feeling of uncertainty. Powerful forces are at work which strike at the very roots of the TNC. Yet, simultaneously, many of the key factors which underlie the growth of this dominant institution of the twentieth century remain in evidence. Which of these sets of forces will triumph is of course uncertain but the main analytical pitfall is that of voluntarism, in which the forces of centralization which have become so dominant over the past century are merely wished away.

NOTES

1. As we saw in Chapter 2 others describing these events have characterized it in slightly different ways. Piore and Sabel refer to the new era as one of "flexible

specialization" whilst Perez calls it "systemation".
   2.   See Piore and Sabel (1984) and Brusco (1982).
   3.   In 1987 Ford began the attempt to introduce a new flexible labour process in its Western European plants. In the United Kingdom this brought it into conflict with the craft unions which had evolved during the period of machinofacture.
   4.   It is often thought that the site of least-cost is characteristically the low-wage developing economies. This may have been true for most of the IACs whose industrial sectors were not especially efficient. But (at least until the sharp appreciation of the Yen in 1986-1987), in many cases it was Japan and the South-East Asian NICs such as Hong Kong, the Republic of Korea, Singapore and Taiwan Province - whose wages were not especially low when compared to India, Bangladesh and China - which were the sites of least cost.
   5.   This is especially the case in relation to its share of global FDI where Japan is a late entrant. But even in the trade arena, its proportion of trade to GDP is lower than that of the Federal Republic of Germany.
   6.   See Chandler (1977) for a detailed discussion of the historical evolution of these characteristics of machinofacturing production.
   7.   Of which there are three - design, machinofacturing (where the physical processes occur) and coordination.
   8.   For the case of Volkswagen, in which the savings of direct labour in production were to some extent outweighted by the expansion of indirect labour, see Chapter 5. For a description of IBM's highly automated but relatively inflexible plant in the United States, see Financial Times, 23 January, 1987.
   9.   Morgan (1986).
   10. See Fransman (1984) for the case of Singapore.
   11. See, for example, Beynon's account of the nature of industrial relations on the shopfloor in Ford of Great Britain during the late 1970s (Beynon, 1984)
   12. An interesting case can be cited here to illustrate the complexities of this process of interior determination. We interviewed H Kamata, author of a chilling account of the intensity of working conditions and the pervasiveness of Toyota's managerial control over the social and personal lives of its workforce in the early 1970s. Kamata acknowledged that he had had access to the Andon switches which would have brought the production line to a halt. But why had he not used it, despite his graphic

account of the unpleasant conditions of working life at that period? "What would my workmates have thought of me?" was the reply, despite the fact that Kamata recounts a level of exhaustion amongst his workmates which most Western workers would find intolerable.

13. See Cusumano's careful and detailed recounting of these events (Cusumano, 1985).

14. Peet (1983) shows how this relocation in the United States is clearly explained by the pattern of industrial conflict. Massey and Meegan (1982) argue a similar case for the United Kingdom.

15. Dore (1984).

16. A more cynical view would be that these decisions are legitimized consensuously.

17. See footnote 11.

18. Dore in Kamata (1982).

19. Financial Times, 4 December 1987.

20. In 1987, 36 percent of personal computers sold in the United States were sourced from abroad (many selling under United States brandnames), up from 1.3 percent in 1982. In the same period the proportion of foreign-assembled computer terminals rose from 24 to 46 percent, and that of inexpensive telephone equipment rose from 33 to 65 percent (Financial Times, 20 May 1987).

21. Piore and Sabel (1984).

22. For example, in pre-1980 glass-container production, the switch from one specification of container to another was associated with two hours of machine downtime and a further six hours of spoiled output as the machine-timing was set and reset.

23. As we saw in Chapter 1, 350 TNCs account for over one-quarter the global GDP.

24. To continue with the illustration of glass container production (footnote 20), the switch to electronic control allows for the precise retiming of machinery and thus cuts out the six hours of wasted production arising from the utilization of the previous vintage of electro-mechanical machine controls.

25. An important caveat is due here. Our argument is that this arises partly because of the changing politics of location which results from the inherent unevenness in the transition between machinofacture and systemofacture. As this unevenness dampens in future decades, it is conceivable that a renewed round of trade liberalization will ensue.

26. This latter feature is a particularly important characteristic of the new electronics technology in

garments manufacturer, since typically the savings on materials costs arising from the utilization of CAD terminals exceed the total costs of labour in production (Hoffman and Rush, 1985).

27. The combined effects of low stocks and flexibility in production have important implications for company profitability. One industry source estimates that the cost of these inventories, "stock-outs" (customers being unable to obtain the garments they wanted) and excess end-of-season stocks of poorly-selling items accounts for around 25 percent of total industry expenditure. (Frazier, 1986).

28. Business Week, August 26 1985.

29. Financial Times, 5 February 1986.

30. This is a common complaint of Japanese firms operating abroad. One consumer electronics firm we visited recounted its difficulties with a supplier. Experiencing problems with the quality of these components it adopted the same strategy as they used in Japan and sent back the faulty components to the supplier so that the source of the problem could be identified and then rectified. But the United Kingdom supplier was surprised to receive the shipment saying that since they were substandard they should be thrown away - "what's the point of sending them back to us?".

31. New York Times, 18 February 1987.

32. Sabel (1986).

33. ibid. p. 46.

34. This proximity is often a mixed blessing - in the words of a popular Mexican phrase "Pity Mexico; it is so far from God and so near America!"

35. Eatwell (1985).

36. ibid. and Thurow (1985).

37. For an illustration of this process in the Computer Aided Design sector, see Kaplinsky (1983).

38. Brusco (1982) and Piore and Sabel (1984).

39. Here the analysis of Palloix (1977) - discussed in Chapter 1 - is particularly illuminating. He draws our attention to the existence of three different circuits of internationalization, in finance, in production and in trade, and argues that no one form should necessarily prevail. What we can observe when technological joint-ventures or technology-swapping agreements substitute for FDI is a retreat away from internationalization through the circuit of productive capital.

40. Altshuler et al (1984).

41. An interesting development in recent years - charted in earlier chapters for the auto industry - is the

growth by some of these developing country firms into TNCs as their access to foreign markets has become progressively blunted.

Abbreviations

AGV	Automatically Guided Vehicle
CAD	Computer Aided Design
CIM	Computer Integrated Manufacturing
CNC	Computer Numerical Control
DCs	Developing Countries
DNC	Direct Numerical Control
FDI	Foreign Direct Investment
FMS	Flexible Manufacturing System
GM	General Motors
IACs	Industrially Advanced Countries
NC	Numerical Control,
NICS	New Industrializing Countries
NIDL	New International Division of Labour
OECD	Organization of Economic Cooperation and Development
QDC	Quick Die Change
RG	Rover Group
SPC	Statistical Process Control
TNCs	Transnational Corporations

Bibliography

Abernathy, W. J. (1978). <u>The Productivity Dilemna: Roadblock to Innovation in the Automobile Industry</u>. Baltimore: Johns Hopkins University Press.
Abernathy, W. J. Clark., K. and Kantrow, W. (1983). <u>Industrial Renaissance: Producing a Competitive Future for America</u>. New York: Basic Books.
Adam, G. (1975). "Multinational Capital and Worldwide Sourcing", in Radice (ed).
Aglietta, M. (1979). "The theory of capitalist regulation", <u>New Left Review</u>,
Altshuler, A., Anderson, M., Jones, D. T., Roos, D. and Womack, J. (1984) <u>The Future of the Automobile</u>. Boston: MIT Press.
Baba, Y. (1985). <u>Japanese Colour Television Firms' Corporate Decision-Making from the 1950s to the 1980s: Oligopolistic Corporate Strategy in the Age of Microelectronics</u>. D. Phil dissertation, Brighton: University of Sussex.
Babbage, C. (1832). <u>On the Economy of Machinery and Manufactures</u>. London: Charles Knight.
Basile, A. and Germidis, D. (1984). <u>Investing in Export Processing Zones</u>. Paris: OECD.
Berg, M. (1985). <u>The Age of Manufactures</u>. London: Fontana.
Berry, B. (1986). "Honda Goes America", <u>Iron Age</u>, 16 May.
Beynon, H. (1984). <u>Working for Ford</u>. 2nd edition, Harmondsworth: Penguin.
Bowles, S. S., Gordon, D. M. and Weisskopf, T. E. (1983). <u>Beyond the Wasteland: A democratic alternative to economic decline</u>. New York: Doubleday Press.
Brett, E. A. (1985). <u>The World Economy Since the War</u>. London: Macmillan.
Bruce, P. (1983). "Strong Future Seen for Steel in Cars",

Financial Times, 18 August.
Brusco, S. (1982). "The 'Emilion Model': Productive Decentralization and Social Integration", Cambridge Journal of Economics, vol 2.
Callahan, J. (1985). "Chrysler's Sterling Height's Plant", Automotive Industries, 4 October.
Caves, R. E. (1982). Multinational Enterprise amd Economic Analysis. Cambridge: Cambridge University Press.
Chandler, A. D. (1962). Strategy and Structure. Cambridge, Mass.: Harvard University Press.
Chandler, A. D. (1977). The Visible Hand. Cambridge, Mass.: Harvard University Press.
Cohen, G. A. (1983). "Forces and Relations of Production", in Mathews, B. (ed), Marx: A Hundred Years On. London: Lawrence and Wishart.
Cole, R. E. and Yakushiji, T. (1984). The American and Japanese Auto Industries in Transition. Ann Arbor: Center for Japanese Studies, University of Michigan.
Cole, R. E. et al. (1986). "Participants Report on a Survey of the North American Automotive Supplier Industry", Industrial Technology Institute. Ann Arbor: University of Michigan.
Crisp, J. (1986). "A Rapid Increase in Demand: Vehicle Components", Financial Times, 4 April.
Crouch, C. and Pizzone, A. (eds). The Resurgence of Class Conflict in Western Europe since 1968. 2 vols. London: Macmillan.
Cusumano, M. A. (1985). The Japanese Automobile Industry: Technology and Management at Nissan and Toyota. Cambridge, Mass: Harvard University Press.
Delcrenzo, M. (1986). "Van Nuys Union OKs pact in bid to save plant", Automotive News, 9 June.
Dodwell Marketing Consultants. (1983). The Structure of the Japanese Auto Parts Industry. Tokyo: Dodwell Marketing Consultants.
Dohse, K., Jurgens, U. and Malsch, T. (1984). From "Fordism" to "Toyotism"? The Social Organization of the Labor Process in the Japanese Automobile Industry. Berlin: International Institute for Comparative Social Research.
Dore, R. (1982). "Introduction" in Kamata, H. (1982).
Dore, R. (1984). The Social Sources of the Will to Innovate. London: Technical Change Centre.
Dosi, G. (1982). "Technololgical Paradigms and Technological Trajectories", Research Policy, Vol. 11, No. 3,

Ealey, L. (1984). "Planting Roots in America", *Automotive Industries*, May.
Ealey, L. (1985a). "Twelve Foreign Car Makers to Enter U.S. by 1980", *Automotive Industries*, December.
Ealey, L. (1985b). "U.S. Built Hondas, Nissans, Retain Cost Edge", *Automotive News*, 6 June.
Eatwell, J. (1985). "Recognising Economic Reality", *The Listener*, 5 January.
ECE. (1983). *Techno-Economic Aspects of the Industrial Division of labour in the Automotive Industry*. New York: United Nations Economic Commmission for Europe.
Einzig, P. (1957). *The Economic Consequences of Automation*. London: Secker and Warburg.
Ernst, D. (1985a). "Automation and the Worldwide Restructuring of the Electronics Industry: Strategic Implications for Developing Countries", *World Development*, Vol. 13, No. 3, pp 333-352.
Ernst, D. (1985b). *Crisis, Automation and the International Division of Labor and Capital*. Frankfurt am Main: Campus.
Evans, D. E. and Kaplinsky, R. (eds) (1985). "Crisis or Slowdown", *IDS Bulletin*, Vol. 16, No. 1, Brighton: Institute of Development Studies, University of Sussex.
Federal Task Force. (1983). "An Automation Strategy for Canada", *Report of the Federal Task Force on the Canadian Motor Vehicle and Automotive Parts Industries*. Ottawa.
Finger, J. M. (1975) "Tariff Provisions for Offshore Assembly and the Exports of Developing Countries", *The Economic Journal*, June, pp 365-371.
Finger, J. M. (1976). Trade and Domestic Effects of the Offshore Assembly Provisions in the US Tariff", *The American Economic Review*, September, pp 598-599.
Fleming, A. (1986). "Rewriting the Rules", *Automotive News*, 19 May.
Flynn, M. S. (1984). "The Competitive Status of the U.S. Automotive Industry", *Industrial Technology Institute, University of Michigan*. Michigan: mimeo.
Franko, L. G. (1975). *Multinational Enterpise, The International Divission of Labour in Manufactures and the Developing Countries*. WEP 2-28/WP4, Geneva: ILO.
Fransman, M. (1984). "Promoting Technological Capability in the Capital Goods sector: The Case of Singapore", *Research Policy*, 13, pp 233-54.
Frazier, R. (1986). "How Industry Can Deliver the Quick Response", *Apparel International*, February, pp 4-7.

Freeman, C. (1984). "Prometheus unbound", <u>Futures</u>, No 15, pp 494-507.
Freeman, C. Clark, J. and Soete, L. (1982) <u>Unemployment and Technical Innovation: A Study of Long Waves and Economic Development</u>. London: Frances Pinter.
Frobel, F., Heinrichs, J. and Kreye, O. (1980). <u>The New International Division of Labour</u>. Cambridge: Cambridge University Press.
Garner, R. (1983). "Electronics at Centre of Research Activity", <u>Financial Times</u>, 12 December.
Giersch, H. (ed) (1979). <u>On the Economics of Intra-Industry Trade: A Symposium</u>. Tubingen: J. C. B. Mohr.
G.M. Workers Voice. (1985). "The Crisis is Theirs - Refuse to Pay for It", <u>G.M. Workers Voice</u>, No. 1, January.
Glynn, A., Hughes, A., Lipietz, A. and Singh, A. (1986). <u>The Rise and Fall of the Golden Age: An Historical Analysis of Postwar Capitalism in the Developed Market Economies.</u> mimeo.
Gooding, K. (1986), "Vehicle Components", <u>Financial Times</u>, 1 March.
Griffiths, J. (1986). "New Materials", <u>Financial Times</u>, 4 April.
Guelden, M. (1986). "Malaysian auto is caught between success, failure", <u>Automotive News</u>, 16 June.
Helleiner, G. K. (1973). "Manufactured Exports from Less-Developed Countries and Multinational Firms", <u>Economic Journal</u>, 83, pp 21-47.
Henderson, J. and Cohen, R. (1979). "Capital and the Work Ethic", <u>Monthly Review</u>, November, pp 11-26.
Hoffman, K (1985a). "Microelectronics, International Competition and Development Strategies: The Unavoidable Issues - Editor's Introduction", <u>World Development</u>, Vol. 13, No. 3, pp 263-272.
Hoffman, K. (1985b). "Clothing, Chips and Competitive Advantage: The Impact of Microelectronics on Trade and Production in the Garment Industry", <u>World Development</u>, Vol. 13, No. 3, pp 371-392.
Hoffman, K (1985c). <u>Managing Technological Change: The Impact and Policy Implications of Microelectronics</u>. Report to the Inter-Ministerial Working Group on the Management of Technical Change. London: Commonwealth Secretariat.
Hoffman, K. and Rush, H. (1985). <u>Microelectronics and Clothing: The Impact of Technical Change on a Global Industry</u>. mimeo, Geneva: ILO.
Inagami, T. (1984). "The Japanese Will to Work", <u>The</u>

Wheel Extended, Vol. XIV No. 1, Special Issue on Behind the Japanese Corporation: Management and Philosophy, pp 78-86.

International Trade Commission (ITC). (1985). The Internationalization of the Automobile Industry and Its Effects on the US Automobile Industry. Washington DC: US International Trade Commission.

Japan Economic Institute. (1984). "U.S.-Japan Competition in Motor Vehicle Parts", JEI Report , No. 48A.

Jarret, J. P. (1979). Offshore Assembly and Production and the Internalization of International Trade within the Multinational Corporation. Ph. D. dissertation, Harvard University.

Johnson, R. (1986). "Canada wants autopact rules to apply to Asian makers there", Automotive News, 28 April.

Johnston, W. B. (1981). "Relocating Automobile Production to the Developing World: The Multinational View", Background Paper for International Policy Forum, Future of the Automobile Program. Cambridge, Mass.: MIT.

Jones, D. T. (1985). The Import Threat to the UK Car Industry. Brighton: Science Policy Research Unit.

Jones, D. T. and Womack, J. P. (1985). "Developing Countries and the Future of the Automobile Industry", World Development, Vol. 13, No. 3, pp 393-408.

Kahn, H. (1985). "Europe, U.S. lag behind Japanese", Automotive News, 30 September.

Kamata, H. (1982). Japan in a Passing Lane. Harmondsworth: Penguin.

Kaplinsky, R. (1982). Computer Aided Design: Electronics, Comparative Advantage and Development. London: Frances Pinter.

Kaplinsky, R. (1983). "Firm Size and Technical Change in a Dynamic Context", Journal of Industrial Economics, Vol. XXXII, No. 1, pp 39-60.

Kaplinsky, R. (1984). Automation: The Technology and Society. Harlow: Longmans.

Kaplinsky, R. (1985). "Electronics-based Automation Technologies and the Onset of Systemofacture: Implications for Third World Industrialization", World Development, Vol. 13, No. 3, pp 423-440.

Kaplinsky, R. (1986). Changes in Economies of Scale: The Implications for Appropriate Technology. Washington: Appropriate Technology International.

Kaplinsky, R. (1987). Microelectronics and Employment Revisited: A Review. Geneva: ILO.

Knights, D., Willmott, H. and Collinson, D. (eds) (1985).

Job Redesign: Critical Perspectives on the Labour Process. Aldershot: Gower.
Krebs, M. (1985). "Cut costs or lose business, OEMs warned", Automotive News, 4 November.
Krebs, M. (1986). "Problems hamper GM's Hamtrack Plant", Automotive News, 26 May.
Kriedte, P., Medick, H. and Schlumbohn, J. (1981). Industrialization Before Industrialization. Cambridge: Cambridge University Press.
Landes, D. S. (1969). The Unbound Prometheus: Technological change and industrial development in Western Europe from 1750 to the present. Cambridge: Cambridge University Press.
Lipietz, A. (1987). Mirages and Miracles: The Crisis of Global Fordism. London: Verso Press.
Littler, C. (1985). "Taylorism, Fordism and Job Design", in Knights et al (eds).
Maddison, A. (1982). Phases of Capitalist Development. Oxford: Oxford University Press.
Marglin, S. A. (1976). "What do bosses do? The origins and functions of hierachy in capitalist production", in A. Gorz (ed), The Division of Labor. Brighton: Harvester Press.
Marx, K. (1947). The Poverty of Philosophy. London: Lawrence and Wishart.
Marx, K. (1876). Kapital. Harmondsworth: Penguin.
Massey, D. and Meegan, R. (1982). The Anatomy of Job Loss: The how, why and where of employment decline. London: Methuen.
McCosh, D. (1985). "Molded Chassis in Works", Automotive News, 26 August.
McEwan, A. (1982). "Slackers, Bankers, Marketers: Multinational Firms and the Pattern of US Foreign Direct Investment; A Working Paper", Cambridge, Mass: Dept of Economics, University of Massachusetts.
McElroy, J. (1984). "Increasing Productivity without Automation", Automotive Industries, June.
Merwin, J. (1986). "A Tale of Two Worlds", Forbes, 16 June.
Morgan, I. P. (1986). "The Purchasing Revolution", Imede perspectives for managers No 7, August. Lausanne.
Mullins, P. J. (1985). "Saturn Counts Down Through GM's Europlants", Automotive Industries, January.
Nag, A. (1986). "Auto Makers Discover Factory of the Future is Headache Just Now", Wall Street Journal, 13 May.
Nayyar, D. (1978). "Transnational Corporations and

Manufactured Exports from Poor Countries", *Economic Journal*, 88, pp 59-84.

Nelson, R. and Winter, S. (1977). "In Search of a Useful Theory of Innovation", *Research Policy*, Vol. 6, No. 1, pp 36-76.

O'Brien, P. and Alieu, R. (1983). *International Industrial Restructuring and the International Division of Labor in the Automotive Industry*. Vienna: Global and Conceptual Studies Branch, Division of Industrial Studies, UNIDO.

O'Connor, D. C. (1985). "The Computer Industry in the Third World: Policy Options and Constraints", *World Development*, Vol. 13, No. 3, pp 311-332.

Odaka, K, et al. (1983). "Ancillary Firm development in the Japanese Automobile Industry", mimeo.

Pagano, U. (1985). *Work and Welfare in Economic Theory*. Oxford: Blackwells.

Palloix, C. (1977). "The Self Expansion of Capital on a World Scale", *The Review of Radical Political Economics*, Vol. 9, No. 2, April, pp 105-111.

Peet, R. (1983). "Relations of Production and the Relocation of United States Manufacturing Industry since 1960", *Economic Geography*, Vol. 59, No. 2, pp 112-143.

Perez, C. (1985). "Microelectronics, Long Waves and Structural Change: New Perspectives for Developing Countries", *World Development*, Vol. 13, No. 3, pp 441-463.

Perez, C. (1986). "The New Technologies: An Integrated View", mimeo, Brighton: Science Policy Research Unit, University of Sussex.

Piore, M. J. and Sabel, C. F. (1984). *The Second Industrial Divide: Possibilities for Prosperity*. New York: Basic Books.

Radice, H. (ed) (1984). *International Firms and Modern Imperialism*. Harmondsworth: Penguin.

Rosenberg, N. and Frischtak. (1984). "Technological innovation and long waves", *Cambridge Journal of Economics*, Vol. 8, pp 7-24.

Rowand, R. (1985). "The Think-Tanker", *Automotive News*, 30 December.

Sabel, C. F. (1986). "Changing Models of Economic Efficiency and Their Implications for Industrialization in the Third World", in Foxley, A., McPherson, M. and O'Donnell, G. (eds), *Development, Democracy, and the Art of Trespassing: Essays in Honor of Albert O. Hirschman*. Notre Dame: University of

Notre Dame Press.
Sabolo, Y. and Trajtenberg R, with Sajhau, J. P. (1976). The Impact of Transnational Enterprises on Employment in Developing Countries: Preliminary Results. WEP L-28/WP6, Geneva: ILO.
Schonberger, R. J. (1982). Japanese Manufacturing Techniques: Nine Hidden Lessons in Simplicity. New York: The Free Press.
Sciberras, E. (1979). "Technology transfer to developing countries - implications for member countries' Science and Technology Policy", in Television and Related Products Sector Final Report. Paris: OECD.
Sharpston, M. (1975). "International Sub-contracting", Oxford Economic Papers, 27, April, pp 94-135.
Silva, F., Ferri, P. and Enrietta, A. (1984). Impact of Microelectronics 'New Technologies' on the Automobile Industry, Turin: mimeo.
Sinclair, S. (1983). The World Car: The Future of the Automobile Industry. London: Euromonitor Publications Ltd.
Smith, A. (1776). An Enquiry into the Nature and Cause of The Wealth of Nations. Harmondsworth: Penguin.
Smith, A. (1983). "Tough stance adopted on components", Financial Times, 1 March.
Snowdon, M. (1986). "The Japanese Approach to Productivity and Quality - A European View", speech to International Association for Vehicle Design.
Sobel, R. (1985). Car Wars: Why Japan is Building the All-American Car. New York: McGraw Hill.
Society of Motor Manufacturers and Traders (SMMT). (1986). World Automotive Statistics. London: Society of Motor Manufacturers and Traders.
Stavro, B. (1985). "Made in the U.S.A'", Forbes, 22 April.
Taylor, F. W. (1903). Shop Management. Reprinted in Taylor, F. W. (1947). Scientific Management, New York: Harper and Brothers.
Taylor, F. W. (1911). The Principles of Scientific Management. New York: Harper and Brothers.
Tharakan, P. K. M. (1979). The International Division of Labour and Multinational Companies: Symposium Organised by the European Centre for Study and Information on Multinational Corporations. Farnborough: Saxon House.
Thurow, L. (1985). "America, Europe and Japan", The Economist, 9 November.
Tolliday, S. and Zeitlin, J. (eds) (1987). The Automobile

Industry and its Workers: Between Fordism and Flexibility. Cambridge: Polity Press.

Transnational Information Exchange. (1985). "The Circle game", TIE-Europe, No 16., Amsterdam.

UNIDO. (1985). Industry in the 1980s: Structural Change and Interdependence. New York: United Nations.

United Nations Centre on Transnational Corporations. (1979). Transnational Corporations in World Development: A Reexamination. New York: United Nations.

United Nations Centre on Transnational Corporations. (1983). Transnational Corporations in World Development: Third Survey. New York: United Nations.

Ure, A. (1835). The Philosophy of Manufactures. London: Charles Knight.

Wantuck, K. A. (undated). "The Japanese Approach to Productivity", The Bendix Corporation, mimeo.

Watanabe, S. (1984). "Microelectronics and Employment in the Japanese Automobile Industry", ILO WEP 2.22/WP 219, Geneva: ILO.

Wilkins, M. (1974). The Maturing of Multinational Enterprise: American Business Abroad from 1914 to 1970. Cambridge, Mass: Harvard University Press.

Winters, D. (1984). "Still cheap but no longer third rate, Mexico nears big time", Wards AutoWorld, August.

Womack, J. (1986a). Multinational Joint Ventures in the Motor Vehicle Sector, Cambridge, Mass: Center for Technology Policy and Industrial Development, MIT.

Womack, J. (1986b). Prospects for the U.S. Mexican Relationship in the Motor Vehicle Sector, Cambridge, Mass: International Motor Vehicle Program, MIT.

Zoia, (1986). "Japanese Cost Advantage Holding Firm", Automotive News, 26 June.

Index

Action Plate Method, 130, 147

AGV, 144, 147, 152, 202, 207, 212, 219(n28)

AIAG, 262-263

Andon, 133, 147, 337-338

Automation, 55(n44),
 of assembly, 144, 207-209, 245-247,
 electronics-based, 33, 39-40, 41, 54-61, 101, 182, 184-191, 333-335,
 experimental nature, 150, 217-218,
 and flexibility, 139-145, 160-165, 202-203,
 in Japan, 138-152, 160-165,
 in United States, 187-195,
 vintages of, 56
 in Western Europe, 188,

Benetton, 331, 353-354

CAD, 60, 150, 267-268, 159, 162, 187, 190, 212, 251, 252, 264, 269, 270, 317, 333, 353

CIM, 77, 150, 152, 169, 175, 190, 191, 208, 211, 212-213, 333, 335, 353

Costs of production
 lower in Japan, 115-121, 133(n13), 216

Crisis, 1, 19-21, 31, 49,
 and long waves, 32-36

Culture, 43, 339-340

Design
 relationship between suppliers and assemblers, 244-253, 262-264,
 design for build/assembly, 246-248
 See also CAD

Deskilling, 47, 51-52, 330

Die-change, 123-126, 145, 224, 275

Diversification, 169, 271

Division of labour
 in international auto industry, 26-27,

in labour process, 47, 51-4, 126-127

Downtime, 51-52, 122-126, 145, 225, 350

Economies of scale, 15, 38, 104, 169(n48), 169-174, 342-353, 357,
international integration, 65-68, 170-171, 350-353

Electronics
importance of, 33-35, 54-60,
in product, 100(n29), 134(n32), 199-200,
and systemic automation, 60,
See also Automation

Excess capacity, 91-92, 97-98
Exterior conditioning, 43, 338

Factory of the Future, 212-213, 272

FDI
in DC component production, 306-309,
disarticulated, 6-7, 9, 11-12, 16, 18, 26, 41,
and exports of components, 309-318,
horizontal, 6, 10, 15, 27,
by Japanese auto assemblers, 88-94, 293-294,
by Japanese component firms, 157, 293-294
relocation back to IACs, 313-318,
by Republic of Korea auto assemblers, 92-94, 293
types of, 6-10,

vertical, 6, 8, 12
by Western European auto assemblers, 89, 206,

Flexible
automation, 54-61, 142-145, 160-165,
technologies, 37, See also Automation,
work practicies, 123-127

Flexibility
in process, 103(n28), 121-124,
in product mix, 123-127, 139-142,
in work organization, 50-54

Flexible specialization, 21(n27), 36-40, 331(n1), 357-358,

FMS, 162-165, 170, 172, 187, 197, 202, 277

GATT, 24-25, 83, 86, 342

Golden Age, 20, 31, 33, 342

Habituation, 41, 42-44

Handicraft
and international integration, 64-69,
and putting-out, 44-45,
transition to manufacture 39, 44-45, 64-69, 329

Heartland technologies, 33-36

History of the auto, 73-75, 96

Ideology, 43, 335, 339-340

Import penetration, 12-13,

86, 345(n20)

Industrial relations, 224-225, 338-339

Industrialization,
export of auto components, 300, 312-313,
export-oriented, 2, 183, 356
import substituting, 2, 356-358,
in developing countries, 2-4, 300, 355-360

Interfirm relationships,
in Japan, 152-158,
new pattern of, 61-64,
transfer of, 335-337
in United States, 237-244,

Interior determination, 43, 339-340

Inventory turns, 129-131

ISDN, 334

JIT, 51-53, 63, 68-69, 89, 90, 183, 231, 252, 272, 273, 288-290, 293(n8), 296(n15)
and economics of location, 69, 291-293
and flexible automation, 139-142, 146-152,
and inventories, 50(n36), 63, 127-131, 146-152,
in Japanese auto industry, 127-138, 142-160,
and labour process, 50-54, 127-138,
in non-Japanese component sector, 253-265,
and quality, 131-134,
in Rover Group, 201-203,
in United States, 197-198,
223,
vulnerability to interuptions, 130, 308-309

Joint ventures, 15-16, 205, 221-223, 266, 277-280, 292, 310-311

Kanban, 130, 144, 147(n29)

Labour process, 60,
and automation, 335,
definition of, 41-42,
differences between Toyota and Nissan, 50(n34), 114, 139, 150,
and flexibility, 50-51,
Fordist, 38(n18), 46-47, 48, 53-54, 127, 182,
in handicrafts, 46,
in Japan, 121-138,
in machinofacture, 47-49,
and quality, 52-53,
in systemofacture, 50-54
in the three eras, 63-69,

Local content, 87, 95, 303

Location
economics of, 26, 68, 153-155, 255-260, 287-294, 346-355,
politics of, 26, 69, 342-345, See also Protectionism

Long waves, 32-36,
and flexible specialization, 38-40

Machine tools, 140-142, 162, 171-172

Machinofacture, 21, 39,
and international integration, 64-69,
transition to

systemofacture, 49, 64-69, 330-332

Manufacture, 39, 45(n26),
and international integration, 64-69,
transition to machinofacture, 45-48, 64-69, 330-332

MAP, 191, 211, 217, 264

Market structure, 79-82,

Mass production
transition from, 36-40

Model T, 61, 74, 120

Modular assembly, 105, 144-145, 186, 248, 249

Multi-tasking and skilling, 54, 68, 126-127

New materials, 105, 199-200

NIDL, 6, 7-10, 17, 18, 24, 26-27, 32, 47, 50, 67, 73, 100, 101, 110, 175, 306, 316, 330

Number of component suppliers, 151-153, 243-244, 262

Productivity growth, 21-23, 115-121, 206-209

Protectionism, 18, 342, 345, 340, 358,
and components, 292-3,
in 1930s, 74,
OMA, 25, 86(n15)
reemergence of, 24-25, 82-96,
VERS, 24, 25, 86, 87, 88-90, 96

QDC, 143

Quality, 222-223, 233(n2), 349,
in Japan and United States 158
and labour process, 52-53,
quality circles, 53, 132-133,
and sourcing policies, 132-133,
and zero-defects, 131-134,

R&D, 53, 57, 63, 94, 100(n29), 101, 136, 159, 160, 162, 166-168, 170-174, 182, 190, 191, 208, 218, 231, 239-241, 249-251, 260-278,
and concentration, 266-267,
and economies of scale, 349
in electronics and new materials, 167-169,
in Japanese components industry, 166-169, 172-173,
"leading-edge" projects, 189-190, 211-212
in new products, 166-169
in United States, 186-188,

Robots, 114, 139-140, 159, 162-163, 169, 199-200, 204, 215-216, 269-270, 271-272

Sourcing
global, 12-13, 100, 183, 298,
multi-sourcing, 166-167, 231-232, 238,
offshore, 196(n5), 264, 287-294, 298-300, 301-306, 309-318,
single-sourcing, 152-159,

203, 237-240, 335-337

SPC, 183, 197, 223, 225, 235

Subcontracting, 16, 27, 105-106, 152-158

Supplier-assembler relationships, 152-158, 166-167, 203

Technological change
 in Europe and United States, 184-201,
 in process, 187-198,
 in product, 198-201,
 types of, 33-34, 136-138
 and types of components, 102-109, 265-267,

Technological determinism, 33, 42

TNCs
 declining role of United States TNCs, 10-14,
 and exports from developing countries, 9,
 history of, 10-11,
 and industrialization in developing countries, 309-310, 361-364,
 and protectionism, 344-345,
 and R&D, 268-269,
 role of, 3-6, 355(n30),
 role in auto industry, 26-27,
 share of production and employment, 4-5

TOP, 191, 211, 264

Toyota City, 129, 153

Trade in autos, 73-76, 98-100

UAW, 88, 213, 215, 225

World Bank, 3, 92(n22)

World Car, 8, 98-100, 101, 110, 246, 346,

World Factory, 7-8, 346